China's Asymmetric Statecraft

Contemporary Chinese Studies

This series provides new scholarship and perspectives on modern and contemporary China, including China's contested borderlands and minority peoples; ongoing social, cultural, and political changes; and the varied histories that animate China today.

Alison R. Marshall, *Cultivating Connections: The Making of Chinese Prairie Canada*
Ruoyun Bai, *Staging Corruption: Chinese Television and Politics*
Christopher G. Rea and Nicolai Volland, eds., *The Business of Culture: Cultural Entrepreneurs in China and Southeast Asia, 1900–65*
Eric Hyer, *The Pragmatic Dragon: China's Grand Strategy and Boundary Settlements*
Ning Wang, *Banished to the Great Northern Wilderness: Political Exile and Re-Education in Mao's China*
Jennifer Y.J. Hsu, *State of Exchange: Migrant NGOs and the Chinese Government*
Norman Smith, ed., *Empire and Environment in the Making of Manchuria*
Joseph Lawson, *A Frontier Made Lawless: Violence in Upland Southwest China, 1800–1956*
Victor Zatsepine, *Beyond the Amur: Frontier Encounters between China and Russia, 1850–1930*
Patrick Fuliang Shan, *Yuan Shikai: A Reappraisal*
Selina Gao, *Saving the Nation through Culture: The Folklore Movement in Republican China*
Andres Rodriguez, *Frontier Fieldwork: Building a Nation in China's Borderlands, 1919–45*

For a complete list of the titles in the series, see the UBC Press website, www.ubcpress.ca.

China's Asymmetric Statecraft

Alignments, Competitors, and Regional Diplomacy

YUXING HUANG

UBC Press • Vancouver • Toronto

32 31 30 29 28 27 26 25 24 23 5 4 3 2 1

Printed in Canada on FSC-certified ancient-forest-free paper (100% post-consumer recycled) that is processed chlorine- and acid-free.

Library and Archives Canada Cataloguing in Publication

Title: China's asymmetric statecraft : alignments, competitors, and regional diplomacy / Yuxing Huang.
Names: Huang, Yuxing, author.
Series: Contemporary Chinese studies.
Description: Series statement: Contemporary Chinese studies | Includes bibliographical references and index.
Identifiers: Canadiana (print) 20220411913 | Canadiana (ebook) 20220411956 | ISBN 9780774868112 (hardcover) | ISBN 9780774868129 (paperback) | ISBN 9780774868136 (PDF) | ISBN 9780774868143 (EPUB)
Subjects: LCSH: China – Foreign relations – 1949- | LCSH: China – Foreign relations – Asia. | LCSH: Asia – Foreign relations – China.
Classification: LCC DS777.8 .H83 2023 | DDC 327.5105 – dc23

UBC Press gratefully acknowledges the financial support for our publishing program of the Government of Canada (through the Canada Book Fund) and the British Columbia Arts Council. Publication was also made possible with financial support from Tsinghua University.

Printed and bound in Canada by Friesens
Set in Garamond and SimSun by Artegraphica Design Co.
Copy editor: Frank Chow
Proofreader: Dallas Harrison
Indexer: Margaret de Boer

UBC Press
The University of British Columbia
2029 West Mall
Vancouver, BC V6T 1Z2
www.ubcpress.ca

To my parents,
Huang Xiaopeng and Zhai Zhen

Contents

Tables

Acknowledgments

This book project began under the direction of Robert Ross, Timothy Crawford, and Peter Krause at Boston College, to whom I am very grateful for contributing to the first draft of the manuscript. Since our first contact in 2009, Bob Ross has been a constant source of encouragement in my academic career. As supervisor of my dissertation research, he not only stimulated my research interest in international relations theory and Chinese foreign policy but also encouraged me to compare and contrast Chinese experiences with those of great powers in the West. Tim Crawford taught me how to uncover patterns in the dynamics of international relations by using process-tracing techniques and structured, focused comparisons. Peter Krause enabled me to articulate and refine my theories in the political science discipline. I am indebted to all my dissertation committee members, as they provided me with a stimulating and congenial environment in which to grow as a scholar. Although Vojtech Mastny was not a member of the committee, he also nurtured my interest in developing general theories based on multi-sided archives. As a young political scientist, I hope the quality of my research will meet the high standards of senior historians like Vojtech Mastny.

As a faculty member, I undertook extensive revisions of the book manuscript between 2016 and 2022. I am very grateful for the support of my research from Tsinghua University's Department of International Relations, Faculty of Social Sciences, and Center for Faculty Development. As my undergraduate supervisors and current colleagues, Yan Xuetong and Chen Qi have stimulated my interest in international relations, supported me to establish myself in the field, and encouraged me to revise and publish this book. Their guidance, encouragement, advice, and care have always helped me to maintain momentum. I am also indebted to Sun Xuefeng, Zhao Kejin, and Tang Xiaoyang (directors of the Department of International Relations from 2016 to 2018, 2018 to 2021, and 2021 to the present, respectively) for their support. I am grateful to He Maochun, who encouraged me to conduct research based on multilingual sources, and to Wu Dahui, Pang Xun, and Liu Feng, who enabled me to better (re)organize the arguments presented in the book. Finally, I am deeply thankful to Tian Jing for inspiring my intellectual growth and guiding my career development.

Pertinent research was conducted in North America, Europe, and China. It was my good fortune to have opportunities to examine scholarly and documentary sources at the libraries of Boston College, Emory University, George Washington University, Georgetown University, Harvard University, Johns Hopkins University, University of Michigan, University of Toronto, Freie Universität Berlin, Humboldt-Universität zu Berlin, Staatsbibliothek zu Berlin, Universität Trier, China Foreign Affairs University, Chinese Academy of International Trade and Economic Cooperation, and Tsinghua University. Archives that provided primary sources included the US National Archives and Records Administration; the Kennedy, Johnson, Nixon, and Ford Presidential Libraries; the North Atlantic Treaty Organization Archives; Bundesarchiv (Berlin and Freiburg im Breisgau); the Foreign Ministry Archive of the People's Republic of China; and nine provincial/municipal archives in China. I would like to express my sincere gratitude to the librarians and archivists at the above institutions, especially Anne Kenny (Boston College) and Nancy Hearst (Harvard University), as they made significant contributions to the completion of my manuscript.

During the writing process, I had the privilege of discussing my research with colleagues from North America, Europe, and Asia. I appreciate the incisive comments and helpful advice from Robert Art, Thomas Berger, William Burr, Chen Ge, Chen Hao, Dai Chaowu, Gerald Easter, David Engerman, Jennifer Erickson, Manuel Fröhlich, Stacie Goddard, Sebastian Heilmann, Hu Weixing, Seth Jacobs, William Keylor, Mark Kramer, Jonathan Laurence, Li Danhui, Lian Yuru, Liang Zhi, Shirley Lin, Liu Yawei, Sean Lynn-Jones, Hanns Maull, Niu Jun, Lindsey O'Rourke, David Pomfret, Galia Press-Barnathan, Priscilla Roberts, Jürgen Rüland, Shen Zhihua, Tang Shiping, Mario Telò, Xia Yafeng, Wang Li, Odd Arne Westad, Seanon Wong, Yin Qingfei, and Zhu Liqun. I also thank Rachel Farmer,

Pamela Lord, William Mayborn, and Sophie Rosales, who proofread portions of the manuscript at different stages of my research.

I wish to express my gratitude for the generous financial support provided by Boston College, the Bradley and Fortin Foundations, the Gerald R. Ford Presidential Foundation, Deutscher Akademischer Austauschdienst (DAAD), Stiftung Mercator, Tsinghua University, and the Cyrus Tang Foundation, without which this book would not have been possible.

I would like to express my gratitude to Randy Schmidt at UBC Press, who believed in the theoretical and policy value of this book project. I am grateful not only to him but also to the anonymous reviewers who, on his request, provided significant insights on how to improve the quality of the book. I am equally thankful to the editorial office and the Publications Board at UBC Press for their unanimous support for this project. I thank Megan Brand for shepherding this book through the production process and Frank Chow for his meticulous copy-editing.

I would like to express gratitude to my parents, Huang Xiaopeng and Zhai Zhen, for persevering with me through years of instability during my research and writing. I dedicate this book to them. Finally, I thank my wife, Ruolan, who enriches my life. As a thoughtful critic, she hopes the book will mark the beginning of a fresh chapter in my life as a scholar of international relations. Any credit given to this work must be attributed to the considerable efforts of the aforementioned people and institutions. Those who provided assistance and advice must nonetheless be relieved of responsibility for any remaining errors.

Note on Romanization, Names, and Translation

I use the Hanyu Pinyin romanization system to denote the standard Mandarin pronunciation of Chinese characters, with the exception of a few names widely used in the West (e.g., Chiang Kai-shek). In the text, I place family names first for Chinese, Japanese, and Korean figures (e.g., Mao Zedong, Kishi Nobusuke, and Kim Il-sung). Translations of all the Chinese quotations and sources are mine unless otherwise noted.

Abbreviations

AAA	Anti-aircraft artillery
ABM	Anti-ballistic missile
ASEAN	Association of Southeast Asian Nations
BCP	Burmese Communist Party
CBS	Columbia Broadcasting System
CCP	Chinese Communist Party
CENTO	Central Treaty Organization
CFMA	Foreign Ministry Archive of the People's Republic of China
CIA	Central Intelligence Agency
CMC	Central Military Commission
CSTO	Collective Security Treaty Organization
CYWJ	*Chen Yun wenji* (*Chen Yun's Collected Works*)
DRV	Democratic Republic of Vietnam
DSDUF	Declassified and Sanitized Documents from Unprocessed Files
DWJJ	*Da waijiaojia Zhou Enlai* (*Zhou Enlai: A Great Diplomat*)
DXPNP	*Deng Xiaoping nianpu, 1904–1974* (*A Chronicle of Deng Xiaoping's Life, 1904–1974*)
FBIS	Foreign Broadcast Information Service

FRUS	*Foreign Relations of the United States*
GRFL	Gerald R. Ford Presidential Library
HKDSJ	*Zhongguo hangkong gongye dashiji, 1951–2011* (*A Chronicle of Major Events of Chinese Aviation Industry, 1951–2011*]
JFJB	*Jiefangjun bao* (*People's Liberation Army Daily*)
JGYLMZDWG	*Jianguo yilai Mao Zedong wengao* (*Manuscripts of Mao Zedong since the Founding of the Nation*)
JJDA	*1958–1965 Zhonghua renmin gongheguo jingji dang'an ziliao xuanbian* (*Selected Archival Materials on the PRC's Economic Affairs, 1958–1965*)
JSP	Japan Socialist Party
LDP	Liberal Democratic Party (Japan)
MTGX	*MeiTai guanxi zhongyao ziliao xuanbian, 1948.11–1996.4* (*Selected Important Materials on US-Taiwan Relations, 1948.11–1996.4*)
MZDNP	*Mao Zedong nianpu, 1949–1976* (*A Chronicle of Mao Zedong's Life, 1949–1976*)
MZDSX	"Mao Zedong sixiang wansui" ("Long Live Mao Zedong Thought")
MZDWJ	*Mao Zedong waijiao wenxuan* (*Mao Zedong's Selected Works on Diplomacy*)
MZDZ	*Mao Zedong zhuan, 1949–1976* (*Biography of Mao Zedong, 1949–1976*)
NIE	National Intelligence Estimate
NRZNP	*Nie Rongzhen nianpu* (*A Chronicle of Nie Rongzhen's Life*)
NSC	National Security Council
NSF	National Security Files
PDHNP	*Peng Dehuai nianpu* (*A Chronicle of Peng Dehuai's Life*)
PLA	People's Liberation Army
PRC	People's Republic of China
RAC	Remote Archives Capture
RBWT	*Riben wenti wenjian huibian* (*Collected Documents on Japan*)
RMNL	Richard M. Nixon Presidential Library

RN	*Cankao xiaoxi* (*Reference News*)
SAARC	South Asian Association for Regional Cooperation
SAM	Surface-to-air
SCO	Shanghai Cooperation Organization
SEATO	Southeast Asia Treaty Organization
SLWM	*Sulian duiwai maoyi jiben tongji, 1954–1975* (*The Foundation of the Foreign Trade Statistics of the Soviet Union, 1954–1975*)
UAV	Unmanned aerial vehicle
WJS	*Zhonghua renmin gongheguo waijiaoshi* (*A Diplomatic History of the People's Republic of China*)
WWJDSJ	*Zhongguo waiwenju wushinian dashiji* (*A Chronicle of Major Events of China International Publishing Group over Fifty Years*)
YZWT	*Yinduzhina wenti ziliao: Jianpuzhai wenti dashiji (1954 nian zhi 1972 niandi)* (*Materials on the Question of Indochina: A Chronicle of Major Events on the Question of Cambodia, 1954–1972*)
ZELJSHDJS	*Zhou Enlai junshi huodong jishi, 1918–1975* (*A Chronicle of Zhou Enlai's Military Activities, 1918–1975*)
ZELNP	*Zhou Enlai nianpu, 1949–1976* (*A Chronicle of Zhou Enlai's Life, 1949–1976*)
ZELWJ	*Zhou Enlai waijiao wenxuan* (*Zhou Enlai's Selected Works on Diplomacy*)
ZELWJHDDSJ	*Zhou Enlai waijiao huodong dashiji, 1949–1975* (*A Chronicle of Major Events of Zhou Enlai's Foreign Affairs Activities, 1949–1975*)
ZELZ	*Zhou Enlai zhuan* (*Biography of Zhou Enlai*)
ZGDWGXWJ	*Zhonghua renmin gongheguo duiwai guanxi wenjian ji* (*Documents on Foreign Relations of the People's Republic of China*)
ZSGX	*E'luosi jiemi dang'an: ZhongSu guanxi* (*Sino-Soviet Relations: Declassified Documents from Russian Archives*)

China's Asymmetric Statecraft

INTRODUCTION
Understanding China's Regional Diplomacy

"China" in Chinese means "Middle Kingdom" and originally referred to the region in which the emperor lived. As the prominent American sinologist John King Fairbank (1907–91) noted, the Middle Kingdom perspective is a useful one for scholars seeking to understand how Chinese leaders view the world beyond their country.[1] European great powers weakened the Asian tributary system, hitherto dominated by China, in the late nineteenth century. The Chinese revolution of 1911, moreover, ended the Qing Dynasty, thus initiating a new chapter of Chinese modernization. However, China's Nationalist and Communist leaders alike were significantly influenced by traditional Chinese culture, not least the Middle Kingdom perspective, from which, consciously or not, they viewed China's foreign relations. Indeed, these leaders expressed sentiments arising from the Middle Kingdom concept through the use of ideological terminology. For example, as Fairbank observed, the People's Republic of China (PRC) expressed its world view through the lens of Marxism-Leninism.[2] Fairbank's scholarly view thus has significant implications for understanding China's foreign relations. In a dyadic relationship, the concepts of the Middle Kingdom and its "neighbouring states" exist simultaneously. Therefore, scholars cannot construct the concept of the Middle Kingdom without its counterpart – that of its neighbouring states. As such, Chinese regional diplomacy is integral to scholars' understanding of Chinese foreign policy.

As Fairbank put it well, the PRC seriously considered its regional diplomacy toward its immediate neighbours. Wang Jiaxiang, the founding director of the Chinese Communist Party (CCP) Liaison Department, stressed this point in his inaugural speech to the department in March 1951. In his words, "we must pay attention to countries in our neighbourhood, because they are very close to us. Any sign of trouble or changes in these countries will have an immediate impact on us." Wang elaborated his point with an analogy: "If a neighbour comes down with a bad cold, you must avoid catching it."[3] In February 1989, Liu Huaqing, deputy secretary-general of the Central Military Commission (CMC), also underlined the importance of regional diplomacy: "It is very complex, with respect to the situations of our neighbourhood and neighbouring states ... [We] need to make predictions and be prepared for incidents."[4] In October 2013, Chinese president Xi Jinping attended "the Conference on the Diplomatic Work with Neighbouring Countries" in Beijing. According to an official press release, Xi Jinping placed emphasis on the utmost strategic significance to China of its neighbouring countries.[5] The immediate audiences to China's rise are the country's weaker neighbours. Therefore, understanding Chinese regional diplomacy is crucial to understanding the implications of China's ascent.

How does China manage relationships with its immediate neighbours? According to Fairbank, Chinese traditional statecraft carries considerable significance for scholars' understanding of contemporary foreign conduct. In ancient Asia, China tailored its regional diplomacy through the lens of "asymmetric statecraft," i.e., how a strong concentration of power engages with multiple weaker neighbours, whereby selective and uniform strategies played crucial roles. Ancient Chinese leaders sometimes adopted selective strategies, such as the *fen er zhi zhi* (divide-and-rule) strategy. For example, the Han Dynasty exploited internal discord between the Xiongnu (Hsiung-nu) by cooperating with the Southern Xiongnu, sending expeditions to outflank the Northern Xiongnu.[6] The Sui Dynasty adopted the *li qiang he ruo* (splitting the strong while cooperating with the weak) strategy toward tribal groups under the rule of the Tujue (Turks)[7] and exacerbated divisions in the Tujue Khanate to a far greater extent by joining forces with the Eastern Tujue Khanate against the Western Tujue Khanate.[8] All these strategies exemplify the practice of selective strategies, but Chinese leaders also adopted uniform strategies at times. The aim of *huai rou yuan ren* (cherishing men from afar), for instance, was to educate foreign leaders in China's neighbourhood. To consolidate a Sinocentric interstate order, China adopted a strategy of *hou wang bo lai* (giving much and receiving little) toward its weaker neighbours. For example, the Hongwu Emperor, the founding emperor of the Ming Dynasty, compiled a list of fifteen countries, including Korea, Japan, and Vietnam, that were "not to be invaded" without legitimate reasons.[9] The list itself demonstrates Chinese patterns of uniform strategies – attempts to treat all weaker neighbours in much the same way.

Since 1949, divergent perspectives – Chinese traditional cultures, modern sovereign norms, and Marxism-Leninism – have been reconciled with the practice of Chinese regional diplomacy. On the one hand, equality among sovereign states has become a key element of modern international law. As a member of the international community, the PRC publicly accepted this norm and developed the Five Principles of Peaceful Coexistence. Meanwhile, Marxism-Leninism has also been a guiding principle of the PRC's foreign relations. As a socialist country, the PRC emphasizes upholding of the principles of both internationalism and patriotism.[10] Thus, its foreign policy statements usually avoid mention of traditional Chinese statecraft concepts such as selective or uniform strategies. On the other hand, the PRC's principal leaders have proven to be receptive to notions of traditional Chinese statecraft, as demonstrated by their understanding of Northern Song Dynasty historian Sima Guang's book on governance, *Zizhi tongjian (Comprehensive Mirror in Aid of Governance)*. This general chronicle of Chinese history, based on records from the reign of King Weilie of the Eastern Zhou Dynasty to the reign of Emperor Shizong of Later Zhou, covering a period of 1,362 years, summarizes the lessons of statecraft. According to official accounts, Mao Zedong reviewed the entire book seventeen times during his life, and Deng Xiaoping read the chronicle "countless times."[11] Moreover, in his speeches, Xi Jinping has frequently referred to Chinese classical works, including *Zizhi tongjian*.[12] The PRC thus accepted the norms of the modern sovereign system, used Marxist-Leninist terminology, and practised foreign policy through the lens of traditional Chinese statecraft.[13] Consequently, the world beyond China needed to deal with the paradox of how to reconcile these divergent perspectives toward an understanding of the PRC's foreign policy, particularly its regional diplomacy toward immediate neighbours.

One way of coping with this difficulty is by identifying certain factors of enduring relevance and treating them as the starting point for analyzing Chinese regional diplomacy. Two constant factors in particular are worth noting: 1) China's neighbours can generally be considered weaker powers, and 2) Chinese regional diplomacy needs to deal with more than one weak neighbour simultaneously. One scholar analyzes the features of Chinese regional diplomacy by referring to the case of South Asia:

> During the 1959–60 period, China peacefully settled all the issues that had arisen between Kathmandu and Peking [Beijing], and on almost all issues it showed the spirit of accommodation, generosity, and reasonableness towards Nepal. By doing so, Peking tried to demonstrate that it was prepared to settle issues peacefully and indirectly suggested that in its border dispute with India, the latter was to be blamed. This was, in fact, a part of China's diplomatic game by which it sought to extend influence in Nepal and to isolate India from there.[14]

The author argues that China adopted a "selective strategy" toward India and Nepal. This case raises an important research question: under what circumstances did China treat weaker neighbours either the same way, i.e., through uniform strategies, or try to differentiate among them through selective concessions or targeted coercion, i.e., selective strategies? In other words, when does China adopt uniform or selective strategies toward its multiple weaker neighbours? The term "uniform strategies" refers to those Chinese attempts to treat weaker neighbours in the same manner, whereas the term "selective strategies" refers to the Chinese approach of differentiating among many weaker neighbours by either offering selective concessions or applying targeted coercion. A systematic analysis of Chinese regional diplomacy suggests that China adopts uniform strategies in some regions and selective strategies in others. Why does China practise its regional diplomacy in different ways?

This question is one of both theoretical and policy significance. On the theoretical side, Chinese regional diplomacy provides scholars with an opportunity to generalize about a great power's patterns of behaviour. On the policy side, it offers policy makers a basis for understanding Chinese geopolitical positions and ambitions. For example, security conflicts exist between China and its weaker neighbours in the South China Sea and South Asia. Although the ascent of China has increased the power gap between it and its weaker neighbours in these two regions, it never settles the territorial disputes among them. In managing such conflicts, however, China produces different patterns of regional diplomacy in these regions. In the South China Sea, China seeks to maintain a uniform strategy toward Vietnam, the Philippines, and Malaysia; in South Asia, by contrast, China practises selective strategies – carefully maintaining the status quo with India and enhancing Pakistan's positions. Understanding the implications of Chinese behaviour would be particularly useful for the United States and its allies in Asia. Therefore, this book seeks to construct a theory that better explains China's regional diplomacy, shedding light on contemporary debates about Chinese regional diplomacy in the new era.

Theoretical Motivations

The major theoretical motivation behind this book is to better explain China's regional diplomacy toward its immediate neighbours. Academic interest in Chinese regional diplomacy is indeed surging, but existing explanations fail to adequately address the core question of uniform or selective strategies. Scholars either examine China's policy toward one particular weaker neighbour – thus missing the connections among China's strategies toward multiple weaker neighbours in a regional context – or argue that external threats or domestic-ideological factors drive Chinese regional diplomacy. Adding to international relations theories that focus on external threats, domestic politics, and ideology, this book proposes a regional competition theory, which argues that both the number of regional competitors and alignment relationships shape a great power's regional diplomacy with respect to uniform strategies or selective strategies. The external threat theory, the domestic-ideological theory, and the regional competition theory are introduced here and presented in full in Chapter 1.

The external threat theory views a state's foreign policy as a response to external threat, defined mainly by the military strength of the state's main enemies. This theory addresses the principal question of restraints on Chinese regional diplomacy by focusing on the international distribution of military strength. However, it inadequately explains Chinese regional practices for two reasons. First, China may adopt similar regional strategies when its external threat perception changes. For example, China began to view the Soviet Union as its primary threat after the Sino-Soviet border clash in 1969, but it did not change its policies toward its weaker Indochinese allies – North Vietnam (officially, the Democratic Republic of Vietnam or DRV) and Cambodia – at the same time. Instead, it maintained its uniform strategies toward these weaker allies both before and after the Sino-Soviet border conflict. In other words, the external threat theory cannot adequately explain the continuity of Chinese regional diplomacy. Second, China may adopt a different regional strategy even as its external threat perception remains the same. For example, from 1958 to 1959, China had substantial military capabilities in South Asia, whereas the Soviet Union did not have any military presence in the region. A country without military capabilities (the Soviet Union) could not threaten one with military capabilities (China), but Soviet aid packages to China's South Asian neighbours led to Sino-Soviet competition in the region. Accordingly, China changed its regional diplomacy from uniform strategies to selective strategies. The external threat theory cannot fully account for the change in China's South Asian policy between 1958 and 1959. This example also suggests that, whereas military strength is a crucial means of dealing with regional competition, it is not the only one.

The domestic-ideological theory examines domestic bases of foreign policy and does a good job of advancing the understanding of internal-international linkage. This theory suggests persuasively that domestic problems exacerbate a state's security problems, and it explains why China adopts different strategies given similar international conditions. Nonetheless, the theory has two limitations in explaining Chinese regional practices. First, it inadequately explains why China adopts selective strategies toward multiple weaker neighbours given the domestic-ideological conditions at a particular historical moment. For example, from 1973 to 1975, China continued with its Cultural Revolution to resist American "imperialism" and Soviet "revisionists." Constant domestic-ideological priorities, however, cannot fully explain China's selective strategies toward the DRV and Cambodia: circumscribing the DRV's armed struggle in South Vietnam but encouraging the armed struggle in Cambodia. Second, the theory does not adequately explain why China may adopt similar strategies toward multiple weaker neighbours under significantly different domestic-ideological conditions. For instance, China's domestic conditions in the two periods 1956–57 and 1960–61 were significantly different. In the first period, China stressed economic construction, whereas in the second period, it emphasized class struggle. However, China made territorial concessions to Burma in both periods even though economic crisis occurred only during the second period.

The external threat theory and the domestic-ideological theory provide key insights into asymmetric statecraft and Chinese regional diplomacy but have certain limitations in explaining the practice of Chinese asymmetric statecraft. The regional competition theory proposed in this book can help to overcome these limitations. A great power is a nation-state with independent offensive military capabilities superior to those of any other state in a region; a small power is one that does not possess this degree of military strength. From a great power perspective, a regional competitor is a state that does not share common objectives and that has independent capabilities in the region. Offensive military capabilities and foreign assistance are two major means of competition. Alliance or alignment involves some level of commitment and an exchange of benefits for allied countries. In particular, an alignment amounts to mutual expectations between two or more states that they will have each other's support in disputes or wars with other states.

The regional competition theory involves several hypotheses.

If a great power confronts a single regional competitor, its asymmetric statecraft toward weaker non-allied neighbours serves as a signal to its regional competitor. By communicating a particular image, the great power can 1) more effectively deter the competitor, 2) enhance its strength without major resistance from that competitor, and 3) weaken the competitor's potential or existing alliances. Therefore, the great power projects and maintains a consistent image to the competitor by establishing a pattern of behaviour through uniform strategies.

If a great power confronts multiple regional competitors, this situation may challenge the power gap between the great power and the weaker non-allied powers. The great power hence bases its asymmetric statecraft toward weaker powers on the degree of its regional competitors' involvement. The greater the number of regional competitors and weaker powers in a region, the greater the possibility of differing degrees of involvement. The great power thus adopts a selective strategy toward multiple weaker neighbours.

If a great power is an alignment leader, it needs to solve two types of problems: 1) the collective action problem, which occurs when members of an alliance are engaged in a struggle against a potential enemy, and each member wishes to benefit from the public goods (such as security) that the alignment offers but expects other members to assume the greater responsibility; and 2) "commitment problems," which occur when allies share the expectation of fighting a potential enemy, but each one faces the abandonment/entrapment dilemma. A lower degree of commitment to allies would increase the chance of being abandoned by allies in the event of conflict. A higher degree of commitment to allies would increase the chance of being entrapped by allies out of their interests.

The alignment leader's confrontation of a regional competitor signifies that the latter is the former's main rival. The alignment leader therefore seeks to mobilize all available resources against the regional competitor. As this gives weaker allies the incentive to be free riders in this conflict, the alignment leader faces collective action problems. Consequently, it must offer greater incentives to weaker allies by adopting selective strategies in dealing with them.

When confronting multiple, as opposed to single, regional competitors, the alignment leader resists free-riding regional competitors amid great power conflict. Weaker allies demand concessions that, if refused, will likely result in the less committed among them abandoning the alignment leader in the event of conflict or entrapping the alignment leader in some conflict only for the weaker allies' interests. To avoid this type of commitment problem, therefore, the alignment leader needs to adopt uniform strategies that demonstrate an impartial level of security commitment benefiting all members of the alignment.

The regional competition theory is a dynamic theory that accounts for foreign policy variation, for three reasons. First, in dyadic relationships, the concept of competition implies the existence of different objectives. A particular state's objectives are frequently subject to change. A changing relationship between two states, based on an analysis of their objectives, can therefore occur even more frequently. Second, regional competition is based on the distribution of offensive military strength and assistance capabilities at the regional level. A global shift in this balance occurs less frequently – over decades – than a regional shift, which can occur in the space of a few years. By using the concept of regional competition, scholars can discuss how changes in the regional balance of power affect foreign policy. Third, the regional competition theory examines both systemic and process variables. The distribution of capabilities is a systemic variable, while relationships are process variables. The regional competition theory classifies relationships as asymmetric relationships, competitive relationships, and alignment relationships. The existence of asymmetric relationships is a basic premise of this research project, whereas competitive relationships and alignment relationships are explaining factors to account for policy changes. Countries in a specific region that have different objectives and independent capabilities have competitive relationships. In the event of armed conflict, countries with expectations of mutual support have alignment relationships. Together, independent capabilities, competitive relationships, and alignment relationships explain a great power's asymmetric statecraft. In brief, the number of regional competitors a great power has and its alignment relationships shape the great power's asymmetric statecraft, in terms of uniform strategies or selective strategies, toward multiple weaker neighbours.

This book conducts in-depth analysis of three historical cases: China's policies in East Asia from 1955 to 1965; in South Asia from 1955 to 1963; and in Indochina from 1962 to 1975. On the one hand, because China enjoyed tremendous advantages over its weaker neighbours in Asia during these periods, records of Chinese regional diplomacy provide opportunities for scholars to develop theories of asymmetric statecraft. On the other hand, in each case, China interchangeably adopted uniform strategies or selective strategies. Because the number of China's regional competitors was subject to change, each case demonstrates how this changing number affected China's regional diplomacy toward its neighbours. Moreover, differences across cases demonstrate how alignment relationships also shaped China's regional diplomacy. In the first two time periods, China's targets were weaker non-allies, whereas in the third period, China's targets were its allies. The empirical record for the three cases includes a total of thirty-one Chinese policies toward particular weaker neighbours and eleven Chinese diplomatic manoeuvres in the three distinct regions. This selection of cases enables me to use process-tracing techniques and structured, focused comparison to examine causal relationships between independent variables and the dependent variable. By analyzing extensive primary documents and scholarly works, I will demonstrate how the number of regional competitors and alignment relationships shapes a great power's asymmetric statecraft, based on Chinese regional diplomacy during the Cold War. Chapter 1 will include an in-depth discussion of how these cases were selected.

Historical Significance

This book evaluates the regional competition theory by analyzing extensive archival and media sources, drawing on a wealth of archival evidence, much of it previously inaccessible. Archival sources include those of the Chinese Foreign Ministry; nine provincial and municipal archives in China; Russian and German archives; the US National Archives; the Kennedy, Johnson, Nixon, and Ford Presidential Libraries; and the NATO Archives in Brussels. It also develops arguments by analyzing obscure Chinese-language publications on the Chinese Communist Party and China's contemporary foreign relations from various libraries in China and the United States. Finally, it analyzes China's recent regional practices through an investigation of official publications, semi-official media sources, scholarly articles, and online sources. Detailed discussions of archival sources are presented at the beginning of the Bibliography. The archival sources enabled me to provide historical narratives that contrast with traditional views of the Cold War dynamics in Asia. Conventional wisdom defines the Cold War in terms of the US-Soviet bipolar rivalry. Rather, by dividing

Asia into the maritime East Asia, South Asia, and Indochina, this book considers different features of competition in different subregions in Asia. When China was a Soviet ally between 1955 and 1958–59, the US-China confrontation reflected US-Soviet rivalry. After the 1958–59 period, Sino-Soviet policy differences changed the landscape and resulted in the US-Soviet-Chinese triangular competition in East Asia and South Asia. After the 1964–65 period, this triangular competition extended to Indochina. When the US military withdrew from Indochina in 1973, the Sino-Soviet competition became the defining feature of Cold War tensions in Asia.

Between 1955 and 1965, Japan and Taiwan were mainland China's weaker neighbours in East Asia.[15] Meanwhile, the United States was China's regional competitor. Japan was a defeated power without substantial military strength, and Taiwan depended on American aid for its survival. During this period, the United States established military bases in Japan and Taiwan. Between 1955 and 1958, Beijing interchangeably applied pressure on or sought compromises with both Tokyo and Taipei. However, these pressures and compromises formed a larger, single, uniform strategy that Beijing applied to both Japan and Taiwan. In the summer of 1958, the Soviet Union emerged as a new competitor in East Asia, and China became increasingly concerned about the degree of both American and Soviet involvement in the region. Between 1958 and 1965, Beijing adjusted its policy, adopting selective strategies toward Japan and Taiwan in order to maintain its power advantage over these weaker neighbours.

India, Pakistan, Afghanistan, Burma, and Nepal were China's non-allied neighbours in South Asia. Between 1955 and 1963, the United States was China's regional competitor, providing aid to the South Asian countries in order to limit Chinese influence. Between 1955 and 1959, China adopted uniform strategies toward, and sought compromises with, its weaker South Asian neighbours in an effort to dissuade their alignment with the United States. In the autumn of 1959, the Soviet Union became a regional competitor to China by extending aid in South Asia to weaken Chinese influence. Accordingly, between 1959 and 1963, China began assessing the degree of American and Soviet involvement in South Asia and adopted selective strategies toward its weaker neighbours in that region, countering the impact of American and Soviet aid while strengthening its own power advantages.

Between 1962 and 1975, North Vietnam and Cambodia were China's weaker Indochinese allies. The United States was China's regional competitor in the 1960s. During South Vietnam's disputes with North Vietnam and Cambodia, US support for South Vietnam made the Indochina conflict part of the broader US-China competition. Between 1962 and 1965, China adopted selective strategies toward North Vietnam and Cambodia to encourage Cambodia's armed struggle with the United States. In the spring of 1965, the Soviet Union became a regional competitor with China by extending aid to the two Indochinese countries. The Soviet aid helped China to counter US influence by supporting Chinese allies, but it also weakened Chinese influence by offering those allies new sources of external support and realignment options. China accordingly adopted uniform strategies toward North Vietnam and Cambodia to prevent their realignment with the Soviet Union. The US commitment to the complete withdrawal of armed forces from Indochina in 1973 left the Soviet Union as China's sole regional competitor. China then adopted selective strategies toward its weaker allies to pre-empt Soviet expansion in Indochina.

Policy Implications

The major policy motivation of this book is to contribute to the contemporary debate on China's regional diplomacy. The regional competition theory has policy implications to account for China's regional behaviour.

Chinese scholars have arrived at two important conclusions with respect to Chinese regional diplomacy. First, China is able to exert critical influence in its neighbourhood. For example, Chinese cooperation with the Association of Southeast Asian Nations (ASEAN) has shaped the regional order in Southeast Asia.[16] Also, as a great power neighbouring South Asia, China has strengthened the "8+1" cooperative mechanisms in the multilateral framework of the South Asian Association for Regional Cooperation (SAARC).[17] According to Yan Xuetong,

> from a geographical perspective ... it is more likely that our country can successfully shape the neighbourhood than the global environment. If we can concentrate our resources on shaping the neighbourhood, it will reduce direct pressures from the periphery ... Our economic strength, particularly trade abilities, is global; but both military strength and political power are still regional. Therefore, [we] should take active initiatives on global economic and trade affairs, but not get involved in political-military affairs beyond our neighbourhood.[18]

Second, Chinese scholars emphasize the close connections between Chinese regional diplomacy (*zhoubian waijiao*) and major-power diplomacy (*daguo waijiao*). These connections can be analyzed in three ways. First, third parties complicate China's conduct of diplomacy vis-à-vis the United States. These third parties, usually China's weaker neighbours, can be either US allies or friends of China.[19] Second, the US military presence in the Asia-Pacific region could be used during American allies' security conflict with China. Consequently, in the eyes of many Chinese analysts, the US forward defence in Asia has demonstrated a tendency directed against China in the context of US-China power competition.[20] Third, the United States has deliberately fostered a degree of tension in East Asia, maintained and strengthened its military presence there, and exploited small powers' suspicions of China's rise to induce their greater political, economic, and security cooperation with the United States.[21]

US policy has resulted in two critical implications for Chinese regional diplomacy. On the one hand, China was aware that the United States would, to some extent, encourage China's neighbours to implement assertive policies vis-à-vis China. For example, Sino-ASEAN security problems, beyond those concerning territorial settlements in the South China Sea, could reflect the instability emanating from a power struggle between China and the United States. Moreover, new problems could potentially arise in Sino-ASEAN relations if the United States, China, and ASEAN maintain their current pace of power accumulation.[22] Likewise, China was also sensitive to Indian attempts to establish strategic superiority over Pakistan through US-India cooperation.[23] On the other hand, China has understood the irreplaceable role of the American military presence in Asia with respect to protecting Chinese interests. The US presence, a source of reassurance for many of China's neighbours amid their engagements with China, ensured regional stability and cooperation. Therefore, China made no attempt to exclude American influence in Asia but instead emphasized the United States' "constructive" role on the Chinese periphery.[24]

Despite the consensus on China's ability to exert critical influence in its neighbourhood, and on the close connections between China's regional diplomacy and major-power diplomacy, Chinese scholars debate whether China should develop distinctive policies toward multiple weaker neighbours. Some argue that China should adopt uniform strategies that make no distinction among all such neighbours. According to Sun Xuefeng and Chen Hanxi, China should "exercise self-restraint" toward small powers in the Chinese neighbourhood, with the goal of maintaining stable US-China relations.[25] Xue Li argues that China should uphold a "principle of universal benefits" and make "appropriate concessions" to obtain the support of weaker neighbours.[26] In Zhang Yunling's view, China has always adopted uniform strategies toward weaker neighbours. "When the South China Sea disputes escalated in 2013, China took various initiatives toward ASEAN – upgrading a free-trade zone, constructing a community of shared future for all humankind, negotiating a Code of Conduct of the South China Sea, and promoting the conclusion of treaties of good neighbourliness and friendship."[27] As he puts it, China should establish more mechanisms with practical implications with ASEAN members, in pursuit of common security.[28] According to Fang Changping and Zheng Ling, China must avoid any selective treatment of ASEAN members.[29] This view is shared by Luo Shengrong and Zhao Qi, who emphasize that China should simultaneously promote cooperation with Vietnam, the Philippines, Malaysia, and Brunei toward stable relationships in the South China Sea.[30]

By contrast, other Chinese scholars emphasize the virtues of selective strategies.[31] Gao Cheng points out that "China can develop distinctive policies toward neighboring countries, in accordance with their political and economic relationships with China." China "needs to further investigate the nature of each bilateral relationship and accordingly develop selective policies to deal with them."[32] In particular, China should "cautiously hedge against" the Philippines and Vietnam and "actively cooperate with" Malaysia.[33] Zhou Fangyin argues that China should adopt a selective strategy – specifically, identifying targets, choosing windows of opportunity to implement policies, stepping up targeted pressures on specific countries, and avoiding uniform pressures.[34] He suggests that China establish deterrent postures in some cases while exercising self-restraint in others. In his view, Japan and the Philippines would be targets of coercion, whereas other regional audiences would be targets of reassurance.[35] In brief, as Wei Ling has suggested, China selectively engages with different countries on different issues while cooperating with weaker neighbours. Therefore, China should tailor its selective strategies in a more nuanced way by making distinctions between different countries to reflect their engagement on different issues.[36]

In light of the debate, Qi Huaigao and Ling Shengli suggest a potential way of reconciling these divergent perspectives. According to Qi Huaigao, China should adopt different policies in different regions: it should adopt uniform strategies in Southeast Asia – promoting strategic trust with ASEAN countries in order to lay the foundations for multilateral cooperation – while adopting selective strategies in South Asia.[37] On the one hand, China should respect Indian influence over Nepal, Bhutan, and Bangladesh. On the other, China should honour its commitment to Pakistan, an "all-weather" friend.[38] Ling Shengli examines Chinese regional diplomacy in Southeast Asia, Northeast Asia, South Asia, and Central Asia. After discussing Chinese practices in these regions, Ling emphasizes that China should seek overall cooperation with Southeast Asian countries but keep an eye on India.[39] The scholarly debate does not end here, but it has become evident in recent years that Chinese scholars are aware of the significance of selective diplomacy in Chinese foreign relations.

One defining feature of Chinese regional diplomacy is its continuity. This book therefore evaluates the regional competition theory based on China's foreign policy toward its weaker neighbours during the Cold War and the post–Cold War period, with a view to the future. Owing to its non-alignment policy, China has not given security commitments to any of its neighbours in the post–Cold War era. It enjoys tremendous advantages in the South China Sea, where the United States is its only regional competitor. China has tried to maintain a uniform strategy toward Vietnam, the Philippines, and Malaysia in order to communicate a consistent image to the United States. Meanwhile, both the United States and Russia have been China's regional competitors in South Asia, and India has received extensive assistance from both countries. Such foreign aid has provided India with the capability to challenge China. Therefore, China has engaged in selective strategies in South Asia – maintaining the status quo with India and enhancing Pakistan's position.

Plan of the Book

This book is organized as follows.

The Introduction examines policy debates on Chinese regional diplomacy within Chinese scholarly and policy communities and thus frames research questions on asymmetric statecraft.

Chapter 1 defines relevant concepts of asymmetric statecraft theory, summarizes current explanations of Chinese regional diplomacy from perspectives of the external threat theory and the domestic-ideological theory, and assesses the virtues and limitations of these two theories. It also proposes the hypotheses of the regional competition theory and provides procedures for evaluating the theory.

Chapters 2 to 4 examine China's Cold War diplomacy in East Asia, South Asia, and Indochina, using comparative case studies and process-tracing methods to assess the explanatory power of the regional competition theory.

Chapter 5 applies the theory to explain Chinese regional diplomacy in Southeast Asia and South Asia in recent years and predicts future Chinese behaviour with respect to shaping regional geopolitical maps of Asia.

The Conclusion summarizes major theoretical findings, identifies theoretical implications of historical research and area studies, and discusses future research on asymmetric statecraft.

1
A Regional Competition Theory of Asymmetric Statecraft

The term "asymmetric statecraft" refers to a great power's regional diplomacy toward more than one immediate neighbour in a particular region. The external threat theory and the domestic-ideological theory, as discussed below, are two major theories that explain asymmetric statecraft. The external threat theory emphasizes the restraints that the international distribution of military power imposes on foreign policy. The domestic-ideological theory stresses the implications of domestic political processes and normative concerns for changes in foreign policy. Both theories provide key insights in explaining asymmetric statecraft, but each has its limitations with respect to accounting for Chinese regional diplomacy.

In this chapter, I will propose relevant concepts, summarize current explanations of Chinese regional diplomacy from the perspectives of the external threat theory and the domestic-ideological theory, and assess the virtues and limitations of these two theories. I will then propose a regional competition theory of asymmetric statecraft to overcome these limitations and discuss the procedures for evaluating it. I will argue that the number of a great power's regional competitors and its alignment relationships shape its asymmetric statecraft, in the form of uniform strategies or selective strategies, toward multiple weaker neighbours.

Defining Asymmetric Statecraft

Scholars have different understandings of asymmetry. David Baldwin offers a few notions, namely causal asymmetry; imbalance of influence; unequal benefits; and uneven distribution of power resources.[1] Baldwin's discussion offers incisive and trenchant guidance on defining asymmetry. As Baldwin well argues, each notion has its virtues and limitations. Since scholars are hard put to provide operationalization of asymmetry based on the first three notions, I begin with a definition of asymmetry based on the uneven distribution of power resources. I define asymmetry as the power gap between a great power and a small power with respect to their offensive military capabilities.

Scholars have discussed three important differences between a great power and a small power. First, a great power is a nation-state with superior offensive military capabilities relative to other states in a region. In an anarchic international system, a nation-state runs the risk of war with other states. Therefore, military strength not only guarantees a state's survival but also enables the state to exert influence beyond its own borders.[2] By contrast, a small power's inherent military weakness forces that power to rely on ambiguous foreign assistance for survival.[3] This describes a scenario wherein a great power can produce offensive weapons, whereas small powers must depend on others to obtain them. For example, although India has been under greater scrutiny in the post–Cold War era, much of its weaponry, according to the *Economist* in 2016, was in fact outdated or ill maintained. On paper, India's air force was the world's fourth largest, with approximately 2,000 aircraft in service, but only 60 percent were typically fit to fly.[4] To a large extent, the disappointing situation was caused by Indian dependency on foreign supplies of its military hardware. Over 60 percent of India's armaments come from Russia. Since 2017, the Indian military has conducted negotiations with twenty-four arms suppliers, nineteen of them foreign corporations. As over 80 percent of its ammunition reserves do not meet Indian Defence Ministry standards, it would be impossible for the Indian military to conduct sustained fighting for more than ten days.[5] In other words, India lacks the capability to launch attacks without foreign support or sufficient military stocks. Such limited capability suggests that India is currently not a great power.

Second, a great power can independently decide its own foreign policy, whereas a small power has a limited degree of policy autonomy. For example, the United States formed balancing coalitions in Europe and Asia during the Cold War. In its asymmetric relationships, the United States deployed armed forces to guarantee the security of weaker allies. Meanwhile, it obtained forward bases, offered by its weaker allies, to project and extend American power. Of course, as Brantly Womack emphasizes, a small power does possess a certain degree of autonomy, so a great power is unable to unilaterally determine an asymmetric relationship.[6] As I have argued elsewhere, small powers, meanwhile, are by no means passive pawns on the chessboard.[7] For example, during the Cold War, Japan invited the United States to deploy armed forces on its territories to deter potential communist invasions. However, this initiative on Japan's part did not change the essentially asymmetric interdependence of the US-Japanese alliance. It was thus the United States that stationed troops and constructed bases in a foreign country, thereby extending US power. As Japan was unable to expand its own power by constructing bases in the United States, it depended on the United States to construct its security policy. With respect to Japan's case, it is neither GDP nor GDP per capita that defines a great power. For instance, prominent theorist Jack Levy does not regard Japan as having been a great power during the Cold War.[8]

Third, geographical features shape the effectiveness of offensive military power projection.[9] For example, the Soviet Union was a European great power in the 1950s, having deployed thousands of tanks and millions of troops in this region. However, it had no military presence in South Asia, which suggests that it lacked the capability to wage war in this region. Therefore, the Soviet Union was not a great power in South Asia in the 1950s. Similarly, China was able to send hundreds of thousands of troops to Indochina in the 1960s, but the Soviet Union sent only 1,165 advisers there. Therefore, China was a great power in the region, but the Soviet Union was not. In brief, a great power is defined in a particular region, and a small power is a nation-state of a particular region.

The foregoing discussion suggests that "region" is both a geographical and a political concept. Muthiah Alagappa defines a region in terms of geographical proximity, security interdependence, and common or similar historical and cultural experiences.[10] Alagappa's clear definition offers brilliant insights – as neighbouring states are more likely to develop closed security interdependence relationships – but different dimensions of the definition merit closer study. For example, China and Pakistan share a common border. The degree of their security interdependence is sufficiently high for Pakistan to be considered an "all-weather" friend of China. However, China and Pakistan do not share similar historical or cultural experiences. Confucianism is an influential political thought in China, a socialist state, whereas Islam is the state religion of Pakistan. In a similar vein, the United Kingdom and New Zealand share common historical and cultural experiences, but they are thousands of miles apart and without substantive security interdependence. Therefore, a definition of region should mainly consider geographical proximity and security interdependence. As Barry Buzan nicely puts it, "in security terms, 'region' means that a distinct and significant subsystem of security relations exists among a set of states whose fate is that they have been locked into geographical proximity with each other."[11]

Buzan convincingly places emphasis on security interactions between states in a specific region, whereas William Wohlforth, Samuel Huntington, and Brantly Womack, among other scholars, raise a new dimension by stressing interactions between regional powers and extra-regional powers. They discuss how regional balancing occurs. As Wohlforth argues, international politics is local, because it would be difficult, even for a great power, to project its power. The most potent threat or opportunity arises from a state's neighbourhood.[12] In an article with Stephen Brooks, Wohlforth argues that "were any of the potential challengers to make a serious run at the United States, regional balancing efforts would almost certainly help contain them, as would the massive latent power capabilities of the United States, which would be mobilized as necessary to head off an emerging threat."[13] Likewise, Huntington articulates his views as follows: "For the secondary regional powers ... [a] superpower's intervention is a resource that can potentially mobilize against their region's major power. The superpower and the secondary regional powers will thus often, although not always, share converging interest against major regional powers."[14] Womack agrees by underlining the importance of extra-regional powers.[15] In other words, interactions among great powers significantly shape, or even regulate, patterns of regional competition.

In a specific region, asymmetric relationships exist between one great power and several small powers. According to Womack, the representative scholar for studies of asymmetric relationships, existing scholarship on asymmetry simplifies international politics by mainly focusing on bilateral asymmetric relationships.[16] The scholarship seeks to understand patterns of interactions between a great power and a small power. In other words, the one-to-one asymmetric relationship is the primary research focus of existing scholarship. Theories in connection with the one-to-one asymmetric relationship are particularly useful for understanding many important international actors, behaviours, and events.[17] However, because one region might include multiple great powers and several small powers, the assumption of international politics as a set of one-to-one asymmetric relationships is incomplete. Accordingly, I propose a typology of asymmetric relationships based on numbers of great powers and small powers (Table 1.1).

Traditional inquiries about asymmetric relationships have examined the features of one-to-one asymmetric relationships but often overlooked the

Table 1.1 A typology of asymmetric relationships

	One great power	*Multiple great powers*
One small power	One-to-one asymmetric relationship (e.g., US-South Korea)	N-to-one asymmetric relationship (e.g., Chinese, Japanese, and Russian relationships with Korea in the late nineteenth century)
Multiple small powers	One-to-N asymmetric relationship (e.g., US-NATO members)	N-to-N asymmetric relationship (e.g., French, German, and Russian relationships with Eastern Europe, 1933–39)

three other types. An N-to-one asymmetric relationship can be a function of a symmetric relationship. A small power's relationships with multiple great powers usually reflect competition among the great powers over that small power. For instance, Korean relationships with China, Japan, and Russia in the late nineteenth century were an extension of those great powers' relationships. In this case, asymmetric relationships are attached to a symmetric relationship of great powers. I will therefore not discuss an N-to-one asymmetric relationship in the following sections. Meanwhile, an N-to-N asymmetric relationship can be divided into a set of one-to-N asymmetric relationships. For example, between 1933 and 1939, France, Germany, and Russia competed over small Eastern European powers. The asymmetric relationships can be divided into a set of asymmetric relationships of France–small powers, Germany–small powers, and Russia–small powers. I will explore an N-to-N asymmetric relationship through an investigation of a set of one-to-N asymmetric relationships. In summary, one-to-one and one-to-N are the most critical types of asymmetric relationships. Statecraft associated with the former type has been well researched, but statecraft in connection with the latter type merits closer study.

Traditional inquiries into asymmetric statecraft seek to understand a great power's coercion and accommodation toward a single weaker power. Scholars have interchangeably used the terms "appeasement" and "engagement" to discuss "accommodation."[18] The three concepts exhibit three common features. First, the core policy objective is to remove causes of tension without prompting a target's further demands.[19] Second, the main policy form is making "unequal or unilateral concessions."[20] Third, these policies usually involve highly asymmetric concessions made under conditions of relatively symmetric capabilities.[21] In other words, accommodation should be analyzed in terms of power relationships. The three above-mentioned features show the fundamental characteristics of accommodation as a foreign policy medium, but they do not discuss a great power's unequal or unilateral concessions to a small power.

Based on these discussions of accommodation, I propose accommodation as an attempt to satisfy a target's grievances in the interest of avoiding conflict. In particular, accommodation occurs in three situations: 1) a state makes asymmetric concessions under conditions of relatively symmetric capabilities; 2) a great power makes symmetric concessions to a small power; and 3) a great power makes unfavourable asymmetric concessions to a small power. The last is the least likely scenario in international politics and thus will be of greater theoretical significance. Typical forms of accommodation include reducing the size of military forces deployed on a neighbour's border, ceding territories in disputed areas, exercising restraint on subversive activities, making trade concessions, offering loans at attractive interest rates, and allowing local currency as a method of payment.

Coercion is the antonym of accommodation. As Lawrence Freedman argues, the key component of coercion is an overt military threat.[22] Freedman captures the essential features of coercion, but the actual concept of coercion would involve additional forms of a similar nature. Scholars have discussed both military threats and economic sanctions as major forms of coercion, for various political purposes.[23] This definition performs a useful service for the study of coercive diplomacy. Based on these definitions, I propose that to better discuss non-military means and covert threats, coercion should include two additional forms: subversion and diplomatic isolation. "Subversion" refers to interventions by one state through exploitation of the political divisions of another state. Suppose we have states A and B and non-state actors C and D within state B. D is the dominant political force in B, while C is challenging D's dominance. If A supports C in challenging D, then A is coercing B through subversion. "Diplomatic isolation," involving at least three states (A, B, and C), occurs in two scenarios. First, if B and C have an adversarial relationship, whereas neither A and B's relationship nor A and C's relationship is adversarial, then A's effort to seek cooperation with C at B's expense is A's coercion against B. Second, if A and B have an adversarial relationship, but neither A and C's nor B and C's relationship is adversarial, then A's effort to reduce the level of B-C cooperation is A's coercion against B. Accordingly, coercion takes four major forms – military threats, economic sanctions, subversion, and diplomatic isolation. I will use "coercion" and "pressure" interchangeably in the following discussions.

In addition, maintenance of the status quo is a state's attempt to preserve existing political or economic relationships without additional costs. For example, a state may neither increase nor decrease the size of its forces toward another country; it may neither raise more demands nor change previous stances in territorial disputes with another country; and it may neither impose trade sanctions on nor offer trade concessions to another country. Different understandings of "status quo" lead to different definitions of "status quo maintenance." For example, assuming T1 and T2 are two points on a time axis, a state may successfully change the status quo of T1 within a short period of time by adopting a "fait accompli strategy" and attempt to defend the new status quo at T2.[24] If a scholar defines the status quo according to the T1 situation, then the state's policy can be considered a policy to revise the status quo. If, however, a scholar defines the status quo according to the T2 situation, then the state's policy can be considered a policy to maintain the status quo. To avoid different understandings of "status quo maintenance," I begin my investigation starting from the point when asymmetry is established.

If two states are connected by an alignment relationship, I will examine how the level of alignment commitment affects foreign strategies. Security commitment is essential to an understanding of alignment relationships. A unilateral enhanced security commitment means one state's accommodation of its allies, whereas a unilateral decreased level of security commitment implies one state's pressure on allied states. An unchanged level of security commitment reflects one state's maintenance of the status quo vis-à-vis allies.

In conclusion, accommodation, coercion, and status quo maintenance are a great power's three major statecraft choices toward a small power.

If a great power engages with more than one small power in a region, the great power will adopt either a uniform strategy or a selective strategy toward the small powers. A uniform strategy refers to a great power's attempts to treat multiple small powers in generally the same way through uniform coercion, uniform accommodation, or uniform status quo maintenance. A selective strategy refers to a great power's attempts to differentiate multiple small powers through selective concessions or targeted coercion.[25] If a great power (A) engages with two small powers (B and C), A's use of either uniform strategies or selective strategies is as shown in Table 1.2.

Table 1.2 Asymmetric statecraft of a great power (A)

Uniform strategies	*Selective strategies*
Accommodation of B and C	Accommodation of B + coercion toward C
Coercion toward B and C	Accommodation of B + maintenance with C
Maintenance with B and C	Coercion toward B + maintenance with C

The puzzle of why a state chooses uniform strategies or selective strategies is of conceptual significance for two reasons. First, conventional wisdom assumes accommodation and coercion as a simple dichotomy; a selective strategy, however, advances an understanding that peacemaking and war making are not mutually exclusive. Second, and more importantly, the puzzle challenges the useful but incomplete approach of bilateral analysis of international politics. It requires more than one small power as a target to discuss one-to-N asymmetric relationships. In a one-to-one asymmetric relationship, scholars examine statecraft in terms of accommodation or coercion. In a one-to-N asymmetric relationship, they examine statecraft in terms of uniform strategies or selective strategies.

I will provide five caveats in order to better discuss the use of uniform strategies and selective strategies. First, I will discuss a great power's regional diplomacy toward its immediate neighbours. As discussed above, a region consists of a group of countries with close security interactions. This suggests that a great power should possess the capability to affect its neighbours in the region that defines the great power. For example, during the Cold War, China was unable to exert significant security influence in Africa, Latin America, or the Middle East because it did not belong to those regions; China's policies toward countries in these regions are therefore not discussed in this book. China's security interactions with its neighbours were more intensive, but during the Cold War its security interactions with Thailand, the Philippines, Indonesia, and Ceylon (Sri Lanka) were limited for various reasons. Thailand was an important state on the Chinese cultural periphery, but it did not share a common border with China. China could have exerted influence on Thailand through the Laotian left wing (the Pathet Lao). However, its impact on Thai foreign policy was limited due to the Pathet Lao's entrapment in the Laotian civil war. It was not until the late 1970s that China possessed the capacity to directly shape Thai foreign policy.[26] Likewise, the security interactions of the People's Republic of China (PRC) with the Philippines and Indonesia were limited because Chinese naval and air forces were unable to conduct extended military operations in the South China Sea. China was unable to shape Ceylon's security policy through use of force along a common border or its limited trade relationship with this island in the Indian Ocean. This book does not seek to explain the PRC's practices where its security interactions with regional audiences were inadequate.

Second, I seek to understand state behaviour, and non-state actors can, of course, be important policy instruments in a state's foreign policy.[27] For example, the Burmese Communist Party (BCP) was a factor in the state-to-state relationship between China and Burma during the Cold War. China imposed restraints on the BCP when it sought to constrain Burma's alignment with the United States in the 1950s, but during the Chinese Cultural Revolution in the 1960s, China exerted pressure on the Burmese government through its support for the BCP. I will not discuss how China affected the BCP through the Burmese government but rather how China affected the Burmese government through the BCP.[28]

Third, I will discuss uniform and selective strategies by making a distinction between allied states and non-allied states. According to Glenn Snyder, "alignment amounts to a set of mutual expectations between two or more states that they will have each other's support in disputes or wars with particular other states."[29] Therefore, alignment includes alignment *against* as well as *with,* by identifying potential opponents as well as friends.[30] By Stephen Walt's definition, alignment involves some level of commitment and an exchange of benefits for allied countries.[31] Therefore, alignment relationships overdetermine foreign policies. A state should practice selective strategies toward one allied state and one non-allied state. For example, during the Cold War, North Korea was a Chinese ally, whereas South Korea was a Chinese enemy, and China adopted selective strategies toward the two countries. This book does not examine the reasons for this. In discussions of uniform and selective strategies, scholars must pinpoint cases where a great power needs to engage with multiple allied states or multiple non-allied states.

Fourth, I will discuss a great power's alignment strategies when its weaker allies assume obligations of mutual assistance against a common enemy in a region. For example, during the Cold War, the United States extended its alignments in Asia and Europe. US Asian allies did not pledge continued support vis-à-vis each other, but US European allies assumed responsibilities for mutual assistance in the event of war. I will examine asymmetric relationships only in the latter case. Another case can be seen in Chinese alignments. China, North Korea, and the Democratic Republic of Vietnam had a common enemy – the United States – in the 1960s. However, mutual assistance between North Korea and the DRV was negligible because these weaker powers were unable to provide it. Consequently, I will refrain from discussions of this case. By contrast, after 1962, the United States became the common enemy of China, the DRV, and Cambodia. China provided aid to the DRV and Cambodia; the DRV exploited Cambodian territory to launch attacks against US armed forces; and Cambodia exploited the DRV's military presence to contend with South Vietnam, a US ally. In sum, China, the DRV, and Cambodia fought against common enemies on a single battlefield. This case meets the standard of mutual alignment commitment. I will discuss cases where the weaker allies of a great power render aid to each other.

Finally, I will not examine a small power with low foreign policy autonomy. For example, Sikkim and Bhutan, China's neighbours, had always been under Indian control during the Cold War. Sikkim was a protectorate of India, and India's financial and technical underwriting of Bhutan's first two five-year plans was 100 percent. At Bhutan's request, India dealt with China on territorial issues on Bhutan's behalf.[32] Consequently, Sikkim and Bhutan were unable to make their own foreign policies, and China's policies toward them were therefore subordinate to China's India policy. China had no specific policy toward either Sikkim or Bhutan.

Existing Explanations of Chinese Regional Diplomacy

Asymmetric statecraft is a great power's particular form of foreign policy. Current theories of foreign policy shed light on it from the external threat and domestic-ideological perspectives.

First, structural realism, offensive realism, defensive realism, institutional realism, and liberal institutionalism offer explanations of foreign policy from the external threat perspective. Structural realists emphasize an international distribution of military power as a necessary but insufficient condition for explaining foreign policy.[33] Based on structural realism, offensive realists explain foreign policy through the lens of revisionist motivations,[34] whereas defensive realists explain foreign policy, with a focus on security demands, through that of a broken balance of power.[35] Institutional realists argue that international regimes may alter actors' definitions of interest, calculations of how to maximize their interest, and/or the power capabilities of different actors.[36] Liberal institutionalism emphasizes that institutions may reduce transaction costs in a variety of ways, such as by providing information, and therefore institutions shape the threat perception and behaviour of states.[37] To secure legitimate national interests, a great power creates and maintains international institutions and thus exercises self-restraint and makes concessions to small powers.[38]

Second, proponents of neoclassical realism, the two-level game theory, and constructivism think highly of domestic politics as a necessary condition for explaining foreign policy. As Thomas Pedersen argues, domestic structural factors shape ideational factors and thus explain foreign policy.[39] Therefore, the theory, which stresses the importance of domestic political processes and elite perceptions, inevitably connects with ideational factors. Ideology is conceived as a set of normative values and relatively enduring beliefs that refer to ideas of what ought to be.[40] As neoclassical realists put it, external threats are processed through a lens of domestic politics. Therefore, foreign policy is a function of the preferences of political elites and social groups.[41] Ideological divisions among states affect a state's alliance behaviour when forging a balancing coalition. Ideological competition also has an impact on a state's deterrent strategies and outcomes.[42] According to the two-level game theory, policy makers need to conduct negotiations at both the national and the international levels, striking a balance between the needs of the two, and therefore may produce suboptimal policies.[43] According to constructivists, identities and values are more important determinants of policy than the constraints and opportunities of an external environment.[44] Ideology provides a value system for elites that enables them to create transnational affiliations. These normative networks provide a basis for identifying with certain foreign states and being averse to others. Therefore, elites with different ideologies make different strategic choices.[45]

The external threat theory and the domestic-ideological theory provide key insights into asymmetric statecraft and Chinese regional diplomacy. These theories, however, have certain limitations in explaining the practice of Chinese asymmetric statecraft. The external threat theory addresses the principal question of constraints on foreign policy by focusing on the international distribution of military strength. However, it provides an inadequate explanation of Chinese regional practices for three reasons. First, China may adopt similar regional strategies when its external threat perception changes. The external threat theory cannot adequately explain the continuity of Chinese regional diplomacy under different threat perceptions. Second, China may adopt a different regional strategy even when its external threat perception is unchanged. The external threat theory cannot fully explain how a country without military capabilities threatens a country with military capabilities in a region. Military strength is a crucial means to regional competition but not the only one. Finally, China did not join regional institutions until the late 1990s. Neither institutional realism nor liberal institutionalism can adequately explain Chinese threat perception or regional diplomacy during the Cold War.

The domestic-ideological theory examines domestic bases of foreign policy and explains well why a great power adopts different strategies given similar international conditions. Nonetheless, it has two limitations in explaining Chinese regional practices. On the one hand, it inadequately explains why China adopts a selective strategy toward multiple weaker neighbours given the domestic-ideological conditions at a particular historical moment. On the other hand, the theory does not sufficiently account for China's similar foreign strategies toward multiple weaker neighbours despite significantly different domestic-ideological conditions.

The External Threat Theory

Many China security experts provide incisive explanations of Chinese regional diplomacy through the external threat lens. If an adversarial great power exercises significant influence over a weaker neighbour of China, then China will regard that small power as being exploited by the adversarial great power as a forward base directed against China. This concern is most likely to lead to Chinese pressure on the small power. If, by contrast, an adversarial great power has disputes with China's weaker neighbour, then China is most likely to exploit such differences out of self-interest. As David M. Lampton puts it, China's regional objective is not to dictate outcomes so much as to prevent others in the region from undertaking activities that threaten core Chinese interests.[46] With respect to China's East Asia policy, Robert S. Ross and other scholars argue that the Chinese peaceful offensive in the 1950s was used as a wedge to weaken the US alliance system in Asia.[47] A. Doak Barnett and Akira Iriye hold that mainland China exerted pressure on Japan and Taiwan when the two weaker powers consolidated security ties with Washington.[48] M. Taylor Fravel and Zhang Shuguang contend that declining Chinese strength was the main cause of the Chinese initiations of crises in the Taiwan Strait.[49]

These explanations offer great insights into Chinese behaviour in the context of Sino-American confrontation. However, the theory does not adequately explain how China was constrained by a militarily weak power in East Asia. It was China, rather than the Soviet Union, that had a substantial military presence in East Asia during this period. According to US intelligence analyses, China had the capacity to launch an amphibious assault by an estimated 75,000 to 100,000 troops.[50] Meanwhile, between 1958 and 1965, the Soviet Union had no military presence in East Asia. As will be discussed, divergent Sino-Soviet policy objectives in East Asia constrained Chinese strategic options in the Taiwan Strait. Soviet attempts to get involved in the Taiwan Strait area contributed to Chinese policy adjustments and decisions to end the crisis in October 1958. The external threat theory, therefore, is inadequate to explain how a country without military capabilities in East Asia (the Soviet Union) was able to constrain the options of a country with military capabilities in the region (China).

Scholars have also examined China's South Asia policy from the external threat perspective. Allen S. Whiting identifies the "joint Russo-Indian threat" as the motivation for Chinese use of force against India.[51] John W. Garver argues that US support of Tibetan insurgents heightened the level of China's perceived threat.[52] Fravel suggests that a decline in Chinese bargaining power with India provides one explanation for the escalation of the country's South Asia policy – on concluding that India was strengthening its relatively strong position, China attempted to use force to either halt or reverse its own decline.[53] According to Fravel, the Indian forward policy changed the local military balance. In particular, transportation was a source of Chinese vulnerability: "Tibet lacked communication links with China proper and Xinjiang ... Even after three roads connecting Tibet to Qinghai, Gansu, and Xinjiang were constructed in the 1950s, transportation difficulties remained, as many of the roads were not passable in winter and were often in disrepair."[54] Based on Fravel's account, China was militarily too weak to contend with India in disputed border areas. India's attempts to strengthen its bargaining power, therefore, prompted assertive Chinese responses.

The above arguments capture the most important dynamics in the regional competition in South Asia between 1959 and 1963. China was in competition with both the United States and the Soviet Union, neither of which, however, had any substantial military presence in South Asia during this period. If a great power is defined in terms of offensive military capabilities in a region, therefore, neither the United States nor the Soviet Union was a great power in South Asia. China, by contrast, had substantial military capabilities in the region. According to US intelligence analyses, China "could support about 300,000 men in the fighting area (170,000 in combat), assuming no interdiction of their road net."[55] The external threat theory does not adequately explain how the two countries without military capabilities (the United States and the Soviet Union) threatened a country with military capabilities (China) in South Asia. If China's perceived threats were genuine, what were the sources of its threat perception? As I will argue, American and Soviet aid to South Asian nations shaped China's perception with respect to sources of regional instability and thus circumscribed China's regional choices.

Another shortcoming of the external threat theory is that it underestimates Chinese advantages over its South Asian neighbours. The theory persuasively identifies weak logistical capabilities in the Sino-Indian border region as a major problem for China, but the situation changed quickly in the mid-1950s. China completed two major roads for vehicle transport (the Qinghai-Tibet and Sichuan-Tibet roads) connecting Tibet to inland China on December 25, 1954.[56] The PRC's deputy premier, Chen Yun, explained Chinese logistical capabilities in his letter to Premier Zhou Enlai: "From January to April of the next year [1956], along the Qinghai-Tibet road, [we can] deliver 12,500 tons of food to stabilize the price level in Tibet. Meanwhile, we can deliver 12,000 tons of other materials to construct airports in Tibet."[57] Moreover, between 1957 and 1958, China completed the Xinjiang-Tibet road. The three major roads solved the main obstacles to military mobilization in Tibet, and they enabled the Chinese to stockpile substantial supplies of food and ammunition there. In addition to these transportation advances, the Lhasa revolt in 1959 presented opportunities for China. By 1952, the Dalai Lama's local government in Tibet (the Kashag) had amassed over 15,000 tons of food.[58] Hypothetically, if a war lasted six months (180 days) in Tibet and one soldier consumed one kilogram of food per day, then 15,000 tons of food could support over 83,000 troops. Scholars may not know the exact amount of food the Kashag had collected by 1959, but undoubtedly the People's Liberation Army (PLA) was able to use it in the aftermath of the 1959 Lhasa revolt. Assuming no external involvement, the overall Chinese military superiority, the Chinese road network in Tibet, and the collapse of the Kashag rendered Chinese military strength sufficient to meet its security needs in South Asia.

Indochina was another critical region in Chinese regional diplomacy. Scholars have also explained China's Indochina policy by focusing on US and Soviet constraints on Chinese behaviour in the region. As Ross emphasizes, China adamantly opposed the establishment by any power of dominant influence in a country of Indochina and possessed both the will and the capacity to inflict great cost on any such power that challenged Chinese interests.[59] According to Zhang Shuguang, China supported North Vietnam in the 1960s to "resist both threats [from the United States and the Soviet Union]."[60] Anne Gilks and Nicholas Khoo further argue that the Sino-Soviet conflict determined China's Vietnam policy when the Soviet Union became China's principal rival.[61] From Lien-Hang T. Nguyen's perspective, China "no longer wanted a unified Vietnam under the control of Hanoi, given the deterioration of Sino-Vietnamese relations and the strengthening of Soviet-Vietnamese relations."[62] Moreover, as Zhai Qiang argues, "China's handling of the Cambodian conflict from 1970 to 1975 was conditioned primarily by its competition with the Soviet Union and North Vietnam in Indochina."[63] Robert A. Scalapino, Brantly Womack, and Zhang Xiaoming also underline the importance of China's stepping up of pressure on Vietnam with the object of resisting Soviet expansion in Indochina.[64]

The above analysis persuasively demonstrates Soviet and US constraints on China, but its applications of the external threat theory leave three issues unsolved. First, the external threat theory does not explain how a militarily weak power in Indochina (the Soviet Union) weakened the position of a militarily strong power in the same region (China). It was China rather than the Soviet Union that had a substantial military presence in Indochina. From 1965 to 1968, China deployed 320,000 troops to North Vietnam for air defence, railway and road construction, and logistical support.[65] Beijing was able to send hundreds of thousands of troops, whereas Moscow sent only 1,165 advisers.[66]

Second, the external threat theory underestimates the limitations of Soviet-Vietnamese cooperation. In November 1969, the DRV's political and military headquarters in South Vietnam delivered instructions of General Vo Nguyen Giap, the DRV's principal military leader, to local commanders in South Vietnam. Hanoi's private assessment was that the Soviet Union had "overestimated the capabilities of the Americans, and feared a nuclear confrontation with them ... [T]he USSR aided us because they wanted to gain profits from the diplomatic bargaining with the Americans"; the DRV should therefore not rely on the Soviet Union.[67] As China well understood, during the war with the United States, Soviet-Vietnamese differences prevented Hanoi from becoming a Soviet instrument to challenge China.

Third, the external threat theory underestimates the degree of the DRV's dependence on China. The DRV expanded its military forces – from 195,000 at the beginning of 1965 to 350,000 in May 1965 and to 400,000 by the end of 1965.[68] However, the DRV's armed forces were still too weak to contend with the United States. Given the Sino-Vietnamese alignment, the DRV was unable to threaten an alignment leader (China) without substantive external support. On the one hand, Soviet-Vietnamese cooperation did not sufficiently meet the DRV's demand during the war with the United States. On the other, heavily bombed by US air strikes over the years, the DRV needed Chinese deterrence of US intervention between 1964 and 1972. The DRV was unable to impose threats on China given the Sino-Vietnamese alignment vis-à-vis the United States.

The Domestic-Ideological Theory

The domestic-ideological theory explains Chinese foreign policy through three specific mechanisms: normative views, domestic mobilization, and regime security. With respect to normative views, as Chen Jian argues, three fundamental and interrelated rationales dominated Chinese foreign policy: 1) the revolutionary nationalism of the Chinese Communist Party (CCP), 2) its sense of responsibility toward an Asia-wide or worldwide revolution, and 3) its determination to maintain the inner dynamics of the Chinese revolution.[69] According to Lorenz M. Lüthi, the Taiwan Strait Crisis in 1958 was "a function of the Great Leap Forward," and elsewhere "domestic developments alone determined the timing of the shelling of Jinmen."[70] "During 1959, Mao's criticism of Nikita Khrushchev's conduct in international affairs changed from the rejection of peaceful coexistence to radical support for world revolution."[71] Prior to the Sino-Indian war in 1962, "Mao was more than happy to carp at the Soviet archrevisionist for his wobbly support of revolutionary China against bourgeois India."[72] Chen Jian, Lorenz Lüthi, and Lien-Hang T. Nguyen emphasize that Chinese support for the DRV was a means of promoting "continuous revolution" and competing with the Soviet Union for the leadership of the communist world.[73] In addition to the arguments on communism, Alastair Iain Johnson examines the impact of nationalism. As he puts it, China was sensitive to territorial issues because the territorial integrity of the state was central to establishing the legitimacy of the PRC in 1949. As a new state with many borders, China was more risk-acceptant about consolidating its territorial integrity.[74] Following this line of reasoning, Manjari Chatterjee Miller develops a "generalizable" theory of "post-imperial ideology." According to her, Chinese victimhood in the postcolonial era prevented Chinese accommodation of India during border negotiations in 1960.[75]

Besides normative considerations, political mobilization furnishes thoughtful understanding of Chinese foreign policy. Chen Jian, Hosoya Chihiro, and Thomas Christensen provide insights to this effect. From Chen's perspective, "Beijing's leaders used force always for the purpose of domestic mobilization."[76] Hosoya Chihiro and Thomas Christensen examine the validity of this argument based on China's East Asia policy.

Hosoya argues that Chinese domestic political changes brought about changes in China's Japan policy.[77] Christensen examines the linkage between domestic ideological pressures and external threats by showing different Chinese concerns during the Taiwan Strait Crises in 1954 and 1958. In 1954, grave Chinese concern over Taiwan's inclusion in the US-sponsored formation of an alliance system triggered Chinese military operations.[78] In 1958, however, Chinese leaders initiated a crisis in the Taiwan Strait in order to mobilize resources for domestic purposes, notably the "Great Leap Forward."[79]

The arguments about normative views and domestic mobilization underscore the importance of active initiatives taken by Chinese leaders to shape foreign policy. By contrast, arguments about regime security focus more on passive responses of Chinese leaders with respect to adjusting foreign policy. John Garver analyzes the impact of Tibetan instability on Sino-Indian relations. Difficult situations in Tibet and the Fourteenth Dalai Lama's asylum in India resulted in a sharp deterioration in Sino-Indian relations and contributed to Chinese border offensives in 1962.[80] Fravel explains Chinese policy shifts in this way:

> China offered concessions in territorial disputes with Tibet's neighbors in exchange for assistance in suppressing the revolt and bolstering domestic instability. In early 1962, China's leaders confronted an economic crisis and famine following the Great Leap Forward along with ethnic unrest in Xinjiang ... Facing these challenges to territorial integrity, China compromised again. In both rounds of compromise in the 1960s, improved ties with neighbors were more important than holding out for maximal claims on its land border.[81]

The domestic-ideological theory performs a useful service for two reasons. First, it advances understandings of internal-international linkage, and it persuasively suggests that domestic problems exacerbated Chinese security problems. For example, economic problems caused by the Great Leap Forward sparked grave Chinese concerns about international security and thus had an impact on foreign policy. Second, the theory enables a more dynamic way to account for policy changes, and it convincingly explains why China adopted different strategies given similar international environments. For example, the theory takes into account the nuanced but crucial impact of Sino-Soviet ideological differences on Chinese regional diplomacy.

Nonetheless, the domestic-ideological theory offers insufficient explanation of Chinese regional diplomacy for two reasons. First, it does not account for Chinese selective strategies given domestic-ideological situations at a historical moment in China. For example, given China's domestic and ideological conditions in 1958, mainland China still adopted a selective strategy toward Japan and Taiwan. In a similar vein, China, India, and Burma shared the same "McMahon Line," drawn by the British, which carried colonial implications for all three countries, but between 1959 and 1963 China adopted a selective strategy toward India and Burma. Likewise, between 1973 and 1975, China continued with the Cultural Revolution, and the Chinese domestic-ideological need to resist American "imperialism" and Soviet "revisionists" persisted throughout the period. Constant domestic-ideological priorities, however, cannot fully explain China's selective strategies toward the DRV and Cambodia. China circumscribed the DRV's armed struggle in South Vietnam but encouraged the armed struggle in Cambodia. The domestic-ideological theory, therefore, does not fully explain Chinese selective strategies toward multiple weaker neighbours.

Second, the domestic-ideological theory offers little guidance in explaining similar Chinese strategies under different domestic-ideological conditions. For instance, China's domestic conditions in the two periods 1956–57 and 1960–61 were significantly different. In the former period, China stressed economic construction, whereas in the latter period it emphasized class struggle. Although an economic crisis occurred only in the second period, China made territorial concessions to Burma in both periods.

The Regional Competition Theory

The external threat theory and the domestic-ideological theory offer brilliant insights into the asymmetric statecraft of a great power, but both have their limitations in explaining Chinese regional diplomacy. Based on these two theories, I propose a regional competition theory. I argue that the number of a great power's regional competitors and its alignment relationships shape its asymmetric statecraft, with respect to uniform strategies or selective strategies, toward multiple weaker neighbours. In what follows, I define "regional competitors," propose hypotheses of the regional competition theory, and offer a research design through which to assess the theory's explanatory power.

Regional Competitors and Alignment Relationships

In view of the theory development in international relations, working with a limited number of variables is the key, according to Morton A. Kaplan. He argues that "the central variables will include the major kinds of actors participating in international politics, their capabilities, including military capability, their motivations, their goals orientations, and their style of strategic and political activity."[82] I agree with him. As discussed above, nation-states are actors of the regional competition theory, and the dependent variable is a great power's regional diplomacy, that is, asymmetric statecraft. Accordingly, I need to identify the features of regional competitors in order to discuss their motivations and capabilities.

From a great power perspective, a regional competitor is a state that does not share common objectives and has independent capabilities in the region. A discussion of regional competitors therefore requires at least two states with different objectives. The regional competition theory emphasizes one or several dyadic competitive objectives at a specific historical moment in a specific region. A discussion of regional competitors also considers the means to achieve specific policy ends. The external threat theory defines capabilities in terms of military strength. Based on that theory, and following Hans J. Morgenthau, I add the capability of providing military or economic assistance as an alternative means to achieve foreign policy objectives.[83] This view is shared by Stephen Walt, who argues that aid can strengthen weaker states whose goals complement one's own. Providing assistance could be an effective way to convey friendly intentions, whereas refusal to offer support would be viewed as a sign of hostility.[84]

Based on these views, I argue that offensive military capabilities and foreign assistance are two major means of competing. On the one hand, military capabilities enable a state to exert greater influence by inflicting serious damage on adversaries or competitors. On the other hand, providing aid enables a state to maximize influence by enhancing the capabilities of allies, partners, or friends. Providing and receiving aid usually suggest a greater degree of cooperation between a donor and a recipient. Military and economic assistance are two major forms of aid, but the distinction between them is usually unclear.[85] A donor's military assistance may contribute to a recipient's military capabilities, and a donor's economic assistance may help a recipient accumulate funds toward a more substantial military build-up. Therefore, both military and economic assistance are means for the donor to exert influence over the recipient.

The power asymmetry between a great power and a small power amplifies the political implications of foreign assistance. A great power's assistance to a small power has dual implications – accommodation and coercion. If a small power agrees voluntarily to align its foreign policy with a great power's foreign policy in return for a stipulated benefit – foreign assistance – such assistance strengthens cooperation between the small power and the great power.[86] For purposes of survival, however, in an anarchic system a great power depends on its military strength, whereas a small power depends on foreign assistance. Therefore, a small power could claim that it "voluntarily" adopted a specific policy in order to obtain foreign assistance from a great power. However, the "voluntary policy" might be proposed in the first place by the small power in view of the great power's preferences.

A great power's regional competitor must possess independent capabilities. Dependency usually takes two forms: 1) limited resources, and 2) prior consultation with other states before taking action. For example, India assisted Nepal in the 1950s but also received a much higher level of assistance from the United States and the Soviet Union. Therefore, India's ability to assist Nepal was not independent. Similarly, the United Kingdom assisted India and Pakistan in the 1950s but always coordinated with the United States beforehand.[87] This coordination was rooted in the fact that the United Kingdom also received American assistance in various forms; thus, the British ability to assist South Asia was not independent.

In conclusion, the formation of a competitive relationship requires two conditions: 1) competing policy objectives, and 2) the use of policy instrument(s) to achieve the objectives. A competitive relationship does not exist in the absence of competing policy objectives, and neither can it be formed if one side does not attempt to weaken the other side's influence or constrain the other side in some way. The regional competition theory does not seek to explain how one or several competitive relationships form. Rather, it seeks to examine the impact of the competitive relationships. For example, Chapter 2 does not seek to explain origins or causes of the Sino-Soviet split. Rather, it examines impacts of the Sino-Soviet competition in East Asia.

From a great power's perspective, if there is more than one regional competitor, then collaborative involvement is possible. Collaborative involvement implies that the regional competitors take actions toward the same effect in regional competition. If one great power has two regional competitors, then collaborative involvement, to a high or low degree, can be measured in the following order: 1) the two regional competitors resort to coercion against the great power; 2) one regional competitor resorts to coercion against the great power, while the other regional competitor assists the great power's weaker neighbours; and 3) both regional competitors assist the great power's weaker neighbours. In the final case, the amount of assistance determines the degree of collaborative involvement.

A great power's choices are circumscribed not only by its regional competitors but also by its allied states. The impact of alignment relationships can be observed in three aspects. First, states entering an alignment may redefine their self-interests and embrace at least some of the partners' interests as their own.[88] Second, alignments increase policy coordination costs among allied states. Allied states might abandon some of their own favoured policies and adopt policies of their allies that are costly to themselves. Military coordination can also be costly. It suggests that allied joint forces will fight more effectively but less so if allied states must fight without help from others.[89] Third, an allied state would have to face the "abandonment/entrapment dilemma." Abandonment means defection by allies in the event of war, while entrapment means being dragged into a conflict over an ally's interests that one does not share. A strong commitment to an ally reduces the risk of abandonment but encourages that ally to run greater risks against an adversary, and it thus increases the risk of entrapment. A weak commitment to an ally reduces the risk of entrapment but casts doubt on one's loyalty, and it thus increases the risk of abandonment.[90]

In conclusion, to conduct its regional diplomacy, a great power needs to consider both its regional competitors and its allies. An alignment relationship overdetermines a great power's policies toward one allied state and one non-allied state. Consequently, the great power always adopts a selective strategy in this case. I will therefore discuss a great power's policies toward multiple weaker allies or weaker non-allies. In each case, the great power behaves differently when it faces one or multiple regional competitors. In other words, I will discuss how the number of a great power's regional competitors and its alignment relationships (independent variables) shape its asymmetric statecraft (the dependent variable), with respect to uniform strategies or selective strategies, toward multiple weaker neighbours. It is worth noting that collaborative involvement is not an independent variable. If a great power confronts only one regional competitor, collaborative involvement does not exist, whereas if a great power confronts more than one regional competitor, collaborative involvement is possible. Therefore, collaborative involvement is only one consequence, when one independent variable (the number of regional competitors) has one specific value.

Hypotheses

How does a great power practise asymmetric statecraft vis-à-vis multiple weaker non-allies? From a great power perspective, when confronting a single regional competitor, the potential challenge comes from that competitor's support for weaker powers. Therefore, to prevent potential challenges, the great power's asymmetric statecraft must address the intentions of the regional competitor.

By communicating a particular image to the regional competitor, the great power can take the upper hand in the competition. First, the great power may seek to communicate high resolve by taking coercive measures against weaker powers. Such an image serves as one facet of a "general deterrence" against the competitor.[91] If the regional competitor correctly perceives the image, then it is less likely to challenge the great power. In other words, the great power can more effectively and more efficiently deter the regional competitor's potential support for weaker neighbouring powers. For example, the Soviet Union was the United States' regional competitor in Europe in the 1950s. The effectiveness of the "rolling back" policy that the United States adopted toward Eastern Europe was undermined by the Soviet military presence. Although unable to change regimes in Eastern Europe, the United States nevertheless successfully established a general deterrence. In view of the United States' high resolve, therefore, the Soviet Union did not exploit its geographical proximity and conventional military superiority by launching attacks in Western Europe.

Second, a great power may seek to communicate a defensive posture by maintaining the status quo with weaker powers. If its regional competitor correctly perceives a defensive stance, then it is less likely to worry about the great power's capabilities and intentions and hence less likely to try to deter the great power from taking coercive measures. The great power can therefore enhance its strength, such as by rearmament or alignment formation, without major resistance from its competitor. For example, the United States was the Soviet Union's only regional competitor in Europe in the 1950s. By adopting a policy of peaceful coexistence – joining the Geneva Conference, withdrawing troops from Austria, and promoting trade with Western Europe – the Soviet Union eased tensions with the United States and was able to buy time for its own military modernization programs without provoking dramatic US responses. For example, in the 1960s, the number of Soviet intercontinental ballistic missiles (ICBMs) grew sixfold within six years (Table 1.3).

Table 1.3 Number of Soviet ICBMs, 1960–65

Year	*Number of Soviet ICBMs*
1960	35
1961	50
1962	75
1963–64	100
1964–65	200

Source: Adapted from *The Military Balance* (London: Institute for Strategic Studies, 1963–66)

Third, a great power may seek to project an image of moderation by making concessions to weaker powers. As long as its regional competitor correctly perceives the image, the great power can minimize the regional competitor's influence in two ways: 1) by constraining the regional competitor from forming an adversarial alliance, or 2) by eliciting concerns on the part of the regional competitor about the cohesiveness of its alliances. In both cases, the regional competitor understands that the weaker power might well accept the great power's offer of closer cooperation. For example, Leonid Brezhnev, General Secretary of the Central Committee of the Communist Party of the Soviet Union, told the Party Central Committee in December 1966: "It is our undeniable obligation, as well as an important aspect of our foreign policy, to exploit contradictions within the imperialist camp."[92] Guided by this principle, the Soviet Union launched a peaceful offensive toward Western Europe through oil exports. Table 1.4 shows Soviet oil exports to major trade partners in Western Europe in the 1970s, when the United States was the Soviet Union's only regional competitor in Europe. The Soviet oil exports ameliorated Western European economic pain, established a moderate Soviet image of the United States, and sparked grave American concern about the cohesiveness of the Atlantic Alliance.

Projecting a particular image to the regional competitor is important, but maintaining a consistent image of the competitor is always difficult. One policy may project different images. The great power may seek to demonstrate its resolve, but its competitor may interpret coercion either as a bluff or as a threat. The great power may seek to demonstrate defensive postures, but its competitor may interpret maintenance as a cover for offensive postures. The great power may seek to demonstrate its moderation, but its competitor may interpret accommodation as a sign of weakness.

TABLE 1.4 Soviet oil exports to Western Europe, 1971–76 (in 10,000 tons)

	1971	*1972*	*1973*	*1974*	*1975*	*1976*
France	453.9	307.8	534.8	136.0	330.7	572.9
Austria	112.8	96.7	125.0	97.0	132.7	151.3
Belgium	203.9	251.6	167.3	175.2	125.5	208.2
Spain	21.4	78.4	51.0	135.1	172.4	200.2
Italy	900.2	843.0	865.2	678.8	688.3	1,198.2
Holland	163.1	243.3	320.0	297.5	309.0	267.4
Germany[1]	609.2	619.5	584.9	634.0	763.4	713.2
Finland	856.7	862.7	1,002.8	917.3	876.8	962.0

1 Federal Republic of Germany (West Germany).
Source: Hu Yanfen, "Sulian de shiyou waimao zhengce" [The Soviet oil export policy], in *Liangci shiyou weiji dui shijie jingji de yingxiang* [Impact of two oil crises upon world economy], ed. Institute of Southeast Asia of Yunnan Province and Institute of Southwest Asia of Yunnan University (1983), 172, available at the Library of the Chinese Academy of International Trade and Economic Cooperation, Ministry of Commerce of the People's Republic of China.

Therefore, the great power needs to project and maintain a consistent image toward the competitor. One way is to establish a pattern of behaviour through uniform strategies.[93] A selective strategy weakens a consistent image. A great power is therefore more likely to maintain a consistent image toward the regional competitor through its uniform strategies toward multiple weaker neighbours.

If the number of regional competitors increases from one to several, how does a great power engage with multiple weaker non-allies? A great power will change its regional diplomacy when the number of regional competitors increases. Given multiple regional competitors, the source of potential challenges becomes uncertain. Maintaining power advantages helps the great power to manage the higher degree of uncertainty. The collaborative involvement of multiple regional competitors can challenge the power gap between the great power and weaker powers in the short run. The worst-case scenario for the great power would be for all the weaker powers, having received support from multiple regional competitors, to challenge the great power's advantages and so weaken its influence in the short run. From the great power's perspective, therefore, concern over maintaining the existing regional power gap between weaker powers replaces concern over manipulating the images it projects to a particular competitor. The great power bases its asymmetric statecraft toward weaker powers on the degree of collaborative involvement of its regional competitors. The greater the number of regional competitors and weaker powers in a region, the greater the possibility of a different degree of collaborative involvement. The great power is more likely to accommodate one weaker power when the degree of collaborative involvement is low. In this situation, the accommodation will not change the existing power gap between the great power and weaker powers but rather enable the great power to concentrate resources in places where the challenges are more serious. The great power is more likely to use coercion against one weaker power when the degree of collaborative involvement is high, to prevent the unfavourable trend of changing a regional distribution of capabilities. The great power thus adopts a selective strategy toward multiple weaker neighbours.

An example is German regional diplomacy in the 1930s. Between 1933 and 1938, British defence commitments did not go beyond the Franco-Belgian-German border, so Britain did not compete with other powers in Eastern Europe. Both France and Russia were Germany's regional competitors in Eastern Europe. Although the Nazi ideology undoubtedly shaped German policies toward weaker neighbours in Eastern Europe, French and Russian involvement also played a crucial role. Czechoslovakia was an ally of France and Russia, whereas Poland had territorial disputes with Czechoslovakia and Russia. The 1935 Franco-Soviet Treaty of Mutual Assistance resulted in a sharp decline in Franco-Polish relations and improved German-Polish relations. Under these conditions, Germany adopted a selective strategy toward Czechoslovakia and Poland. Germany threatened to invade Czechoslovakia and eventually dismembered this weaker neighbour. Meanwhile, Germany made considerable concessions to Poland. In the spring of 1936, it agreed to a generous settlement of the controversial issue of payments for a railway service through the "Polish corridor." The "corridor," inhabited by a Polish majority, divided the bulk of Germany from its province of East Prussia. Berlin paid 1.8 million Reichsmarks (RM) in May 1936 and 1.5 million RM monthly thereafter. These economic concessions also served as political acknowledgment of Poland's right to control the corridor.[94] Moreover, Germany imposed constraints on Nazi activities in Danzig, exchanged intelligence with Poland, and promised to side with Poland in the event of a Polish-Soviet conflict.[95] The high degree of French and Russian involvement thus contributed to German selective strategies toward Czechoslovakia and Poland.

If a great power is an alignment leader, how does it manage such alignments when facing a regional competitor? In an asymmetric alignment, power asymmetry exists between one great power (an alignment leader) and several weaker allies. As Kenneth Waltz argues, "in alliances among unequals, alliance leaders need worry little about the faithfulness of their followers, who usually have little choice anyway."[96] As James Morrow puts it, in an asymmetric alignment, "deals between major and minor powers are natural ... [T]he minor power will make autonomy concessions to the major power in return for the security the major power can provide." Consequently, asymmetric alignments are more common and last longer than symmetric alignments.[97] These arguments identify important features of an asymmetric alignment, but they are incomplete without an answer to the question of why an alignment leader sometimes adopts different strategies to make an asymmetric alignment work.

An alignment leader needs to solve two types of problems. Collective action problems involve situations where allies engage in a struggle against a potential enemy, and each member wishes to benefit from public goods (such as security) offered by the alignment, while at the same time expecting other allies to assume a greater responsibility.[98] For example, the United States and its NATO allies always hold different views on sharing the burden of the Atlantic Alliance. The United States complains about the inadequate defence contributions of its European allies, whereas European countries complain about US control over their defence policies. Between 2017 and 2020, the US-German disputes over defence burden sharing reflected the underlying problems of the Atlantic Alliance's collective actions.

The alignment leader of an asymmetric alignment also needs to work on commitment problems. Commitment problems arise from a situation where allies share the expectation of fighting a potential enemy, but each member of the alliance faces the abandonment/entrapment dilemma. For example, Germany and Austria-Hungary forged a balancing coalition prior to the First World War. This meant that, on the one hand, unless it provided a strong commitment to Austria-Hungary, Germany faced the prospect of being abandoned, and, in the event of war, would have had to deal with an all-out attack by Britain, France, and Russia. On the other hand, were it to provide a strong commitment to Austria-Hungary, Germany needed to minimize the risk of being entrapped by this ally; a strong commitment from Germany would embolden Austria-Hungary to initiate hostilities in the Balkans, leading to an all-out German confrontation with Britain, France, and Russia. Germany was never able to solve the abandonment/entrapment problem.

The alignment leader and weaker allies in an asymmetric alignment have different sources of vulnerability. The alignment leader is most vulnerable when it has more than one regional competitor and is uncertain about which among them is the main competitor. By mobilizing all available resources against one competitor, the alignment leader enables another regional competitor to be a "free rider" in the struggle. By not doing so, however, the alignment leader allows a regional competitor more opportunities to develop capabilities or to form an adversarial alignment. For example, prior to the Second World War, France had two regional competitors in Eastern Europe – Germany and Russia – and was the alignment leader of the Franco-Polish-Romanian alignment. Therefore, if France were to mobilize Poland and Romania against Germany, Russia would benefit from the Franco-German confrontation. By not doing so, however, France would give Germany a greater opportunity to embark on rearmament programs. The situation of multiple competitors, therefore, presented France with significant challenges with respect to effective alignment management.

Weaker allies, by contrast, are most vulnerable during a great power confrontation. If weaker powers are on the winning side, the outcome of the great power confrontation will significantly weaken their capabilities; if they are on the losing side, they will disappear from the new international order. For instance, during the Cold War, Western European states sought alignments with the United States. However, they were far more vulnerable than the United States because, in the event of a US-Soviet confrontation, Western Europe would have become a major battlefield. Western European states thus needed US protection for their security, but they also needed to avoid a US-Soviet showdown. As a result, Western European states welcomed the US military presence on their territories but displayed considerable reservations concerning US deployment of medium-range missiles.

One regional competitor constitutes the main rival of the alignment leader, who accordingly sets about mobilizing all available resources against that competitor. What likely follows is a great power confrontation between the alignment leader and its regional competitor, which weaker allies are keen to avoid. It is in such a situation that weaker allies have the incentive to become free riders. The alignment leader then faces the challenge of collective action problems, which necessitate offering selective incentives. This entails selective security commitments to weaker allies in order to encourage them to contend with the regional competitor. The alignment leader may adopt distinctive policies toward certain "good allies," such as raising its level of support for them, and toward "bad allies," such as maintaining or even decreasing its level of support. These selective strategies generate peer pressure among weaker allies, giving them additional incentives to enlist support from the alignment leader. Such strategies help the alignment leader to resolve free-rider problems. For example, the Soviet Union's having been a regional competitor of the United States in Europe for decades engendered the primary incentives for US support for NATO. Rather than use NATO as a substitute for the Anglo-American special relationship, however, the United States treated the United Kingdom as a "model ally" to encourage other European allies to follow Britain's example. When confronting a single regional competitor, therefore, an alignment leader is most likely to adopt selective strategies toward multiple weaker allies.

If the number of regional competitors increases, the alignment leader cannot be certain about which one is its main rival. It hence has fewer incentives to mobilize all available resources, because it does not want any regional competitor to act as a free rider in a great power confrontation. However, commitment problems remain important to the alignment leader. On perceiving that it seeks to avoid a great power confrontation, its weaker allies have even greater incentives either to entrap or to abandon the alignment leader for the sake of their own interests. Less committed allies will use those that are most committed as reference points for demanding a greater security commitment from the alignment leader. Should they not achieve this objective, they will likely opt for realignment. Under this scenario, the alignment leader's use of selective strategies toward its weaker allies would only offer incentives, or even excuses, for entrapment or abandonment. The alignment leader must therefore adopt uniform strategies to demonstrate impartiality in its security commitment to each ally, which benefits all members of the alignment. Although uniform strategies alone cannot resolve the abandonment/entrapment dilemma and its associated problems, they will reduce the likelihood of weaker allies' realignment. For example, in the 1920s, France needed to work out the commitment problems of its alignment relationships with Poland and Romania. In August 1929, Poland sought to obtain more concrete French support for its security. France, however, deemed the creation of military stockpiles in Poland too costly; moreover, it rejected the Polish request in order to avoid "establishing a dangerous precedent."[99] In other words, France sought to avoid creating incentives for other weaker allies, presumably Romania, to make similar demands. If France did not accommodate Romania by providing the same support it would have given to Poland, Romania would likely have abandoned France. Therefore, if it has multiple regional competitors, an alignment leader is more likely to adopt uniform strategies toward multiple weaker allies.

In summary, the four main hypotheses of the regional competition theory of asymmetric statecraft are as follows:

H1 If there is only one regional competitor, then a great power is more likely to adopt uniform strategies toward weaker non-allies, because it seeks to communicate a consistent image toward the regional competitor.

H2 If the number of regional competitors increases, then a great power is more likely to adopt selective strategies toward weaker non-allies, because it seeks to maintain its regional advantages over the weaker powers in the short run.

H3 If there is only one regional competitor, then a great power is more likely to adopt selective strategies toward weaker allies, because it seeks to solve collective action problems.

H4 If the number of regional competitors increases, then a great power is more likely to adopt uniform strategies toward weaker allies, because it seeks to solve commitment problems.

Table 1.5 summarizes the four hypotheses:

Table 1.5 Hypotheses of the regional competition theory

Scenario	*Non-allies*	*Allies*
One competitor	Uniform strategies	Selective strategies
More than one competitor	Selective strategies	Uniform strategies

Theoretical Implications

In the evolution of international relations, changes in the international distribution of military power usually take place over a long historical period, and the international distribution of military power is therefore a relatively constant factor. By contrast, changes in foreign policy can occur over a relatively short time period, so using a constant factor to account for foreign policy changes presents a significant challenge to structural realists.[100] Both the external threat theory and the domestic-ideological theory have made significant contributions to resolving this problem. The external threat theory is more dynamic than that of structural realism by virtue of discussing perception, which is subject to change in different historical contexts. The domestic-ideological theory is more dynamic than that of structural realism by virtue of examining normative views, domestic mobilization, and regime security. Both theories seek to use more dynamic independent variables in explaining foreign policy variation.

The regional competition theory considers the virtues of both existing theories and seeks to address certain analytical inadequacies of each. Like the external threat theory, the regional competition theory identifies military power as a crucial means of achieving foreign policy objectives; it also considers competing objectives among nations. Unlike external threat theory, however, it views foreign aid as an alternative powerful means of achieving foreign policy objectives. It explains how a militarily weak power can exert significant influence on the security policy-making of a militarily strong power when the weak power has means, other than military strength, to neutralize the political influence of that strong power. Like the domestic-ideological theory, the regional competition theory neither assumes nation-states as unitary actors nor assumes that they pursue similar objectives. Competing objectives could involve many critical issues – security, regimes, or ideologies. Unlike the domestic-ideological theory, the regional competition theory does not take different political processes or leaderships into account, the object being to develop a more generalizable theory of foreign policy.

The regional competition theory is a dynamic theory with which to account for foreign policy variation for three reasons. First, in dyadic relationships the concept of the competitor requires different objectives. Because one state's objectives are frequently subject to change, a changing relationship between two states, based on an analysis of their objectives, can occur even more frequently. For example, between 1939 and 1941, the changes in German and Soviet objectives redefined their relationship in three successive stages – rivalry, cooperation, and confrontation. Therefore, by using the concept of the competitor, scholars can discuss how changes in policy objectives affect foreign policy.

Second, regional competition is based on the distribution of military strength at the regional level. A global shift in the balance occurs less frequently – over decades – than a regional shift in the balance of offensive military capabilities, which can occur over a few years. For example, the United States changed the global balance of power over the course of four decades (1898–1945), whereas Nazi Germany changed the regional balance of Europe in six years (1933–39). Therefore, by using the concept of regional competition, scholars can discuss how changes in the regional balance of power affect foreign policy.

Third, the regional competition theory examines both systemic and process variables. The distribution of capabilities, a systemic variable, involves both the ability to hurt (military strength) and the ability to assist (foreign aid). Meanwhile, competitive relationships and alignment relationships are process variables. In this regard, I agree with Glenn Snyder, who argues persuasively that "introducing relationships explicitly into neorealist theory permits a richer, more detailed analysis of interactions between particular states than is possible from only structural or unit perspectives."[101] The regional competition theory simplifies "relationships" into "asymmetric relationships," "competitive relationships," and "alignment relationships." The existence of asymmetric relationships is the premise of the theory, whereas competitive relationships and alignment relationships are factors subject to change. Countries in a specific region that have different objectives and independent capabilities define competitive relationships. In the event of armed conflict, countries with different expectations of mutual support define alignment relationships. Independent capabilities, competitive relationships, and alignment relationships together explain a great power's asymmetric statecraft. In brief, the number of a great power's regional competitors and its alignment relationships shape its asymmetric statecraft, in terms of uniform strategies or selective strategies, toward multiple weaker neighbours.

Based on current scholarship in foreign policy, the regional competition theory seeks to explain a new puzzle of uniform versus selective strategies. It proposes a new concept of regional competitors, and it identifies new causal mechanisms to explain asymmetric statecraft. As discussed in the Introduction, this book seeks to develop a theory of asymmetric statecraft that better explains the historical records of China's regional diplomacy and thus contributes to the contemporary debate in this regard. If the regional competition theory can better explain China's regional diplomacy, the book will have achieved its main objective. Meanwhile, I have generated hypotheses based on illustrative examples from Europe and the United States in periods other than the Cold War. Therefore, the book does not rule out the possibility that the regional competition theory could become part of a more generalized one. I would be glad to examine pertinent empirical research that other scholars may conduct toward refining the regional competition theory with a view to applying it to explanations of great powers in other regions. A more detailed discussion of the generalizability of the regional competition theory is found in the concluding chapter.

Research Design

As discussed above, a region consists of states with high degrees of security interdependence. This study divides Asia into three regions – the maritime East Asia, South Asia, and Indochina – and examines China's asymmetric statecraft in each region in turn between 1955 and 1975. In East Asia, mainland China's policy targets were two weaker non-allies, Japan and Taiwan. China and Japan would have concluded a normalization agreement if not for US-China rivalry in the region, and mainland China would have "liberated" Taiwan during the Chinese civil war without American intervention. Mainland China therefore had to make its East Asia policy an adjunct to its American policy. In South Asia, China had five weaker non-allies: India, Pakistan, Afghanistan, Burma, and Nepal.[102] China had territorial disputes with each of them, and each received aid from the United States and/or the Soviet Union. China sought to settle territorial disputes in its favour but also had to engage with American or Soviet challenges in the neighbourhood. There were therefore close connections between Chinese regional diplomacy and its great power diplomacy. In Indochina, China developed alignment relationships with the DRV and Cambodia. The Sino-Vietnamese alignment was operative in the 1950s, and China and Cambodia began handling common security challenges after 1962. China and the United States began competing over the future course of Indochina in the early 1960s, and the Soviet Union joined the competition after 1965, but none of them wished to run the risk of a great power confrontation. China therefore had to make its alignment policies an adjunct to its American/Soviet policy.

I select these cases to develop the regional competition theory for three reasons. First, China possessed advantages over its neighbours in three respects.

- The overall military balance favoured China. The size of the PLA was 5.29 million in 1950, 4.80 million in 1953, 3.83 million in 1956, and 2.38 million in 1958.[103] The military forces of China's neighbours were far smaller: 200,000 for Japan, 600,000 for Taiwan, 500,000 for India, 400,000 for North Vietnam, and 50,000 for Cambodia.[104] Table 1.6 further demonstrates Chinese advantages in terms of defence budget.
- China was able to design and produce major weapons for ground forces independently, whereas most of its neighbours did not have such a capability. For example, the Chinese army in Tibet was furnished with

120 mm mortars, 82 mm mortars, 75 mm recoilless rifles, and 40 mm rocket launchers, whereas the Indian army was furnished with "World War I rifles."[105] China also possessed nuclear capability by October 1964 and the ability to launch nuclear missiles by October 1966.[106] During the Cold War, none of China's neighbours had such capabilities.

- China was able to project military strength beyond its borders. In August 1954, it had the capability to mass-produce aircraft.[107] The Chinese air force possessed 3,000 aircraft in 1954 and 4,000 in 1955.[108] As discussed above, from 1965 to 1968, China deployed 320,000 troops to the DRV for air defence, railway and road construction, and logistical support. By contrast, none of China's neighbours was able to project military strength beyond its own border.

Second, the cases enable me to conduct comparative case studies and use process-tracing techniques to examine casual mechanisms of the regional competition theory. Stephen Van Evera provides a list of eleven

Table 1.6 Comparison between mainland China's defence budget and those of its neighbours, 1954–65

Year	*Mainland China*	*Japan*	*Taiwan*	*India*
1954	2,363	484.8	80.0	503.0
1955	2,642	457.1	110.9	524.0
1956	2,487	457.1	114.4	624.0
1957	2,240	446.6	126.2	567.0
1958	2,033	451.0	207.2	621.0
1959	2,358	462.3	219.2	577.0
1960	2,358	455.9	203.3	582.0
1961	2,033	472.7	214.2	625.0
1962	2,315	517.0	245.5	862.0
1963	2,700	390.0	249.4	1,409.0
1964	2,962	553.0	267.6	1,380.0
1965	3,527	623.0	285.5	1,346.0

Note: Amounts are in millions of dollars. The fixed exchange rate between China's renminbi and the US dollar was 2.46:1. The data for Japan, Taiwan, and India are at 1960 prices and 1960 exchange rates.
Source: Xu Guangyi, ed., *Dangdai Zhongguo jundui de houqin gongzuo* [Logistical work of armed forces in contemporary China] (Beijing: Zhongguo shehui kexue chubanshe, 1990), 304; *SIPRI Yearbook of World Armaments and Disarmament, 1969/70* (Stockholm: Almquist and Wiksell, 1970), 272–75.

case-selection criteria. My case selection conforms to the first nine criteria on his list.[109] I conduct in-depth analysis of three historical cases – China's policies in East Asia during 1955–65; in South Asia during 1955–63; and in Indochina during 1962–75 – and thus break the case of Chinese regional diplomacy into three sub-cases. As discussed above, the external threat theory and the domestic-ideological theory should explain these cases, but neither theory can do so adequately. Therefore, these cases provide an empirical foundation for challenging current theories and developing new theories. As Table 1.7 shows, I have selected cases with diverse values for the variables of the regional competition theory. In each case, China interchangeably adopted uniform strategies or selective strategies. In other words, the dependent variable varies in each case.

In each case, the first independent variable (the number of China's regional competitors) is subject to change. Between 1955 and 1958, the United States was China's sole competitor in East Asia, but between 1958 and 1959, the Soviet Union proved to be a new competitor there. Between 1955 and 1959, the United States was China's only regional competitor in South Asia, but the divergence in Sino-Soviet objectives in 1959 made the Soviet Union a new competitor there. China's regional competitors in Indochina also changed. Between 1962 and 1965, the United States was China's only regional competitor, but different Sino-Soviet attempts to resolve the Indochina conflict between 1964 and 1965, along with Soviet aid to the DRV and Cambodia, made the Soviet Union China's new regional competitor. The Soviet Union then became China's only regional competitor in Indochina after the US withdrawal from the region in 1973. Each case thus demonstrates how the changing number of regional competitors affected China's regional diplomacy toward its neighbours.

Table 1.7 Applications of the regional competition theory to three historical cases of Chinese diplomacy

Scenario	*Non-allies*	*Allies*
One competitor	China toward East Asia, 1955–58 China toward South Asia, 1955–59 *Uniform strategies*	China toward Indochina, 1962–65 China toward Indochina, 1973–75 *Selective strategies*
Multiple competitors	China toward East Asia, 1958–65 China toward South Asia, 1959–63 *Selective strategies*	China toward Indochina, 1965–72 *Uniform strategies*

In each case, the second independent variable (China's alignment relationships) is a constant factor, but differences across cases demonstrate how such relationships shaped China's regional diplomacy toward its neighbours. In the first two cases, mainland China's targets were weaker non-allies: Japan and Taiwan in East Asia and five weaker audiences – India, Pakistan, Afghanistan, Burma, and Nepal – in South Asia. In the third case, China's targets were its allies: China, the DRV, and Cambodia all fought on the same side between 1962 and 1975.

It is worth noting that, according to the definitions of Snyder and Walt, alliance or alignment amounts to mutual expectations between two or more states of support for each other in disputes or wars with other particular states. The nature of security commitments with respect to mutual interests, however, suggests that operationalization of the alliance/alignment concepts may not be rigorous. Scholars sometimes need to conduct ad hoc analyses for a better understanding of whether states indeed have mutual expectations of support during an armed conflict, as alignments may exist without an alliance treaty. For example, this book discusses China's alignments with the DRV and Cambodia. No alliance treaty regulated their security relationships, but their joint armed struggles on the same side suggest the existence and practice of security commitments to each other. An alliance treaty, moreover, does not necessarily define a security relationship. For instance, the Sino–North Korean alliance treaty concluded in 1961 is still operative, in theory, in the post–Cold War era. However, China does not regard the treaty as a security guarantee to North Korea. In the past decade, China has always viewed Sino–North Korean contacts as "normal" in a "state-to-state relationship" and opposed North Korean nuclear programs. North Korea, meanwhile, refuses to accept any potential Chinese security guarantee. In the post–Cold War era, therefore, China and North Korea have not been allied with each other.

Accordingly, any change in an alignment relationship carries rich and subtle meanings. For example, Chapter 3 discusses the Sino-Pakistan relationship between 1955 and 1962, when the two states were not aligned with each other. After the Sino-Indian border conflict of 1962, China and Pakistan gradually developed security commitments based on mutual interests, and they formed a balancing coalition after 1963. In practice, China deterred India's invasion of Pakistan during the Indo-Pakistani War of 1965 by presenting India with an ultimatum. In the post–Cold War era, however, China not only adopted a non-alignment policy but also publicly denied that the Sino-Pakistan friendship would be directed against any third party. In particular, China would not commit itself to Pakistan in the Indo-Pakistani conflict over Kashmir.[110] In other words, in the post–Cold War era, China and Pakistan have not been aligned with each other.

In each empirical case, I will apply process-tracing techniques to assess the regional competition theory. Process tracing examines the process whereby initial case conditions are translated into case outcomes.[111] Researchers should therefore clarify each step of a causal mechanism and verify each stage of the process by providing evidence.[112] As process tracing is a useful technique in developing and evaluating theories, I will apply it in the case studies.[113] For example, the United States' escalation of the Indochina War and Sino-Soviet competition are two potential explanations that account for changes in China's Indochina policy between 1964 and 1965. Tracing the process of China's subtle policy changes can help scholars to assess which explanation is more convincing. The United States launched air strikes against the DRV in August 1964, while the Soviet Union provided extensive aid to the DRV in February 1965. As Chapter 4 shows, it was in May 1965 that China changed its Indochina policy. In October 1964, China used military forces to guarantee the DRV's border but did not similarly accommodate Cambodia. China thus adopted selective strategies toward its weaker allies. In May 1965, however, China reiterated its guarantee with respect to the North Vietnam border and extended the border guarantee to Cambodia – in other words, it adopted uniform strategies toward these weaker allies. This example suggests that the US escalation of the Indochina War does not adequately explain China's new policy and that Sino-Soviet competition offers a better explanation. Besides evaluating the explanatory power of the external threat theory and the domestic-ideological theory, I will conduct comparative case studies to evaluate the regional competition theory. Each case covers a time period of eight to twelve years. I will therefore trace how Chinese regional diplomacy was conducted in the time period under investigation and thus evaluate how well the regional competition theory explains the record of Chinese regional diplomacy.

Third, assessing the explanatory power of the regional competition theory requires a systematic investigation of primary and secondary sources. This requirement is closely related to the process-tracing technique. To better trace a process, researchers should be relentless in obtaining diverse evidence, be familiar with the environment in which evidence is produced, be careful in precisely interpreting evidence, and be aware of potential biases in evidence collection and/or interpretation.[114] In other words, high-quality process tracing requires a researcher to have a good knowledge of the history of the chosen cases, a good knowledge of relevant theories to be evaluated, and a strong capacity for combining empirical findings with general knowledge.[115] It is therefore insufficient for a scholar to examine only secondary sources in conducting process-tracing analysis. At the same time, however, it would be difficult for a political scientist to examine primary sources for theory development. Jack Levy nicely summarizes the reasons for a political scientist to examine archival sources and the problems involved:

> One problem that political scientists must confront in their use of secondary sources is that the implicit (or explicit) theoretical questions that guided the historian's study may have been quite different from the questions the political scientist wants to answer, and this may limit the utility of particular secondary sources for the political scientist ... Insisting that the political scientist work the archives and in addition read all relevant secondary sources, and do this for enough cases to facilitate the ability to generalize, is impractical.[116]

Levy convincingly points out that scholars should exploit extensive sources to assess theories. For the regional competition theory, for example, extensive sources would enable scholars to make fair judgments on competitive relationships and alignment relationships. However, Levy well understands that archival research is a labour-intensive task and therefore argues it would be extremely difficult – "impractical" in his words – to develop and examine theories based on primary sources. In view of the necessity of archival research, I will attempt to overcome the difficulties that Levy has well explained. In each empirical case, I will reach theoretical conclusions based on a wide range of sources from Chinese, Russian, German, American, and NATO archives. A more detailed discussion of the features of these archival sources is found in the Bibliography. In brief, these archival sources provide opportunities for me to evaluate the regional competition theory based on China's regional diplomacy.

First, Chinese sources provide direct evidence for an investigation of Chinese regional diplomacy. The Foreign Ministry Archive of the People's Republic of China offers key documents concerning records of conversations between Chinese and foreign leaders. The archive also provides documents concerning implementation of Chinese foreign policy. Moreover, each provincial or municipal archive in China has a complete set of documents from the CCP Central Committee and the State Council. Local archives offer records of Chinese leaders' speeches at internal party meetings and CCP Central Committee directives related to foreign affairs, all of which enable me to examine Chinese leaders' perceptions at the national level. In addition to the unpublished archives, I will exploit published chronologies, collected speeches, and biographies of major Chinese leaders and published and unpublished documentary sources in various Chinese and American libraries.

Second, Russian and German archival sources provide indirect support for understanding Chinese regional diplomacy. During the Cold War, the Soviet Union and East Germany were allies of the PRC and the DRV. Sino-Soviet, Soviet–East German, Sino–East German, and East German–DRV records of conversations offer new opportunities for scholars to advance understandings of Chinese regional diplomacy. Soviet archives reveal the rise and fall of Sino-Soviet relations and the nature and limitations of Soviet-Vietnamese cooperation. In addition, because the Soviet Union and East Germany maintained various intelligence exchange channels on a regular basis, East German archives reveal the dynamics of Sino-Soviet relations and features of China's Soviet policy. I will analyze Russian and East German archives to discuss Chinese regional diplomacy.

Third, US and NATO archives provide evidence for important observations and critical assessments of Chinese regional diplomacy. The United States and its allies collected evidence and conducted analysis, based on a wide range of sources, with respect to China, the Soviet Union, and many other countries in Asia. These sources involve records of conversations between Chinese or Soviet leaders and foreign leaders and offer key information about military deployment and foreign aid. I will extensively exploit archival sources at the US National Archives and Records Administration and the Kennedy, Johnson, Nixon, and Ford Presidential Libraries, and I will compare and contrast them with evidence from Chinese, Russian, and German archives.

It is worth noting that governments sometimes release archival sources on a selective basis. Despite the limitations of the archival access, however, the wealth of historical evidence enables me to treat various theoretical and empirical claims with caution and examine instrumental motives behind historical narratives and personal accounts. As conclusions can still be incomplete, I welcome scholars to present more evidence for further discussions of theories of asymmetric statecraft, based on records of Chinese regional diplomacy.

2
East Asia, 1955–65

The global confrontation between the United States and the Soviet Union, demonstrated by clashes in East Asia between the United States and People's Republic of China (PRC) in the 1950s, was a main feature of the Cold War. The United States forged a balancing coalition with Japan and Taiwan and treated the alliances as instrumental in its containment policy toward China. Beijing understood the nature of the cooperation among Washington, Tokyo, and Taipei, and the Chinese Communist Party (CCP) investigation bureau discussed a potential US-orchestrated plan to divide China into six areas. According to the CCP estimate, the Japanese and the Nationalists in Taiwan would jointly work under American leadership in intelligence and propaganda.[1] The Korean War led to the deterioration of Sino-American relations to a level that generated deep hostility between China and the US-sponsored alliances. By significantly bolstering its military capability during the Korean War, however, mainland China gained tremendous advantages over its neighbours Japan and Taiwan.

Between 1955 and 1958, the United States was China's sole competitor in East Asia, and mainland China adopted uniform accommodation strategies toward Japan and Taiwan to weaken their alliance relationships with the United States. In 1958, the United States suspended Sino-American ambassadorial talks. To make the United States resume the talks, China imposed sanctions on Japan and launched a vicious attack on the Nationalist-controlled Jinmen Islands (Quemoy Islands). Between 1958 and 1959, the Sino-Soviet alliance relationship became progressively hostile. Sino-Soviet competition weakened mainland China's advantages over Japan and Taiwan, while the United States continued to be China's competitor. Consequently, between 1958 and 1965, mainland China adopted selective strategies toward Japan and Taiwan in accordance with the United States' and Soviet Union's degrees of involvement in East Asia. Between 1959 and 1962, China conducted only "friendship trade" with Japan in an attempt to support Japanese social democrats and exert pressure on the Japanese government. Meanwhile, mainland China proposed cross-strait trade with Taiwan in an attempt to weaken the US-Taiwan alliance. The Sino-Soviet border clashes in 1962, however, encouraged Taiwan's possible launch of invasions of the mainland. Although the United States upped the ante in the Taiwan Strait area, it was reluctant to give further aid to Japan. Under these circumstances, mainland China prepared for war against Taiwan but made trade concessions to the Japanese government. Thus, in light of the competition with both Moscow and Washington, Beijing developed distinctive policies toward Taipei and Tokyo.

Uniform Strategies, 1955–58

Soviet and American Involvement in East Asia, 1955–58

East Asia had different implications for the Soviet Union and for China. Distant from Soviet political and economic centres, the Soviet Far East was connected with Europe by a railway, a sea line of communication, and an air route. By the end of 1951, Soviet industrial capabilities in East Asia produced only 15 percent of the Soviet industrial output.[2] By contrast, China possessed a strategic rear, a long, unbroken stretch of coastline, and excellent seaports. The Soviet Union thus proposed a division of labour in the Sino-Soviet alliance. Soviet leader Joseph Stalin suggested to CCP vice chairman Liu Shaoqi in July 1949 that Moscow assume greater responsibilities toward the West and that China concentrate more resources in colonial and semi-colonial areas in the East.[3] Stalin re-emphasized this point during his meetings with Wang Jiaxiang, head of the CCP Liaison Department, in May 1951: "You understand the situation in Asia and the Question of the East better than us. [We] mainly depend on you in solving these problems. We better understand Europe and the West."[4] In comparison with the Soviet Union, China's major limitation was its inadequate military strength. The Soviet Union would not be able to offset its geographical limitations in Asia until it improved Chinese strategic strength, and it therefore provided extensive aid to China. Table 2.1 shows the major

Table 2.1 Soviet loans to China, 1950–55 (in millions of rubles)

Year	*Military loans*	*Economic loans*
1950	1,200.0	–
1951	1,926.0	38.0
1952	1,036.0	–
1953	610.0	–
1954	546.0	290.3
1955	970.0	–
Total	6,288.0	328.3

Source: Shen Zhihua, *Wunai de xuanze: lengzhan yu ZhongSu tongmeng de mingyun, 1945–1959* [Reluctant choices: the Cold War and the fate of the Sino-Soviet alliance, 1945–1959] (Beijing: Shehui kexue wenxian chubanshe, 2013), 329–30.

Soviet assistance packages to China between 1950 and 1955. The Soviet Union offered armaments and also set the foundations for a modern Chinese industrial system. This ardent Soviet backing soon gave China sufficient military power over its weaker neighbours.

The Sino-Soviet alliance also demonstrated the two countries' common policy objectives in East Asia. With respect to Japan, China and the Soviet Union would

> undertake to carry out jointly all necessary measures within their power to prevent a repetition of aggression and breach of the peace by Japan or any other State which might directly or indirectly join with Japan in acts of aggression. Should either of the Contracting Parties be attacked by Japan or by States allied with Japan and thus find itself in a state of war, the other Contracting Party shall immediately extend military and other assistance with all the means at its disposal.[5]

Meanwhile, the Soviet Union became mainland China's principal arms supplier for its goal of "liberating Taiwan." The Korean War forced Beijing to postpone implementation of its military plans in the Taiwan Strait but strengthened the Sino-Soviet alliance. Soviet aid rapidly enabled China to possess the military capability necessary to contend with the United States.

Chinese policy choices were also circumscribed by Soviet technologies and Sino-Soviet trade, however. Soviet technology transfers contributed

TABLE 2.2 Sino-Soviet trade, 1954–65

Year	*Trade value*[1]	*Share*[2]	*Year*	*Trade value*[1]	*Share*[2]
1954	1,291	53.1	1960	1,664	43.7
1955	1,786	56.9	1961	828	28.2
1956	1,524	47.5	1962	702	26.4
1957	1,365	44.0	1963	601	20.6
1958	1,539	39.8	1964	445	12.9
1959	2,097	47.9	1965	407	9.6

Notes:
1 In millions of US dollars.
2 Percentage of China's total trade with foreign countries.
Source: Meng Xianzhang, ed., *ZhongSu maoyi shi ziliao* [Sources on the Sino-Soviet trade history] (Beijing: Zhongguo duiwai jingji maoyi chubanshe, 1991), 580, 610.

to China's mass production of aircraft but also drew China closer to the Soviet Union. The Soviet Union provided China with licences to mass-produce aircraft, including the MiG-15 in 1953, the MiG-17 in 1954, the MiG-19 in 1957, the Tu-16 in 1959, and the MiG-21 in 1961.[6] It also provided naval equipment to China. Between 1953 and 1955, the Soviet Union supplied eighty-one battleships, including thirty-two finished products (four destroyers, two medium-sized submarines, four large-sized submarines, and twenty-two high-speed torpedo boats) and forty-nine semi-finished products (four frigates, three medium-sized submarines, four large-sized submarines, four port-minesweepers, ten river-minesweepers, and twenty-four large-sized torpedo boats). In 1959, it promised to supply five different types of naval equipment (missile submarines, medium-sized submarines, large-sized missile torpedo boats, small-sized missile torpedo boats, and hydrofoil boats) and two types of missiles (submarine-launched missiles and anti-ship missiles).[7] Additionally, in October 1957, it agreed to assist with China's nuclear and ballistic missile programs.[8] Finally, the Soviet Union provided complete factories to China through Sino-Soviet trade. Soviet aid contributed considerably to Chinese economic construction but, as Table 2.2 demonstrates, this trade dependency put China in considerable debt to the Soviet Union. At one time, the level of Sino-Soviet trade accounted for over 50 percent of China's overall trade volume, and it did not decrease significantly until after 1960.

In addition to the Soviet Union, the United States was a critical factor in shaping Chinese foreign policy. The fundamental interests of the United States and China were at odds in East Asia. Tables 2.3 and 2.4 show major

US assistance packages to Japan in the 1950s. During this period, the United States urged Japan to follow its trade embargo policy against China, which obstructed Japanese economic development. According to US intelligence estimates, roughly 25 percent of Japanese coking coal and 6 percent of its iron ore requirements were supplied from China, and alternative sources would be more expensive, thereby hiking steel production costs.[9] In response, China's trade representative Lei Renmin pointed out that "the price of her [Chinese] coal shipped to Japan is about US$20 cheaper per ton than the price Japan has to pay for coal imported from the western hemisphere. If not for artificial barriers, I believe China's coal would help reduce costs in Japanese industry and improve the living standards of the Japanese people."[10] As the Sino-American political confrontation caused US-Japanese economic tensions, Sino-Japanese trade became an important Chinese policy instrument toward the US-Japan alliance.

The question of Taiwan, like that of Japan, was a matter concerning mainland China's security. Unlike the question of Japan, however, the

Table 2.3 US assistance to Japan, 1951–54 (in millions of dollars)

Year	*Military*	*Economic*	*Total*
1951	78.6	190.5	269.1
1952	150.0	4.4	154.4
1953	300.0	–	300.0
1954	111.7	–	111.7

Source: Memo, Lay to the National Security Council, June 23, 1953, *Foreign Relations of the United States* [hereafter *FRUS*], *1952–1954*, vol. 14, *China and Japan* (Washington, DC: US Government Printing Office, 1985), 1437. James S. Lay was the executive secretary of state.

Table 2.4 US military assistance to Japan, 1950–59 (in millions of dollars)

Year	*Army*	*Navy*	*Air Force*	*Total*
1950–57	578.2	351.9	255.1	1,185.2
1958	15.7	69.5	46.6	131.8
1959	9.3	29.5	45.5	84.3
Total	603.2	450.9	347.2	1,401.3

Source: Dispatch, US Embassy in Tokyo to the Department of State, July 26, 1957, *FRUS, 1955–1957*, vol. 23, *Japan* (Washington, DC: US Government Printing Office, 1991), 430.

question of Taiwan was also an issue of Chinese sovereignty. American Taiwan policy was undetermined between 1949 and 1950, when the United States deployed only one aircraft carrier, one heavy cruiser, one light cruiser, and twelve destroyers in East Asia.[11] The outbreak of the Korean War, however, led to a significant shift in US policy toward Taiwan. Between 1951 and 1964, American economic aid totalled $1.5 billion, the largest such program per capita worldwide.[12] "In FY 1950–1954 the US programmed some $942 million in materiél and training for the [Nationalist] forces ... This program plus economic assistance and direct forces support has made possible the development of a reorganized army of 21 infantry and 2 armored divisions, a small navy of 3 destroyers, 6 destroyer escorts, and 82 other combatant vessels."[13] Between 1951 and 1958, it delivered 1,117 aircraft to the Nationalists in Taiwan, including 269 F-84Gs and 388 F-86Fs.[14] The United States also deployed seven aircraft carriers, three heavy cruisers, forty minesweepers, 600 aircraft, and one battalion of Special Forces in the Western Pacific during the Taiwan Strait Crisis in 1958,[15] as well as 4,500 troops and a few dozen surface-to-surface tactical missiles.[16] The US military presence thus became the key deterrent to Beijing's use of force. In short, between 1955 and 1958, China and the Soviet Union shared common strategic objectives in East Asia, and the United States was China's only regional competitor.

Political-Economic Concessions in East Asia, 1955–58

The history of Japanese invasions of China and the protracted conflict in Korea caused China genuine concern over the US-Japanese alliance. Zhou Enlai stressed that the United States "is rearming Japanese militarists, organizing an aggressive bloc in the Pacific [region], and gravely threatening the security of Asian nations."[17] Liao Chengzhi, who was in charge of China's Japan policy, offered a similar line: "Yoshida [Shigeru]'s government is reviving Japanese militarism, following US imperialists' instructions, and taking a hostile attitude toward the PRC by concluding the so-called 'Sino-Japanese peace treaty' with Chiang Kai-shek's reactionary and remnant cliques."[18] Despite these public statements, China was well aware of the possibility of driving wedges between Japanese political forces through "non-official" Sino-Japanese trade. According to Zhou's private analysis of 1952, the Japanese leadership was divided into two factions: "Yoshida and his stooges are following American imperialists, destroying peace pacts, rearming, and turning Japan into a market of American imperialism. However, American imperialism has reduced their profits by tightly controlling Japanese major industries ... The Japanese bourgeoisie receives this with great dissatisfaction. Therefore, another faction is opposing Yoshida by refusing American offers. Some [people] hope to resume Sino-Japanese trade."[19] Under these circumstances, China concluded non-official trade agreements with the Japanese in June 1952 and October 1953. The Chinese trade delegations were supported by the PRC, whereas the Japanese trade delegations opposed their government's embargo policy. China adopted a harder line, but Japan replied with stronger embargo policies. As a result, only 5 percent and 38.8 percent of the proposed trade volumes respectively were realized under the two trade agreements.[20]

Taiwan was another focal point of the Sino-American confrontation. China never gave up its military plans to occupy the Nationalist-controlled offshore islands, but US interventions complicated the situation. Secretary of State John Foster Dulles announced on August 3, 1954, that the United States had committed to protecting the islands of Taiwan and Penghu against mainland Chinese attacks through its navy and air force. According to Dulles, the United States had no formal defence treaty with the Nationalists for the defence of Taiwan, but, he emphasized, the defence of Taiwan might be grouped with the defence of Korea and Japan.[21] A tight cluster of American allies thus forced China to act decisively on its own doorstep. On August 8, Mao Zedong, China's principal leader, approved the plan to conduct military operations in the Taiwan Strait.[22] On September 3, the shelling of the Nationalist-controlled Jinmen Islands began, demonstrating China's high resolve with respect to US intervention in the strait.

The "artillery diplomacy" did not prevent the conclusion of a US-Taiwan mutual defence treaty, however. It was clear that the United States would never give up its military presence in East Asia and that assertive policies toward Tokyo and Taipei on the part of mainland China would push them closer to Washington. Beijing therefore set new policy courses. On December 11, 1954, Peng Dehuai, the PRC's defence minister, submitted a report to Mao on attacking the Yijiangshan Islands, two tiny islands in the Dachen Archipelago. Mao suggested that Peng "reconsider" the timing of military operations,[23] but he came under heavy pressure from his military to proceed with the attacks. On January 17, 1955, Mao, believing that the following day would still be "too early" to conduct military operations, suggested postponing them for as long as "two or three months." Due to Peng's persistence, Mao finally agreed to the launching of attacks,[24] but he explicitly permitted a complete withdrawal of Nationalist troops from the Dachen Archipelago.[25] To communicate a consistent image to the United States, a change in China's policy toward Japan followed immediately. In its internal analysis, China would "strive for [political forces], including the haute bourgeoisie, in order to promote internal divisions of Japan to a greater extent."[26] The means to achieve this objective was "significant expansion of Sino-Japanese trade in concert with diplomatic struggle."[27] In January 1955, China began negotiations with Japan over a new trade agreement,[28] and in March the CCP Politburo proposed that the objective of China's Japan policy was to achieve normalization of Sino-Japanese relations.[29]

Meanwhile, China's US policy underwent a marked shift from coercion to accommodation. On February 2, 1955, Zhou wrote to Mao recommending positive feedback on a Soviet proposal to convene an international conference on the question of the Far East, and Mao concurred.[30] On February 6, Zhou explained the plan to the Indian ambassador in Beijing, saying that "it would be feasible to reduce tensions in the Far East, including tensions in the Taiwan Strait area, through a Geneva-type international conference."[31] On April 5, the CCP Politburo issued a guideline stating that no public objection should be raised to the relaxation of tensions in the Taiwan Strait.[32] On August 1, Indian mediation paved the way for Sino-American ambassadorial talks in Geneva. From the Chinese perspective, these talks "should be in preparation for Sino-American negotiations, at the level of Foreign Minister, over relaxation of tensions in the Taiwan Strait area."[33]

The United States maintained a strong naval and air presence in Japan and Taiwan, whereas Beijing sought to drive a wedge between the US-sponsored alliances through its accommodation of the American allies. From the spring of 1955 onward, China began adopting a uniform accommodation strategy. On April 15, Zhou explained the new policy to Burma's Premier U Nu: "I believe that the Chinese people would forgive Chiang [Kai-shek] ... if he agrees to peaceful unification of China";[34] he underlined the concrete meaning of forgiveness to Pakistan's Premier Muhammad Ali Bogra by suggesting Chiang as a PLA (People's Liberation Army) marshal.[35] In addition to making political concessions, Beijing sought to reduce military tensions in the Taiwan Strait area. On October 3, the Central Military Commission (CMC) submitted a report on launching attacks over offshore islands and deploying the PLA's air force in Fujian Province, but Mao temporarily shelved the report.[36] Beijing also aimed to detach Taipei from Washington through accommodation. When Indian diplomat Krishna Menon – a broker of the Sino-American ambassadorial talks – was in Beijing, the CCP leadership invited all available prominent political figures in the pre-1949 Nationalist government to attend a welcoming reception for him. Zhou explained to Soviet chargé d'affaires Yakov Lomakin that the United States was specifically fearful of a cross-strait understanding, and the invitations to Nationalist political figures were designed to arouse US suspicions in this regard.[37] The immediate objective of Beijing's accommodation, therefore, was to induce American concern over the cohesiveness of its alliances.

Since Japan was also an American ally, Chinese regional diplomacy that did not accommodate Japan would undermine the effectiveness of China's policy vis-à-vis the United States. Therefore, mainland China adopted a uniform accommodation strategy toward both Taiwan and Japan. Chinese accommodation of Japan consisted of three parts. First, China pushed forward its trade relations with Japanese governments. On May 4, 1955, it concluded the third non-official trade agreement, which, unlike with the first two, both the Chinese and the Japanese governments explicitly guaranteed.[38] According to Chinese sources, the objective of the development of Sino-Japanese trade relations was to "encourage Japanese people's anti-American sentiment and strive for Japanese neutrality." In order to detach Japan from the United States, China needed to "strengthen lines of communication with Japanese industrial and commercial circles ... and shift the focus of struggle toward US imperialism."[39] Table 2.5 shows the significant development of Sino-Japanese trade from 1954 to 1958.

Second, Zhou exhibited a reasonable attitude and willingness to compromise with respect to the Tokyo-Taipei peace treaty, concluded in 1952. "The abrogation of the [Japanese] peace treaty [with Taipei] would not be a precondition of the Sino-Japanese normalization. Rather, it would be

Table 2.5 Sino-Japanese trade, 1954–58 (in millions of dollars)

Year	*Trade value*
1954	35.17
1955	83.31
1956	128.40
1957	114.73
1958	80.65[1]

Note:
1 The figure for 1958 covers the first three months.
Source: Shen Jueren, ed., *Dangdai Zhongguo duiwai maoyi* [Foreign trade of contemporary China], vol. 2 (Beijing: Dangdai Zhongguo chubanshe, 1992), 371.

the objective and result of the Sino-Japanese normalization."[40] In other words, mainland China would push Sino-Japanese relations forward despite the existence of the Japan-Taiwan treaty. If the treaty were to be abrogated, China would further accommodate Japanese interests. Third, in December 1955, China decided to treat Japanese war criminals in its custody leniently. None of the Japanese officials was sentenced to death or life imprisonment, and only a few were sentenced to fixed terms of imprisonment.[41]

The Chinese uniform strategy had a potent political effect between 1956 and 1957, when the United States became snarled in a greater conflict between its interests and those of its allies. Japanese prime minister Hatoyama Ichirō expressed his willingness to pay a visit to China, and Chiang Kai-shek voiced opposition to the deployment of US ground forces in Taiwan.[42] These developments demonstrated the allies' reluctance to support the United States. In Mao's words, neither Japan nor Taiwan wished to "lift the [American] sedan chair."[43] Consequently, China continued to practise its uniform accommodation strategy.

Regarding Taiwan, the mainland presented a clearer proposal than previous offers in May 1956. Zhou pointed out that Chiang Kai-shek could keep his armed forces as long as he agreed to unification.[44] Mao's main term was to sever US-Taiwan diplomatic relations. Under this condition, "everything in Taiwan shall be kept. It would be necessary to obtain Mr. Chiang's permissions on the timing of democratic and socialist reforms." Mao additionally emphasized that Chiang could "take anti-communist policies to deal with the Americans and internal [divisions]. Taiwan can send some people to the mainland. A secret tour is possible when a public one would be inconvenient."[45] In May 1955, the mainland had proposed giving Taiwan the status of a "province" rather than an "autonomous region."[46] In the spring of 1957, however, it agreed to a status for Taiwan as a "region with [a] high degree of autonomy"[47] and was also prepared to make economic concessions in order to "allay hostility and enhance understandings, in collaboration with the work of peaceful liberation of Taiwan."[48]

China's Japan policy was on the same parallel. In October 1956, Mao pronounced the United States the "number one enemy" and sought to unite with Japan against it.[49] China's accommodation of Japan took several concrete forms. First, the Taipei-Tokyo peace treaty waived Japanese war reparations to China, but Taipei was unable to represent the Chinese people as a whole in this respect. Zhou, however, agreed to "consider reasonable articles in the Taipei-Tokyo Treaty" if Tokyo and Beijing concluded a peace treaty.[50] In other words, Beijing would be willing to consider the Japanese stance on war reparations if Tokyo abrogated its treaty with Taipei. Second, Zhou responded in a moderate tone to the notion of Japanese rearmament, proposing a "reduction in the size of [Chinese] military forces, if the Americans withdraw their military forces from Japan." China would "not oppose Japanese self-defense forces as long as they [were] not under American command."[51] In other words, China would not oppose the development of Japanese armed forces in the context of a non-military US-Japanese alliance. Third, Mao agreed to revise Article 1 of the Sino-Soviet Treaty of Friendship, Alliance, and Mutual Assistance, which was directed against Japan: "China would cancel the clause regarding the Sino-Soviet military alliance when Japan becomes fully independent ... and concludes a non-aggression pact with China."[52] In other words, China was prepared to weaken the US-Japanese alliance at the expense of the Sino-Soviet alliance.

Developments in Taiwan and Japan in 1957 did not bring about any change in the Chinese uniform accommodation strategy that year. In May, the United States deployed missile troops in Taiwan, but Beijing did not take any countermeasures, other than publicizing an opposition statement. As Zhou explained to Soviet ambassador Pavel F. Yudin, "our statement sought to reveal American aspirations of turning Taiwan into military bases. We do not need to impose counterthreats."[53] Mao also explained this policy to Soviet leader Kliment Voroshilov: "[We need] to further develop the contradiction between Chiang Kai-shek and the Americans; and reconcile our differences with Chiang."[54] Following this direction, Zhou not only emphasized the high degree of autonomy Taiwan would enjoy after unification but also proposed providing financial assistance to Taipei. "If Chiang Kai-shek agrees to peaceful liberation of Taiwan, we will acknowledge his leadership. His armed forces would be kept ... We will also provide financial resources to him. In this circumstance, he will become a patriot rather than a traitor."[55]

Japanese prime minister Kishi Nobusuke tilted toward the United States to an even greater extent than Chiang. On June 2, 1957, he paid a visit to Taipei during which he announced support for an invasion of the mainland by Chiang.[56] Despite this, Beijing's policy of accommodation did not change. When receiving Japanese veterans, Defence Minister Peng Dehuai suggested in particular "reducing the size of Chinese naval forces, if Japan becomes fully independent." "We can cooperate with Japanese friends: you develop more naval forces, whereas we develop more ground forces."[57] Deputy Premier Chen Yi emphasized the importance of foreign trade when the Chinese and Japanese were negotiating their trade agreement in

December: "Foreign trade can provide possibilities in foreign relations. Foreign trade has economic, political and diplomatic implications ... We should begin with foreign trade and then turn to foreign relations. Diplomatic relations will follow foreign trade and cultural relations."[58] Beijing thus provided iron, coal, salt, and soybeans because, as the CCP vice chairman, Zhu De, explained, Japan would "tilt toward China politically as long as both sides can do business on a larger scale."[59]

China's policies toward these weaker US allies remained unchanged at the beginning of 1958. In February, Mao assessed that Taiwan represented only a "second-degree threat, since less powerful military technology is concentrated there."[60] On March 8, he considered the possibility of deploying PLA aircraft to the Taiwan Strait but did not follow through. As Mao wrote to Peng, "the deployment [of air power] should follow your advice for its preparation; but it should be decided later when the actual deployment occurs."[61] Meanwhile, Sino-Japanese trade relations continued to improve, and the two countries reached a new trade agreement on March 5. China would provide iron, coal, and other raw materials in exchange for Japanese steel of various types to the value of £100 million sterling between 1958 and 1962. In 1958, both sides also concluded a trade agreement in the amount of £10 million sterling of exports from each side.[62] Chen Yi announced the Chinese government's support for these agreements on March 7.[63] However, the deterioration of Sino-American relations in March 1958 necessitated changes in Chinese regional diplomacy.

Economic Sanctions and Shelling over Jinmen Islands, 1958

The United States and China began their ambassadorial talks in Geneva in 1955 with different objectives. The United States would impose restraints on Chinese use of force by suggesting a joint communiqué to this effect, a proposal that China firmly rejected. Zhou remarked that the joint communiqué would "enable the US to freeze the status quo in the Taiwan Strait area and convey an impression to the public of the relaxation of tensions there ... [In the new circumstance,] the US could strengthen its military presence on Taiwan, Jinmen, and the Mazu Islands." Zhou vehemently denounced the US "plot," which would "tie Chinese hands."[64] The Sino-American ambassadorial talks could not produce a satisfactory settlement, but the fact that the talks continued implied the possibility of a tacit understanding between Beijing and Washington on the East Asia situation. The risk of the United State's abandonment of its allies, moreover, would further estrange Japan and Taiwan. In other words, the Sino-American ambassadorial talks were bound to weaken US-sponsored alliances. When the United States found it impossible to impose restraint on the Chinese use of force, it prepared to reduce the level of the talks in order to cement its position with its allies. On December 12, 1957, US ambassador to Czechoslovakia U. Alexis Johnson, the US representative in the US-China ambassadorial talks, informed his Chinese counterpart, Wang Bingnan, that he would send his aides to continue talks. The all-out rejection he received from Wang was an attempt on the part of China to maintain the ambassadorial level of contact.[65] The United States turned a deaf ear, however, and on March 12, 1958, it reiterated its decision in a formal diplomatic note.[66]

The dramatic change in Sino-American relations inflicted serious damage on Beijing's uniform accommodation strategy toward Tokyo and Taipei. The American decision to end the ambassadorial talks implied that the United States wanted to reassure its allies, which raised the prospect of a more cohesive US-sponsored alliance system. The continuation of Chinese accommodation, therefore, would strengthen the American allies' capabilities and thus enhance the strength of the alliances. Accordingly, the Chinese leadership began considering exerting pressure on both Japan and Taiwan. In March, Mao queried "whether it would be appropriate to trade with Japan on a large scale."[67] In reply, Zhou suggested that China should "concentrate forces on isolating the war clique of American imperialism and place Japanese potential imperialists on special alert." He emphasized that some Japanese political forces sought "militarization"; therefore, "the precondition of conducting trade with Japan is not to make a loss [*bu chi kui*]."[68]

At this critical juncture, Tokyo's political commitment to Taipei propelled Beijing's policy shift. On March 30, Prime Minister Kishi expressed his attitude toward the Sino-Japanese trade agreement of March 5. He claimed that the Japanese government would never acknowledge the PRC, would deny any privileges to Chinese trade delegations or commercial branches, and would disavow any right to raise the PRC national flag in Japan.[69] In response, Beijing stated that the Sino-Japanese trade agreement could not be implemented until the Japanese government "removed all obstacles."[70] The Chinese statement marked the beginning of Chinese trade sanctions against Japan. As Zhou explained to Yudin, "we have decided to step up pressures upon the Japanese ruling clique ... We can only achieve our objectives through struggle. We will not achieve any objective if we do not solve the main problem through excessive concessions or compromises."[71] Later Zhou was more emphatic with respect to greater severity: "The Japanese ruling clique is short-sighted, [because] it interprets our struggle as a means to shape Japanese election results. Of course, these struggles would affect elections, but this was not the main objective ... We have prepared for the continuation of their policies for two or three years. We will sever all contacts, official and semi-official, with them."[72]

In addition, China "prepared for tensions with the United States."[73] On June 30, it presented an ultimatum demanding resumption of the ambassadorial talks: "It is necessary [for the United States] to send a representative at the ambassadorial level within 15 days to resume talks. Otherwise, the Chinese government would be of the opinion that the US is determined to break off the Sino-American ambassadorial talks."[74] Again the United States ignored the Chinese ultimatum, forcing the Chinese to look for new points of American weakness. On July 16, Chen Yi met the ambassadors from seven Asian and African countries and issued a warning: "The Americans and British have been everywhere attacking other people's weak points without realizing that they themselves have many soft underbellies."[75] As Chinese pressure on Japan was too weak to draw the United States back to the negotiating table, China prepared to initiate a crisis in the Taiwan Strait, and Mao deployed air power in Fujian Province on July 17.[76] The announcement on July 18 of Mao's decision to shell the Jinmen Islands marked the beginning of Beijing's uniform coercion policy toward Tokyo and Taipei.[77] The United States proposed resumption of ambassadorial talks on July 28 and attempted to get in touch with Chinese counterparts on August 4, but to no avail.[78] Chinese artillery diplomacy was already under way. Between August 4 and 13, the PRC deployed 520 MiG-17 and J-5 fighters in the Taiwan Strait.[79] The US reply to the Chinese ultimatum had come too late.

China gained more flexibility with respect to the United States, however. Prior to the outbreak of the Taiwan Strait Crisis, Mao had not committed to the use of force in taking the Nationalist-controlled Jinmen Islands. Nonetheless, on August 20, according to Mao's instructions, China was to

> immediately concentrate forces to launch surprise attacks against Nationalist troops on the Jinmen Islands (excluding those on Mazu Islands) and blockade the Jinmen Islands for three months. The enemy might withdraw from the Jinmen Islands or flounder under great handicaps. [China should] consider amphibious landings based on conditions in that circumstance. Take one step and look around before taking another. The first step is to encircle and blockade [the enemy] and shell for three days. Observe the response of the international audience and the enemy, and then bomb [the Jinmen Islands], if appropriate.[80]

Chinese artillery diplomacy became operational on August 23, with the PLA firing more than 30,000 rounds that day.[81] The immediate consequence of the shelling was resumption of the Sino-American ambassadorial talks in September 1958. It was not only a critical event in Sino-American relations but also a turning point in Sino-Soviet relations. The US military presence prevented the Chinese takeover of the Jinmen Islands, and the development of Sino-Soviet differences caused China to end the crisis.

Sino-Soviet Policy Differences in East Asia

1955–58

The Soviet Union provided political support and extensive assistance for mainland China's Taiwan policy, but Beijing and Moscow had differences on the question of Taiwan. First, the PRC regarded Taiwan as an inalienable part of Chinese sovereign territory, whereas the Soviet Union considered Taiwan a burden on the Sino-Soviet alliance. In June 1956, Nikita Khrushchev, first secretary of the Communist Party of the Soviet Union, received Liu Yalou, first commander-in-chief of the PLA Air Force. Khrushchev stated that "Chiang Kai-shek has fled to Taiwan. He looks like useless potato peelings to be thrown out. I think he is tying Taiwan to his hands. [Let's] throw him into the Pacific Ocean." Liu, however, believed Khrushchev was wrong: "Taiwan does not look like potato peelings. Rather, it is an inseparable part of the People's Republic of China. How can [we] throw it out?"[82] Second, the PRC adamantly opposed any prospect of political divisions in China, whereas the Soviet Union was willing to consider a political settlement, including that of "one China, one Taiwan." In May 1956, when the standing committee of the International Committee of the Red Cross invited Beijing and Taipei to attend its conference, the invitation to the latter did not bear Taiwan's official name of "the Republic of China (ROC)" but rather "Formosa." Moscow voted for the proposal, which suggested that the Soviet Union would support Taiwan's participation in the International Committee of the Red Cross's sponsored activities, as long as Chinese Nationalists would identify themselves as representatives of "Formosa." Both Beijing and Taipei strongly objected to this. Washington supported Taipei's stance, but Moscow did not vote for Beijing's position. Beijing was incensed at the Soviet vote, with Zhou inscribing three large exclamation marks on a Chinese Foreign Ministry report.[83] Later Zhou directly expressed to his

Soviet counterparts his displeasure at this "incorrect" policy – the PRC would never join an international organization or attend an international conference at which Taiwan was also present.[84] Indeed, the United States noted this difference between China and the Soviet Union:

> Peiping [Beijing] is apparently becoming increasingly concerned that the "two Chinas" concept may be gaining wider international support. A number of recent bloc actions can be interpreted as constituting at least a temporary acceptance of the present situation in other divided countries; Peiping [Beijing] may have wanted to make it clear that this acceptance by no means extends to the situation in China.[85]

Sino-Soviet disagreement was also apparent in the case of Japan. China and the Soviet Union were both concerned about the US-Japanese alliance, but the question of Japan involved the Soviet nuclear policy. The Soviet Union agreed to offer "models of atomic weapons" to China in October 1957, but Moscow was genuinely worried that Soviet assistance to Chinese nuclear programs would lead to a nuclearized Japan.[86] In February 1958, therefore, the Soviet Union proposed a nuclear-free zone in East Asia that would cover both China and Japan. Zhou's reply hinted at some reservations: "This would be a very good idea ... If the zone could be successfully constructed, Japan and the Philippines would be further separated from the United States. If the zone cannot be constructed, the propaganda [of the Soviet proposal] can help us obtain support from more pacifists, especially those in Japan."[87] Zhou's "agreement" could not reconcile different Sino-Soviet considerations, however. The Soviet Union had attempted to prevent Japanese acquisition of nuclear weapons, but its proposal also implicitly suggested the possibility of cutting off aid to Chinese nuclear programs, while China would prefer to have Soviet aid at its disposal. On February 1, after discussions with other Chinese leaders, Zhou emphasized to his Soviet counterpart that the proposed nuclear-free zone should include Japan, mainland China, and Taiwan. Foreign powers would not be permitted to establish missile bases or to test or store nuclear weapons. If Japan would not commit to this, China would be free of any obligation. In Zhou's opinion, the United States would never allow Japan to assume the proposed responsibility, and so "the [Soviet] proposal will probably become a piece of propaganda. However, as the Soviet official note mentioned, it would be good even if the proposal were purely for propaganda use."[88] These exchanges revealed to China the existence of differences with the

Soviet Union, and it began limiting its policy briefings to the latter. Consequently, the Soviets expressed displeasure over the Chinese failure to consult with them when China changed abruptly from soft to hard tactics vis-à-vis Japan.[89]

Despite these differences, cooperation still characterized Sino-Soviet relations in the summer of 1958. In May, the Soviet Union and the United States prepared for talks in Geneva on nuclear arms control. The US-Soviet discussion presented China with both challenges and opportunities. An agreement between the two countries might bring about the end of Soviet aid to Chinese nuclear programs, but the Soviet Union might take further steps to help China before assuming new responsibilities vis-à-vis the United States. Of course, China would not be bound by any agreement that it was not a party to, including those involving nuclear provision and storage. Therefore, as Chen Yi concluded during his talk with Soviet diplomats on July 12, 1958, "the Soviet Union can transfer these [nuclear] weapons to China and observe tests in China. Undoubtedly, this situation would be disadvantageous to the United States and other major powers in the West."[90] Indeed, Moscow sent three Soviet nuclear scientists to China that summer. They identified potential locations for nuclear plants in Qinghai Province and submitted a report to the Chinese government that "paved the way for and accelerated the development of Chinese nuclear programs."[91] Sino-Soviet military cooperation was well under way.

1958–59

Sino-Soviet military cooperation was of mutual interest, but there were disputes over forms of cooperation. A dispute over naval cooperation marked the beginning of a changing relationship. The Soviet Union proposed joint ownership of naval facilities in China, which would give it part ownership of the Chinese armed forces and military facilities, but China was persistent about exclusive rights. In July 1958, Mao criticized Ambassador Yudin in increasingly shrill language:

> You never trust the Chinese! You only trust the Russians! [To you] the Russians are first-class [people,] whereas the Chinese are among the inferior who are dumb and careless. Therefore [you] came up with the joint ownership and operation proposition. Well, if [you] want joint ownership and operation, how about hav[ing] them all – let us turn into joint ownership and operation [of] our army, navy, air force, industry, agriculture, culture, [and] education. Can we do this? Or, [you] may have all of China's more than ten thousand kilometers of coastline ... You may accuse me of being a

nationalist or another Tito. My counter argument is that you have extended Russian nationalism to China's coast.[92]

The diplomatic confrontation led to Khrushchev's secret visit to Beijing on July 31, 1958. Khrushchev explained to Mao that the Soviet Union had no intention of controlling China through the establishment of a "joint fleet." Temporarily mollified, Mao explained China's Japan policy to Khrushchev, emphasizing that trade sanctions against Japan had been in force for three months and that he would be prepared to sustain them for another three months. Zhou suggested a coordinated policy with the Soviet Union, with China applying informal pressure on Japan and the Soviet Union stepping up formal pressure. Khrushchev's silence implied reservations on his part.

The shelling of the Jinmen Islands exacerbated Sino-Soviet relations. On August 11, 1958, Zhou sent Khrushchev a list of Chinese requests, demanding thirty MiG-19C aircraft and 32,000 C-5 missiles within a month.[93] China had already decided to shell the Jinmen Islands by this time, but it did not inform the Soviet Union of its military plans. The United States immediately intervened in the Taiwan Strait once the shelling started. Still in a nuclear standoff with the United States, the Soviets were concerned that the shelling by their Chinese allies might draw them into a military confrontation with the Americans, despite assurances from China that it would "assume the whole responsibility and not entrap the Soviet Union."[94] On December 18, 1959, a Soviet report commented on Sino-Soviet relations as follows: "One cannot regard as normal the situation, when we, [as] China's allies, do not know what the Chinese comrades may undertake tomorrow in the area of foreign policy. Indeed, all countries of the socialist camp are linked not only by [the] common ideas and goals, but also by [the] alliance commitments."[95]

US naval and air forces deterred Chinese attempts to take the Jinmen Islands. In order to relax tensions, Mao propounded the famous "noose policy" on September 5, 1958:

At present, America commits itself to an "all-round contract" policy along our coast. It seems to me that the Americans will only feel comfortable if they take complete responsibility for Jinmen and Mazu, or even for such small islands as Dadan, Erdan, and Dongding. America gets into our noose. Thereby, America's neck is hanging in China's iron noose. Although Taiwan is [for the Americans] another noose, it is a bit farther from [the mainland]. America now moves its head closer to us, since it wants to take responsibility for Jinmen and other islands. Someday we will kick America, and it cannot run away, because it is tied up by our noose.[96]

This comment suggested that Mao might not take the Jinmen Islands, but he had not made a final decision to end the crisis. On September 7, he instructed the PLA to escalate military operations: "The artillery troops at the frontline of Xiamen should conduct a punitive attack the next day [September 8] ... on a larger scale compared to that of [August] 23. The estimate shall be 30,000 rounds."[97] The PLA blockaded the Jinmen Islands by taking additional measures on September 14, unleashing an artillery bombardment of Nationalist transport docks and air-drop zones on the offshore islands. The PLA Air Force expanded its patrol area and attacked Nationalist transport aircraft and fighters. Its naval forces attacked Nationalist warships in Liaoluo Bay.[98] China also made diplomatic attempts to take the offshore islands on September 15. During the resumed Sino-American ambassadorial talks, Beijing proposed that "if the Kuomintang [Nationalist] troops are willing to withdraw from these islands on their own initiative, the Government of the People's Republic of China will not pursue them [Nationalist troops]."[99] In other words, mainland China would take the Jinmen Islands to end the crisis. The United States might have accepted the proposal, but Taiwan refused to consider it. Therefore, mainland China continued the shelling in order to turn the military pressure on Taiwan into political pressure on the United States.

It was at this critical moment that Moscow stepped into the crisis. On September 16, Khrushchev proposed sending Tu-16 bombers to the Taiwan Strait: "If China believes it necessary and makes requests, the Soviet Union will send Tu-16 bombers, equipped with missiles and Soviet pilots, to launch heavy blows against aggressive troops along the Chinese coastal areas. Attacks on Nationalist troops would apply pressure on the US and let it perceive our capabilities."[100] However, Khrushchev did not mention who would be in charge of the Soviet air forces. As Mao informed Yudin in July, "if your army operates on our territory ... it must be commanded by us."[101] Khrushchev's omission, therefore, made the Chinese leadership wary about Soviet intentions. A letter from Zhou to Mao suggests disagreement with Khrushchev's advice: "[We] need to consider whether the timing would be appropriate. It would complicate the current situation if Soviet air power entered China ... China and the Soviet Union should find another appropriate moment to talk about when the Tu-16s would be under our command." Mao was equally nervous about the "form of the Sino-Soviet cooperation," and he urged Zhou to "carefully study" whether the Soviets would send "volunteer troops," "mercenaries," or "state troops" to China.[102] It is somewhat odd that one communist leader should think that his communist comrade would send "mercenaries." Mao may have suspected that Khrushchev would exploit the opportunity presented by tensions in the Taiwan Strait to extend Soviet influence in East Asia.

The Sino-Soviet disagreement became more problematic when Khrushchev's additional proposals made Mao even more suspicious. Secretary of State Dulles proposed a ceasefire in the Taiwan Strait on September 18, 1958. China immediately informed the Soviet Union that it would oppose Dulles's proposal by attacking the Nationalists on the Jinmen Islands.[103] From the Chinese perspective, shelling the Jinmen Islands was a continuation of the Chinese civil war: because the PRC would not be fighting over anything to do with the United States, the Chinese artillery diplomacy did not relate to a "ceasefire." Had China agreed to the American-proposed ceasefire, it would have implicitly acknowledged an American "right" to intervene in Chinese domestic affairs. Moreover, China informed the United States that it had "waited a considerable length of time for a peaceful withdrawal [of] Chiang Kai-shek's troops from the islands."[104] This suggests that the PRC had still not completely given up its plan to take the Jinmen Islands, having made every effort to enlist Soviet support for its opposition to the American ceasefire proposal and for Chinese takeover of the islands.

The Soviet counterproposal on September 27 reflected Sino-Soviet disagreements, however. The Soviet Union proposed an international conference outside the purview of the United Nations to end the crisis and an additional letter to the United Nations secretary-general to obtain support within the United Nations.[105] The Soviet proposal of an international conference indicated Chinese acceptance of a ceasefire and internationalization of the Taiwan issue. Although the Soviet Union was a permanent member of the UN Security Council, China had been labelled as an aggressor by the United Nations during the Korean War, and Beijing did not want the Taiwan issue to be connected with the United Nations in any way. Therefore, neither point of the Soviet proposal was acceptable to China, which replied as follows: "In addition to Soviet public support for our country, it seems unnecessary to propose any concrete advice. The Soviet Union should also convey its patience if other sides suggest Soviet mediation ... It is too early for the Soviet Union to propose an international conference. Issues [to be discussed at the conference] should be further studied."[106]

US and Soviet involvement complicated the situation in the Taiwan Strait area. China was unable to take the Jinmen Islands given the American military presence. Meanwhile, if China maintained the tension in the

Taiwan Strait, the Soviet Union would seize the opportunity to exert greater influence. Soviet troops in the Taiwan Strait area would side with China, at least temporarily, but such troops on Chinese territory would undoubtedly give Khrushchev greater leverage. Also, the Soviet Union might cooperate with the United States, in the name of the United Nations, to restrain Chinese freedom of action in East Asia. Zhou therefore communicated to his Soviet counterpart on September 27 that the PLA would blockade the Jinmen Islands but not conduct amphibious operations.[107] The CCP Politburo soon made the final decision. As Mao pointed out, "the guideline has been set ... [L]et Chiang Kai-shek's troops stay on Jin[men] and Ma[zu] ... We will negotiate with him to solve the problem of Jin[men], Ma[zu], Tai[wan] and Peng[hu]."[108] Mainland China published a "message to compatriots in Taiwan" on October 6 that formally ended the crisis. Chinese concern over Soviet exploitation of the Sino-American confrontation contributed to the decision to end the crisis.

Besides Taiwan, China and the Soviet Union also held different positions on revision of the US-Japanese security treaty. The Chinese artillery diplomacy indirectly moved the US-Japanese negotiations forward. China published its first statement opposing revision of the treaty on October 11, 1958, whereas the Soviet Union did not publish a similar statement until December 2.[109] During this period, in November, the Soviet Union suggested China publish a Sino-Soviet joint statement on the US-Japanese treaty revision negotiations, but the advice was politely declined by the Chinese.[110] Then, on December 31, Khrushchev additionally expressed a wish to promote "Soviet-Japanese cooperation in accordance with the principle of peaceful coexistence." He specifically regarded such cooperation as "a significant contribution to peace in the Far East and the world." To prevent a sharp decline in Sino-Soviet relations, Moscow did not publish Khrushchev's statement until January 18, 1959.[111]

Undoubtedly, Soviet-Japanese relations were better than Sino-Japanese relations. Table 2.6 shows the significant development of Soviet-Japanese trade while China was engaging in a struggle against "Japanese militarists." Soviet-Japanese trade reduced the effectiveness of Chinese sanctions, and Khrushchev explicitly opposed Chinese policy. He did not support China's low flexibility as seen in the linkage between Sino-Japanese trade and Japanese diplomatic acknowledgment of the PRC, whereas Zhou's reply cited the need to launch trade sanctions and curtail personnel exchanges. In Zhou's words, "the Sino-Japanese relationship was different from the Soviet-Japanese relationship. The Japanese government follows the United States to promote the concept of 'Two Chinas' ... Our relationship with

Table 2.6 Soviet-Japanese trade, 1958–62 (in millions of rubles)

Year	*Trade value*
1958	33.9
1959	51.1
1960	123.9
1961	161.6
1962	232.9

Source: Foreign Trade Institute of the PRC Foreign Trade Ministry, ed., *Sulian duiwai maoyi jiben tongji, 1954–1975* [The foundation of the foreign trade statistics of the Soviet Union, 1954–1975] [hereafter *SLWM*] (Beijing: Renmin chubanshe, 1977), 58.

Japan should be treated coldly [*leng yi leng*]."[112]

The competing Sino-Soviet objectives in East Asia were a cause of Soviet attempts to cut off aid to China. From 1958 to 1959, the Soviet Union refused to offer China assistance with respect to aviation research institutes, aviation forging and casting equipment, and nuclear submarines.[113] On June 20, 1959, moreover, it refused to offer "models of atomic weapons," and on August 23 it withdrew 233 nuclear scientists. At this time, China had completed only seven of thirty pre-arranged nuclear projects.[114] Sino-Soviet differences became a source of confrontation when Khrushchev visited Beijing on September 30, 1959. China requested Soviet assistance in accordance with the Sino-Soviet agreement signed in 1957,[115] but the Soviet Union demanded policy coordination between the two countries. Chinese and Soviet policies were fundamentally at odds, and neither country made real compromises.[116] The immediate consequence of the summit meeting was that Sino-Soviet competition replaced Sino-Soviet cooperation in East Asia. The United States was a Chinese regional competitor, and significant Sino-Soviet policy differences made Moscow an indirect ally of China's enemies in East Asia.

Selective Strategies, 1959–65

Strong Pressures on Tokyo, Secure Deals with Taipei, 1959–62

The low ebb in Sino-Japanese relations in 1959 was mainly due to the revision of the US-Japanese security treaty. In the context of the Sino-

American confrontation, such revision implied a strengthening of the US alliance with Japan. According to Zhou's analysis, "American [military] forces occupy Okinawa and Bonin Islands, deploy nuclear weapons, and have established hundreds of military bases in Japan. The US will use Japan as a vanguard during wartime."[117] In November 1959, Japanese foreign minister Fujiyama Aiichiro claimed that the security treaty would include a "Far East clause," and the geographical definition of "Far East" would include Chinese coastal waters, notably the Taiwan Strait.[118] Japan's stance therefore precluded any resumption of Sino-Japanese official trade. China would not lift sanctions unless "the Kishi government gives up its plan to launch attacks on Chinese coastal areas, backed by the US-Japanese military alliance."[119]

Although Sino-Japanese semi-official trade had been curtailed, China took every opportunity to step up pressure on the Japanese government through non-official trade with Japanese political factions. As the Liberal Democratic Party (LDP) government was being challenged by the Japan Socialist Party (JSP), China moved to cement relations with the JSP through its general secretary, Asanuma Inejiro. Asanuma had once stated that "Japan under no circumstances should retract the commitments and obligations" of the Tokyo-Taipei peace treaty, and that the treaty should "be respected in all circumstances,"[120] but he had gradually changed his position after 1954. In March 1959, he stated in Beijing that "American imperialism is the common enemy of the Chinese and Japanese people," a statement that triggered serious protests from the Japanese government. It was only under these circumstances, however, that the All-China Federation of Trade Unions would agree to do business with the General Council of Trade Unions of Japan, over which the JSP held significant sway.[121] This trade policy was an important instrument of Chinese regional diplomacy. In Zhou's words, "trade would be permitted, but ... economic struggle must follow political struggle."[122]

The United States and Japan concluded a new security treaty on January 14, 1960. Unlike the old treaty, concluded in 1951, it explicitly committed the United States to Japan's defence.[123] China responded with firm opposition – "the conclusion of the Japanese-US alliance treaty represents the revitalization of Japanese militarism and Japanese public participation in the US aggressive military bloc"[124] – and revised its defence guidelines. The CMC concluded that China should "make every effort to defend northeast China and the Shandong Peninsula" in the event of war.[125] China had previously used Sino-Soviet cooperation as a deterrent against the US-Japanese alliance and therefore sought Soviet support in concert with

Japan policies.[126] Differences in Sino-Soviet policy worked against China, however. The Soviet Union sought reduction of armed forces, whereas China emphasized "continuation of enhancing the defensive strength of the socialist camp."[127] In February 1960, both sides published different positions on disarmament.[128] The United States directly supported Japan, and Sino-Soviet differences worked to Japan's advantage. Under pressure from the United States and the Soviet Union, China adopted a more assertive policy toward Japan, maintaining its hardline trade policy and establishing a "North Sea Fleet."[129]

Meanwhile, the United States reduced its degree of involvement in the Taiwan Strait. During the Taiwan Strait Crisis in 1958, Secretary of State Dulles refused to provide escorts for Nationalist warships within twelve nautical miles of Chinese sovereignty.[130] He also publicly commented on the Nationalists' "foolishness" in concentrating large numbers of troops on the Jinmen Islands.[131] In this circumstance, Mao stressed, "we can cooperate with Chiang and his son, as long as they can resist America." If the United States cut off its aid to Taiwan, the mainland would be willing to provide the same amount.[132] According to Zhou's detailed explanations, by the end of 1958, US-Taiwan relations were snarled in "five contradictions": 1) the United States proposed Nationalist troop withdrawals from the Jinmen Islands, whereas Taiwan persisted in holding them; 2) the United States proposed the political formula of "two Chinas," whereas Taiwan stressed the concept of "one China"; 3) the United States was willing to invite both mainland China and Taiwan to the United Nations, whereas Taiwan emphasized the "Republic of China" as sole representative of the Chinese nation; 4) the United States could find a new agent to work for its interests in Taiwan, whereas Chiang Kai-shek consolidated his control over Taiwan; and 5) the United States might treat the question of Taiwan as a matter of trusteeship and provide support to Taiwan independence movement leaders such as Liao Wenyi, whereas Chiang Kai-shek countered that movement. In conclusion, Zhou believed that these US-Taiwan contradictions were greater than the cross-strait contradiction.[133]

The escalation of US-Taiwan disputes implied weakness in Taiwan's challenge to the mainland. The Conlon Report, released in September 1959 by the Committee on Foreign Relations of the US Senate, proposed three policy changes: 1) concluding a treaty of commerce with Beijing; 2) promoting the withdrawal of Nationalist troops from offshore islands; and 3) supporting Beijing as a permanent member of the UN Security Council.[134] Secretary of State Christian Herter, Dulles's successor, claimed that the report did not represent the Department of State's current view but did not deny its significance as reference material.[135] Washington's adoption of these policies could have rendered Taipei's survival problematic, but it would also have implied "two Chinas" as a political reality. The PRC Foreign Ministry's analysis was as follows:

> Regarding the Chinese representation at the United Nations, the nature of the problem is to engage in a struggle against the United States ... The US is exploiting the United Nations admission to create "two Chinas." They have proposed a number of plans, such as "neutrality in Taiwan," "the Republic of Taiwan," "trusteeship in Taiwan," or making the PRC and Chiang's representatives two member states in the United Nations.[136]

The report concluded that Beijing should not attend any international conferences or join any international organizations where Taipei represented "China." In other words, Beijing would allow Taipei to represent "China" in certain international organizations as it would not seek to join those organizations in the first place. Although Beijing had made every effort to take over the Jinmen Islands in 1958, in October 1960 Mao proposed sending ammunition and food to Nationalist forces on the islands.[137] In January 1961, Chen Yi expanded the accommodation policy by stressing that compromises should be permitted beyond those necessary and that the mainland should strive toward fifteen to twenty years of peace for socialist construction.[138] This implied that China would not use military forces in the Taiwan Strait during the time period that Chen specified.

It was at this time that the Soviet Union presented significant challenges to China's foreign policy. The Sino-Soviet ideological confrontation at the Bucharest Conference – partially a reflection of Sino-Soviet policy differences over international affairs – convinced Beijing that Moscow was part of "a united front against China."[139] Soviet policies in the aftermath of the conference confirmed Chinese suspicions. In July 1960, the Soviet Union exerted pressure on China by completely cutting off aid, refusing to send the 900 experts as previously agreed, withdrawing the 1,390 Soviet experts in China, and breaking 343 contracts and agreements.[140] According to Zhou's detailed report,

> China will be affected in many aspects after the withdrawal of Soviet experts – construction, scientific cooperation, special military technology, peaceful use of atomic energy, cooperation with some Eastern European countries, overseas students, propaganda, international conferences, diplomatic exchanges, foreign trade ... In terms of foreign trade, we are indebted to them

in the sum of 1.6 billion rubles. We need to pay 2.3 billion rubles back, if we include the 0.7 billion rubles of loans in due course.[141]

The Sino-Soviet split forced China to reorient its foreign trade with the West, and for economic reasons Japan was the most likely trade partner.[142] Ikeda Hayato's replacement of Kishi Nobusuke as Japanese prime minister in 1960 also provided China with an opportunity to set new policy courses. Given the US-Japanese alliance, however, China was reluctant to abandon its trade sanctions against Japan and would continue to select Japanese trade partners on its own political terms. In 1960, it proposed "friendship trade" with selected Japanese companies, having identified a few "friendship organizations," such as the Japanese-Chinese Association for Trade Promotion. China would do business only with companies that had been "introduced" (*jieshao*) by these friendship organizations, its main political condition being their attitude toward the US-Japanese alliance. A large number of these companies' employees "have participated in the struggle or offered financial support [to the anti-treaty movement], and [they] will continue to adopt friendly attitudes in future." China would break commercial contracts if a trade partner changed its political stance,[143] and it refused to respond to any overtures from companies without an introduction from a friendship organization.[144] The "friendship trade" was a new form of Chinese pressure on the Japanese government. In Ikeda's words, "this type of [Chinese] classification of trading firms as 'friendly' and by implication 'unfriendly,' would divide the business community of Japan much as Korea is divided by the 38th parallel."[145]

In the summer of 1961, three factors contributed to the practice of China's East Asia policy. First, the Sino-Soviet split offset China's military advantages, especially naval and air strength. According to Marshal Ye Jianying, China was unable to obtain naval equipment from the Soviet Union. Consequently, "the percentage of warships and aircraft at full readiness [had] been in decline due to insufficient materials and accessories."[146] The Soviet Union also weakened China economically and flaunted the achievements of Soviet-Japanese trade when China applied economic pressure on Japan. As Soviet diplomats told their Chinese counterparts, "the Soviet Union has placed an order for 30,000-ton oil tankers, 12,000-ton cargo ships, electrical equipment, and industrial chemical equipment. Conducting trade was to the Soviet advantage from an economic perspective."[147] Second, the United States encouraged Japan to develop its military strength. According to Chinese estimates, by the end of 1961, the United States would have established Japanese military installations on which

268,000 troops would be stationed, a 130,000-ton fleet, and 1,100 combat aircraft.[148] Third, the question of Taiwan made Sino-Japanese relations even more problematic. In mid-1961, the United States called the issue of the PRC's representation at the United Nations an "important question" that should be decided by a two-thirds majority of members present and voting. Beijing criticized Tokyo as an American "lackey"[149] for supporting the proposal, and it was not until April 1962 that the Chinese propaganda line toward Japan moderated.[150]

The issue of China's UN representation raised the level of tension in the Sino-Japanese relationship but reduced that in the Taiwan Strait. In the summer of 1961, both the United States and Taiwan expressed their differences publicly, and Washington concluded that both Beijing and Taipei were firmly opposed to a "two Chinas" policy.[151] Caught in a dilemma due to its alliance with Taiwan even as world support for the PRC's UN membership was growing, the United States sought to keep Taiwan in the United Nations and invite the mainland as a new member. On June 27, US media proposed two seats in the United Nations for Beijing and Taipei, both of which expressed official opposition to the proposal on June 29 and June 30, respectively.[152] As US-Taiwan tensions meant that Taiwan would be unable to pose any challenge to offset mainland China's power advantage, Beijing maintained its accommodation policy toward Taipei. The CMC decided in August that in order to maintain stability in the Taiwan Strait, the PLA would "not actively attack Nationalist troops." Chinese shelling over the Jinmen Islands was thus transformed from firing ammunition to firing "propaganda shells."[153] The mainland also re-emphasized its willingness to provide economic aid. In September, Liu Shaoqi stressed that "we have told Chiang Kai-shek that we can provide financial aid as the Americans have done. Why do you accept American money rather than Chinese money? We have also told him – 'you can rule Taiwan if you want, as long as you sever the tie with Americans.'" Zhou continued: "Like us, Chiang opposed the creation of 'two Chinas.' Therefore, the US has difficulties in the United Nations."[154] China's domestic economic difficulties did not prevent Beijing from making repeated attempts to promote national unification by providing financial assistance to Taipei.

Playing Taipei Off against Tokyo, 1962–65

There were three major developments in East Asia between 1962 and 1965. The first was Chinese concern over US-Soviet cooperation against China. Before 1960, the Chinese had established only eight checkpoints along its

3,084-kilometre border with the Soviet Union.[155] Sino-Soviet border clashes in 1962 signalled a dramatic change in the situation. In the first few months of that year, China had to deal with serious economic problems. Soviet consulates in Yining and Urumqi issued visas to Chinese citizens of Uighur and Kazakh ethnicity who wished to leave for the Soviet Union in search of better lives. The Soviet visa policy encouraged thousands of Chinese citizens to leave Xinjiang for Soviet Central Asia. The situation on the Sino-Soviet border spun out of control on April 27 and 28, when Chinese local administration collapsed in three border counties and the Chinese population fell significantly in Tacheng (68 percent), Yumin (over 50 percent), and Huocheng (38 percent).[156] In the ensuing months, the Chinese established fifty-eight checkpoints along the Sino-Soviet border.[157]

The Soviet Union exerted pressure not only in Xinjiang but also in Mongolia. In 1961, Moscow granted Ulan Bator credits worth $135 million for the Mongolian Third Five-Year Plan (1961–65).[158] In March 1963, a Soviet broadcast claimed that the Mongolian army had received modern aircraft and tanks in recent years.[159] In July, the Soviet Union and Mongolia reached an agreement that would allow Soviet troops to strengthen Mongolian forces along the southern border.[160] As Mongolia bordered only the Soviet Union and China, the agreement was clearly directed against China. In October, a number of Soviet military officers openly advocated direct military action against China before China came into possession of any nuclear capabilities. These Soviet officers thought that Khrushchev was making a mistake by not attacking China and believed that the Soviet army could defeat China in four days.[161] This serious deterioration in Sino-Soviet relations sparked genuine concern in Beijing about the negative impact of US-Soviet cooperation on China. CCP Politburo member Peng Zhen concluded on August 7, 1965, that "this modern revisionism is seeking to complete US-Soviet cooperation in order to dominate the world ... Modern revisionists have become accomplices of American imperialism. [We] need to make preparations. Modern revisionism will cooperate with American imperialism when the latter launches attacks against us. We should be careful about a pincer movement in both flanks."[162]

The second major development was that Taiwan was receiving indirect Soviet support and direct American aid. The Sino-Soviet clashes hence offered Taiwan new opportunities to launch incursions into the mainland. Both China and the Soviet Union were aware of the new situation, in which Moscow had become Taipei's indirect ally. According to Zhou, "Americans and Chiang [Kai-shek] are exploiting our difficulties to carry out provocations, and the Soviet leadership clique takes similar measures to create difficulties for us."[163] Indeed, the United States and Japan held similar views on the impact of Sino-Soviet relations on cross-strait relations. Counsellor of the Japanese Embassy in Moscow Okada asked in a conversation with Ilya Safronov, deputy chief of the Far Eastern Division of the Soviet Foreign Ministry, how the Sino-Soviet alliance treaty would operate in the event of a Nationalist invasion of mainland China. Safronov made a clear distinction between Soviet commitments to Eastern European allies and to China. He stressed that under the Warsaw Pact a *casus belli* would arise if any third power attacked the countries concerned, whereas the Sino-Soviet treaty was directed specifically against Japan or allies of Japan. Okada and the US Embassy in Moscow thus concluded that the distinction between Soviet security commitments left Moscow with a free hand in the event of a resumption of Chinese civil war.[164] In other words, Moscow would side with Beijing if it regarded Taipei as a Japanese ally but would not support Beijing otherwise.

Nationalist troops in Taiwan would never be able to launch military incursions into the mainland without American support. The US attitude toward Taiwan's counteroffensive plan was two-faced. During the Sino-American ambassadorial talks, the United States attempted to reduce tensions in the Taiwan Strait by imposing restraints on the Nationalists,[165] but it also provided additional military and economic assistance to Taiwan in the final months of 1962. Both sides reached a new military assistance agreement on September 11, 1962. The United States delivered F-104Cs on December 12 and offered $50 million in economic assistance to Taiwan.[166] Tables 2.7 and 2.8 show US military and economic assistance to Taiwan. In April 1965, the United States agreed to provide annual aid of $50 million for the next five years.[167] Soviet indirect support and American direct aid so encouraged Taiwan's adventurism that from 1962 to 1965, the Nationalists launched 130 offensives along the entire Chinese coast – from the Shandong Peninsula to Hainan Island.[168]

The third major change was estrangement between the United States and Japan. After the conclusion of the US-Japanese security treaty in 1960, the United States did not increase the size of its deployment in Japan,[169] and by 1961 it had reduced the number of its military bases to two naval bases and six air bases.[170] It also reduced military and economic assistance to Japan "with the objective of ultimate termination."[171] The US thus reduced the degree of its support for Japan while seeking to maximize its economic interest in the country. On the one hand, it urged Japan to follow the embargo policy against China. On the other hand, it had a clear trade advantage over Japan. Table 2.9 shows Japan's trade deficits with the

Table 2.7 US aircraft deliveries to Taiwan, 1961–65

Year	*Number of aircraft*
1961	10
1962	9
1963	26
1964	49
1965	46

Source: Yao Jun, ed., *Zhongguo hangkongshi* [A history of China's aviation] (Zhengzhou: Daxiang chubanshe, 1998), 596.

Table 2.8 US economic assistance to Taiwan under the Agricultural Trade Development and Assistance Act of 1954, 1960–65 (in millions of dollars)

Year	*Amount of assistance*
1960	7.6
1961	28.0
1962	59.3
1963	93.7
1964	26.2
1965	56.1

Source: Du Jidong, *Meiguo dui Taiwan diqu yuanzhu yanjiu 1950–1965* [US assistance to Taiwan, 1950–1965] (Nanjing: Fenghuang chubanshe, 2011), 95.

Table 2.9 Japanese trade balance with the United States, 1958–62 (in millions of dollars)

Year	*Exports*	*Imports*	*Balance*
1958	666	987	–321
1959	1,029	1,079	–50
1960	1,149	1,447	–298
1961	1,055	1,837	–782
1962	1,358	1,574	–216

Source: Aaron Forsberg, *America and the Japanese Miracle: The Cold War Context of Japan's Postwar Economic Revival, 1950–1960* (Chapel Hill: University of North Carolina Press, 2000), 10.

United States. In order to offset those deficits, Japan desperately needed to expand its trade with China.

Between 1962 and 1965, Taiwan presented a greater challenge to the mainland, whereas Japan became a secondary problem in Chinese regional diplomacy. Accordingly, Beijing maintained its selective strategies, but changed the targets of its concessions, increasing pressure on Taipei while accommodating Tokyo. The tensions in the Taiwan Strait area triggered Beijing's pressure on Taipei. As Chen Yi assessed the situation on May 29,

1962, "the first possibility is the creation of some incident in the Taiwan Straits. Thinking particularly about the Chinese economic situation is difficult, they [the Americans] may attempt to have Chiang Kai-shek land on the mainland and start a civil war."[172] US moderation at the Sino-American ambassadorial talks temporarily prevented escalation of the Taiwan Strait Crisis, but mainland China had to remain vigilant. "American imperialism ... may encourage Chiang Kai-shek residual bandits' military adventurism to invade the mainland at any time."[173] The 100,000 Chinese troops deployed in Fujian Province in the summer of 1962 were not deployed elsewhere until the autumn of 1963.[174]

Taiwan's attempts to exploit the Indochina conflict led mainland China to step up the pressure on Taiwan. In March 1963, Chen Cheng, a principal Nationalist leader, visited South Vietnam with a promise of military support, in an attempt to establish a military base there for operations against mainland China.[175] Beijing responded promptly on March 29, deploying additional aircraft in the Taiwan Strait.[176] Other major moves included deployment of at least forty-one aircraft and reactivation of two coastal airfields near the Taiwan Strait as operational fighter bases.[177] Indeed, mainland China's internal estimates were even more serious. In December 1963, Zhou witnessed military exercises of the South China Fleet, and relayed Mao's instructions to Wu Rulin, commander of the fleet:

> The US will send six or seven divisions to us when it wages a local war against us. Chiang Kai-shek and [South Vietnamese president] Ngo Dinh Diem will send a dozen divisions respectively. [They will] exploit railways, military and commercial ports of Zhanjiang, and [transfer their forces] to Liuzhou, in order to prepare for operations against us. It is estimated that [they] can even pose a direct threat to our Third Line Rear. In addition, Chiang Kai-shek would also launch invasions in the southeastern coastal area. The British in Hong Kong could cooperate with them as well. We are not afraid of [their collaboration]. Chairman Mao, with great resolve, has decided to reconstruct [China] after fighting the war. The CCP central leadership has agreed with Chairman Mao. Therefore, according to Chairman Mao's instructions, the South China Fleet should be aware of the imperative to comprehensively prepare for war ... You should place an emphasis on fighting in the western part of Hainan Island and the Beibu Gulf ... The CCP Central will establish the Beibu Gulf strategic headquarters if the enemy conducts amphibious attacks in Zhanjiang or wages a local war on a larger scale.[178]

The Indochina conflict provided incentives for mainland China to stand firm against Taiwan. In July 1964, Nationalist naval forces, in the guise of Japanese fishing vessels, conducted small-scale amphibious attacks along the Chinese coastal areas. Marshal He Long, vice chairman of the CMC, gave mainland Chinese naval forces new guidelines on launching active attacks against the Nationalists beyond the twelve-nautical-mile limit of China's claimed sovereignty.[179] The South China Fleet put the guideline into practice. Two Nationalist patrol vessels approached Shantou on August 5, 1965. In response, the South China Fleet launched attacks thirty nautical miles from the mainland that sank both ships on the high sea.[180] The Chinese navy also destroyed a Nationalist patrol vessel and a gunboat in November 1965.[181]

Moreover, mainland China sought to isolate Taiwan diplomatically. In 1963, Beijing was informed of France's willingness to establish diplomatic contacts. The French, however, provided a unique formula for severing ties with Taipei, whereby Paris would recognize Beijing and wait for Taipei to sever diplomatic ties. French president Charles de Gaulle thus assumed no responsibility for expelling Chiang's representatives from France: if Chiang refused to withdraw his diplomats from Paris, de Gaulle would not withdraw French diplomats from Taipei; if Chiang kept consular officers in Paris, de Gaulle would do likewise in Taipei.[182] The PRC's practice for the previous fourteen years had been that Beijing would establish diplomatic contacts only after its counterpart had severed ties with Taipei. The French position thus presented significant challenges to China. Establishment of diplomatic relations with France risked Mao's prestige, because if Chiang had chosen to remain in Paris, Mao would have had to end the relationship with de Gaulle to avoid the two-Chinas scenario. Nevertheless, Mao agreed to the French formula in order to exert additional pressure on Chiang, and this decision paid off when Taipei, on its own initiative, ended its relationship with Paris. Mao told the heads of Japanese youth delegations after the battle that "Chiang Kai-shek, an American lackey, is our enemy ... [You] say your government is so bad, [but] I think it [the Japanese government] is better than the US government ... better than our old friend Chiang Kai-shek as well."[183] In Mao's view, the Sino-Soviet split had weakened China's capabilities, and Beijing should henceforth deal with the challenges of the US-Taiwan alliance rather than US-Japanese alliance.

Mainland China therefore employed selective strategies – pressure on Taiwan and accommodation of Japan. In December 1961, Prime Minister Ikeda wanted to send LDP adviser Matsumura Kenzo to Beijing for trade talks, but his Chinese counterparts were cautious. It was not until August 26 the following year that Matsumura received Zhou's invitation to Beijing. This was a strong signifier of the changing character of China's Japan policy. In September 1962, China abandoned all preconditions for improved Sino-Japanese relations. It demanded neither immediate abrogation of the peace treaty between Tokyo and Taipei nor Japanese support for the PRC's representation at the United Nations. In particular, China agreed to "unconditionally extend the scope of friendly companies," suggesting a critical change in China's "friendship trade policy."[184] In November 1962, China and Japan reached a long-term memorandum trade agreement. When Taipei ended its contract to buy 300,000 tons of chemical fertilizer from Tokyo, Beijing immediately offered Tokyo a new contract for 700,000 tons.[185] In view of China's economic difficulties in 1962, this was significant when the Japanese sought to promote trade on a larger scale. This change in Chinese trade policy paved the way for significant development in Sino-Japanese trade, as Table 2.10 shows. China promoted trade relations for political purposes. Zhou cordially received former Japanese prime minister Ishibashi Tanzan, saying that "we always propose friendship not only between Chinese and Japanese people. [Chinese and Japanese] governments should gradually move towards friendship ... We have waited and placed great hope in Ikeda."[186] The two countries reached agreements on exchange of correspondents and liaison offices in April 1964.[187]

Table 2.10 Sino-Japanese trade, 1959–65 (in millions of dollars)

Year	*Trade value*
1959	0.00
1960	0.19
1961	36.09
1962	73.79
1963	129.26
1964	302.09
1965	454.26

Note: The data cover both the "friendship trade" (1960–65) and the "memorandum trade" (1962–65). The former refers to Chinese trade with partners "introduced" by friendly organizations in Japan. The latter refers to Chinese trade with partners to meet the demand specified in the semi-official trade agreement signed in 1962.
Source: Shen, *Dangdai Zhongguo duiwai maoyi,* 371.

China's support for Japan was also seen in its changing attitude toward Soviet-Japanese territorial disputes over "northern territories" – Iturup, Kunashir, Habomai, and the Shikotan Islands – which were under Soviet administrative control. The Soviet Union agreed to transfer Habomai and the Shikotan Islands to Japan, which laid the foundation for the establishment of diplomatic relations between the Soviet Union and Japan in 1956. However, in January 1960, when the United States and Japan undertook revisions to their security treaty, the Soviet Union refused to carry out the transfer.[188] The *People's Daily* published an editorial on March 22, 1960, claiming that Habomai and the Shikotan Islands were Soviet territories and that the Soviet Union was unable to transfer these islands to Japan not only because of the US-Japanese security treaty revisions but also because of the absence of a Soviet-Japanese peace treaty.[189] In July 1964, however, China changed its stance and supported Japanese claims to the northern territories. When Mao and Zhou received the JSP delegation on July 10, they stressed China's opposition to territorial ambitions and divisions of other countries' territories, resolutely supporting Japan's demand for the return of the northern territories. The Soviet ambassador to China immediately lodged a protest with the Chinese government.[190]

On November 9 that same year, Sato Eisaku became prime minister of Japan and tilted toward the United States, but China continued to promote Sino-Japanese relations. In April 1965, during the tenth-anniversary celebration of the Bandung Conference, Zhou received a Japanese representative and said that "we always take the initiative in developing Sino-Japanese relations." When Japan proposed contacts through the Japanese and Chinese consulates in Switzerland, Zhou proposed contacts at the level of foreign minister or premier.[191] He later admitted that he wanted to start the process of Sino-Japanese rapprochement when Sato began his tenure,[192] implying that China sought Sino-Japanese cooperation and compromises in the first few years of Sato's government.

China's East Asia policy between 1955 and 1965 supports hypotheses of the regional competition theory. Between 1955 and 1958, the United States was China's sole competitor. China adopted either a uniform accommodation policy or uniform coercive diplomacy toward the United States' weaker allies and sought to present a consistent image to the United States. Between 1958 and 1959, the Soviet Union proved to be a new competitor in East Asia. The Sino-Soviet conflict changed the strategic calculus of China's regional diplomacy. Between 1959 and 1965, China adopted selective strategies toward the United States' weaker allies, based on the degree of US and Soviet involvement in East Asia, to maintain its regional advantages. In other words, China's regional diplomacy was shaped by a foreign power's military presence on the Chinese periphery and its assistance to China's weaker neighbours. China's switch from uniform strategies to selective strategies demonstrated the proactiveness and flexibility of its asymmetric statecraft.

3
South Asia, 1955–63

During the Cold War, China engaged with five weaker neighbours in South Asia: India, Pakistan, Afghanistan, Burma, and Nepal. From 1955 to 1959, the United States was China's only regional competitor, while China and the Soviet Union acted in concert. China adopted uniform strategies toward all five of these South Asian neighbours in order to constrain their alignment options vis-à-vis the United States and to send consistent messages to Washington. In 1958 and 1959, however, Sino-Soviet disagreements over India transformed the Soviet Union into a new regional competitor. Soviet assistance to China's weaker neighbours became a source of Soviet leverage against Chinese influence, while Soviet and American "collusion" presaged a possible diminution of China's influence over its South Asian neighbours. Accordingly, based on the degree of US-Soviet collaborative involvement, China implemented selective strategies from 1959 to 1963, which it executed in two phases. In the first phase, from 1959 to 1961, China maintained the status quo with India, Pakistan, and Afghanistan but offered additional concessions to Nepal and Burma. In the second phase, from 1962 to 1963, China made Pakistan and Afghanistan new targets of accommodation and India a target of pressure. China's selective strategies seriously undermined the Soviet and American positions and maintained Chinese regional advantages over its South Asian neighbours.

Uniform Strategies, 1955–59

American and Soviet Involvement in South Asia

The decline in British influence in the aftermath of the Second World War enabled India to play a critical role in South Asia. Britain's withdrawal in 1949–50 consigned Sikkim and Bhutan to India's control, and in 1950 India and Nepal concluded a mutual defence treaty stipulating "effective countermeasures" against a "foreign threat."[1] The common struggle against British rule also fostered cordial relations between India and Burma. India and Pakistan, meanwhile, each controlled parts of Kashmir, but both advanced territorial claims to the former princely state as a whole. Moreover, there was, and still is, dispute in Afghan-Pakistani relations over what is known as the Pashtunistan question. Consequently, India and Afghanistan formed a balancing coalition against Pakistan, their common regional antagonist.

Indo-Pakistani rivalry weakened the capabilities of both states, resulting in their constant need for foreign supplies. The United States and the Soviet Union began providing aid to South Asia in the 1950s. As Table 3.1 shows, India increasingly relied on foreign assistance for its economic development, and between 1953 and 1957 it received comprehensive economic

Table 3.1 The role of foreign assistance in India's five-year plans, 1951–66 (in 100 million rupees)

Period	*Total budget*	*Foreign assistance*	*Share of foreign assistance (%)*
1951–56	196.0	18.8	9.6
1956–61	460.0	94.8	20.6
1961–66	750.0	220.0	30.0

Source: Zhanhou diguo zhuyi jingji bianxiezu, ed., *Zhanhou diguo zhuyi jingji* [Economics of imperialist countries in the postwar era] (Shanghai renmin chubanshe, 1972), 301.

Table 3.2 US aid to Pakistan, 1951–70

Period	*US aid commitment ($ million)*	*US share of total aid commitments (%)*
1951–60	964.9	68.4
1961–70	2,961.2	50.6

Source: Arshad Zaman, "Economic Relations between Pakistan and the United States: Aid, Trade, and North-South Relations," in *United States–Pakistan Forum: Relations with Major Powers,* ed. Leo E. Rose and Noor A. Hussain (Lahore: Vanguard Books, 1987), 60.

assistance packages in the amount of $700 million from the United States and $393 million from the Soviet Union.[2] Table 3.2 shows that the United States was also Pakistan's most important supplier of aid from 1950 to 1970: "In FY 55 US will program assistance for Pakistan of about $50 million in contrast to the $29 million proposed initially ... Total [of economic assistance] in excess of $105 million includes $5.5 million flood relief, $5.3 million technical assistance, $20 million defense support funds for economic development, $75.6 million consumer goods and industrial raw materials."[3]

Afghanistan, Burma, and Nepal received less economic aid from the United States and the Soviet Union. From 1954 to 1959, the Soviet Union committed approximately $300 million in aid to Afghanistan and also offered "an $80 million grant – the first that the USSR has made outside its satellites." By contrast, the US economic program in this regard from 1952 to 1959 "totaled about $150 million,"[4] and by June 30, 1960, the United States had committed approximately $162 million in economic assistance, including $23 million worth of wheat.[5] Meanwhile, the United States provided Burma with ten reconditioned patrol boats for use in protecting shipments of rice and other goods, at a cost of approximately $3.5 million.[6] However, the problem of rice export competition arose between the United States and Burma as the US rice disposal programs in Asia made it extremely difficult for Burma to obtain hard currency through rice exports. Consequently, the Soviet Union "promised to take all Burmese rice not sold elsewhere." In addition, it would "offer Soviet assistance in the establishment of industrial plants, agreeing to accept rice in payment, even on a deferred basis, if necessary."[7] To counter the Soviet moves, the United States offered "up to $25 million in dollar assistance and $17.3 million in local currency loans"[8] – offers that were crucial in view of Burma's weak economic base. To Nepal, the United States provided approximately 80 million Nepali rupees (NPR), while the Soviet Union provided negligible assistance.[9]

The United States and the Soviet Union also became prime arms suppliers in South Asia. India and Pakistan were embroiled in territorial disputes, but since neither was able to mass-produce modern armaments, they sought foreign assistance. By December 31, 1953, India's purchases of military equipment from the United States, including twenty-six C-119 aircraft and 100 medium tanks, amounted to $36.3 million, while the equipment Pakistan purchased from the United States – including 352 medium tanks, seventy-five 90 mm Gun Carriages (M36), and various types of ammunition (up to 90 mm diameter) – totalled $26.5 million.[10] The total value of US military aid intended for Pakistan during the period

1950–58 was $411.6 million. The United States also maintained a military advisory group of about 100 personnel in Pakistan.[11] Meanwhile, the Soviet Union exploited the opportunity that Afghan-Pakistani territorial disputes offered to cement its position in Afghanistan. From 1954 to 1958, Afghanistan received loans from the Soviet bloc totalling $158 million, including some $25–35 million for arms, and Afghan military forces received military training from "more than 400 Soviet bloc technicians."[12]

In conclusion, American and Soviet involvement in South Asia exhibited three features. First, unlike the situation in Europe, neither the United States nor the Soviet Union maintained a strong military presence in South Asia; instead, aid was the primary means for achieving their considerable influence in the region. Second, India, Pakistan, and Afghanistan were the primary focus of US-Soviet competition; neither the United States nor the Soviet Union had much interest in vying for Burma or Nepal. The overall volume of foreign assistance to Nepal was hence much smaller than to other South Asian countries, and it did not include military aid from the United States or the Soviet Union. Third, among these South Asian nations, Pakistan tilted toward the United States, while Afghanistan followed the Soviet foreign policy line. As a critical player in South Asia, India adopted a non-alignment policy and sought aid from both the US and the Soviet sides. This, in turn, suggested particularly fierce US-Soviet competition over India.

US-Soviet competition constrained China's South Asia policy and reflected Sino-American competition. India, Burma, and Pakistan were not members of the Soviet bloc, and each had territorial disputes with China. However, all three countries acknowledged the People's Republic of China (PRC) as the sole legitimate government of the Chinese nation, and thus became the primary focus of Sino-American competition in South Asia. For example, in response to the Indian famine of 1951, China provided 660,000 tons of grain in emergency assistance, while the United States provided 2 million tons.[13] Moreover, according to a People's Liberation Army (PLA) estimate, 15,000 Chinese Nationalist troops had established military bases in Burma with American support.[14] In view of the Nationalist element, both the PRC and Burma opposed the United States.[15] However, Burma's government was under challenge from the Burma Communist Party (BCP), and the overseas Chinese community in Burma wielded considerable economic power. Consequently, the Burmese government's concern over possible intervention by the PRC in support of the BCP – either in an armed struggle or in the national elections – drew Burma closer to the United States.

China and the United States also competed over Pakistan, which exported cotton for hard currency. China was Pakistan's largest foreign market for cotton in 1952,[16] but in 1954 Pakistan joined the Southeast Asia Treaty Organization (SEATO) and the Central Treaty Organization (CENTO) and thus became an American ally. The US-Pakistan alliance would help Pakistan to gain American aid, and it would also drive a wedge between the United States and India. Nevertheless, the US-Pakistan alliance caused genuine concern in China on the part of China. In Chen Yi's words, "we must be fully aware of the existence of an imperialist encirclement from South Korea to Pakistan. US imperialism is establishing military bases everywhere against us."[17]

To deal with the American challenge, China pursued a cooperative policy with the Soviet Union. The Chinese and Soviet stances in South Asia were not identical. On his visit to Indian-controlled Kashmir on December 10, 1955, Nikita Khrushchev publicly treated it like an Indian state.[18] By contrast, China took a neutral stance on the Kashmir issue.[19] Moscow's subsequent tilt toward Beijing was demonstrated by Soviet deputy premier Anastas Mikoyan's visit to Pakistan in March 1956, when Mikoyan expressed his country's willingness to change its Kashmir policy and provide aid to Pakistan. In his words, "the Kashmir issue should be decided by Kashmir's people, not by us." He stressed that Khrushchev would be prepared to visit Pakistan at any moment.[20] The Soviet policy adjustment offered better terms for Sino-Soviet cooperation in South Asia. Geng Biao, the PRC's ambassador to Pakistan, reported a conversation with his Soviet counterpart in a cable to Zhou Enlai on April 6, 1956. It conveyed the Soviet Union's view of Pakistan as the weakest link in CENTO and SEATO and hence the view that the Sino-Soviet alliance should seek a breakthrough in Pakistan. The Soviet Union also perceived Pakistan's "anxiety" vis-à-vis the Soviets and Pakistan's "dependency on China on important questions." Therefore, "China will be the major force undertaking activities in Pakistan and the success will be shared by us."[21] This left the United States as China's only regional competitor in South Asia.

China's Political-Economic Concessions in South Asia

Sino-Indian negotiations in 1954 marked the beginning of China's uniform accommodation strategy in South China. The "McMahon Line" – the border between India and Tibet imprecisely drawn by British colonial authorities – was neither known to nor approved by the Chinese Nationalist government. In February 1951, after driving the Tibetan administration out of the area below the "McMahon Line,"[22] India proposed making the

"McMahon Line" one part of the Sino-Indian border, but it was not until the summer of 1954 that China began considering the issue of its border with India. As Zhou pointed out, "the 'McMahon Line' existed not only on the Sino-Indian border, but also on the Sino-Burmese border ... The Chinese government [the PRC] cannot acknowledge the legitimacy of the line, but ... it did not intend to advance its forces below the line."[23] In other words, China would implicitly acknowledge Indian administrative control below the "McMahon Line." Moreover, improved transportation between Tibet and the Chinese hinterland gave China tremendous advantages over its neighbours. In October 1954, therefore, Mao Zedong promised Indian prime minister Jawaharlal Nehru a reduction of armed forces in Tibet: "We have deployed only around 10,000 troops in Tibet, with 10,000 additional troops in the Qamdo area that are constructing roads. They will return [to inland China] when the roads are completed."[24] Cooperation between China and India thus reduced Indian incentives to cooperate with the United States.

China's accommodation of India did not imply Chinese pressure on Pakistan. When Nehru told Zhou in June 1954 that "Pakistan's incumbent government will always follow the United States. Pakistan should not be included in any agreement associated with a peace zone,"[25] Zhou demurred, saying that "the PRC's policy toward Southeast Asia is peaceful coexistence. We take this attitude toward India, Indonesia, and even Pakistan."[26] During that visit to India, Zhou declined Nehru's invitation for him to visit Kashmir.[27] China had adopted a neutral stance with respect to the former princely state. During a visit by Pakistani leaders on October 7, 1954, Zhou said, "we oppose [the US-Pakistan alliance], but we do not emphasize this." He went on to promise that "we can find a way to remove the [source of the] fear. We would like to take the same approach to work with Pakistan as what we do with India ... If someone is isolating Pakistan in Asia, we will oppose it ... China is taking a neutral stance and calmly dealing with the Kashmir issue."[28] China wanted this issue to be peacefully resolved without foreign intervention. The primary objective was to prevent the United States from exploiting the dispute in order to expand its influence.

Meanwhile, China also pursued an accommodation policy vis-à-vis Burma to prevent its alignment with the United States. As Zhou promised Burmese prime minister U Nu, "China's policy toward Burma would be identical with its policy toward India." China would be willing to offer "a political guarantee" of "peaceful coexistence." Moreover, as Zhou made clear, the PRC would never support the BCP's attempts to overthrow the

Burmese government by launching an armed struggle. "Revolutions can never be exported. Otherwise, revolutions will fail. Communists in different countries can achieve their success by their own efforts. They should not expect foreign support." The PRC even suggested arms sales to the Burmese government.[29] The accommodation policy was not implemented, but the suggestion itself reflected the PRC's support for Burma. Finally, China imposed restraints on the political activities of overseas Chinese. In Mao's words, "illegal activities or revolutions may occur in every country. It is the business of those countries. Overseas Chinese should not participate ... We will not establish Chinese Communist Party [CCP] committees in overseas Chinese [communities] and have disbanded existing committees."[30]

Afghan and Nepalese diplomatic recognition of the PRC in 1955 provided an excellent platform for China to practise the uniform accommodation strategy to an even greater extent. China pursued four specific initiatives: 1) it promoted trade with and provided aid to its South Asian neighbours; 2) it sought compromises with Burma during border negotiations; 3) it provided aid to Nepal that was not at Indian expense; and 4) it accommodated India by allowing the Fourteenth Dalai Lama's visit to New Delhi. These policies would enable the PRC to create and expand a "peace zone," exploit differences between South Asian countries and the United States, and reduce the degree of American involvement in South Asia. Zhou analyzed the significance of a peace zone on June 7, 1955:

> The United States is encircling the Soviet and other People's Democracies, but breakthroughs are available everywhere from the East to the West. We should strive for more breakthroughs. The most critical issue of the world struggle today is to expand a peace zone. After the Geneva Conference last year, Chinese and Indian Premiers issued a joint communiqué and mentioned the establishment of a peace zone. The peace zone has been rapidly expanding in the past year. This is to our advantage. But the war-clique is fearful, because the peace zone cuts off their encirclement. This trend can postpone [the] outbreak of war.[31]

In an attempt to expand the peace zone, China conducted trade with Burma on special terms. In 1953, Burma had proposed that rice should account for 75 percent of its exports to China. At that time, China "remove[d] the rice from trade [agreements] ... [because it] did not need the rice"[32] and preferred a much smaller volume of trade in mutually agreed items. The Chinese stance changed in 1955. The US rice disposal program from 1953 to 1955 resulted in lower rice prices and "left Burma with about 20 per cent of its crop unsold."[33] Consequently, Burma lost a large portion of its traditional rice market and a substantial amount of foreign exchange. China seized the opportunity by providing for a 20 percent cash payment to import rice from Burma.[34] Deputy Premier Chen Yun explained the policy as follows:

> We buy cotton from Egypt, and by following the same principle, we buy cotton from Pakistan and import rice from Burma. This is to their advantage. Our purchase of their goods makes it difficult for the US to bargain [with these countries] on price ... Imperialism cannot cut prices at will. This is our support to them. The price will go up when Minister Ye or his deputies arrive. Otherwise, the price will go down.[35]

Following this line of reasoning, Ye Jizhuang, the PRC's foreign trade minister, and his deputy, Li Zheren, explained Chinese economic statecraft in South Asia. Ye stressed the relationship between price negotiations and foreign strategies. According to him, China should

> offer a higher price than the international market price to import their goods, provide a lower price than the price on the international market to export goods of their interests, and provide complete sets of light industry equipment on a deferred basis and favourable terms ... to coordinate with foreign policy activities and expand the peace zone. [We will] sacrifice the trade with some Afro-Asian countries ... [We] should give priority to India, Indonesia, Syria, and Lebanon and seek governmental trade agreements with Pakistan, Nepal, Afghanistan, Cambodia, and Saudi Arabia.[36]

Meanwhile, Li emphasized the relationship between the scale of trade and foreign relations:

> We need to positively and gradually expand the trade with them to enlarge the peace zone ... India: The trade relationship is falling behind the political relationship. [Therefore, we] must make every effort to find various possibilities to expand the trade ... Burma: Premiers of both countries have agreed that China will annually import 150,000 tons of rice from 1955 to 1957. [We] must consolidate the trade relationship and enhance cooperation through annual rice agreements ... Pakistan has a relatively bad political attitude toward us, [but we] should strive for its side with peace and neutrality

> [through trade agreements] ... Afghanistan and Nepal have relatively friendly political attitudes toward us, [and] small-scale trade can be possible.[37]

Political concerns with respect to expanding a peace zone in an attempt to weaken American influence drove Chinese economic practice. As Zhou made clear, "the practice of expanding the peace zone entails adopting a policy of peace, upholding national independence, non-participation in adversarial alliances, and opposing foreign military bases on one's own territories ... The peace policy has greatly contributed to prevention of war. We, with enthusiasm, fully support this policy, based on an adequate estimate."[38] In 1956, China offered economic assistance to Pakistan to alleviate famine. Chinese assistance packages included 60,000 tons of rice at "a reasonable price" and an additional 4,000 tons of rice as free assistance.[39] This suggests that China understood Pakistan's attempts to direct the US-Pakistan alliance against India rather than China. Also, China paid close attention to the spillover effect of Chinese aid, because Burma exported rice to Pakistan. Zhou gave a detailed explanation to U Hla Maung, Burma's ambassador to China, on August 4, 1956: "[China has] told [Pakistan that] the rice price offered to Pakistan must be on the same price terms as that of the world market. Otherwise, other countries will blame us." China subsequently offered additional rice to Pakistan in the form of free assistance.[40] In other words, China provided aid to Pakistan and protected Burma's economic interests.

A more significant attempt at accommodation was apparent in Chinese efforts to reach a border agreement with Burma. Border disputes occurred throughout the northern, central, and southern sectors. In the northern sector, the British had extended the "McMahon Line" from the Sino-Indian border to the Sino-Burmese border. Having acknowledged Chinese sovereignty over the villages of Hpimaw (Pianma), Gawlum (Gulang), and Kangfang (Gangfang) (PGG), Britain nonetheless occupied them. In the central sector, Britain had acknowledged Chinese sovereignty over Nanwan (the Meng mao triangular area) but occupied it in the guise of a permanent lease. In the southern sector, the British drew the "1941 line" that divided the Panhung-Panlao (Banhong-Banlao [BB]) tribal region where China had a claim. The Chinese Nationalist government had acknowledged the line in 1941, but the PRC did not accept it. Moreover, the PLA occupied a vast area west of the line. In November 1955, Chinese and Burmese troops fired at each other in the southern sector. The aftermath of the conflict might have seen Burma tilt toward SEATO for the sake of US protection, but instead the border incident pushed forward Sino-Burmese border negotiations. In March 1956, Zhou approved two negotiating plans drafted by the PRC's Foreign Ministry. The first proposed administration based on the line of actual control. Both sides sent police to the border area to maintain order. The second plan proposed troop withdrawals over a three-to-five-kilometre area based on the line of actual control. Both plans implied that China would not be prepared to give up the area west of the "1941 line."[41]

The Sino-Burmese border incident strengthened US-Burma cooperation, which in turn resulted in Chinese compromises with Burma. June 1956 saw further Sino-Burmese border clashes.[42] Meanwhile, the United States decided to offer new aid packages to Burma.[43] In this circumstance, Zhou suggested to U Hla Maung PLA troop withdrawals from west of the "1941 line" in exchange for the PGG villages.[44] The proposal was to Burma's advantage. The area of the PGG villages was not specified during the conversation but would cover only about 130 to 180 square kilometres. By contrast, the Chinese troop withdrawal from the "1941 line," whereby China would unilaterally withdraw from a 1,300-square-kilometre area to facilitate further border negotiations, was finalized during the conversation.[45] Zhou also expressed explicit concerns about "imperialist exploitation" of the border issue, to which U Hla Maung replied that

> the Burmese government is of the opinion that this [the border issue] is a matter of Sino-Burmese relations ... Someone suggests Burma's participation in SEATO and even claims that SEATO should be responsible not only for its member states but also for other states not in the region. However, Burma's government still considers this [the border issue] as a problem in our bilateral relations.[46]

Zhou responded that "this is the correct position. Otherwise Burma will not be a country that is friendly to us."[47]

Nonetheless, given the Sino-Burmese border disputes, Burma and the United States had incentives to strengthen their cooperation. In September 1956, the United States provided additional military assistance to Burma and sent military advisers dressed in civilian clothing.[48] There were reports that it might provide economic aid in the amount of $42.3 million and deliver free military assistance in the amount of $19 million.[49] In light of this, Zhou believed that the Sino-Burmese border settlement should be based on a "realistic attitude," with the object of "reaching an understanding." Therefore, China should not "make excessive demands."[50] Indeed, Zhou proposed a settlement based on two concessions. First, China would use the triangular area (the central sector) in exchange for the BB tribal region.[51] Second, the Sino-British agreement in 1941 mentioned that China possessed mining rights in the Lufang areas of Burma; if the border issues could be solved, China would relinquish the rights in July 1957.[52] At this time, China had certain reservations regarding application of the watershed principle, the size of the PGG villages, and the claims of the BB tribes,[53] but it had already made unilateral concessions to Burma, namely the "1941 line" and mining rights in the Lufang areas. In response, Burma's deputy premier, U Ba Swe, told Mao that "Burma will not join any military alliance and will not become an anti-China military base for imperialists."[54]

In addition to Burma, China made considerable concessions to Nepal, though *not* at India's expense. After 1955, Nepal persistently demanded Chinese economic assistance.[55] From the Chinese perspective, "Nepal is adopting a policy of peace and independent development. Nepal is dissatisfied with Indian control and is in fear of American and British influence. Nepal is willing to ... obtain Chinese and Soviet aid in order to independently develop its economy." Therefore, China would offer assistance to Nepal in order to encourage the struggle against imperialism; meanwhile, it would "take care of the Indo-Nepalese relationship."[56] "Sino-Nepalese relations should not go above Indo-Nepalese relations. We need to obtain Indian prior understandings with respect to certain important affairs in connection with India."[57] In September 1956, China offered Nepal 20 million rupees in cash and 40 million rupees' worth of machinery, equipment, materials, and other commodities.[58] However, it exercised self-restraint in two aspects. First, it would not send advisers to Nepal, suggesting instead that Nepal should invite Indian advisers. Second, the amount of Chinese assistance to Nepal would not exceed that of Indian assistance. China emphasized to both Nepal and India that China's assistance to Nepal must be based on the unity of the three countries.[59]

It was also the Chinese opinion that Sino-Indian cooperation would weaken American influence in South Asia. As Zhou pointed out, India, a nationalist country, was the PRC's "partner (*tongmengjun*) against imperialism."[60] Accordingly, China accommodated India by permitting the Fourteenth Dalai Lama's visit to New Delhi. The "democratic reform" in Tibetan ethnic areas in Sichuan, Qinghai, and Gansu Provinces had sparked armed conflicts in March 1956, and it was in that context that India had issued an invitation to the Dalai Lama to attend the celebrations of the 2,500th year of Buddhism. To avoid Sino-Indian conflict, therefore, the PRC's Foreign Ministry approved the visit on September 10, 1956.[61] Moreover, China exercised restraint with respect to Sino-Indian disputes, which occurred throughout western, central, and eastern sectors of the Sino-Indian border. The size of the central sector was limited. The western sector (Aksai Chin) was under Chinese control, and the eastern sector (territories below the "McMahon Line") was under Indian control. According to India, China should abandon its claims in the eastern sector based on the "McMahon Line," withdraw from Aksai Chin, and abandon claims to the western sector as well. In reply, China expressed willingness to engage in border negotiations.[62]

The Lhasa revolt in March 1959 did not change Chinese efforts toward accommodation. In its aftermath, Mao Zedong believed that the Dalai Lama had "communicated with India" before the incident,[63] but he still wished to compromise with Nehru. In his view, "we should temporarily not report Nehru's speeches on the Tibet revolt, because we will engage in debates with him if we do so. We should avoid debates, make observations for a period, and leave adequate room [for further engagement]."[64] The deterioration of Sino-Indian relations offered the United States a new opportunity. On April 24, 1959, Pakistan suggested Indo-Pakistani co-operation against "threats upon the subcontinent."[65] The United States supported the Indo-Pakistani joint defence proposal. To prevent a further sharp decline in Sino-Indian relations, Mao reduced the PLA's size in Tibet in order to allay "Indian fears."[66] He suggested to Nehru that

> the enemy of the Chinese people is in the East. American imperialism has established many military bases in Taiwan, South Korea, Japan, and the Philippines. These bases are directed against China. The Chinese main concern and the main struggle are in the East – the hostile American imperialism in the Western Pacific region, rather than India or any country in Southeast Asia or South Asia. The Philippines, Thailand, and Pakistan have joined SEATO, which was directed against China. However, we do not treat them as enemies. India, a country outside of SEATO, is a Chinese friend rather than an enemy. China will not be foolish enough to have a two-front war – one with America in the East and the other with India in the West.[67]

Zhou put Mao's instruction into practice. The original draft of a Foreign Ministry instruction stated that "we should take a cold and detached attitude toward India if it does not change its anti-China policy." The sentence was completely rewritten by Zhou on August 4, 1959, to read "we should give a positive answer to India at an appropriate moment if India has the willingness to get in touch with us."[68] The Sino-Indian border clashes occurred on August 25, 1959, when troops on both sides fired shots at each other. In the aftermath of the conflict, Pakistani president Ayub Khan visited New Delhi on September 1 and proposed Indo-Pakistani "joint defence."[69] In view of the situation, China wished to ease tensions with India through negotiations. On September 8, Mao told Afghan deputy premier Mohammad Naim Khan that "we would welcome it if Nehru can maintain his neutrality policy ... We wish to reach compromises with Mr. Nehru and solve the problem based on friendship. We do not want India to fall in American hands." Accordingly, Mao hoped that Naim Khan could "construct a bridge" for meetings between Zhou and Nehru.[70] It is unclear exactly what proposals China was prepared to make at this time, but it is evident that China would make considerable efforts to achieve agreements with India without applying pressure.

Triangular Competition in South Asia, 1959–63

American and Soviet Involvement in South Asia

During the Cold War, South Asian nations relied on foreign assistance, whereas the United States and the Soviet Union remained strategically and economically self-sufficient. Therefore, Washington and Moscow exerted influence in South Asia by providing aid. Table 3.3 shows the volume of American and Soviet economic aid to India from 1958 to 1964.

Table 3.3 US and Soviet economic aid to India, 1958–64 (in millions of dollars)

Year	*United States*	*Soviet Union*
1958	305.1	20.0
1959	366.7	430.0
1960	758.4	–
1961	594.4	125.0
1962	766.8	–
1963	714.6	–
1964	689.8	210.0

Source: Shaheen Irshad Khan, *Rejection Alliance? A Case-Study of U.S.-Pakistan Relations, 1947–1967* (Lahore: Ferozsons, 1972), 68; Foreign Trade Institute of the PRC Foreign Trade Ministry, ed., *Sulian duiwai maoyi jiben tongji, 1954–1975* [The foundation of the foreign trade statistics of the Soviet Union, 1954–1975] [hereafter *SLWM*] (Beijing: Renmin chubanshe, 1977), 155–57.

In April 1961, the United States indicated its "willingness to commit up to $1 billion in the next two years in support of India's external resource requirements in the Third Five-Year Plan period." The US commitment to Pakistan would "be of the order of magnitude of $250,000,000."[71] The Kashmir dispute had never been fully settled, however. To deal with Pakistan's recalcitrance, the United States provided aircraft to India through the United Kingdom. In June 1962, the United States offered a loan of F-104 fighters for British defence if Britain delivered a Lightning Mark II squadron to India.[72] The United States was also willing to share half the hard currency cost of one Lightning Mark II squadron and to finance 75 percent of the further development cost of the Orpheus engine. In addition, it offered to sell India nine C-130 transports for rupees.[73]

The Soviet Union also dramatically enhanced India's strategic importance between 1958 and 1962 by providing additional aid.[74] In June 1959, the Soviet government offered a credit of 1,500 million rubles toward India's Third Five-Year Plan and an additional credit of 500 million rubles at the end of July 1960. In both cases, Moscow offered easy terms and conditions.[75] In February 1961, it promised to offer 600 million rupees' worth of new aid packages.[76] Meanwhile, the Soviet Union directly contributed to India's military buildup. In October 1960, the two countries concluded a contract for India's purchase of eight Antonov An-12 aircraft capable of carrying heavy machinery and equipment at high altitudes. The total value of the contract was about 100 million rupees, repayable in six installments in non-convertible Indian rupees under the terms of the Indo-Soviet trade agreement. It was agreed that the interest on unpaid balances would not exceed 2 percent per annum.[77] In addition, the favourable Soviet terms would include a 40 percent cheaper price, unlimited spare parts, payment in rupees, and possible licensing agreements.[78] From October 1960 to May 1962, the Soviet Union offered 94 aircraft to India, including 32 An-12 transports, 26 MiG helicopters, 12 MiG-21 fighters, and 24 Ilyushin Il-14 transports.[79] Consequently, "the AN-12's, MI-4's, IL-14's and HF-24 engines ... introduced some 200 Soviet technicians into Indian defense installations."[80]

The United States and the Soviet Union wielded almost equal influence in the case of India, but not in other South Asian nations, where they held somewhat uneven sway. The Kashmir dispute and increased US aid to India created new opportunities for the Soviet Union to drive a wedge into the US-Pakistan alliance. In 1959, it offered Pakistan $3 million in economic assistance.[81] In 1961, during negotiations over the Soviet-Pakistani oil-prospecting agreement, the Soviet Union presented "three

Table 3.4 Soviet economic aid to Afghanistan, 1958–64 (in millions of dollars)

Year	*Amount of aid*
1958	15.0
1959	129.0
1960	46.0
1961	200.0
1962	–
1963	150.0
1964	41.0

Source: SLWM, 155–57.

Table 3.5 US and Soviet aid to Nepal, 1958–63 (in millions of Nepali rupees)

Year	*United States*	*Soviet Union*
1958–59	17.951	–
1959–60	56.225	–
1960–61	86.997	8.456
1961–62	–	–
1962–63	46.800	15.000

Source: John W. Garver, *Protracted Contest: Sino-Indian Rivalry in the Twentieth Century* (Seattle: University of Washington Press, 2001), 142.

rates of interest [on loans]. For communist countries the rate of interest was 2%; for neutralist countries the rate was 2-½%; and for Western committed countries the rate was 4%." Although Pakistan was an American ally, the Soviet Union agreed to 2.5 percent interest on its $30 million credit to Pakistan.[82] For Pakistan, the amount of Soviet aid was far less than that from the United States, and Pakistan was aware of the political motivations behind such aid. The Soviet Union also provided aid to Afghanistan, and Table 3.4 shows the amount of such aid from 1958 to 1964. Moreover, the United States and Soviet Union had become involved in Nepal and Burma to a limited extent. Table 3.5 shows US and Soviet aid to Nepal, but other than $6.4 million in 1962, the Soviet Union did not provide aid to Burma from 1958 to 1972.[83]

Sino-Soviet Policy Disagreements in South Asia

The transformation from Sino-Soviet cooperation to Sino-Soviet competition between 1958 and 1959 constituted the most significant change of international politics in South Asia. As discussed above, China and the Soviet Union had different concerns regarding the Kashmir issue. Neither India nor Pakistan was an immediate Soviet neighbour. The US-Pakistan alliance, therefore, had limited impact on Soviet security. Soviet support for India, meanwhile, would strengthen bilateral relations and prevent complete Soviet dependency on China. By contrast, both India and Pakistan were immediate neighbours of China, and each had territorial disputes with the PRC. If China supported India's stance on Kashmir, Pakistan would stand behind the United States' containment policy against China.

Therefore, China sought to strike a balance between India and Pakistan. In spite of these differences, the Soviet Union did not challenge China. Indeed, until 1958, Sino-Soviet cooperation was the linchpin of China's South Asia policy.

In the aftermath of the Lhasa revolt in March 1959, the Fourteenth Dalai Lama's exile in India added fuel to Sino-Indian territorial disputes. From the Indian perspective, giving political asylum to the Dalai Lama conformed fully to international law; from the Chinese perspective, however, India's tolerance of the Dalai Lama's anti-China activities on its territories constituted intervention in Chinese domestic affairs. As deterioration of Sino-Indian relations provided the United States with an opportunity to accelerate Indo-Pakistani cooperation, China needed greater Soviet support to deal with the prospect of an Indo-Pakistani joint defence. China therefore collaborated with the Soviet Union to a greater extent with respect to South Asia, referring repeatedly to "class interests" in order to obtain Soviet support. In May 1959, Zhou Enlai conducted two conversations with Soviet diplomats and diplomatic representatives of socialist countries. According to Zhou, the nature of the Tibet issue reflected "class struggle," and Indian interventions in Tibet demonstrated its "class instinct."[84] The Soviet Union, moreover, supported these Chinese stances by publishing Khrushchev's interview with R.K. Karanjia, editor-in-chief of *Blitz,* on May 7. According to Khrushchev, "based upon all available sources on the question of Tibet, it is evident that the incident [in Tibet] was caused by hostile elements, who opposed any new development."[85] On the same day, as Soviet ambassador Pavel F. Yudin told Zhou, the *People's Daily* commentaries on Nehru were "well written in all aspects" by presenting "indisputable historical facts and logics of political lives."[86] Of course, Soviet support for China was conditional on expectations of rapid improvement in Sino-Indian relations. As Yudin told Deputy Premier Chen Yi on May 8, "China and India have convergent interests in promoting peace and preventing international conflict"; however, "imperialist enemies (especially the United States) would exploit the continued tension of Sino-Indian relations out of self-interests, which would be disadvantageous to China and interests of the whole Socialist Camp."[87] The Soviet Union therefore sought to reconcile Sino-Indian differences.

Contrary to its expectations, the Soviet Union soon found itself in a quandary in the summer of 1959, when Sino-Indian relations deteriorated dramatically. At that time, the Soviet Union was providing aid to both China and India; China was a Soviet ally, whereas India was a Soviet non-allied state. In the aftermath of a potential Sino-Indian armed conflict, to honour its commitments to China, the Soviet Union would have to exert pressure on India by cutting off aid, which would mean a complete loss of Soviet political capital in India. In order to preserve its credibility with India, therefore, the Soviet Union needed to exert pressure on China by manipulating its alliance commitments, which, however, would weaken the cooperative basis of the Sino-Soviet relationship. While the Soviet Union was faced with this dilemma, armed conflict between China and India occurred on August 25, 1959. At this critical moment, Khrushchev was in the midst of preparations for his visit to the United States, scheduled for September 15, 1959. To the Soviet Union, cooperation with the United States outweighed the significance of Sino-Soviet collaboration. When it chose to accommodate India, it relinquished the possibility of preserving its former influence in China.

The Sino-Indian border clash became a turning point in Sino-Soviet relations in the context of regional competition in South Asia. The Soviet Union voiced disagreement with Chinese positions on September 8, 1959, expressing the opinion in a letter to the CCP's Central Committee that demarcation of the Sino-Indian border was difficult due to the mountainous areas along said border, and blaming China for the clash, which had resulted in Indian casualties. More importantly, the Sino-Indian conflict complicated the situation prior to Khrushchev's visit to the United States. It was then that the Soviet Union would publicly announce its "regret" regarding the border conflict. After receiving the Soviet letter, China immediately proposed postponing publication of the Soviet statement, but the Soviet Union published it in *Pravda* on September 9, ahead of the scheduled publication date of September 10.[88] The Soviet Union claimed it had "friendly" relations with both China and India,[89] and the Soviet press presented the case for both sides of the Sino-Indian border dispute by publishing, without comment, summaries of the exchange of letters between Zhou and Nehru of September 8–9. Although the summary of Zhou's letter was twice as long as that of Nehru's, both Chinese and Indian positions appeared to have been fully covered.[90] The Soviet announcement was an immediate source of dispute during the Mao-Khrushchev summit in October 1959. On October 2, the two leaders held a critical discussion on Sino-Soviet relations. Mao criticized the Soviet declaration because it "made all imperialists happy," but Khrushchev disagreed. Both sides engaged in an intensive debate. Chen Yi was "outraged" at the Soviet declaration that "the aggravation of [the] relationship with India was our [Chinese] fault." Khrushchev countered: "I am also outraged by your declaration that we are time-servers. We should support Nehru, to help him stay in power."[91] The Sino-Soviet dispute implied that both sides had competing objectives in South Asia.

Sino-Soviet competition reshaped China's South Asia policy. Between 1955 and 1959, China's regional diplomacy had been defined by US-China rivalry. China had used uniform strategies toward weaker neighbours to send consistent messages to the United States. In the aftermath of the October 1959 Mao-Khrushchev summit, however, challenges to China could come from both the United States and the Soviet Union. The worst-case scenario for China would be one where all of its South Asian neighbours received support from both the United States and the Soviet Union in the short run. In return, the small powers might make their territories available to the United States or the Soviet Union for power projection. As Sino-Soviet competition weakened Chinese advantages over its South Asian neighbours, maintaining such advantages became China's prime regional objective. China would therefore adopt selective strategies based on the degree of US-Soviet involvement.

Selective Strategies, 1959–63

Maintaining the Status Quo with Three Neighbours, Securing Borders with Others, 1959–61

There were varying degrees of US-Soviet involvement in different countries of South Asia. India received the largest amount of assistance from both sides. Pakistan received sizable American assistance and, after 1956, additional Soviet assistance. Afghanistan received economic assistance from both sides and was the third-largest recipient of Soviet foreign aid after 1955.[92] By contrast, from 1955 to 1959, Burma and Nepal received much less American assistance and scant Soviet assistance. Moreover, the US-Burma relationship soured in November 1959, when the United States sold rice to India (150,000 tons), Indonesia (75,000 tons), Ceylon (10,000 tons), and Pakistan (10,000 tons). The large share of Burma's traditional market that the US rice disposal programs took caused considerable resentment.[93]

In these circumstances, China put the five neighbours in two categories: 1) India, Pakistan, and Afghanistan, and 2) Nepal and Burma. The first three countries had received extensive external aid and were more likely to develop their own capabilities by exploiting foreign support; they were also more likely to make their territories available for foreign use. China therefore maintained the status quo with these states in order to concentrate available resources on weakening foreign influence elsewhere. Nepal and Burma had received only limited amounts of foreign aid and were less likely to challenge China or offer foreign powers the use of their territories. China therefore accommodated these two countries in order to consolidate its regional advantages. In other words, competition with both the United States and the Soviet Union drove China to change its regional diplomacy from uniform strategies to selective strategies.

The Sino-Soviet summit meeting on October 2, 1959, demonstrated competing Chinese and Soviet objectives in South Asia. The first sign of Chinese policy change toward India occurred two days after the Mao-Khrushchev meeting. Zhou received Indian communists on October 3 and proposed "two approaches" to deal with India – accommodation (*rangbu*) and struggle (*douzheng*):

> India, a nationalist country, has two faces. If it continues to adopt peaceful neutrality and nationalist independent policy ... then some minor accommodation (*gebie rangbu*) is necessary. We have done that at the Bandung Conference. However, if after we have offered concessions they still refuse our friendship, [or if they] turn into reactionaries, then it is incorrect to make concessions. Therefore, we should leave some room for [Indian political] forces that take neutral stances and actively strive for their support. However, on the other hand, [we should] resolutely conduct struggle.[94]

Zhou's suggestion of Chinese policy changes was later confirmed by Mao's concrete proposal on November 3. Mao suggested mutual force reduction along the Sino-Indian border based on a "customary line."[95] The proposal suggested that China would neither acknowledge the "McMahon Line" in the eastern sector nor withdraw troops from the western sector. The essential point of this proposal, therefore, was to maintain the status quo. On November 16, Nehru made a counterproposal suggesting a mutual troop withdrawal from the western sector but not the eastern sector.[96] The Indian proposal was hence to no avail, because Nehru's suggestion implied that a Chinese unilateral troop withdrawal from the western sector would take place in parallel with an Indian consolidation of its territorial control of the east.

From the Chinese perspective, competition with the Soviet Union changed the role of Soviet aid to India from that of an anti-American instrument to a form of restraint on Chinese interests. During a meeting with Mao on November 12, Wang Jiaxiang, head of the CCP Liaison Department, asserted that Soviet public statements since September 1959 had effectively "destroyed the Sino-Soviet relationship and made trouble for the Sino-Indian friendship." Wang received Mao's full support. As Mao stated, China "was showing a brave face on two sides: one to Khrushchev and the other to [US president Dwight] Eisenhower."[97] On November 19, Zhou explained Mao's statement at the State Council of the PRC: "[We must] stand up to imperialism as well as to incorrect ideas and wrong behaviours by Socialist countries ... If they [the Socialist countries] are wrong, we should not follow them."[98] He and his deputies also explained the Chinese bottom line. According to Chen Yi, "we do not want to push Nehru to the West"; however, "the unity with Nehru has a limit. We should not cede our territories."[99] Moreover, Zhou would not accommodate (*rangbu*) Nehru; rather, he would "expose Nehru's mistakes and his reactionary side."[100] From 1959 to 1960, Chinese economic difficulties were in sharp contrast to India's improved conditions due to foreign support. It was thus difficult, if not impossible, for China to accommodate India with the strategic objective of maintaining Chinese advantages in South Asia.

The new feature of competition in South Asia in 1960 was firmer resolve on the part of both China and the Soviet Union. On January 26, Zhou met with Soviet ambassador Stepan Chervonenko, first criticizing Soviet neutrality in the Sino-Indian border dispute. Zhou later told Chervonenko that China would neither accommodate Nehru nor use possible concessions as a means of keeping India from "turning to the right,"[101] which by Chinese definition meant the Americans. Three days later, Chen Yi explained the Sino-Burmese non-aggression pact, concluded on January 28, to Chervonenko: "The non-aggression pact required that neither side would join an alliance directed against the other. This is a blow to SEATO." He did not mention, however, that the non-aggression pact also prevented Burma from seeking an alignment with the Soviet Union against China. Moreover, Chen Yi made clear that China would never make new concessions to India:

> The "McMahon Line" was part of the Sino-Burmese border in the northern sector ... [W]e try to avoid the term in our agreement. Rather, we prefer a customary line ... We would welcome Nehru's reference to the Sino-Burmese agreement as a precedent ... The final border settlement should be based on a customary line. This question has been submitted to Nehru. Therefore, the Sino-Burmese border agreement dealt a damaging blow to India.[102]

Chinese and Soviet assessments of India were thus at odds. During the Warsaw Pact meeting in February 1960, the PRC, an observer at the meeting, publicly criticized certain "reactionary forces" in Asia who were deliberately exploiting border issues by adopting anti-China policies to court imperialism. This reproof undoubtedly constituted Chinese reaction to the Soviet stance on India. China also castigated the Soviet Union, saying that by continuing to support India, it would be emulating "imperialists" that "sow discord and create anti-China schemes in an attempt to isolate China."[103] Khrushchev shrugged off the Chinese warnings, however, and expressed his resolute support for Nehru. In the Soviet-Indian joint communiqué, signed on February 16, he "highly endorsed" Nehru's positions with respect to India's non-alignment policy and non-participation in military alliances. On behalf of the Soviet government, he claimed that Nehru had made a "significant contribution" to world peace and honoured the Soviet commitment by providing 1,500 million rubles to India.[104] The Soviet-Indian joint communiqué thus highlighted Sino-Soviet competition in South Asia.

There were three critical competitive dyadic relationships in South Asia: US-Soviet competition, Sino-American competition, and Sino-Soviet competition, the last being a new element in the regional arena. China and the United States had assessed the Soviet Union differently. The Chinese leadership believed that the Soviet Union would seek compromises with the West at China's expense.[105] The United States and its allies, on the other hand, clearly misconstrued Sino-Soviet competition. NATO's Committee of Political Advisers reported on April 12, 1960, that

> the Chinese continue to acknowledge Soviet leadership of the bloc. The two regimes are bound together by a common dedication to the cause of Communism; by a common hostility to the West; by continuing Chinese dependence on the Soviet Union for military, economic, and technological aid as well as for aid and support against the United States and its Asian partners; and by the importance for the Soviet Union of a large friendly presence in her rear ... The Soviet government has adopted a non-committal position on the Sino-Indian border dispute.[106]

Neither the Chinese nor the US perception was accurate. China underestimated the implications of US-Soviet competition, whereas the United States underestimated the hostility between China and the Soviet Union. These inaccurate perceptions demonstrated the complex nature of regional competition in South Asia.

China's maintenance of the status quo was best demonstrated during the Sino-Indian border negotiations in New Delhi in April 1960. Prior to

Zhou Enlai's visit to New Delhi, he had conveyed messages to Soviet leaders through Andrei Ledovskii, Soviet ambassador to Burma. From Zhou's perspective, Nehru was reluctant to settle the Sino-Indian border issues because he sought to "gain advantages from both sides – seeking money from the US and attempting to obtain aid from the Soviet Union."[107] Zhou also told U Nu, who sought to mediate the Sino-Indian border conflict that it was "impossible for China to make concessions." Zhou compared the Sino-Burmese border settlement with the Sino-Indian border conflict, and criticized India's stances. As he concluded, the troop withdrawal on the Sino-Indian border would be "a matter for the Indians," because the Indian troops were "beyond the so-called 'McMahon Line.'"[108] During the negotiations with India, Zhou requested simultaneous resolution of the disputes over the eastern and western sectors. He suggested that Nehru abandon territorial claims in the western sector in exchange for the unchanged Chinese position in the eastern sector.[109] China sought to maintain the status quo with respect to administrative control: "Both sides will maintain the existing administrative lines before reaching an agreement. In the eastern sector, we will acknowledge the existing line of Indian administrative control. In the western sector, India should acknowledge the line of Chinese administrative control."[110] No concrete agreement was arrived at. After the negotiations, China stopped patrolling the Sino-Indian border.[111] In sum, China demonstrated a defensive posture before and after the Sino-Indian border negotiations.

In this complex situation, Pakistan presented China with both challenges and opportunities. The Indo-Pakistani joint defence plan could become a real threat to China in the long run. However, US and Soviet support for India could place the US-Pakistan alliance in jeopardy and thus lead to Pakistan's isolation. In February 1960, Pakistan proposed border negotiations with China.[112] From the Chinese perspective, Pakistan might quite possibly use such negotiations to obtain more assistance from both the United States and the Soviet Union. China would hence be a means rather than an end for Pakistan. China was therefore reluctant to accept Pakistan's offer, choosing instead to maintain the status quo by claiming that there was no border dispute and expressing hopes of "friendly coexistence."[113] China would neither cooperate with India against Pakistan nor cooperate with Pakistan against India.[114] In other words, China took an even-handed approach to maintaining the status quo with both India and Pakistan.

China took a wait-and-see approach to the Sino-Pakistani border settlement because the disputed border was close to the Indo-Pakistani disputed area of Kashmir. By early 1961, China had not completely lost hope of reaching a border agreement with India. In February 1961, as Zhou pointed out to a Nepalese delegation in Beijing, "General Ne Win paid a visit to China during the last Spring Festival and signed the Sino-Burmese border agreement. The Nepalese delegation has paid a visit to China during this Spring Festival and is negotiating over border issues as well ... We hope to solve border issues with another country next year. Therefore, we can solve one problem every year."[115] In other words, China would settle border issues with either Pakistan or India in 1962. The delay in Sino-Indian negotiations suggested that Pakistan might be a new Chinese partner in border talks. However, China was fully aware of the resolute Indian opposition to Sino-Pakistani border negotiations. When Zhou received the Indian Foreign Ministry's secretary-general, Ratan Kumar Nehru, in July 1961, Nehru claimed that India had received both American and Soviet assistance, possibly to convey a strong negotiating position. He reiterated that Kashmir belonged to India rather than to Pakistan, and therefore neither China nor Pakistan had any right to discuss the territories (Kashmir) of a third country (India). As he stated to Zhou, "if I were you, I would tell them [Pakistan] that I refuse to negotiate, because you [Pakistan] are not a legitimate government over the territory [Kashmir]."[116] Zhou took a non-committal, wait-and-see stance. During Sino-Nepalese border negotiations, King Mahendra of Nepal conveyed a message from Pakistani president Ayub, who wished to promote Sino-Pakistani border negotiations. Zhou, however, would have to "be cautious because the question involves India."[117] As Zhou well understood, Sino-Indian relations would cross the Rubicon once Sino-Pakistani border negotiations began.

In addition, China sought to maintain the status quo with Afghanistan, another receptive audience of foreign influence. As Afghanistan had territorial disputes with both Pakistan and China, the Sino-Indian border clashes elicited particular concern on the part of the Afghans with respect to China. In order to prevent a sharp decline in Sino-Afghan relations, China sought to conclude political agreements with Afghanistan. On July 28, 1960, Chen Yi suggested either a friendship treaty or a non-aggression pact between the two countries.[118] Unlike a friendship treaty, a non-aggression pact would include a specific clause on non-participation in adversarial alliances directed against the other contracting party.[119] Afghanistan opted for the non-aggression pact, which was signed by both sides on August 26. Chen Yi expressed his gratitude to his Afghan counterpart, Prime Minister Mohammed Daoud: "The conclusion to be drawn from the pact is your support of us. We will repay the support with friendship. China is a large country with a huge population. Many people, for example,

Indians, are in fear of our sheer strength. But by concluding a non-aggression pact Afghanistan shows it is not afraid of us. Therefore, we can tell this to those who fear us."[120] Meanwhile, in view of the Afghan-Pakistani conflict over Pashtunistan, China tried to avoid Pakistan's isolation by providing reassurance. Chen Yi explained Chinese maintenance of the status quo as follows: "[We] will not conduct secret diplomacy [toward Afghanistan and Pakistan]. What we have told Afghanistan can be told to Pakistan as well ... You [Pakistan] take a friendly attitude toward us. We hope [you will] also be friendly to others and Afghanistan."[121]

By contrast, China sought a diplomatic breakthrough with Nepal and Burma through accommodation. On December 20, 1959, the PRC's Foreign Trade Ministry proposed a selective foreign aid policy:

> The double-faced nature of the ruling class of nationalist countries should be taken into account with respect to [the PRC's] aid to these countries. [We] should develop a distinctive policy toward them in accordance with their attitudes toward us and our foreign policy. This will be beneficial to their anti-imperialist struggle, their friendship with us, and the development of their national economies.[122]

In addition to the foreign aid policy, Chinese territorial compromises with Nepal and Burma contrasted sharply with China's maintenance of the status quo with India, Pakistan, and Afghanistan. Zhou issued two invitations on December 22, 1959, one to Nepal's prime minister, Bishweshwar Prasad Koirala, to discuss border issues that could be "easily resolved,"[123] the other to the Burmese prime minister, General Ne Win, to "push forward concrete discussions and a settlement of the border issue."[124] Chen Yi explained the reason for these invitations as follows: "Now [we are engaging in] a struggle of isolations and counter-isolations. You [Nehru] do not come to Beijing, but others will come ... Nepal's Premier will come."[125]

Koirala visited Beijing in March 1960. China made two particular concessions. First, on the border issue, China proposed that the northern and southern slopes of Mt. Everest, based on a "customary line," would henceforward belong to the two countries, respectively. Accordingly, China would cede to Nepal three pieces of territory that had been claimed by the Qing Dynasty. China also proposed that each country hold a 50 percent ownership of Mt. Everest.[126] Second, China increased the amount of its assistance to Nepal. In October 1959, Nepal requested Chinese supplementary assistance in the amount of 40 million rupees,[127] and in March

1960 China increased the amount to 100 million rupees.[128] However, China also tried to maintain the existing Sino-Indian relationship. The amount of Chinese assistance to Nepal would therefore continue to be less than the amount of Indian assistance. This was a matter of choice rather than Chinese capabilities. As Zhou explicitly told Koirala, "we do not want to compete with India [in Nepal]." Koirala was persistent in his demand that the amount of Chinese assistance be at least equal to that from India. Zhou neither approved nor rejected the request. Rather, he encouraged Koirala to raise more demands in the future.[129]

Between 1960 and 1961, China continued to accommodate Nepal. On June 28, 1960, a skirmish occurred on the Sino-Nepalese border when PLA soldiers mistook a group of Nepalese men for Tibetan insurgents. China apologized for the incident, offered compensation to Nepal, and promised to halt military operations within ten kilometres of the Chinese side of the border.[130] In February 1961, China exchanged intelligence with Nepal about its military operations against Tibetan insurgents and offered additional financial assistance.[131] In August, Zhou conveyed a message to King Mahendra emphasizing that the remaining dispute over the peak of Mt. Everest could be "amicably resolved."[132] During border negotiations in September, Zhou proposed that both China and Nepal declare ownership of the peak, while "[the Chinese ownership] can be larger or smaller." As China would demand less than 50 percent of the peak, a border agreement was reached. Moreover, China gave Nepal additional economic aid – $9.8 million for a road linking Kathmandu with Tibet.[133] China's domestic economic difficulties were therefore no obstacle to its provision of aid to Nepal.

Burma was also the target of Chinese accommodation in three ways. First, China made new concessions to Burma on border issues. During negotiations in January 1960, China finally accepted the watershed principle in the northern sector.[134] In July, it made additional concessions regarding the PGG area in order to conclude a border treaty with Burma.[135] Second, China neither advocated nor supported violent revolutionary changes in Burma. In October 1960, Mao told U Nu that "some troops escaped from Burma and came to us ... They wanted to launch counter-offensives by using arms provided by us. We have told them that we can accept them, but we cannot provide arms. The Sino-Burmese relationship must be friendly." Mao specifically committed to Sino-Burmese "friendship" by refusing to "deliver arms" to the Kachin people in order to strengthen interstate cordial relations.[136] Finally, China rendered economic assistance to Burma. In December 1960, Zhou visited Burma with an official 433-member delegation.[137] During this visit, China granted Burma credit of nearly $84 million.[138] The aid package was so generous that Burma would not need to begin repaying the Chinese loans until 1971.[139] Consequently, China became Burma's largest donor, accounting for 39.6 percent of the total foreign assistance committed to Burma's "four-year plan."[140] Not even economic difficulties stemming from China's Great Leap Forward (1958–62) prevented these generous Chinese aid packages.

War Preparation with India, Peace-Making with Others, 1962–63

Regional developments in South Asia between 1959 and 1961 drew Pakistan closer to China. As Tables 3.6 and 3.7 show, American and Soviet support for India redefined the Indo-Pakistani balance. Although the Indo-Pakistani conflict over Kashmir was not resolved, US economic support enabled India to spend more of its hard currency on advanced weapons from the United Kingdom. Indeed, the United States encouraged Britain to deliver arms to India. Pakistan, meanwhile, was unable to offset Indian capabilities through Soviet assistance, and its strategic environment deteriorated. Pakistan had security concerns over China but, like China, was of the opinion that India's non-alignment policy was a means of obtaining aid from both the United States and the Soviet Union.[141] It was urgent for Pakistan to seek rapprochement with China, which now became the end, rather than the means, of Pakistan's foreign policy. To justify this position to the United States, Ayub pointed to an "increasing threat to Pakistan's security posed by China." Against US advice, therefore, "the best prospect for avoiding difficulties with China lay, he felt, in reaching agreement with the Chinese on the demarcation of the disputed border between Pakistan and China."[142] The greater the United States' support for India, the greater China's significance to Pakistan would be. Pakistan's isolation thus drove it to tilt toward China. Given the Kashmir dispute, Sino-Pakistani cooperation would embitter Sino-Indian relations, whereas Indian cooperation with the United States and the Soviet Union strengthened Sino-Pakistani cooperation. China accordingly began to bring its power to bear on India.

The first concrete Pakistani attempt to improve relations with China occurred in December 1961, when Pakistan rejected the American line on Chinese representation in the United Nations. In January 1962, Indo-Pakistani tension over Kashmir escalated. Pakistan, an American ally, was prepared to fight not only India but also "America, the Soviet Union, and other major powers in the West."[143] It therefore pressed for border negotiations with China in order to avoid isolation. China mentioned two

Table 3.6 **US economic aid to India and Pakistan, 1959–61 (in millions of dollars)**

Fiscal year	*Country*		*Ratio*
	India	*Pakistan*	*(India/Pakistan)*
1959	366.7	235.0	1.56
1960	758.4	301.3	2.52
1961	594.4	172.0	3.46

Source: Khan, *Rejection Alliance?,* 68.

Table 3.7 **Indian and Pakistani defence expenditures, 1959–61 (in millions of rupees)**

Year	*Country*		*Ratio*
	India	*Pakistan*	*(India/Pakistan)*
1959–60	2,670	960.3	2.78
1960–61	2,809	996.4	2.82
1961–62	3,124	971.5	3.22
1962–63	4,739	904.5	5.24

Source: Mohammed Ahsen Chaudhri, *Pakistan and the Great Powers* (Karachi: Council for Pakistan Studies, 1970), 135.

obstacles: the Indo-Pakistani joint defence plan and the US-Pakistan alliance. Pakistan responded that "neither will be an obstacle."[144] This suggests that American assistance to India was the underlying reason why Pakistan sought rapprochement with China at the expense of cooperation with the United States.[145]

By 1962, China was of the opinion that India had become an anti-China instrument of both the United States and the Soviet Union. During a conversation with East German officials in January, Zeng Yongquan, the PRC's deputy foreign minister, labelled the United States, [Yugoslavia's principal leader] Tito, and Nehru as vanguards of imperialists, revisionists, and reactionaries, respectively. In the Chinese assessment, all these forces collaborated with each other against China.[146] In view of the Soviet–East German alliance relationship, Zeng did not mention "the Soviet Union" but used "Tito" instead. This made the Chinese–East German talk easier for all the participants. However, the assessment underlined China's serious concern over India, which had obtained support from both the United

States and the Soviet Union. In March, during the visit of US under secretary of state Chester Bowles to New Delhi, his Indian counterparts urged "secret conversations" "on [US-India] contingency plans for" a potential Chinese invasion.[147] China might not know the details of the US-India talks, but Bowles's visit strongly demonstrated greater American resolve to enhance India's capabilities. According to Zhou, "it is impossible to solve the Sino-Indian border dispute because India would exploit the dispute to court the West and obtain assistance."[148] Meanwhile, China was under pressure from the Sino-Soviet border conflict and Taiwan's amphibious attacks at the same time. In Zhou's words, "the Soviet leadership creates problems for us at the rear. American imperialism is still the enemy and source of external problems [*diguo waihuan*] ... Americans and Chiang [Kai-shek] are exploiting our difficulties to carry out provocations, and the Soviet leadership clique takes similar measures to create difficulties for us."[149] As the Sino-Soviet border conflict in Xinjiang occurred near the western sector of the Sino-Indian disputed areas, Chinese pressure on India was a part of the struggle against both the United States and the Soviet Union. Wang Enmao, the first secretary of the CCP Xinjiang Committee, stated on June 21, 1962, that

> we need to engage in a struggle against the Indian reactionaries in the west. [Moreover, we] will have a struggle against revisionists along the Sino-Soviet and the Sino-Mongolian border ... We [in Xinjiang] will not directly join the struggle against Chiang Kai-shek's bandits in the Southeast, however, our struggle along the Sino-Indian border against Indian reactionaries ... will collaborate with the struggle against American imperialism and Chiang Kai-shek ... Foreign forces have supported the exodus from Tacheng and Yili. When did the anti-revolutionary incidents occur? [They] occurred when American imperialism was supporting Chiang Kai-shek's bandits to launch offensives in the Southeast and the Indian reactionaries were carrying out provocations along the Sino-Indian border. This is not by accident.[150]

The PRC's ambassador to India, Pan Zili, provided a similar line of reasoning. He explained his perspectives to his Soviet "comrades" before leaving for Beijing on July 14, 1962. In his view, "the [Chinese] Nationalists have been in concerted actions with India in order to pose threats to China from different directions."[151] Pan suggested three points. First, India had become a source of threat not because of its own capabilities but because of its cooperation with the United States and the Soviet Union. Second, Taiwan and India had received extensive US aid; therefore, their "concerted actions" reflected the US containment policy against China. Third, Pan expressed Chinese dissatisfaction – even anger – with respect to Soviet support of India. On this topic, Zhou developed a similar argument during his talk with North Korean principal leader Kim Il-Sung: "Tension in the Taiwan Strait this year and the news of Sino-Soviet problems have encouraged India to take joint actions with the Americans and Chiang Kai-shek to carry out border provocations."[152] In the summer of 1962, China explicitly regarded India as a US or Soviet instrument for anti-China purposes.

Accordingly, China's India policy became more assertive. On April 12, 1962, China condemned Indian provocations against the status quo on the Sino-Indian border. China took the first coercive measure against India on April 30 by resuming patrols.[153] On May 11, it also declared that it would resort to "self-defence" against "aggressive Indian military forces on Chinese territories."[154] On May 22, Zhou urged "full preparation" against "Indian armed provocation" by the end of June.[155] In early June, the PLA established a border headquarters in charge of military operations.[156] In September, Zhou formally told the Tenth Plenary Session of the CCP Central Committee that Mao had decided to "cut off the Indian troops' line of retreat."[157] He made clear that "if they [Indians] are actively carrying out provocations, we should completely remove [their outposts]."[158]

China combined a peace-making strategy with a war-making strategy in October 1962. The targets of Chinese accommodation included Pakistan and Nepal. After almost two years of "consideration," China claimed on May 3 that it would soon start Sino-Pakistani border negotiations.[159] According to US estimates, the Sino-Pakistani agreement to start their border negotiations demonstrated that "after the earlier settlements with Burma and Nepal, [China] is reasonable and leaving India the only neighbor in the subcontinent area which is not willing to settle its boundary with [China]."[160] In February 1962, Nepal requested Chinese military assistance;[161] however, it was not until October 6 that China offered Nepal political support, with Chen Yi stating that "the Chinese government and people will stand together with all just countries and people on the side of Nepal forever, if a foreign power invades Nepal."[162] The statement was clearly directed against India, because Nepal bordered only China and India. The Sino-Pakistani border negotiations, which formally began on October 12, 1962, served as a Chinese concession to Pakistan and a coercive measure against India.[163] The negotiations thus paved the way for the Chinese use of force along the Sino-Indian border. The PLA General Political Department issued the following instruction on October 20:

> The Indian provocations have an international background. India became the anti-China vanguard for Americans when the US offered a high price to buy it off ... India always makes loud noises about "Chinese aggression" when the US Congress considers foreign assistance programs. The anti-China policy adopted by India has also been practically supported by the modern-revisionists behind the scene. [Therefore,] we can conclude that the anti-China policy adopted by India is a part of the international anti-China movement supported by both imperialism and modern revisionism.[164]

China launched military offensives on October 20 to teach India a lesson – that any effort to challenge the Chinese established power advantages in South Asia would fail. The Chinese removed Indian outposts beyond the "McMahon Line" within two days. Between November 1959 and September 1962, Indian troops had advanced significantly northward. India therefore demanded a return to the conditions of September 8, 1962, which would imply China's acquiescence to Indian control over the disputed territories in previous years.[165] Zhou described such a demand as "capitulation to India." He proposed negotiations and maintenance of the status quo of November 1959 – before the start of the Indian "forward movement."[166] When the Chinese proposal was rejected, the PLA began the second phase of its military operations.[167] By November 21, it had driven Indian troops in the eastern sector below the "McMahon Line" and moved to the customary line that the PRC had claimed. In the western sector, the PLA removed all Indian outposts in disputed areas. It captured 3,213 Indian military personnel between October 20 and November 21.[168]

During the Sino-Indian confrontation, China reached additional agreements with Nepal and Pakistan. On October 21, 1962, it proposed an additional £700,000 to construct the Nepal-Tibet road.[169] It also presented the following proposals during the border negotiations with Pakistan: 1) the boundary line, with some exceptions, would generally follow the Karakoram watershed; 2) China and Pakistan had some disputes over Khunjerab and other passes, but China would share the passes with Pakistan; and 3) China would take 50 percent of K2 (the Chogori Peak).[170] In addition, China would avoid any mention of Kashmir as an Indian territory in future official or propaganda publications.[171] Zhou then explained Chinese selective strategies to Mongolian leader J. Zedenbal as follows:

> Many ask why there is no settlement of the Indian-Chinese border conflict, because the border question between China and Pakistan is actively discussed[?] We think that Pakistan negotiates with us without submitting

> itself to America and England, although it belongs to an aggressive bloc. India, however, speaks the language of America, although it maintains that it does not belong to any aggressive blocs ... India did indeed declare non-alignment to aggressive blocs, but [it] became ever more dependent on American dollars. India received 640 million dollars from America for military purposes. Nehru's government is turning away from the policy of peace. We must understand imperialism's threat and danger.[172]

Zhou also criticized the alleged "regret" expressed by socialist countries: "I do not understand the word 'regrettable,' that you used regarding the Chinese-Indian border conflict. If this refers to India, it is correct. If you said it in reference to China, in order to make us out to be the guilty [party], then that is false. On this question there are differences of opinion among the fraternal parties."[173] In conventional diplomatic language, "regrettable," a neutral word, implied Soviet refusal to support its socialist ally in the Sino-Indian dispute.

The Sino-Indian border conflict significantly enhanced Chinese cooperation with Pakistan against India. China signed its first official trade agreement with Pakistan in January 1963. It not only "expressed resolute support for Pakistan's struggle to maintain territorial integrity" but also "deeply exchanged ideas with Pakistan about a Chinese interest-free grant."[174] In addition, China concluded a "provisional protocol" with Pakistan on March 2, 1963, ceding 40 percent of the disputed areas.[175] Pakistan's foreign minister, Zulfikar Ali Bhutto, visited China, and Mao observed that "we were of assistance to Pakistan when we waged the war against India." Bhutto replied that "Pakistan is a Chinese ally if viewed objectively."[176] Bhutto's assessment was correct. In February 1964, during Zhou's visit to Pakistan, China promised assistance should Pakistan come under attack.[177] In February 1965, it offered a $60 million loan, and it added $7 million in loans after the outbreak of the Indo-Pakistani War of 1965.[178] More importantly, China deterred India's invasion of Pakistan during the war by presenting India with an ultimatum.[179]

Pakistan's territorial disputes with Afghanistan were not resolved. The development of Sino-Pakistani relations had the potential to arouse Afghan suspicions and enhance its cooperation with India or the Soviet Union. However, Sino-Indian border tensions diverted US and Soviet attention from Afghanistan, which in 1960 requested American assistance in the amount of $350 million. The United States did not respond until June 1962 and rejected the request. In April 1961, the Soviet Union refused to offer more assistance to Afghanistan, which "only real friends and fraternal countries could obtain."[180] Consequently, Afghanistan accepted the development of Sino-Pakistani relations and in fact promoted better relations with China. In April 1960, it had been reluctant to enter into border negotiations with China,[181] but in January 1963 it actually requested such negotiations. In response, China proposed to provide aid to Afghanistan,[182] and it also ceded almost all of the disputed areas to Afghanistan based on a customary line.[183]

China's South Asia policy between 1955 and 1963 offers a second case (after its East Asia policy) through which to examine the validity of the regional competition theory. Between 1955 and 1959, the United States was China's only regional competitor in South Asia. Chinese uniform strategies reduced the likelihood of cooperation between its weaker neighbours and the United States. Divergence in Sino-Soviet objectives in 1959 made the Soviet Union a new Chinese competitor. Between 1959 and 1963, China adopted selective strategies in South Asia in an attempt to consolidate its power advantages over weaker neighbours. A crucial consequence of such selective strategies was Pakistan's non-commitment of its security to the United States. Instead, Pakistan sought to strike a balance by promoting its relations with China. It became the key broker of the US-China rapprochement in the 1970s and the linchpin of Chinese South Asia policy in subsequent decades.

4
Indochina, 1962–75

Between 1962 and 1975, the People's Republic of China (PRC) had two Indochinese allies – North Vietnam (officially, the Democratic Republic of Vietnam or DRV) and Cambodia. Between 1962 and 1965, China and the Soviet Union coordinated their Indochina policies, which left the United States as China's sole regional competitor. Hence, China adopted selective strategies toward its weaker allies by establishing the DRV as an example for Cambodia's conduct of anti-American armed struggle. Between 1964 and 1965, the Soviet Union and China demonstrated their different strategic preferences with respect to resolving conflict in Indochina. The Soviet Union proposed a political settlement through an international conference; China recommended armed struggle. On the one hand, the Soviet Union exploited its aid to the DRV and Cambodia to circumscribe China's Indochina policy. On the other, both the Soviet Union and the United States supported political settlements in Indochina. When the Soviet Union became China's new regional competitor in 1965, Chinese selective strategies toward the DRV and Cambodia were likely to create strong incentives for Cambodia – the less committed ally – to tilt toward the Soviet Union. Consequently, between 1965 and 1973, China adopted uniform strategies toward the DRV and Cambodia, and strengthened its alignment with these weaker allies through commitments to guarantee their borders, which China honoured by also pledging continued support for the two countries despite its rapprochement with the United States. The US withdrawal from Indochina in 1973 implied that the Soviet Union would be China's sole competitor in the region. Between 1973 and

1975, therefore, China adopted selective strategies toward the DRV and Cambodia – by imposing restraints on armed struggle in Vietnam but encouraging it in Cambodia – with the object of counterbalancing Soviet influence.

Selective Strategies, 1962–65

American and Soviet Involvement in Indochina

Indochina became an arena for Sino-American competition after the outbreak of the Korean War. No alliance treaty regulated Sino-Vietnamese relations, but common security interests and ideological affiliations shored up their alignments. China and the DRV hence coordinated their foreign policies in peacetime and made joint military plans in times of war. During the 1954 Geneva Conference, at China's suggestion, the DRV withdrew its military forces from South Vietnam and Cambodia in order to promote the reunification election scheduled to take place in Vietnam in June 1956, when it seemed likely that the DRV's president, Ho Chi Minh, would become the principal leader. However, ardent backing from the United States encouraged Ngo Dinh Diem to appoint himself president of the Republic of Vietnam (South Vietnam), below the seventeenth parallel. It was in this capacity as ruler of South Vietnam that Diem boycotted the national election to reunify the country, as laid down in the Geneva accords. Accordingly, the DRV began to consider the unification of Vietnam through armed struggle, which resulted in closer South Vietnamese cooperation with the United States. The United States provided aid and advisers to South Vietnam, conducted land operations there, and bombed the DRV on South Vietnam's behalf. These US interventions, in turn, drew the DRV and China closer. China deployed armed forces in North Vietnam and provided it with extensive aid. Between 1950 and 1974, Chinese aid to the DRV, in the amount of RMB4.26 billion, was sufficient to equip 2 million men. Chinese military aid packages included more than 2 million rifles, 70,000 artillery pieces, 1.2 billion rounds of ammunition for rifles, 18 million artillery shells, 176 battleships, 552 tanks, 320 Panzers, 170 aircraft, 16,000 vehicles, and 18,420 tons of explosives. The division of Vietnam enhanced China-DRV security interdependence.[1]

The civil war in Laos between 1959 and 1962, meanwhile, bolstered Cambodia's security ties with China. The onset of the war sparked American concern about the DRV's infiltration of South Vietnam through Laos, and the United States provided aid and sent 517 advisers to the Laotian

Table 4.1 US armed forces deployed in South Vietnam, 1960–64 (in thousands of personnel)

Year	*Personnel (thousands)*
1960	0.885
1961	3.205
1962	11.3
1963	16.3
1964	23.3

Source: SIPRI Yearbook of World Armaments and Disarmament, 1972 (Stockholm: Almquist and Wiksell, 1972), 269.

Right Wing.[2] Moreover, as Table 4.1 shows, the US military presence in South Vietnam and Thailand increased significantly between 1960 and 1964. In May 1962, the United States established a new headquarters in Thailand.[3] From the Chinese perspective, the United States would present challenges to Chinese security by establishing forward bases in Indochina. Cambodia had territorial disputes with both South Vietnam and Thailand. From its perspective, Cambodia was the weakest of the three, and, fearing that US intervention would encourage South Vietnamese and Thai regional aspirations directed against it, it tilted toward China under the guise of neutrality. On April 10, 1962, Prince Norodom Sihanouk received the PRC's ambassador to Cambodia, Chen Shuliang. On being presented with Chen's credentials, Sihanouk stated that "I grasp this opportunity of receiving your credentials to solemnly make two specific commitments to China. First, Cambodia will side with China forever and promote and protect the PRC's just cause. Second, Cambodia will be committed to its friendship with the PRC forever and continue to take the existing course of action, regardless of foreign pressures." He continued: "Cambodia should be grateful for Chinese support which brought about peace and tranquility in Cambodia." Chen responded: "China will support Cambodian independence, neutrality, and territorial integrity, in all circumstances."[4]

China adopted three concrete measures in support of Cambodia. First, it urged the DRV to provide Cambodia with an alignment option. During his visit to the DRV in May 1963, Liu Shaoqi, the PRC's president, stated that "socialist countries and the proletariat must unite with oppressed people and nations and form the tightest alignments with them. [We should] make persistent efforts to unite all possible forces to establish and develop the most widely united front against imperialists under American leadership."[5]

The DRV-Cambodia cooperation would thus be in their mutual interests. The DRV sponsored the Viet Cong, which was established on December 20, 1960, and launched armed struggle with the object of regime change in South Vietnam. Exploitation of Cambodian territory would enable the DRV to deliver cadres, troops, armaments, and other logistical support to the Viet Cong. Meanwhile, with the ardent support of Vietnamese communists, Cambodia would improve its position in territorial disputes with South Vietnam and Thailand, and Vietnamese communists began to appear in Cambodia.[6] Second, neither the PRC nor the DRV supported the Left Wing (Cambodian communists) in its proposed armed struggle against Sihanouk's government. Rather, both the PRC and the DRV promoted an anti-America united front with Sihanouk's government by urging the Cambodian communists to cooperate with Phnom Penh.[7] Third, the PRC provided aid to Cambodia. According to US intelligence estimates, by 1964 China had offered military aid sufficient to equip 22,000 men with light and heavy automatic and semi-automatic weapons.[8] By the end of that year, it had agreed to supply Cambodia with enough arms to equip 27,000 men, thereby supplanting the United States as quartermaster for the Cambodian armed forces.[9]

Before 1964, both China and the Soviet Union opposed armed struggle as a means of achieving revolutionary victory in Laos. Rather, they supported a political settlement of the civil war there through the formation of a coalition government. In April 1956, China expressed great satisfaction with the Sino-Soviet common objectives in Indochina,[10] and in October 1959, Mao Zedong and Nikita Khrushchev explicitly acknowledged convergent Sino-Soviet national interests in Indochina. Khrushchev said, "we should advise Vietnamese comrades not to expand military actions in Laos," a sentiment with which Mao was "in complete agreement."[11] After the outbreak of the civil war in Laos, both China and the Soviet Union expressed support for the participation of the Left Wing (the Pathet Lao) in a national coalition government. In May 1961, the Soviet Union, China, and the DRV joined the International Conference on the Settlement of the Laotian Question, during which Zhou Enlai gave his support to the policy coordination of the Soviet Union, China, the DRV, and the Pathet Lao,[12] and the Soviet Union gave its support to the PRC's stance on Laotian non-participation in the Southeast Asia Treaty Organization (SEATO).[13] In March 1962, the Soviet Union, China, the DRV, and the Pathet Lao coordinated their policies during internal meetings. The Soviet Union stressed the importance of the national coalition government and its view that the Pathet Lao should share administrative power with the Right Wing under Prince Boun Oum na Champassak.[14] That summer the Soviet Union, China, and the United States concluded the 1962 Geneva Accord, according to which US armed forces would pull out of Laos. The agreement maintained stability on China's southern borders and reduced Soviet incentives to provide aid to the DRV. By August 1964, only thirty Soviet economic advisers, working on economic construction, remained in the DRV; the Soviet Union had withdrawn all of its military advisers from the DRV's armed forces.[15] Thus, between 1962 and 1965, the United States was China's sole regional competitor.

A Partial Alignment Commitment to Pre-Empt Adversaries

The 1962 Geneva Accord did not solve Laos's problems. During the civil war, the United States had 666 military personnel in Laos, while the DRV had 10,000. The United States withdrew all its troops, but the DRV withdrew only forty "technicians," leaving behind a large number of troops in Pathet Lao–controlled areas.[16] The Geneva Accord paved the way for a Laotian coalition government of the Left, Central, and Right Wings, but it was operative for only eight months, as the Left and Central Wings were in conflict, and the Central Wing was split. By June 1963, realignment in Laos had resulted in the division of the small nation into two distinctive camps: the Right Wing with the majority of the Central Wing versus the Left Wing with the minority of the Central Wing. The former took the upper hand, threatening the DRV's line of communication with South Vietnam; accordingly, the DRV strengthened the Pathet Lao armed forces. The United States had genuine concerns about the situation in South Vietnam and resumed the bombing of areas controlled by the Pathet Lao. Laos's armed conflict thus became once again a source of international conflict between the DRV and the United States. The escalation of the Indochina conflict made redeployment of US armed forces in Laos likely, and in order to protect South Vietnam, the United States might also invade North Vietnam by advancing across the seventeenth parallel. China therefore needed to protect the DRV's security by adopting a more assertive policy toward the United States.

As Chinese allies, the DRV and Cambodia adopted anti-America policies but conducted different forms of struggle. DRV policies directed against the United States were manifested in support for guerrilla forces in South Vietnam. Cambodian policies, by contrast, were directed against American allies. The escalation in the conflict between the United States and the DRV hence implied a potential escalation in Sino-American confrontation, whereby the United States would resolve South Vietnamese–Cambodian and Thai–Cambodian territorial disputes in an attempt to contain China and the DRV. US efforts thus provided an opportunity to settle regional border issues. Cambodia would act as a free rider by exploiting the China-DRV-Cambodia alignment to solve problems unrelated to the other members, and it was therefore reluctant to launch an armed struggle against the United States. Accordingly, China made substantial efforts to enhance the DRV's position vis-à-vis the United States but lesser efforts with respect to Cambodia. China used military forces to guarantee the DRV's border but did not similarly accommodate Cambodia, and it provided large-scale aid to the DRV but only limited aid to Cambodia. China thus adopted selective strategies by using the DRV as an example through which to encourage armed struggle in Cambodia.

With respect to the DRV, China guaranteed the seventeenth parallel between North Vietnam and South Vietnam and provided extensive aid. In May 1963, Liu Shaoqi told Ho Chi Minh that "we will stand together with you. We will be your rearguard if a war comes."[17] Mao also stressed Chinese willingness to provide aid in the form of free assistance. Loans could be easily turned into grants. "Borrowing [money] from China does not matter. You [North Vietnamese] can return it at a time convenient to you. [You can] also not pay it back."[18] This Chinese support significantly pushed armed struggle forward in South Vietnam. In October 1963, DRV prime minister Pham Van Dong declared, for the first time in the country's history, that "the Chinese people have been the most powerful supporters of the patriotic struggle in South Vietnam."[19] The general secretary of the Chinese Communist Party (CCP), Deng Xiaoping, visited Hanoi in February 1964 and vowed that "what China offered in the past were only projects to satisfy your need to begin construction. In the future China will offer assistance in a more comprehensive way."[20] In addition, China contributed directly to the Viet Cong arsenal. Between 1962 and 1964, it provided the Viet Cong with 90,000 rifles, 446 artillery pieces, 21 million rounds of ammunition for rifles, and 76,400 artillery shells.[21] By the spring of 1964, 40 percent of South Vietnam was under either Viet Cong control or predominant influence.[22]

The new situation in South Vietnam provided incentives for the United States to invade North Vietnam. In the summer of 1964, China reiterated its guarantee with respect to the North Vietnamese border. Zhou stated on July 10th that "if the Americans wish to expand the war and invade the DRV, or [if] the Americans expand the war to us, we will not stand idly by. In other words, we will make due preparations if they [Americans] want to have a war like the Korean War."[23] Mao reassured the North Vietnamese: "The DRV and Viet Cong should make preparations. If they [the Americans] conduct landings or bombings, we will fight. If the Americans invade the North, then this is not a matter for you to deal with. It [the United States] must be aware that the Chinese also have legs. If the Americans can send troops, why should not the Chinese? We will take only one step forward toward your [country]."[24] In August, the United States began bombing over North Vietnam following the Gulf of Tonkin incident, when the US Navy claimed it had come under attack by the North Vietnamese. Zhou Enlai commented that "this reckless behaviour by [the United States] in carrying out incessant provocations against a sovereign state [the DRV] is totally unacceptable. We must respond appropriately."[25] According to the PRC statement, "aggression on the DRV amounts to aggression on the PRC. The Chinese people will never stand idly by."[26] China deployed additional armed forces along the Sino-Vietnamese border. US aerial photographs of August 7 showed that the Chinese had deployed thirty-six jet fighter aircraft (MiG-15s and MiG-17s) to Phuc Yen Air Base near Hanoi. At least ten anti-aircraft artillery (AAA) positions, including seventy-five light and medium guns, were established at this airfield.[27]

By contrast, China offered Cambodia only limited support when the latter proposed convening an international conference aimed at achieving a settlement that would guarantee Cambodian territorial integrity. Although China responded favourably on August 27, 1962, the two countries had different considerations with respect to the proposed conference.[28] For Cambodia, it was a critical step toward upgrading China's alignment commitments, but China was unwilling to use military forces to guarantee Cambodia's borders. On November 5, Prince Sihanouk publicly announced that Cambodia would renounce American military aid and warned that further border incidents would lead to an irrevocable break in relations between Cambodia and South Vietnam. Sihanouk implied that American support for South Vietnam during Vietnamese-Cambodian territorial disputes was the main underlying reason for this statement. The Chinese ambassador in Phnom Penh assured Sihanouk that "Cambodia would under no circumstances be abandoned."[29] On November 8, the French ambassador in Phnom Penh visited Sihanouk and held a conversation with Charles Mayer, Sihanouk's press adviser. Sihanouk expressed his readiness to cut off relations with South Vietnam and "request[ed] Chinese Communists to send troops to Cambodia."[30] Cambodia had high hopes of Chinese military intervention, but the Chinese placed limits on its commitment. During his visit to Phnom Penh in February 1963, Liu Shaoqi stated that China would simply sign two documents in support of Cambodian independence.[31] China made no specific response with respect to Cambodian requests to send troops and made clear that it would give only limited economic support to Cambodia. Deng Xiaoping pointed out to Cambodian deputy premier Lon Nol that "China has fallen behind as regards technology ... [You] can see our clothing is of low quality. We have to make great efforts to solve the problems of food, clothing, and daily necessities. We will need about fifty years to overcome economic and technological backwardness."[32] In May 1964, in line with Mao's instructions, the PRC included the DRV's needs in its economic plans, but Mao did not mention Cambodia.[33]

In the aftermath of the Gulf of Tonkin incident, Cambodia took a hard-line policy by refusing United Nations guarantees of its borders. Rather, it would "depend upon itself and the assistance of other friendly countries to guarantee its border security."[34] The Cambodian chargé d'affaires in Laos explained this line of reasoning to his Chinese counterpart: "The US is in fear of China. To small Indochinese nations, China would not only be a force of justice, but also an actual protective force." The Chinese chargé d'affaires did not respond, however.[35] This silence was in sharp contrast to China's repeated public commitments to protect the DRV. The United States correctly understood the limits of Sino-Cambodian alignment, with officials reporting that "we see no evidence" that China had "shown willingness [to] provide economic and military aid and guarantees to the degree hoped for by Sihanouk."[36]

Sihanouk's visit to Beijing in the autumn of 1964 provided additional evidence of this: he failed to achieve a mutual defence treaty with China or obtain any specific Chinese commitment on the Cambodian border.[37] Instead, Mao told him, "only by struggling will you be able to survive. In order to struggle, you need to rely on the vast masses." Mao suggested that Sihanouk follow the line of the *Communist Manifesto,* and he was obviously dissatisfied when Sihanouk replied that he knew the book. "You may know it," Mao retorted, "but you must demonstrate determination to stand on the side of the majority"[38] – thus implying that Sihanouk should follow Ho Chi Minh's example of being "on the side of the majority." If the DRV and Cambodia conducted armed struggle, Indochina would bog down the Americans. Because Sihanouk was reluctant to do so, China provided much less support to Cambodia than to the DRV. Sihanouk said that Cambodia would be grateful if China could state that "any aggression toward Cambodia is aggression toward the PRC," observing that China had already made such a statement with respect to the DRV. China declined this request, however, with Zhou Enlai claiming that Cambodia should withhold an image of "neutrality."[39] Despite the substantial security relationship between China and Cambodia, China still wanted Cambodia to claim itself as a neutral state, which demonstrates Beijing's limited commitment to Phnom Penh.

Sihanouk's activities in Beijing did not improve the situation. In the following week, the leaders of the DRV, Viet Cong, and Pathet Lao also went to Beijing. During their discussions, the DRV and the Viet Cong proposed armed struggle, but Sihanouk sought official statements on maintaining Vietnamese-Cambodian borders. In contrast, China's primary focus was on waging armed struggle against the United States, and it therefore established the DRV as an example for Cambodia. Zhou's strenuous efforts to convince all sides in Beijing to issue a joint declaration against America met with diplomatic snubs from Sihanouk. On October 4, 1964, Zhou addressed Sihanouk:

> Despite no joint declaration, [you have expressed] willingness to move closer toward each other and prepare for a joint declaration. That the declaration would have to be postponed is only a matter of form. [We] have received this with great satisfaction. I would like to sponsor a banquet for all sides for further discussions. The banquet will be held internally, not for publication, in order to avoid suspicions. You could freely discuss [matters] without restraint.[40]

The "satisfaction" Zhou expressed was solely a matter of courtesy. Indeed, he was unsuccessful in promoting armed struggle in Cambodia to the same extent as in Vietnam. Cambodian reservations with respect to Chinese advice appeared to be the primary reason for the absence of a joint anti-American declaration in Beijing, and this affected the Sino-Cambodian alignment. On Sihanouk's return to Phnom Penh, Cambodia publicly acknowledged receiving Chinese military aid.[41] Despite Sihanouk's exaggeration of the extent of Chinese commitments, however, on October 8 Zhou refused specifically to commit China to fully supporting Cambodia.[42] Cambodian reservations with respect to anti-American armed struggle had become an obstacle to such commitment.

Still, China's selective strategies toward the DRV and Cambodia did contribute to Cambodia's more assertive policies vis-à-vis the United States. On October 28, 1964, Sihanouk warned that if another serious border incident occurred, he would break diplomatic relations with the

United States. He also announced a policy of automatic retaliation against South Vietnamese incursions.[43] Sihanouk's Independence Day speech on November 9 was devoted largely to attacking the United States and the West. In particular, he proposed convening an Indochinese People's Conference to draw together all parties or "patriotic" movements of the DRV, South Vietnam, and Laos, with his own Sangkun Reastr Niyum (People's Socialist Community).[44] He also announced on November 14 that the US embassy in Phnom Penh, a hotbed of espionage and subversion, should be closed. On November 17, he attempted to resolve US-Cambodia differences by agreeing to high-level talks with the United States in New Delhi.[45] The talks, however, were nothing more than reiterations of irreconcilable positions. Cambodia required major US concessions on various key issues: "Stop all violations (voluntary or involuntary) of Cambodian soil by American or Vietnamese troops, intervene to stop Khmer Serei broadcasts, stop accusations (including press) that Cambodia is not neutral or that Cambodia permits the VC [Viet Cong] to use its soil, and give Cambodia 'unconditionally' 100 bulldozers, trackers or fuel trucks."

The United States rejected this "obviously unacceptable proposal."[46] It suggested that talks might be resumed at a later date, but Cambodia declared the talks terminated and useless due to the United States' "flagrant bad faith."[47] Thus, Cambodia apparently tilted toward China by adopting an anti-American policy.

Uniform Strategies, 1965–73

Sino-Soviet Differences in Indochina, 1964–65

Before 1964, China was the DRV's "only effective ally." China provided support, both politically and materially, for the DRV's attempt to take over South Vietnam, whereas the Soviet Union offered little material or political support for the war.[48] Meanwhile, both the Soviet Union and China sought to weaken US influence. The Soviet Union, therefore, had neither the capabilities nor the intent to compete with China. Between 1964 and 1965, however, differences between China and the Soviet Union began to appear, and their relationship changed from cooperation to competition. In the aftermath of the Gulf of Tonkin incident, the United States carried out retaliatory air strikes against the DRV. China adopted various propagandistic and military policies in support of the DRV, but Soviet critiques of the United States were limited and marked by a reserve that drew Chinese criticism.[49] In response, the Soviet Union delivered a foreign policy *démarche* to the DRV in a drive to counter China, raising "the possibility that the Tonkin Gulf Incident was attributable to Chinese leaders' divisionary efforts through anti-imperialist forces and their narrow nationalist guideline ... The Soviet Union cannot forgive their acts. Chinese leaders are making every effort to divide world progressive forces by exploiting this event."[50] The Soviet Union was unable to obtain the concurrence of the DRV regarding this assessment, and Moscow realized that, given the competing Sino-Soviet objectives, it lacked the means to influence Hanoi. The Soviet Union therefore began to set new policy courses. On December 3, Leonid Brezhnev offered new Soviet commitments with respect to US air attacks over the DRV: "The Soviet Union cannot stand idly by with respect to the fate of a fraternal socialist country, and is prepared to provide necessary aid."[51]

Premier Alexei Kosygin's visit to Hanoi in February 1965 demonstrated the Soviet Union's willingness to engage in regional competition in Indochina. The Soviet Union offered modern armaments, such as surface-to-air (SAM) missiles and radar, which China could not produce. Table 4.2 shows that Moscow became an increasingly important source for Hanoi to conduct military operations. China also raised the ante. Between 1964 and 1965, Chinese aid increased sharply – by 100 percent of rifles, 33.3 percent of artillery pieces, 160 percent of ammunition for rifles, 350 percent of artillery shells, and 250 percent of electrical equipment to the DRV and

TABLE 4.2 US estimates of Chinese and Soviet weapons to Vietnam, 1963–66

Year	*Recipients*	*Chinese (%)*	*Soviet (%)*
1963	Viet Cong	7	1
	North Vietnamese Army	–	–
1964	Viet Cong	15	2
	North Vietnamese Army	–	–
1965	Viet Cong	21	3
	North Vietnamese Army	90	8
1966	Viet Cong	29	4
	North Vietnamese Army	80	18

Source: Report, US Department of State, November 28, 1967, Gerald R. Ford Presidential Library (GRFL), NSC (National Security Council) Vietnam Information Group Intelligence and Other Reports, 1967–1975, box 8.

Table 4.3 US estimates of Soviet and Chinese military equipment (combat materials) to North Vietnam, 1967–73 (in millions of dollars)

Year	*Soviet Union*	*China*
1967	505	145
1968	290	100
1969	120	205
1970	70	85
1971	145	90
1972	360	200
1973	140	85

Source: Data between 1967 and 1970 are from "Net Assessment of North Vietnamese and South Vietnamese Military Forces," April 10, 1972, Richard M. Nixon Presidential Library (RMNL), NSC Files Vietnam Subject Files, box 115. Data between 1971 and 1973 are from Table 2, "Communist Military and Economic Aid to North Vietnam, 1970–1974," January 3, 1975, Central Intelligence Agency, http://www.foia.cia.gov/document/0001166499.

by 1,000 percent of armaments to the Viet Cong.[52] As Table 4.3 demonstrates, however, the Soviet Union became an alternative source of critical external support for the DRV. Soviet aid had two important implications for China. Although it appeared to be on the Chinese side and against the United States, it would also give the Soviet Union a greater voice with respect to the course of the DRV's foreign policy. Given competing Sino-Soviet objectives, therefore, Soviet aid to the DRV would circumscribe China's foreign policy choices.

At that time, China and the Soviet Union had different views on how to resolve Indochina's problems. The Soviets called for a political settlement through an international conference on the question of Vietnam, whereas China placed heavy emphasis on armed struggles. As both a permanent member of the UN Security Council and a co-chair of the Geneva Conference, the Soviet Union had the capacity to exploit various channels between East and West. China, by contrast, was excluded from the United Nations, and it had neither a special position in the Geneva Conference mechanism nor a diplomatic relationship with the United States. Once negotiations began, therefore, the Soviet Union would be better able than China to affect the course of events in Indochina. Such Sino-Soviet competition engendered strong Chinese opposition to political settlements through negotiations.

As Mao told Soviet premier Alexei Kosygin, "currently guerrilla warfare is the main issue in Vietnam, and political struggle plays a secondary role."[53] After the Mao-Kosygin talks, however, the Soviet Union was still insistent on conducting negotiations.[54] Consequently, Deputy Premier Li Xiannian regarded the Soviet proposal as a "conspiracy":

> It seems US imperialism desperately wants negotiations ... It wants to be out of the current predicament in a more or less graceful way ... Why did Moscow claim to support negotiations at the same time? They are of the same mind to such an extent. We must be alert with respect to this conspiracy ... [The Soviet Union] also utters a few anti-imperialist words, and [it] gives [the DRV] some, but not much, aid, in order to attain the right to speak.[55]

The Soviet Union provided aid not only to the DRV but also to Cambodia. Four aid packages underscored the Soviet commitment to Cambodia. The first, provided in August 1963, included four MiG aircraft and twenty-four anti-aircraft artillery pieces. The second aid, provided in March 1964, included two MiG-17 aircraft, twenty anti-aircraft artillery pieces, eighty-six heavy machine guns, and fifteen 82-millimetre mortars and recoilless guns. A Soviet freighter carrying aircraft arrived in Cambodia on September 27, 1964, with other Soviet military equipment on board, including 85-millimetre anti-aircraft guns, 76-millimetre cannon, mortars, machine guns, and small arms. Soviet technicians also worked at an AAA installation south of Phnom Penh. In March 1966, the Soviet Union offered the third aid package, which included five MiG-17 aircraft, two transports, and some modern anti-aircraft guns. The fourth aid agreement, concluded in February 1968 in the amount of $5.8 million, was the most important of its kind that Cambodia had ever reached with a socialist country. The Soviet Union promised to provide one MiG-15 training plane, one radar installation, a thousand vehicles, armaments for ground forces, and other military matériel.[56] After the coup in Cambodia in 1970, the United States conducted an investigation of Cambodia's arsenal with respect to available Soviet arms, and it found 21 armoured and amphibious personnel carriers, 250 artillery pieces, 3 auxiliary vessels and amphibious craft, 14 jetfighters, and 15 non-jet combat aircraft, trainers, transports, and helicopters.[57] Hence, the Soviet Union's influence was relatively equal to that of its Chinese "comrades." With respect to foreign technicians, in 1967 there were in Cambodia 135 Soviet and Eastern European advisers and 130 Chinese advisers; as for military technicians, there were 30 Soviet and Eastern European advisers and 40 Chinese advisers.[58]

In light of China's confrontation with the United States and competition with the Soviet Union, a new source of Sino-Soviet friction arose in the spring of 1965: the question of whether to support an international conference on the question of Cambodia.[59] On February 11, Sihanouk wrote to the co-chairs of the Geneva Conference, the Soviet Union and the United Kingdom, expressing his willingness to convene the conference immediately. On February 16, he delivered a message to France, India, and the Soviet Union, requesting that these states "immediately" convince the United States and the United Kingdom to accept "without delay and without prerequisites" the conditions relevant to the convening of the Geneva Conference. On February 22, Moscow radio commented on Sihanouk's proposal, claiming that "any sane man" should realize that "immediate peaceful negotiations" constituted the only alternative to expanded war in Vietnam. China reported the Cambodian notes but completely ignored the call for a conference.[60]

The Soviet Union, China, and the United States thus realized the new character of their competition in Indochina. The Soviet ambassador to Luxembourg told his American colleague on March 15 that Beijing, not Hanoi or Saigon, constituted the "real obstacle" to a settlement.[61] General Xu Shiyou, the PLA's commander of the Nanjing Military Region, gave his analysis on April 19: "The situation of the Vietnam War is intensive. It has paved the way from so-called 'special warfare' to a war like the Korean War. Therefore, we should not harbour any illusions regarding US imperialism and modern revisionism ... [which are] the roots of the problem (*huo gen*)."[62] The United States and its allies also carefully assessed the recent development of Sino-Soviet competition in Indochina. A NATO intelligence estimate concluded that "Kosygin's talks in Peking [Beijing] in February 1965 appeared to bear little fruit ... After a short-lived tactical display of unity, Chinese attacks on the new Soviet leaders began following the February 1965 air strikes against North Vietnam. The Chinese have recently accused Moscow of sacrificing the interests of the Vietnamese people to its desire for 'cooperation' with the United States."[63] In this circumstance, China would have to deal with a complex security environment in the spring of 1965, and it began considering a new alignment policy toward the DRV and Cambodia.

An Alignment Guarantee to Prevent Realignments: 1965–70

The situation in Indochina presented significant challenges to China. The United States could invade the DRV in order to cut off its channel to the Viet Cong. The Soviet Union, meanwhile, was providing aid to both the DRV and Cambodia, and it could exploit its status as co-chair of the Geneva Conference to achieve a political settlement of the Indochina conflict. The Soviet Union thus presented the DRV and Cambodia with an alternative source of support should their relationships with China fail. As a dissatisfied Cambodia could cause rifts in the China-DRV-Cambodia alignment, China adopted uniform strategies toward its weaker allies: increasing its level of support for Cambodia by guaranteeing its borders, imposing restraints on Cambodian communists, and providing additional aid.

Cambodia exploited Soviet aid to enhance its strategic importance to China. Sihanouk had made pro-Chinese gestures, yet he also signalled his disagreement with Chinese policies. At the Indochinese People's Conference in Phnom Penh in 1965, he stated that "US military interventions have deprived Vietnam of its right of unification as laid down in the 1954 Geneva Accord. Although Cambodia is a neutral state, we cannot adopt a neutral attitude toward aggressors and those they have oppressed. [We cannot] be neutral when faced with justice and injustice."[64] He argued, however, that the time had come for the DRV and the Viet Cong to reassess their negotiating positions. He claimed that the growing US presence in South Vietnam had dramatically changed the situation and that Vietnamese communists could no longer drive the Americans from South Vietnam through force of arms. The speech was never presented orally due to Vietnamese communist objections.[65] The conference passed an anti-American resolution on March 9, and again Sihanouk demonstrated his ambivalence, labelling the conference a success yet saying he did not agree with the resolution.[66] He wrote to all the Geneva powers on March 15 requesting urgent reconvening of the Geneva Conference to guarantee Cambodia's territorial integrity.[67] The Soviet Union published a note on April 8 in support of the Cambodian position.[68] Several Soviet officials intimated that a Cambodian conference would naturally provide the opportunity for informal talks on other subjects, such as Vietnam.[69] Soviet ambassador to the United States Anatoly Dobrynin indeed hinted that there "might be" "corridor talks" about Vietnam at the proposed Cambodian conference.[70]

In this new situation, Cambodia might push the Geneva Conference proposal forward in the absence of a specific Chinese commitment on Cambodian borders. The United States and the Soviet Union might reach an agreement on resolving the Indochina conflict without taking Chinese positions into account. Cambodia might depend on the Soviet Union to conduct negotiations with the United States if China only maintained its existing level of support for Cambodia. In other words, there was a real danger that Cambodia would abandon China. Accordingly, China established a strong and reliable strategic presence in Indochina to deal with this challenge. The PLA's engineer corps entered the DRV on April 17, 1965.[71] From 1965 to 1968, China deployed 320,000 troops to the DRV for air defence, railway and road construction, and logistical support. The number of PLA troops in the DRV reached 170,000 annually.[72] The Chinese military presence enabled the DRV to send more troops to South Vietnam through Cambodia. It also enabled China to directly protect both the DRV and Cambodia through its armed forces. In mid-April 1965, Zhou Enlai advised Sihanouk that a conference on Cambodia would be pointless, even if conclusions and a resultant agreement should satisfy Cambodia: the United States would exploit the opportunity offered by the conference to talk directly with the DRV as a political manoeuvre. Sihanouk heeded Zhou's advice.[73] On April 24, he announced that the United States, South Vietnam, and Thailand had no right to attend the proposed Geneva Conference as they had not signed the 1954 Geneva Accords.[74] He was also of the opinion that the proposal was "out-dated."[75] Sihanouk was looking for excuses to withdraw the proposal to reconvene the Geneva Conference and immediately enlisted Zhou's support. On April 29, Zhou praised Sihanouk for the "brilliant [decision], pointing to an American 'conspiracy'" with respect to the proposed conference on "the question of Cambodia."[76] Both the United States and the Soviet Union supported the conference proposal, so Zhou's anti-American stance was also clearly directed against the Soviet Union. Sihanouk broke off diplomatic relations with the United States under the pretext of border incidents, and the prospect of a US invasion of Cambodia resulted in China's full guarantee of Cambodia's security, with Zhou cabling Sihanouk on May 20 that "China will never sit idly by if the Americans expand the war to Cambodia."[77] To deter the United States, China used the same language as it had prior to its intervention during the Korean War. China would guarantee Cambodia's security, as it had North Korea's in 1950. Differences in the degree of Chinese commitment to Cambodia and the DRV disappeared. China's border guarantees for both the DRV and Cambodia marked the beginning of its uniform strategies toward its weaker Indochinese allies in 1965.

China's commitment to a definite alignment with Cambodia led to a climax in its relationship with Cambodia. Visiting China in September 1965, Sihanouk denounced American "aggression" in Vietnam and expressed his disapproval of a political settlement. He emphasized his preparations for armed struggle and mobilization of guerrilla warfare.[78] Later Zhou discussed Sihanouk's visit with North Vietnamese prime minister Pham

Van Dong: "The war has been expanded to North Vietnam. It is, therefore, impossible for Laos and Cambodia not to get involved. Sihanouk understands it ... [At] present, China has presented Cambodia with 28,000 pieces of weapons. Sihanouk told me that this amount was enough to equip Cambodian regular and provincial forces and that all US weapons have been replaced."[79] At this critical moment, Cambodia needed to deal with US pressure as well as challenges from Cambodian communists. The PRC therefore provided clear and resolute support to Sihanouk, emphasizing Cambodia's position "on the anti-American front line." As Zhou pointed out on November 13, "Cambodia is a kingdom. Although there are leftists in Cambodia, we will not command them to launch struggle against Sihanouk. It is their [Cambodian communists'] business when they have domestic struggle." Even as he stated that "we indeed oppose [American] imperialism and [Soviet] revisionism and support world revolution," Zhou stressed that this principle should be "flexibly applied" in the case of Cambodia.[80] On November 21, PLA chief of staff Luo Ruiqing reiterated China's commitment to Cambodia at a reception for Cambodian defence minister Lon Nol in Beijing: "If the US dares to spread the flames of war" to Cambodia, China would "not stand idly by" and "assuredly give all-out support."[81] In return, Cambodia agreed to sell 5,000 tons of rice from its coming harvest to the Viet Cong.[82] In Sihanouk's words, "we have given this aid to them by closing our eyes, because we and the Viet Cong have a common enemy, which is US imperialism."[83] Between 1964 and mid-1966, with Chinese support, Cambodia and the DRV enhanced their co-operation against US military operations and Soviet negotiation offers.

The outbreak of the Chinese Cultural Revolution, however, significantly weakened the Sino-Cambodian alignment, for two reasons. First, Cambodia's sustained support to the DRV risked its becoming directly involved in US-DRV military confrontations. Cambodia desperately needed effective deterrence from China against growing US pressure, but the Cultural Revolution seriously undermined the Chinese military position. Domestic instability in China caused doubts in Cambodia about China's capabilities and its resolve to provide effective assistance to Cambodia should the United States launch attacks. Second, the Cultural Revolution led to a "left turn" in China's diplomacy and raised Cambodian suspicion of possible "revolution export" by China. In September 1967, the Cambodian-Chinese Friendship Association in Phnom Penh, under the influence of overseas Chinese, launched political struggles against Sihanouk's government. The Friendship Association's equivalent in Beijing cabled the Cambodian association to present congratulations and celebrate. Sihanouk regarded this as the first official Chinese attack against Cambodia – "China is challenging the right of Cambodia to be master of its own home and is trying to split the people from (? their) Government and link them with its enemies"[84] – and recalled Cambodian diplomats from Beijing.

In the difficult circumstance, Zhou expressed willingness to correct Chinese "mistakes" "at any moment."[85] On October 26, 1967, he told Cambodia's ambassador to China that "we are of the opinion that China and Cambodia have common enemies, who would like to exploit any misunderstanding between us in order to destroy us, one by one ... That the Chinese Friendship Association cabled its Cambodian counterpart was a mistake ... We do not agree with some of their activities either."[86] Zhou also wrote to Sihanouk on November 1, calling for "reestablishment of sincere friendship."[87] In January 1968, on behalf of Sihanouk, Cambodian foreign minister Norodom Phurissara published a joint communiqué with his DRV counterparts in Hanoi, denouncing US "schemes to occupy Indochinese countries to turn them into neocolonies and military bases of the United States." Both sides regarded US negotiation offers as "a maneuver of division" and expressed resolute support for the DRV's preconditions to the talks.[88] These points fully conformed to China's Indochina policy since 1965. The joint communiqué implied that the alignment with China was still the foundation of Cambodia's foreign relations.

To encourage Sihanouk's assertive policies, China imposed additional restraints on the Cambodian communists engaging in armed uprisings in Battambang Province in January 1968. Promoting a united front between the Cambodian communists and Sihanouk's government, Zhou emphasized to the former in November 1968 that it was necessary "to unite with the revolutionary mass all over the world, as well as revolutionary nationalists. [We should] exploit all forces who are amid contradictions with the main enemy and thus treat them as indirect allies."[89] The political report of the CCP's Ninth Party Congress in April 1969, the most "revolutionary" document in the PRC's history, did not mention "revolutionary struggle" in Cambodia, suggesting scant Chinese support of the armed struggle against Sihanouk. In October 1969, Norodom Phurissara, meeting with the Chinese ambassador to Cambodia, Kang Maozhao, addressed recent Cambodian-American armed conflict and pointed out that three tons of medicines from China had been delivered to the Viet Cong. When Phurissara complained about the Cambodian communist armed struggle, Kang emphasized that China did not provide weapons to the communists and would not intervene in Cambodian domestic affairs.[90]

The difficulties of the Sino-Cambodian alignment coincided with problems in the Sino-Vietnamese alignment in two aspects: estimates of Soviet aid to the DRV and terms of US-DRV talks. As Le Duan, the general secretary of the Vietnamese Lao Dong (Worker's Party), told Zhou, "you are saying that the Soviets are selling out Vietnam, but we don't say so."[91] With respect to US offers to negotiate, China and the DRV also had divergent perspectives: China would achieve peace through armed struggle, but the DRV did not oppose a peace agreement through negotiations. Between November 1964 and April 1965, the DRV gradually developed a negotiation proposal with four conditions: 1) US withdrawal and cessation of air attacks "in strict conformity with the Geneva Agreements"; 2) no military alliances, foreign bases, troops, or personnel in Vietnam; 3) settlement of the affairs of South Vietnam "by the South Vietnamese people themselves in accordance with the program of the [National Liberation] Front [i.e., the Viet Cong]"; and 4) "peaceful reunification without foreign intervention."[92]

The DRV was too weak to force the United States to accept these terms, however, and it backed down following the escalation of US bombings over the country. In August 1965, during an interview with a *Le Monde* correspondent, Ho Chi Minh called for withdrawal of US forces but did not label this an "immediate" necessity.[93] In December 1966, the DRV's press representative in Paris, Tran Ngoc Kha, clarified that "the North Vietnamese demand of withdrawal of American troops as one of the basic four points is not meant to be a condition for the opening of peace talks, but a condition for the settlement of peace."[94] US air strikes between 1965 and 1967 inflicted tremendous damage on the DRV. According to Soviet and Eastern European observations, the increasing gravity of food shortages led to serious deterioration of the health and physical stamina of the DRV's combat troops and increased their problems in coping with modern weapons of war. North Vietnamese pilots were having difficulties handling MiG fighters.[95] The US bombardment of Hanoi undermined public morale and effectively sapped the people's will to continue the fight.[96] The damage caused by the air strikes compelled the DRV to drastically revise its peace conditions. In January 1968, it informed the United States, through Romania, that it would enter negotiations with the United States after US bombing had ceased for "a convenient period of time."[97] By March 31, the United States had stopped bombing almost 90 percent of the DRV's population and most of its territory,[98] but not completely, nor did it withdraw its armed forces from Indochina or acknowledge the Viet Cong. In response, the DRV declared "its readiness to send its representatives to make contact with US representatives to decide with the US side on the unconditional cessation of bombing and all other acts by the United States against the DRV so that talks could be begun."[99]

The US military presence in South Vietnam meant the possibility that the United States might defeat the DRV, and Soviet aid to the DRV raised the possibility of the latter's abandonment of China. Despite significant differences between the Chinese and Vietnamese positions, China could accept neither scenario and made an even greater commitment to the DRV. China ran the risk of a higher probability of confrontation with the United States. In May 1965, the DRV demanded Chinese road construction in North Vietnam to compensate for damage caused by US air strikes, and China agreed to send 80,000 troops to construct and repair seven roads.[100] In July, the PLA moved two anti-aircraft divisions and one anti-aircraft regiment to the DRV.[101] Chinese fighters from Hainan Island downed a US F-104 over the Gulf of Tonkin in September.[102] China refused to take joint action with the Soviet Union, but in December 1966 Mao reluctantly told Le Duan that "although we do not agree with [Sino-Soviet] joint action, we can operate in parallel and offer assistance on a bilateral basis."[103]

The DRV's announcement on April 3, 1968, that it was prepared for negotiations with the United States was immediately supported by the Soviet Union but came as a surprise to Beijing. Zhou said to Pham Van Dong that

> the April 3rd statement of the Government of DRV was a surprise not only for the world's people but even for [US president Lyndon Baines] Johnson's opponents. However, in your statement you only used the word "contact." You have had secret contacts before there was limited bombing. Now with this statement you made public those contacts. And, to the world's people, it partly is your compromise, and [it] helps the US solve their difficulties ... It was a [US] wicked and deceitful scheme. In fact, he [President Johnson] doesn't want to give up the war. The [US] statement [of March 31] is only a means for them to overcome the difficult time ... So many people don't understand why the Vietnamese comrades were so hurried in making this statement ... It is the judgment of the world's people ... The situation showed that Vietnamese comrades find it easy to compromise. The world's people can't help thinking that you are facing some difficulties in your struggle. That you changed your positions has increased the number of expected votes for Johnson.[104]

China received the news of the US-DRV negotiations with ill grace. The start of the talks implied that both sides could reach a compromise with Soviet help. China would not be able to bog down the United States, and the DRV would become a pro-Soviet regime. The negotiations seriously undermined the Chinese position in Indochina, as Zhou made clear to Pham Van Dong: "For a long time, the United States has been half-encircling China. Now the Soviet Union is also encircling China. The circle is getting complete, except [the part of] Vietnam."[105] Both the US military presence in Indochina and Soviet assistance to the DRV precluded Chinese pressure on the DRV, however. China was inhibited from imposing sanctions, either by reducing its military or economic support to the DRV or by harassing Soviet aid transiting China to the DRV.[106] In June 1968, it ended up agreeing to the DRV's demand for 107-millimetre rocket artillery pieces and providing all pieces of this type in the PLA's inventory.[107]

Between 1969 and 1970, China had to deal with challenges from both the Soviet Union and the United States. The Soviet Union began looming as a military threat to China after 1968. Table 4.4 shows the growth in Soviet ICBMs (intercontinental ballistic missiles) and divisions in Asia. The Soviet Union did not station the ICBMs or troops in Indochina, but it was after 1968 that Moscow could use its military forces to apply pressure on Beijing by reducing available Chinese strategic resources in Indochina. After the Soviet invasion of Czechoslovakia in August 1968, China began labelling the Soviet Union a "socialist imperialist power." The Sino-Soviet border conflict in March 1969 exacerbated Chinese security problems, leaving China with a deteriorating military balance.[108] In June 1969, Brezhnev proposed an "Asian Collective Security System" at the International Meeting of Communist and Workers' Parties. Chinese leaders immediately perceived that the main Soviet motivation was to "encircle China."[109] Consequently, the Soviet Union rather than the United States was now China's main concern in Asia.[110] This did not mean, however, that challenges emanating from the United States were of secondary importance, coming as they did mainly via Cambodia. Following a coup in Phnom Penh in March 1970 and the removal of Sihanouk from power, Lon Nol, Cambodia's new principal leader, allowed the United States to attack Viet Cong and North Vietnamese bases in Cambodia. The United States initiated air strikes, dealing DRV troops in Cambodia a heavy blow. By May 24, the Americans had captured or destroyed significant amounts of Vietnamese supplies, including 4,551 tons of food, 100 tons of weapons, 1,292 tons of ammunition, and 6,550 tons of equipment, documents, and explosives.[111]

Table 4.4 **Soviet military presence in Asia, 1967–75**

Year	*ICBMs*	*Divisions in the Far East and along the Sino-Soviet border*
1967–68	450–75	15
1968–69	800	15
1969–70	1,050	21
1970–71	1,300	30
1971–72	1,510	33
1972–73	1,530	44
1973–74	1,527	45
1974–75	1,575	45

Source: The Military Balance (London: Institute for Strategic Studies, 1968–76).

The coup in Cambodia also provided China with opportunities, however. After the coup, Sihanouk faced two stark choices – either ending his political life or conducting overseas struggle. Sihanouk represented the sole Cambodian political force that could undermine Lon Nol's legitimacy, and the Cambodian communists represented the only political force that could launch military attacks against Lon Nol's government. The coup therefore presented a new opportunity for Sihanouk and the Cambodian communists to form a united front. Sihanouk paved the way by making such a proposal on March 23, 1970.[112] During Sihanouk's visit to Beijing, China would give refuge to the prince to head a government-in-exile. On May 1, Mao promised to provide free military assistance to Sihanouk and expressed in Beijing his wishes for a larger political basis for Sihanouk's new government.[113] On May 4, Sihanouk formed a coalition government, and appointed Khieu Samphan, a Cambodian communist leader, as deputy premier and defence minister. The government was based on a division of labour: Sihanouk's associates would be responsible for political-diplomatic affairs in China, and the Cambodian communists would be responsible for armed struggle in Cambodia. Zhou explained Chinese views during a talk with Japanese "leftists" in October:

> Our media has reported the PRC's statement in support of the Royal Government of the National Union of Kampuchea. American imperialism, a Republic, is a reactionary country. In contrast, Cambodia, a monarchy, is a progressive [force]. To make the judgment, one must look at the particular policies the ruling class is adopting. Regime type is only a matter of form.[114]

It was therefore Cambodia's foreign and security policies rather than a shared ideology between Cambodia and China that strengthened the Sino-Cambodian alignment.

Despite the renewal of the Sino-Cambodian relationship, the Soviet Union continued to be an alignment option for Sihanouk's government. It did not think highly of Sihanouk's government, but neither could it abandon support for it. The Soviets had two major concerns. First, Lon Nol's pro-American government was in sharp contrast to Sihanouk's anti-American government. The global US-Soviet competition meant that Sihanouk's policies would be to the Soviet advantage. Second, because the DRV supported Sihanouk's government, putting pressure on that government would hurt the Soviet Union's relations with the DRV and strengthen the Chinese position in the China-DRV-Cambodia alignment. Thus, the Soviet Union kept its embassy in Phnom Penh, but its press showed growing sympathy for Sihanouk's government.[115] Asked at a press conference on May 4 which government the Soviet Union recognized as the lawful one, Kosygin gave an evasive answer: "We recognize a neutralist government of Cambodia, the one which pursues a policy of peace and not that of war. And this is the view that we are holding today, too."[116] On May 12, the Russian news agency TASS reported Kosygin's congratulations conveyed to Sihanouk's new government in Beijing.[117] On May 30, the Soviet ambassador in Phnom Penh departed for vacation.[118] The Soviet Ministry of Foreign Affairs invited Sihanouk's representatives to attend a diplomatic reception in Moscow on June 23, paving the way for further development of the relationship.[119]

The Soviet Union presented an alignment option not only for Cambodia but also for the DRV. It provided additional aid to the DRV after the latter's heavy losses in Cambodia. Soviet shipments of war matériel to the DRV reached the third-highest monthly volume ever recorded in May 1970 (134,000 tons), exceeded only by deliveries in May and June 1968. Shipments included 180,000 tons of fertilizer, 373,000 tons of petroleum, 44,300 tons of foodstuffs, and 33,400 tons of general and miscellaneous cargo. The latter category included at least 4,900 tons of vehicles. About 14 tons of military-related cargo were also delivered in May on three Soviet ships, along with a small number of helicopter engines.[120]

The US military operations threatened China, and Soviet aid to the DRV and Cambodia raised the possibility of China's abandonment by its Indochinese allies. The coup in Cambodia drew Sihanouk's government and the DRV much closer, to the extent that the DRV offered Vietnamese advisers to train Sihanouk's troops.[121] Chinese support for Cambodia would thus be a form of support for the DRV, as Sihanouk pointed out on March 8, 1971:

> The help we receive from China is delivered to the Vietnamese border. From there the North Vietnamese transport it to the Cambodian border. It is a very long way, and the Americans constantly bomb our lines for supplies. However, whatever we need we ultimately receive, because China gives us all that we request. We have decided to arm 30,000 men this year, and 40,000 more next year. China will give all the equipment we need for these men.[122]

In practice, China offered more aid than it had earlier promised to Cambodia. The Cambodian communist troops grew from about 3,000 in 1970 to an estimated 85,000 in mid-1971.[123] Chinese assistance not only strengthened Cambodia's positions during the war with the United States but also reduced incentives for Cambodia to enter into closer cooperation with the Soviet Union. China's direct objective was to drive the United States out of Indochina; its indirect objective was to exclude Soviet influence from the region. Its uniform commitment to both the DRV and Cambodia, therefore, was aimed at preventing the defeat of its allies by the United States or the establishment of pro-Soviet regimes on the Chinese periphery.

Aid to Allies, Negotiations with Adversaries, 1971–73

Between 1969 and 1971, China and the United States drew closer to one another. This was partly because, after 1969, China perceived the Soviet Union as a primary threat, and a stable Sino-American friendship could enable China to mobilize available strategic resources against the Soviets. Moreover, the bombing of North Vietnamese military bases in Cambodia in 1970 had been the United States' last attempt to resolve the Indochina conflict through military means. The air strikes weakened the DRV's military presence in Cambodia but also prompted significantly more Chinese aid packages to the DRV. For both the United States and China, therefore, rapprochement was a necessary and urgent move.

China, however, was aware that rapprochement with the United States would hurt its alignment relationships. Both the DRV and Cambodia were in a state of war with America, and any suspicion of Chinese commitment to the United States would push them toward the Soviet Union. China therefore needed to strike a balance between rapprochement with the United States and the concerns of its Indochinese allies. Since selective strategies toward the DRV and Cambodia would provide incentives, or even pretexts, for these weaker allies to abandon China, the PRC maintained its uniform strategies by providing aid to both countries and promoting the overthrow of both the South Vietnamese government under Nguyen Van Thieu and the Cambodian government under Lon Nol.

China and the United States began gravitating toward each other between November 1969 and June 1971. In November 1969, the United States delivered a message to China through Pakistani president Yahya Khan, who conveyed Washington's interest in normalizing relations, as demonstrated by the withdrawal of two of its destroyers from the Taiwan Strait.[124] On December 4, China responded favourably by releasing two American prisoners. Meanwhile, China also issued an invitation to US representatives to visit the PRC's embassy in Warsaw for ambassadorial talks.[125] And on February 20, 1970, China indicated its willingness to receive in Beijing a US representative of "ministerial rank or a special presidential envoy."[126] On March 21, the United States proposed the establishment of a secret channel between the White House and Zhongnanhai.[127] On June 15, National Security Adviser Henry Kissinger proposed to "bring about improvement in US-Chinese relations fully recognizing differences in ideology."[128] Later, on October 25, President Richard Nixon held a conversation with Yahya Khan in which he attempted to open negotiations with China, saying that the United States would "make no condominium [sic] against [China]."[129] China knew full well that it was the pursuit of an Indochina settlement that drove these US initiatives. During Yahya Khan's visit to Beijing, therefore, Zhou Enlai explicitly signalled self-restraint by declaring that China would "not join the [Indochina] war unless America extends the war to China"[130] and that "a special envoy of President Nixon will be most welcome."[131] These secret contacts laid the foundation for people-to-people contact. In March 1971, the Chinese and American teams met at the World Table Tennis Championships in Nagoya, Japan, and the latter expressed willingness to visit the PRC.[132] Accordingly, in April Mao issued an invitation to the American team. On May 10, Nixon proposed a preliminary meeting between Kissinger and Zhou to discuss issues of principal concern, including Nixon's visit to China.[133] On June 4, Kissinger suggested holding concrete discussions with Zhou during the period July 9 to 11.[134] On June 11, China agreed to the arrangement.[135]

The visit of the US table tennis team to China exerted a potent influence on the Soviet Union, the DRV, and Cambodia, all of which began to consider the possibility of Sino-American cooperation. During a talk with American colleagues at the International Control Commission (ICC) who sought information about his "Chinese colleagues" with respect to Chinese road construction in Laos, Colonel Skowron, Polish military adviser to the ICC, replied that "perhaps later they [the Chinese] will be your colleagues but not mine."[136] His comments accurately reflected the Soviet understanding of the Sino-American rapprochement. Although invited, along with the United States, to the ping-pong games, the DRV – a Soviet strategic partner – boycotted the exhibition matches in Beijing, and North Vietnamese media did not report the American visit.[137] The Cambodian response was relatively mild in comparison. On July 3, Sihanouk re-emphasized his determination to oust Lon Nol and "denounced" Lon Nol's "illusions regarding Nixon's visit to China."[138] Sihanouk's statement implied that he had realized the prospect of Nixon's visit to China but hoped China would not invite the president.

China clearly regarded Indochina as the most sensitive issue in the rapprochement process. On June 7, 1971, Marshal Ye Jianying asked the CCP Working Conference

> why is the US approaching us so desperately? ... In Southeast Asia, the US position is getting more difficult every day, particularly with respect to its troop withdrawal from Indochina. In the past, they turned to Soviet revisionists for help. In view of the current situation, [however,] it is impossible to solve problems without Chinese participation. They need us on this matter. This could be the first issue under discussion when they come to negotiate with us.[139]

Therefore, China needed to consider how to accommodate its Indochinese allies while trying to promote a strategic relationship with the United States. During Sino-American secret negotiations in July 1971, it adopted uniform strategies toward the DRV and Cambodia. To retain US credibility in the eyes of American allies, Kissinger stressed continued support to Nguyen Van Thieu of South Vietnam and Lon Nol of Cambodia. He also denounced the DRV's military presence in South Vietnam and Cambodia. Zhou, on the other hand, was committed to regime change in South Vietnam and Cambodia and conducted an oral defence of the DRV.[140] "So long as the war does not cease, we will continue our support. This support is not only for the people of Vietnam, but also the people of Cambodia and Laos."[141] Despite these facts, the change in Sino-American relations made the DRV and Sihanouk skeptical about future Chinese support. On July 16, Beijing announced its invitation to President Nixon to visit China. In response, Hanoi publicly claimed through its official editorial that Washington would "try to achieve a compromise between big powers in an attempt to make smaller countries bow to their agreements."[142] The editorial implicitly but clearly criticized the Chinese "agreement" with the United States concerning the DRV. In private talks, Le Duan was more specific. He was most concerned "about the recent diminishing of worldwide interest in the Vietnam War, resulting from the President [Nixon]'s impending trip to Beijing. He stated that [this] was the most important present problem in continuing the war" and emphasized that "there were a number of critical things he would like to say about the USSR and China, especially the latter, but he felt compelled to remain silent to avoid jeopardizing continued Soviet and Chinese aid without which North Vietnam could not continue to fight."[143] For his part, Sihanouk directly expressed to Chinese leaders his anger over the Sino-American rapprochement: "The US is the Number One imperialist country. It wages aggressive [wars] everywhere! ... Why would China receive the president of such a country! What are you going to talk to him about?"[144] During Nixon's visit to China, Sihanouk paid a visit to Hanoi and published tough words there.

In view of these grievances, therefore, there was a real possibility that the DRV and Sihanouk might tilt toward the Soviet Union. In response, China avoided any selective strategies toward the allies. As Zhou argued privately, "for the present, it is not appropriate to overpraise Vietnam; we should treat her as we do the other two nations [Cambodia and Laos]."[145] China continued to offer extensive aid to the DRV and Sihanouk's government-in-exile, concluding aid pacts with the former on January 22 and the latter on February 11, 1972. Between 1971 and 1972, China offered the DRV 100 aircraft, 180 Hongqi-2 surface-to-air missiles, 2 radars, 20 amphibious tanks, 204 heavy-calibre cannons, and 45,000 shells.[146] Meanwhile, China pledged continued support to Sihanouk's government, which by July 11, 1972, controlled 85 percent of Cambodian territory, with a population of 5 million.[147] According to Sihanouk, Zhou had promised that "we [China] will give you [Cambodia] everything you need to attain final victory as soon as possible."[148] Although its aid packages to the Indochinese allies were generous, China's political support for their policies was circumscribed. Hoan Tung, editor-in-chief of the North Vietnamese daily newspaper *Nhan Dan,* described the consequences of US air strikes in 1972, lamenting that the "capital" that North Vietnam had accumulated for national construction had "gone down the drain."[149] However, Chinese reactions, according to US observations, were "circumspect and limited."[150] In November 1972, Kissinger held a discussion with Foreign Minister Qiao

Guanhua on the question of Indochina. After the talks, he reported to Nixon, on November 13, that Chinese political support for North Vietnam and Cambodia was in decline: "It's the softest I've ever heard them on Vietnam; no particular support for the North Vietnamese ... They as much as said they would use their influence to keep things quiet in Cambodia."[151] The Sino-American rapprochement inevitably weakened China's alignment relationships with the DRV and Sihanouk's government, but Chinese uniform strategies prevented their disintegration.

Selective Strategies, 1973–75

The Sino-American rapprochement suggested US disengagement from Indochina. Table 4.5 illustrates the changing character of the US military presence in South Vietnam. Between 1969 and 1972, the Nixon administration withdrew over 80 percent of US armed forces. In the Paris Peace Accords concluded in January 1973, the United States agreed to the complete withdrawal of American military forces, including military advisers, from Vietnam. In this circumstance, the US Congress cut funds for military activities in Indochina. In May 1973, the House of Representatives registered a solid majority against the funding of American bombing in Indochina, and the Senate forbade the use of force in Indochina without congressional consent.[152] All these signs implied a quick decline of US influence in Indochina.

Table 4.5 US armed forces deployed in South Vietnam, 1965–72 (in thousands of personnel)

Year	*Personnel (thousands)*
1965	184.3
1966	385.3
1967	485.6
1968	536.1
1969	475.2
1970	344.6
1971	157.0
1972	68.5

Source: SIPRI Yearbook of World Armaments and Disarmament, 1972 (Stockholm: Almquist and Wiksell, 1972), 269.

The US commitment to a complete withdrawal of its military forces left Indochina to Sino-Soviet competition, regarding which the Chinese leadership had a clear understanding. In January 1973, CCP Vice Chairman Li Desheng observed that "in the past, the US established SEATO to blockade us. Now the US has failed, while Soviet revisionists are meddling by establishing the so-called 'Asian Collective Security System.' They will replace the US in blockading us. Our foreign policy is to develop relations with Southeast Asian nations in order to break out of the blockade."[153] Moreover, meeting with Australian prime minister Gough Whitlam on October 31, 1973, Zhou Enlai stated that "we take note that Your Excellency has expressed the view that this region should be free of great powers' competition. However, in order to achieve a reduction of tensions, countries and people in the region should make constant efforts against superpowers' power politics and expansionism."[154] China had always labelled the United States and the Soviet Union as "superpowers." However, as the US withdrawal from Vietnam could hardly be regarded as expansionism, Zhou's analysis referred exclusively to the Soviet Union. A pro-Soviet Indochina, supporting the Soviet proposal of an Asian Collective Security System, would threaten Chinese security. The DRV had received extensive Chinese and Soviet aid. North Vietnamese attempts to avoid conflict with the Soviet Union, therefore, made the DRV a free rider in China-DRV-Cambodia alignment. Accordingly, China adopted selective strategies toward its weaker allies. It imposed restraint on the DRV's armed struggle in South Vietnam, and it occupied the Xisha Islands (Paracel Islands) in the South China Sea to circumscribe the DRV's territorial claims. Meanwhile, China supported the armed struggle of Sihanouk's coalition government to overthrow Lon Nol's government, with the object of counterbalancing Soviet influence.

China's selective strategies began after the conclusion of the Paris Peace Accords. China emphasized gaining flexibility, rather than armed struggle, in Vietnam, urging the DRV to abide by the Peace Accords. Mao told Le Duan that "some leftist Communists do not agree [with the Peace Accords]. They say you should continue the warfare ... Their suggestions should not be listened to." Instead, Mao called for peace for six, twelve, or eighteen months. Such a ceasefire, from his perspective, "should not be called an opposition against revolution."[155] The existence of South Vietnam would give the DRV incentives to continually cooperate with China.

More importantly, China used armed forces to drive South Vietnamese troops out of the Xisha Islands in 1974. Pham Van Dong had acknowledged the PRC's sovereignty over the islands in 1958, an act later described as a tactic by the DRV to enlist China's political and material support. In November 1971, Vo Van Sung, the DRV's delegate general in Paris, met with his American counterpart, General Vernon Walters. Vo Van Sung claimed a kingdom called "Nam Viet," which included parts of China's Guangdong, Guangxi, and Yunnan Provinces and autonomous regions. The DRV did not claim any of these territories, but it did lay claim to the Xisha Islands.[156] In December 1973, it would grant "rights" to Italian companies to exploit oil in Beibu Gulf.[157] On December 26, the DRV proposed to China that "the division of Beibu Gulf was not settled due to the war environment." It suggested "negotiations, by governments on both sides, over Beibu Gulf."[158] It was entirely possible that the DRV would present China with a demand regarding the Xisha Islands, which were under South Vietnamese control, during the negotiations. China would therefore not be able to take the upper hand in negotiations with the DRV unless it drove the South Vietnamese from the islands. This step would be critical to China's counterbalance of Soviet influence in Indochina. China agreed to enter negotiations with North Vietnam over the Beibu Gulf on January 18, 1974, and the PLA occupied the Xisha Islands the very next day. The operation resulted in a South Vietnamese military defeat – eighteen dead, forty-three wounded, and forty-eight captured.[159] When the battle was over, the Viet Cong expressed its gratitude to China for the liberation of the islands for the Vietnamese and thus implied a territorial claim on the islands by the communist organization in South Vietnam. China returned the note by denying that the Xisha Islands were the so-called Hoang Sa Islands, as they were called in Vietnamese. Thus, China did not acknowledge any claims of sovereignty over the islands by South Vietnam, the Viet Cong, or North Vietnam.[160] Rather, it used North Vietnam as an example to teach Sihanouk's coalition government a lesson – that following the Soviets would be a mistake.

China still had to deal with Soviet expansionism in the case of Cambodia. The Soviet Union regarded Cambodian communists as a progressive force and the source of Cambodia's military prowess.[161] Because they followed Sihanouk's leadership, the Soviet Union had greater incentive to develop a cooperative relationship with Sihanouk's government once the Cambodian communists had bolstered their capabilities. In August 1973, Soviet media gave greater coverage to Sihanouk and the Cambodian communists, implying further political support.[162] The Soviet Union acknowledged Sihanouk as Cambodian head of state on October 9 and treated his government as the "sole legitimate representative" of the Cambodian nation. It promised to provide all necessary aid and completely cut off official contacts with Lon Nol by withdrawing thirty diplomats and personnel from Phnom Penh.[163] In November, the Soviets issued their first invitation to Sihanouk's representatives to celebrate the October Revolution.[164] The Soviet manoeuvring in Cambodia served as a warning to China. Zhou remarked to Kissinger that "the only thing I wish to bring to your attention is that the Soviet Union wants to have a hand in that pie."[165] Later he explained his point in private to Chinese officials at the Foreign Trade Ministry: "Cambodia ... must be viewed in the general context of world politics with special emphasis on Soviet ambitions."[166] The Soviet Union needed time to expand its influence in Cambodia. The quicker Sihanouk's government could achieve final victory, the greater the probability that China could strengthen its alignment with Cambodia.

China therefore actively supported total victory for the Cambodian resistance movement. Sihanouk explained in his interview with a CBS News correspondent in September 1973 that China would deliver ammunition to Cambodia. There was no lack of weapons for his armed forces, which would launch an attack to take Phnom Penh in the next dry season, between December 1973 and May 1974.[167] In April 1974, Mao encouraged Sihanouk's critical step of besieging Phnom Penh with a concentrated force of 100,000 troops.[168] On May 26, China publicized its first military aid pact with Cambodia since the Paris Peace Accords[169] and also offered strong political support. On October 2, Qiao Guanua, the PRC's deputy foreign minister, pointed out to Kissinger that "the final result [of the situation in Cambodia] is clear; it is only a matter of time ... So now this question is not worthwhile, but it doesn't matter very much. Events have their own laws."[170] In December 1974, US Senator Mike Mansfield paid a visit to Beijing and sought advice from Deputy Premier Deng Xiaoping on the question of Cambodia. Deng stated that "it seems that the only way for Cambodia is to continue to fight its way out with the resistance forces there."[171] This Chinese critical support brought about a Cambodian "general offensive," with the regular armed forces of Sihanouk's government, totalling 200,000, controlling 90 percent of Cambodian territory by the end of 1974.[172] Sihanouk's government ousted Lon Nol's regime on April 17, 1975.

China's Indochina policy between 1962 and 1975 provides an opportunity to examine the regional competition theory. Between 1962 and 1965, the United States was China's only regional competitor, and China adopted selective strategies toward its weaker allies to encourage Cambodia to follow the DRV's armed struggle. Between 1964 and 1965, different Sino-Soviet attempts to solve the Indochina conflict, along with Soviet aid to Indochina, made the Soviet Union China's new regional competitor. Between 1965 and 1973, therefore, China adopted uniform strategies toward its weaker allies to counterbalance American and Soviet influence. After the US withdrawal from Indochina in 1973, China's priority, with respect to the exclusion of Soviet influence in Indochina, was security. Consequently, China adopted selective strategies toward the DRV and Cambodia to circumscribe the former's pro-Soviet policies and to prevent the Soviets from driving a wedge between itself and Cambodia. In the ensuing decade, China counted on Cambodian support to counterbalance Soviet regional influence.[173]

5
Regional Diplomacy in the New Era

Adding to international relations theories that focus on external threats, domestic politics, and ideology, this book proposes a regional competition theory, which posits that the number of both regional competitors and alignment relationships shape a great power's regional diplomacy with respect to its use of uniform strategies or selective strategies. The regional competition theory seeks to make traditional foreign policy theories more dynamic by taking into account foreign aid, competing objectives, and alignment relationships. This book has conducted in-depth analyses of three historical cases: China's policies in East Asia in 1955–65; in South Asia in 1955–63; and in Indochina in 1962–75, using Chinese, Russian, German, American, and NATO archival sources to dissect Chinese regional diplomacy in its immediate neighbourhood. Table 5.1 summarizes Chinese regional diplomacy in these three historical cases – a total of thirty-one Chinese policies toward particular weaker neighbours and eleven Chinese diplomatic conducts in three distinct regions.

In the post–Cold War era, the Chinese did not possess sufficient power advantages over their neighbours in East Asia. During the first decade of the twenty-first century, it was widely believed that the People's Liberation Army (PLA) was no match for the Japan Self-Defense Forces.[1] From 2007 onward, China began to narrow its defence budget gap vis-à-vis Japan, and the Chinese defence budget is currently over three times that of Japan. However, Japan is still able to deny China access to or control of critical areas. An active denial strategy on the part of Japan will capitalize on the

TABLE 5.1 Summary of Chinese asymmetric statecraft, 1955–75

Period	*Target*	*Policies*	*Statecraft*
		Mainland China toward non-allies in East Asia, 1955–65	
1955–58	Japan	Promoting official trade agreements Proposing revisions to the Sino-Soviet Treaty Proposing reduction in the size of Chinese naval forces	Uniform accommodation
	Taiwan	Exercising self-restraint in use of force Promoting political negotiations Proposing trade and economic assistance	
1958	Japan	Imposing trade sanctions	Uniform coercion
	Taiwan	Shelling of the Jinmen Islands	
1959–62	Japan	Establishing a "North Sea Fleet" Promoting only non-official trade	Selective strategies
	Taiwan	Exercising self-restraint in use of force Not competing for seats in international organizations Proposing economic assistance	
1962–65	Japan	Promoting official trade agreements Supporting Japanese claims to "northern territories"	Selective strategies
	Taiwan	Preparing for war and launching naval attacks Severing Taiwan's diplomatic ties with France	
		China toward non-allies in South Asia, 1955–63	
1955–59	India	Proposing "no advancement" below the "McMahon Line" Reducing the size of armed forces in Tibet Allowing the Fourteenth Dalai Lama's visit to India Maintaining neutrality on Kashmir	Uniform accommodation
	Pakistan	Maintaining neutrality on Kashmir Providing economic assistance	
	Afghanistan	Making trade concessions	
	Burma	Seeking territorial compromises Making trade concessions Not supporting Burmese communist armed struggle Imposing restraints on oversea Chinese in Burma	
	Nepal	Providing economic assistance Making trade concessions	
1959–61	India	Maintaining the "administrative line"	Selective strategies
	Pakistan	Denying the existence of border disputes Maintaining neutrality on Pashtunistan	

Period	*Target*	Policies	*Statecraft*
	Afghanistan	Concluding a non-aggression pact Maintaining neutrality on Pashtunistan	
	Burma	Seeking territorial compromises Providing economic assistance Not supporting the Kachin people	
	Nepal	Seeking territorial compromises Exchanging intelligence Providing economic assistance	
1962–63	India	Launching border offensives	Selective strategies
	Pakistan	Seeking territorial compromises Providing economic assistance	
	Afghanistan	Seeking territorial compromises Providing economic assistance	
	Burma	Providing economic assistance	
	Nepal	Providing economic assistance	
		China toward allies in Indochina, 1962–75	
1962–65	DRV	Making border guarantees by use of force Providing large-scale assistance	Selective strategies
	Cambodia	Proposing border settlement through negotiations Providing limited assistance	
1965–70	DRV	Making border guarantees by use of force Providing military and economic assistance Tolerating US-DRV negotiations	Uniform accommodation
	Cambodia	Making border guarantees by use of force Providing military and economic assistance Imposing restraints on overseas Chinese and Cambodian communists	
1971–73	DRV	Providing military and economic assistance Seeking rapprochement with the United States	Uniform maintenance
	Cambodia	Providing military and economic assistance Seeking rapprochement with the United States	
1973–75	DRV	Imposing restraint on the DRV's armed struggle Accepting Nguyen Van Thieu's control of South Vietnam Using armed force in the South China Sea	Selective strategies
	Cambodia	Encouraging Cambodia's armed struggle Promoting regime change to oust Lon Nol Providing military and economic assistance	

country's geography and the defensive potential of its modern weapons.[2] For example, Japan has almost twice as many advanced destroyers as China (thirty-five versus twenty-one) and will soon become the world's second country with operational fifth-generation fighter jets. As Michael Beckley concludes, "Japan retains enduring geographic and technological advantages that will allow it to deny China sea and air control throughout much of the East China Sea for the foreseeable future."[3]

China, by contrast, has since the end of the Cold War been better positioned than its neighbours to compete in Southeast Asia and South Asia. As Kai He well argues, "asymmetric" is the word to describe the relationship between China and Southeast Asian states.[4] China's GDP or military expenditure is many times more than the combined GDP or military expenditure of the Association of Southeast Asian Nations (ASEAN) countries. India is the most powerful state in South Asia, but as Manjeet Pardesi emphasizes, the Sino-Indian relationship is also characterized by asymmetry. The material power gap has become even greater. In 1989, China's GDP and military expenditure were 1.17 times and 1.08 times those of India, respectively. Two decades later, in 2019, they were 5 times and 3.67 times those of India, respectively.[5] A striking feature, however, is that China has not reaped benefits through settlement of security problems with its weaker neighbours. In the South China Sea, China has had territorial disputes with multiple neighbours, and in South Asia it was inevitably involved in the Indo-Pakistani conflict. Meanwhile, China adopted a non-alignment policy of not committing itself to any country. China does not assume any defence responsibility in the event of Indo-Pakistani conflict over Kashmir.[6] During the standoff between the two countries in 2019 and 2020, China emphasized its willingness to "promote friendly relationships with both India and Pakistan."[7] As the conflict escalated, it was clear that China and Pakistan had no mutual security commitment directed against India. In brief, China did not consider Pakistan as an allied state in the post–Cold War era. The most pressing issue for Chinese regional diplomacy, therefore, was how to engage with multiple weaker non-allies in a region.

The end of the Cold War contributed to heightened tension in Sino-American relations. The collapse of the Soviet Union removed the major source of threat from the north, enabled China to concentrate resources on developing its capabilities, closed the gap between Chinese and American capabilities, and engendered greater anxiety among China's weaker neighbours. Concerns over China's obviously greater capabilities and security problems in Asia provided the United States with new opportunities to exert greater influence. The United States hence strengthened its alliance relationships and looked for new allies in the Indo-Pacific region. In other words, China and the United States have engaged in strategic competition in the South China Sea and in South Asia.

The end of the Cold War also created a new situation characterized by the coexistence of cooperation and competition in Sino-Russian relations. There has been enduring tension between the United States and Russia over limitations on anti-ballistic missile (ABM) systems and NATO expansion. Such competition has pushed Russia closer to China, with Russia selling advanced weapons to, and conducting joint military exercises with, China, as well as supporting the creation and operations of the Shanghai Cooperation Organization (SCO). However, Russian and Chinese interests have not been identical with respect to Central Asia, and even as Russia has advanced its cooperation with China, it has sought an alternative linchpin for its Asia policy. Most of China's neighbours are too weak to attract Russian attention, leaving India as the only country with great power potential. Although Russia has usually supported Chinese positions with respect to security problems in Asia, it has provided more advanced weapons to India than China, thus becoming a Chinese regional competitor in South Asia.

The regional competition theory explains China's regional diplomacy during the Cold War and subsequent periods, with a view toward the future. The end of the Cold War did not change three important aspects of regional competition in Asia. First, the United States and Russia continue to be global military powers, and China is essentially a regional great power in Asia. China's power projection abilities are inadequate compared with those of the United States or Russia. Second, China maintains enormous advantages over most of its immediate neighbours. Third, China's weaker neighbours have the ability to reduce Chinese advantages by permitting the establishment of bases on their territories by the United States or Russia or by receiving aid from either.

The remainder of this chapter will discuss features of Sino-American competition, the limitations of Sino-Russian cooperation, and China's regional diplomacy. The United States is China's only regional competitor in the South China Sea, and its military presence is a key factor in explaining China's uniform strategies toward the Philippines, Vietnam, and Malaysia. In South Asia, both the United States and Russia are China's regional competitors, and their arms sales to India have contributed significantly to China's selective strategies toward India and Pakistan. In examining the regional dynamics, the regional competition theory also sheds light on future trends in Chinese regional diplomacy.

Uniform Strategies in the South China Sea

US Involvement in the South China Sea

China has strengthened its capabilities vis-à-vis the United States since the end of the Cold War, and the EP-3 incident in 2001, when a US Navy EP-3 surveillance plane collided with a Chinese fighter jet over the South China Sea, raised the possibility of direct military clashes between the two great powers. In light of China's greater military strength developed in the past three decades, the United States has sought to maintain a stronger naval and air presence in China's neighbourhood. Between 2004 and 2008, it strengthened its forward bases in Guam by redeploying two Los Angeles–class attack submarines, four B-2 bombers, and five F-22 fighters from Pearl Harbor and Alaska.[8] However, the global financial crisis in 2008 both weakened US leadership in global affairs and tilted the Sino-American balance of power toward China. The US response to China's rise, particularly the Obama administration's "pivot" to East Asia, reflected American attempts to maintain regional order in order to preserve its credit with China's neighbours. The US Air Force bolstered its intelligence, surveillance, and reconnaissance capabilities, and the US Navy frequently carried out "freedom of navigation operations," which, in Chinese eyes, challenged Chinese sovereign claims in the South China Sea. These moves, aimed at thwarting Chinese ambitions, made China suspicious of US China policy.

Acutely aware of the changing balance of power vis-à-vis China and in view of its relative decline, the United States attempted to strengthen relations with existing allies and sought potential new allies. It first bolstered ties with the Philippines, conducting joint military operations with that country in 2002. A total of 2,700 American and 2,900 Philippine troops launched the three-week joint exercises on the island of Luzon in the northern Philippines.[9] Both sides upgraded joint military exercises in February 2004, with 2,500 American and 2,300 Philippine troops taking part.[10] In October 2003, the United States increased its aid from $30 million to $55 million, with emphasis on improving the Philippines' amphibious capabilities.[11] Amid tensions between 2012 and 2016, the United States reached new defence agreements with the Philippines, conducted joint exercises, and exchanged intelligence.

The United States also began providing new aid packages to Vietnam. In June 2012, the US Export-Import Bank – the American official export credit agency – provided Vietnam's state-owned enterprises with over $100 million to purchase American-produced satellites.[12] In December 2013, the United States decided to provide $32.5 million worth of aid to ASEAN members for coastal defence and freedom of navigation in the South China Sea. In particular, Vietnam received $18 million for five high-speed cruisers.[13] Like Vietnam, Malaysia also received US military hardware, including eight US-produced F/A-18D Hornet jet fighters.[14]

Finally, the United States enabled its allies to provide aid. For example, Japan became a source of external support for Vietnam. Japan and Vietnam signed a defence memorandum in October 2011,[15] and Japan provided patrol boats to Vietnam in 2013.[16] It also provided significant economic aid to Vietnam – $500 million in loans in January 2013 for economic construction,[17] a new ¥100 billion loan package in September 2015 for infrastructure construction,[18] and ¥90 billion in May 2016 for railway construction in Ho Chi Minh City.[19]

Sino-Russian Cooperation in the South China Sea

The end of the Cold War did not remove sources of US-Russia contention on the questions of ABM systems, Georgia, and Ukraine. From the US perspective, Russia was determined to revise existing borders through the use of force, whereas from the Russian perspective, the United States had attempted to establish forward bases, directed against Russia, in the Russian neighbourhood. This competition with the United States drew Russia closer to China: not only did Russia provide China with advanced military technologies, but the two countries also conducted joint military exercises in Central Asia (2007), the Sea of Japan (2009, 2015, and 2021), the South China Sea (2016), the Baltic Sea (2017), the Southern Urals (2018 and 2019), the East China Sea (2019), Ningxia (2021), and the Sea of Oman (2022). Sino-Russian joint exercises covered a wide range of subjects, including counter–nuclear strike exercises, ABM operations, air defence training, anti-submarine warfare, reconnaissance and annihilation, amphibious attacks, and island occupation.[20]

According to an analysis of official Russian documents, Alexander Korolev argues that Russia adopted a "hedging" strategy in the Sino-Vietnamese disputes in the South China Sea.[21] Although it sold arms to Southeast Asian countries, it was not a Chinese regional competitor in the South China Sea. Russian arms sales to Vietnam included two frigates, six Project 636 Kilo-class submarines, twelve Su-27SK fighters, eight Su-30MK2 fighters, and twelve S-300PMU1 air defence missile systems.[22] Russia also sold eighteen Su-30MKM fighters to Malaysia.[23] In support of Chinese positions, however, Russia opposed US involvement in the South China Sea and refused to conduct joint oil exploitation with Vietnam in

Sino-Vietnamese disputed areas.[24] In May 2012, the Russian ambassador to the Philippines, Nikolay Kudashev, stated that neither Russia nor the United States should become involved in territorial disputes in the South China Sea because neither had a territorial claim.[25] Foreign Minister Sergei Lavrov explained Russia's position in August 2015: "Any parties directly involved in the dispute should seek to work out a settlement to every side's satisfaction under the condition of non-interventions by external powers. We do not believe that internationalization of the dispute would be helpful."[26] In May 2016, China and Russia issued a joint statement, in the name of the SCO, reiterating the Chinese positions on the South China Sea,[27] and in July 2016 Russia decided to conduct joint exercises with China in the South China Sea.[28] As President Vladimir Putin pointed out, these joint exercises would contribute to Sino-Russian security.[29] In brief, Russia and China did not compete over influence in the South China Sea.

China's Uniform Strategies

The South China Sea disputes involved mainland China, Taiwan, Vietnam, the Philippines, Malaysia, Indonesia, and Brunei. Both the mainland and Taiwan claimed territories in the name of "China." Indonesia did not make territorial claims, and Brunei did not have a military presence.[30] Therefore, neither Taiwan, Indonesia, nor Brunei was a target of China's policy in the South China Sea. All other sides had a military presence, projecting their power through airfields. China's military was on Yongxing Island (Woody Island), Vietnam's on Nanwei Island (Storm Island), the Philippines' on Zhongye Island (Thitu Island), and Malaysia's on Danwan Island (Pulau Layang-Layang). After 2014, China constructed new airfields on Yongshu Island (Fiery Cross Reef) and Chigua Island (Johnson Reef). Consequently, Vietnam, the Philippines, and Malaysia became China's policy targets. China was much stronger than these neighbours in the semi-closed marine area.

The territorial disputes in the South China Sea also reflected Sino-American competition for power. Despite Chinese protests, the United States carried out extensive and close-in surveillance of Chinese coastal areas. In addition to fostering Sino-American mutual suspicions, US operation also gave China's weaker neighbours the opportunity to play the US off against China. To reduce their incentives to cooperate with the United States, therefore, China adopted uniform strategies.

As Premier Zhu Rongji emphasized in 2002, China needed to make "friendship investments" in neighbouring countries, such as Vietnam, which would carry "significant political implications."[31] Following this line, China and ASEAN concluded a framework agreement in 2002 on comprehensive economic cooperation, after China took the initiative to eliminate its tariffs to facilitate imports from ASEAN members. China and ASEAN also issued a joint "declaration of the conduct of parties in the South China Sea," emphasizing settlements through negotiations and peaceful means. China's uniform concessions to Vietnam, the Philippines, and Malaysia were made in order to send consistent signals to the United States. According to Deputy Foreign Minister Wang Yi, "the main objective [of the declaration] is to send a clear signal to the outside world that countries in this region are able to successfully solve their problems through negotiations and to achieve peace and stability in the South China Sea through cooperation."[32] China also sought to convince the United States that Vietnam, the Philippines, and Malaysia were not interested in being exploited as US forward bases against China. Moreover, the uniform concessions heightened these countries' dependency on Chinese markets and reduced the United States' manoeuvring room in the Chinese neighbourhood with respect to military deployments.

Although Vietnam, the Philippines, and Malaysia reaped extensive economic benefits from China, none of them abandoned its territorial claims in the South China Sea; in fact, they strengthened their military cooperation in the region. In March 2006, Vietnam and Malaysia established a naval communication channel to demonstrate their determination to cooperate in the South China Sea.[33] In the spring of 2009, the Philippine government ratified the 1982 United Nations Convention on the Law of the Sea (UNCLOS) and asserted its claims to Huangyan Island (Scarborough Shoal).[34] In March 2009, Abdullah Ahmad Badawi, Malaysia's prime minister, toured Danwan and Guangxingzai (Swallow and Ardasier) Reefs to demonstrate Malaysian sovereign claims.[35] China, however, did not exert pressure on its weaker neighbours, other than issuing certain public statements, and maintained its uniform accommodation, continuing for the most part to open its domestic market to these countries until the summer of 2010, which saw direct US intervention.

The US "pivot" to Asia encouraged Vietnam, the Philippines, and Malaysia to form a united front against China. Secretary of State Hillary Clinton claimed during her visit to Hanoi in July 2010 that territorial disputes in the South China Sea involved US national interests.[36] In August, the USS *John S. McCain* (DDG-56) paid a four-day visit to Da Nang, and the USS *George Washington* (CVN-73) conducted joint exercises with Vietnamese naval forces.[37] In October, Vietnam, in its capacity as chair of ASEAN, seized the opportunity to promote the ASEAN Declaration on

Cooperation in Search and Rescue of Persons and Vessels in Distress at Sea. From the Chinese perspective, the document constituted ASEAN's first official statement with respect to member states' potential naval cooperation in the South China Sea.[38] In April 2011, the United States and the Philippines conducted joint military exercises on an unprecedented scale – 2,500 American and 5,000 Philippine combat forces participated.[39] It was in this circumstance that China made its final effort to maintain its uniform accommodation strategy. As Premier Wen Jiabao said to Malaysian journalists, also in April 2011, the Sino-Malaysian "territorial and naval disputes should be settled through peaceful negotiations. We do not support solving bilateral issues through multilateral negotiations. This will make the problem more difficult and more complicated."[40] However, during the ASEAN summit meeting the following month, Vietnam, the Philippines, and Malaysia suggested that ASEAN conduct "internal negotiations" before bringing China into the equation.[41] These three neighbours of China thus sought to entangle ASEAN in the South China Sea disputes out of self-interests, rejecting China's offer of negotiations on a bilateral basis.

Tension in the South China Sea in the summer of 2011 reflected the intensity of Sino-American competition as well. Premier Nguyen Tan Dung reiterated Hanoi's claims to the Nansha Islands (Spratly Islands) on June 9, and Vietnamese live-fire exercises took place between June 13 and 14.[42] The Philippines sought to take the upper hand by changing the name of the South China Sea to the "West Philippine Sea."[43] In light of these developments, the United States proceeded with the scheduled Southeast Asia Cooperation against Terrorism (SEACAT) exercise with the Philippines and Malaysia.[44] Secretary of State Clinton, meanwhile, engaged in serious talks with Philippine foreign minister Albert del Rosario, and she emphasized that the United States would practise freedom of navigation in the South China Sea and honour its alliance commitments to the Philippines.[45] On July 8, with ardent US support, the Philippines informed China that it would submit territorial disputes to the United Nations for arbitration.[46] All of these made China anxious and caused it to view the United States as its major challenger in the South China Sea. Despite China's criticism of joint exercises between the United States and Southeast Asian countries, Michael Mullen, the seventeenth chairman of the Joint Chiefs of Staff, told his Chinese counterpart that the United States would continue conducting military training and joint exercises with other parties in the South China Sea.[47]

It was clear that between 2011 and 2012, China's uniform accommodation of weaker neighbours could not prevent their attempts to enhance cooperation with the United States. In October 2011, Vietnam and the Philippines concluded a naval memorandum on "mutual cooperation and information sharing," and the coast guards of both nations also established communication channels.[48] Vietnam supported the Philippines' proposal to construct a "peace zone" in the South China Sea as a means of territorial settlement, in accordance with international laws.[49] The United States, meanwhile, continued to strengthen its military forces in the region. In November, it began deploying troops to Australia (reaching a total of 2,500 by 2017) and sent more B-52 bombers, F-18 fighters, and RQ-4 Global Hawk unmanned surveillance aircraft to Darwin. US nuclear warships also conducted more military operations in Australia's coastal waters.[50] Vietnamese-Philippine cooperation and the new US deployments increased pressure on China. Deputy Foreign Minister Cui Tiankai commented on February 7, 2012: "Recent events in the Western Pacific Region have occurred in the Chinese neighbourhood. In other words, China does not make troubles for others across the vast ocean. Rather, problems have come to us."[51]

In early 2012, China maintained uniform strategies toward the Philippines, Vietnam, and Malaysia but reversed them from uniform accommodation to uniform coercion. China put pressure on the three countries to demonstrate its resolve vis-à-vis the United States. In April, China seized the opportunity that the Philippines' interception of Chinese fishing vessels presented to set a new policy course, sending "maritime surveillance ships" to protect fishing vessels from attack by Philippine warships. The resulting tensions led to further US involvement, in the form of joint exercises with the Philippines on April 16 and with Vietnam on April 23.[52] The US military operations did not deter China, however. On May 16, it began imposing sanctions on the Philippines. Most Chinese travel agencies suspended tours to the Philippines, and the Chinese General Administration of Customs imposed import restrictions on bananas from the Philippines.[53] On June 21, the State Council of the PRC approved the establishment of Sansha City to administer disputed territories in the South China Sea.[54]

US concerns about regional stability brought about its pivot to Asia, whereas from the Chinese perspective the pivot constituted new US efforts to change the balance of power in its own favour. China was deeply suspicious of underlying US intentions, and Assistant Foreign Minister

Le Yucheng observed that "any form of 'pivot' should be helpful in sustaining the balance rather than breaking it."[55] As long as the United States sustained its support for the Philippines, Vietnam, and Malaysia, China would apply uniform pressure on these weaker neighbours in order to demonstrate its high resolve to the United States. The Philippines sought a settlement through multilateral negotiations, whereas Malaysia was open to both multilateral and bilateral negotiations. On January 22, 2013, the Philippines submitted the South China Sea dispute to an international court and obtained ASEAN's support. China presented demands to the Philippines to withdraw its legal case and applied pressure on Malaysia to thwart ASEAN unity behind the Philippines.[56] In addition, China refused to withdraw its maritime surveillance ships from Huangyan Island, and sent more battleships to Ren'ai Island (the Second Thomas Shoal), which the Philippines claimed.[57]

More importantly, the Philippines-Vietnam-Malaysia united front triggered a more assertive Chinese response – that of land reclamation in the South China Sea. In February 2014, Malaysia, the Philippines, and Vietnam met to coordinate naval policy toward China. They unanimously opposed Chinese territorial claims based on the nine-dash line and called for an early conclusion to negotiations on a Code of Conduct in the South China Sea.[58] From the Chinese perspective, these actions were attempts to coordinate with the US pivot to Asia. Accordingly, a uniform coercive policy toward these weaker neighbours would project a strong Chinese image vis-à-vis the United States. In May 2014, China and Vietnam sent more than a hundred ships during the dispute over moving the Chinese "Haiyang Shiyou 981 oil platform."[59] During the standoff, China began reclaiming submerged features of Chigua Island, which the Philippines had claimed.[60] Chinese military infrastructure quickly developed projection capabilities in the South China Sea. The United States was acutely aware of China's strength, and Secretary of Defense Ash Carter condemned the reclamation of over 2,000 square miles of land within eighteen months, to which China responded that "our [construction] has been lagging, whereas other parties have conducted their constructions for one or two decades. We have just started ... Our limited construction will soon end."[61] In the spring of 2016, China completed a 3,000-metre airstrip on Yongshu Island and a 2,000-metre one on Chigua Island, which would enable China to deploy fighters and fighter-bombers.[62] China's land reclamation not only exerted pressure on its weaker neighbours but also demonstrated its resolve to the United States.

Neither the United States nor the weaker Asian powers were able to prevent Chinese land reclamations, but China was unable to drive the United States from the South China Sea through uniform pressures. Meanwhile, Chinese pressure on its weaker neighbours gave them incentives to strengthen defence ties with the United States. A uniform accommodation strategy would therefore be needed once the airstrip projects were completed. Indeed, China considered a shift in regional diplomacy in the summer of 2014, and that August it proposed a "dual-track" approach to maritime settlement whereby China would solve territorial disputes through bilateral negotiations with other claimants but maintain peace and stability in the South China Sea with all ASEAN countries.[63] This new policy course suggested that China would be willing to discuss territorial disputes in certain multilateral contexts. If peace and stability were to be maintained by China and all ASEAN countries, then China would exercise self-restraint, such as non-use of force, toward a settlement in the South China Sea. Of course, the terms of a peaceful settlement would have to be clarified and agreed to by all relevant parties during China-ASEAN negotiations. The dual-track approach did not have an immediate impact. On the one hand, the United States continued to work on cooperation with the regional united front directed against China. On the other, China did not finish its land reclamation projects in the South China Sea until March 2016. China therefore had to look for new opportunities to work out its uniform accommodation strategy.

Rodrigo Duterte's inauguration as the new president of the Philippines provided China with such an opportunity. Unlike the former president, Benigno Aquino III, Duterte neither implemented the South China Sea Arbitration (*Philippines v. China*) nor maintained the scale of the Philippines' joint military exercises with the United States. These policies significantly improved Sino-Philippine relations and paved the way for Chinese regional accommodation. China began offering training assistance to the Philippine Coast Guard,[64] and it promised to provide $3.4 billion for at least three infrastructure programs in the Philippines.[65] Chinese compromises with Vietnam and Malaysia followed immediately. The Chinese and Vietnamese defence ministers held cordial talks in Beijing and promised to advance cooperation in all aspects and effectively manage their differences.[66] Malaysian premier Najib Razak also paid a visit to China, with the object of promoting economic and defence relationships. Malaysia would purchase four warships from China and allow the first Chinese submarine to exploit the Malaysian docking site.[67] By January 2017, the transformation of China's strategy from uniform coercion to uniform accommodation was complete.

The Declaration of the Conduct (DOC), jointly announced by China and ASEAN in 2002, did not satisfy the ASEAN requirement of maintaining regional stability because the contracting parties deliberately avoided binding commitment to the declaration. Therefore, the Philippines, Vietnam, and Malaysia called for negotiations over binding agreements toward a Code of Conduct (COC) in the South China Sea. China agreed to enter the negotiations in March 2017,[68] and a "framework agreement of the COC" was concluded in May.[69] In August 2017, China proposed negotiations over specific terms of the COC no later than the end of the year. Of course, China had some concerns over "external interventions," and it also suggested "general stability in the South China Sea" as a precondition of negotiations.[70] Despite these concerns, China's participation in a multilateral framework with its three weaker neighbours demonstrated its willingness to accommodate them in a uniform way. As President Xi Jinping told President Duterte, China would "further promote a Chinese-ASEAN community of shared future to establish itself as the model for an Asian community of shared future."[71] In October 2017, Defence Minister Chang Wanquan held talks with ASEAN defence ministers and described China and ASEAN as "a natural community of shared future." China would promote joint naval exercises, anti-terrorist cooperation, and defence communication with ASEAN members.[72] Not only the Philippines but also Vietnam was the target of Chinese accommodation. During his visit to Vietnam in November, Xi regarded the Sino-Vietnamese friendship as "unbreakable" and "steadfast."[73] The joint statement released during Xi's visit stated that both sides would comprehensively enforce the terms of the DOC and reach agreement on the COC as early as possible. To achieve peace and stability in the South China Sea, both sides expressed their willingness to avoid any actions that would complicate or escalate the situation.[74]

Between 2017 and 2018, the United States enhanced its naval and air strength in the West Pacific. According to Secretary of Defense James Mattis, the United States considered China its strategic competitor due to Chinese military presence in the South China Sea.[75] Meanwhile, the United States encouraged Japan to provide more digital reconnaissance equipment to the Philippines and Vietnam.[76] China has not yet solved security problems with its neighbours. US support for these neighbours enhanced their positions during negotiations with the Chinese over the COC, making the negotiations more difficult. As the chairperson of the Foreign Affairs

Committee of the National People's Congress, Fu Ying, pointed out, "the United States armed forces in the Asia-Pacific have been clearly directed against China. The United States has strengthened its alignment relationships and military networks in the surrounding area of the South China Sea." The US military posture, according to Fu, brought about "Chinese concerns of the broken balance of forces in the South China Sea."[77] Indeed, in the South China Sea, US military strength has far exceeded that of China, the Philippines, Vietnam, and Malaysia combined. When asked about the US position on Chinese land reclamation, General Kenneth F. McKenzie Jr., then director of the Joint Staff, stated that "the United States has had extensive experience of destroying small islands in the West Pacific."[78] He might have been referring to American victories over Japan during the Second World War, but the historical analogy implied that the United States could take preventive action against the Chinese naval and air forces. In June 2019, the United States delivered eight, six, and twelve unmanned aerial vehicles (UAV) to the Philippines, Vietnam, and Malaysia, respectively, which would be used to enhance the recipients' reconnaissance capabilities.[79] The US defence cooperation with these countries implied a more serious US-China competition in the South China Sea.

As additional accommodation of weaker neighbours by China in the face of American pressure could be interpreted as a sign of weakness, China adopted a uniform strategy of status quo maintenance in October 2018. It did not propose new forms of accommodation but reiterated its earlier proposals for further talks. China suggested establishing defence communication mechanisms with the Philippines, Vietnam, and Malaysia to avoid accidents in the sea or in the air.[80] In July 2019, the PLA navy conducted joint naval exercises in Qingdao with six ASEAN members, including these three countries.[81] Later, China suggested "institutional" arrangements for military exercises with ASEAN members in the South China Sea.[82] At a China-ASEAN meeting in June 2021, Foreign Minister Wang Yi urged all relevant parties to "exercise self-restraint and avoid unilateral actions."[83] The objective of China's uniform status quo maintenance strategy toward the Philippines, Vietnam, and Malaysia was to weaken the influence of "extra-regional powers" in the South China Sea. As Premier Li Keqiang put it in November 2019, China and ASEAN members should "take care of ourselves" and "act as the drivers of negotiations with a view to exclude interruptions."[84] In November 2020, he emphasized again that China and ASEAN should make progress on the negotiations over the COC in order to "demonstrate to the international society that we have the wisdom and capacity ... to maintain peace and stability in the South China Sea."[85] Thus, the main policy objective of China's uniform strategies toward weaker neighbours was to send consistent signals to the "international society" that Chinese neighbours would not seek further defence cooperation with the United States.

The Chinese conduct in the South China Sea conforms to the hypotheses of the regional competition theory. The United States, China's only regional competitor, contributed to China's use of uniform strategies toward its weaker neighbours Vietnam, the Philippines, and Malaysia: accommodation until 2012, pressure between 2012 and 2016, back to accommodation in 2017, and maintenance of the status quo after 2018. China's South China Sea policy thus reflected its attempts to calibrate its policies toward different neighbours from a regional perspective.

Selective Strategies in South Asia

US Involvement in South Asia

The United States was also a competitor of China in South Asia. In the aftermath of the terrorist attacks of September 11, 2001, it exploited Pakistan's territories to launch invasions of Afghanistan, deploying air forces and using three military bases in Pakistan for various purposes,[86] as well as providing Pakistan with six C-130 transports.[87] In March 2004, the United States accorded Pakistan special treatment as a "non-NATO allied state." In the ensuing five years, it committed to aid of $3 billion and abatement of a debt of $1.5 billion.[88] In 2006, it sold $370 million worth of missiles to Pakistan, including 50 submarine-launched missiles, 50 surface-launched missiles, and 30 air-launched missiles.[89] In 2007, it provided a lease agreement on 26 Bell 412EP helicopters for Pakistani air training.[90] Between 2001 and 2009, the United States also provided Pakistan with 6 surveillance radars, 18 newly equipped F-16 fighters, 60 F-16A/B upgrade assemblies, 20 reconditioned AH-1F Cobra attack helicopters, 6 reconditioned C-130E transports, 8 reconditioned P-3C Orion turboprop aircraft, 115 M-109 self-propelled guns, and 2,007 BGM-71 anti-tank missiles.[91]

Indian support of US military operations in Afghanistan also resulted in generous US aid packages. In 2002, the United States provided India with eight long-range radar systems and conducted its first military exercise with India.[92] Between 2007 and 2008, US military equipment supplied to India amounted to $10 billion, covering twelve C-130J Super Hercules transports ($2 billion), eight P-8I long-range naval patrol aircraft ($2.1 billion), and ten C-17 Globemaster III strategic transports ($4.1 billion).[93] In addition, the United States permitted its allies Israel and Japan to provide military aid to India. In December 2001, Israel offered India the EL/M-2075 Phalcon, an airborne early warning and control radar system that could detect sixty objects within 400 kilometres.[94] Israel also provided India with naval Barak surface-to-air missiles and unmanned reconnaissance aircraft.[95] India also became the largest recipient of Japanese loans between 2004 and 2006.[96]

The changing situation in Afghanistan and the rise of China contributed to the United States' new policy toward South Asia. During the war in Afghanistan, the United States was greatly concerned about Pakistan's secret cooperation with Al-Qaeda and cut off aid to Pakistan in July 2011. Given the Kashmir dispute, the decline in US-Pakistan relations enhanced cooperation between the United States and India, and both countries signed a landmark defence agreement in August 2016. According to the Logistics Exchange Memorandum of Agreement, both sides would exchange logistics support and supplies and services such as food, water, fuel, spare parts, repairs, transportation, communication, and medical services between their armed forces.[97] In September 2017, the United States agreed to provide India with an electromagnetic aircraft launch system, which had been recently equipped for US naval forces.[98] In recent years, US ally Israel provided India with military hardware, in the amount of $1 billion annually, with 131 land-to-air missiles.[99] The Indo-Israeli deal would have been impossible without prior understandings with the United States. Tensions between the United States and Russia led to US sanctions against sovereign countries that had received Russian arms, but, according to the US Department of Commerce, the United States would give India privileges similar to those accorded to NATO allies. The US export control policy suggested that India could get access to US military hardware despite its extensive military cooperation with Russia.[100]

India had territorial disputes with both Pakistan and China, whereas Pakistan and China maintained their close cooperation. US South Asia policy therefore reflected the Sino-American competition to a greater extent. Moreover, China's ascent provided a new foundation for cooperation between the United States and India. The US economic growth rate was lower than that of China, but India was also catching up to China with respect to relative growth. US-India cooperation would offset the impact of China's rise on the United States and, for India, counterbalance the Sino-Indian power gap. That Sino-American competition in South Asia would be of greater importance to both sides, as suggested by the US switch from an Asia-Pacific strategy to an Indo-Pacific strategy.

Sino-Russian Competition in South Asia

Unlike in the South China Sea, where the United States was China's sole competitor, China had a second competitor in South Asia – Russia. The Sino-Russian "partnership of strategic coordination" did not amount to an alliance relationship. Rather, both sides had different concerns with respect to Central Asia. In August 2006, China provided $300 million in loans to Turkmenistan, on favourable terms over a period of two decades, in exchange for annual gas imports of 30 billion cubic metres. In June 2010, China contracted with Uzbekistan for annual gas imports of 10 billion cubic metres. Between 2017 and 2018, according to agreements between China and Kazakhstan, China annual gas imports would reach 5 to 10 billion cubic metres. Consequently, China and Russia would have equal shares of the gas export market of Central Asian countries. This market division would negatively affect Sino-Russian negotiations over the price of Russian gas exports to China and enable Central Asia to develop independent economic and political lines vis-à-vis Russia.[101] China's sharing in the Central Asia market, therefore, was not always compatible with Russian interests.[102] In January 2022, Russia and China once again demonstrated different positions over the domestic unrest in Kazakhstan. According to Russia, at the request of Kazakhstan, Russia and its allies in the Collective Security Treaty Organization (CSTO) sent armed forces to maintain peace and stability in Kazakhstan. In response, China emphasized "respecting Kazakhstan's sovereignty" as a precondition for China to express support for the CSTO's military operations. Meanwhile, China suggested that the Shanghai Cooperation Organization and the CSTO should "strengthen cooperation and coordination."[103] Russia's silence on China's precondition and suggestion imply concern over Chinese involvement in Kazakhstan. Russia should hence cooperate with China, while at the same time avoiding complete dependency.

India was the most likely candidate for great power status in the Chinese neighbourhood and thus became an alternative linchpin for Russia's Asia policy. Russian aid to India was on a large scale over an extended time period. In February 2008, both sides concluded a ten-year defence agreement under which Russia would provide four to five civilian nuclear power plants and transfer pertinent technologies.[104] In addition to economic aid, Russian military aid played a critical role in the Indian arsenal. Between 2001 and 2003, Russia promised to give India the *Admiral Gorshkov* aircraft

Table 5.2 Chinese and Indian percentage shares of Russian arms sales, 2003–10

Year	*China*	*India*
2003	44.2	35.8
2004	46.5	21.3
2005	65.0	13.7
2006	30.6	20.5
2007	20.0	22.2
2008	19.4	19.6
2009	13.1	29.4
2010	10.0	32.4

Source: Ma Jianguang, *E'luosi duiwai junshi jishu hezuo: xianzhuang yu qianzhan* [Russia's foreign technological cooperation: current situations and future trends] (Beijing: Guofang gongye chubanshe, 2013), 203.

carrier, 172 Su-30MKI aircraft, 6 IL-78 tanker aircraft, and 310 T-90 tanks.[105] In 2003, Russia provided India with a lease agreement for four long-range nuclear bombers and two nuclear submarines.[106] In 2006, both sides agreed to jointly produce 1,000 BrahMos cruise missiles within the next ten years.[107] Russia would grant licences for India to produce up to 600 T-90 tanks.[108] It completed 3 frigates for India between 2009 and 2010[109] and in 2012 delivered Mi-17V-5 helicopters and assembled 42 Su-30MKI aircraft for India.[110] During President Putin's visit to India in October 2018, Russia and India concluded an arms sales agreement in the amount of $5 billion. Russia would provide S-400 air defence systems for India to shoot down aircraft or cruise and ballistic missiles at different speeds.[111] In April 2019, India requested an additional 464 T-90MS tanks at a cost of $2 billion. In response, Russia extended the production licence of T-90 tanks in India.[112] Table 5.2 shows that Russian arms sales to India gradually accounted for a larger share of Russian arms exports. Andrei Nikolayev, head of the Duma Defence Committee, once pointed out that Russia would provide only defensive weapons to China but both defensive and offensive weapons to India.[113] The Russian-produced arms offset the Sino-Indian power gap. For instance, in 2009, India deployed 105 Su-30MKI to the eastern sector of the Sino-Indian disputed area.[114] In 2016, it deployed 100 Russian-Indian jointly produced BrahMos missiles to the northeast, directed against China.[115]

There were two aspects to the Sino-Russian competition in South Asia. First, Russia made significant efforts to enhance India's international status. Between 2015 and 2016, Russia and China took different positions on India's application for SCO membership, with Russia supporting it and China demurring.[116] With Russian support, India succeeded in joining the SCO.[117] The fact that the SCO members' joint communiqués ceased to mention United Nations reforms after 2018 suggests that India has become a more important factor in Sino-Russian relations in recent years.[118] Russia invariably expresses support for making India a permanent member of the UN Security Council, which is a far cry from Chinese ideas of future UN reforms. In view of the Sino-Indian security problems, the cooperation between Russia and India was partly directed against China. Second, Russia has not only delivered arms for Indian forces along the Sino-Indian border but also implicitly acknowledged India's positions in its territorial disputes with China. From the Indian perspective, disputed areas exist only in the western sector of the Sino-Indian border, whereas from the Chinese perspective, disputed areas extend from the western sector to the central sector and the eastern sector. In recent years, Russia has scarcely mentioned the central or the eastern sector of the disputed border but claimed to respect Sino-Indian efforts to deal with "the question of Ladakh" (i.e., the western sector).[119] Thus, China had only one regional competitor – the United States – in the South China Sea but two – the United States and Russia – in South Asia.

China's Selective Strategies

Backed by foreign assistance, India attempted to achieve greater power advantages over Pakistan and counterbalance Chinese power advantages. Accordingly, China developed distinctive policies toward India and Pakistan. From the Chinese perspective, Indian challenges were not urgent. In the Sino-Indian border area, India's numerical strength could be offset by China's advantages in missiles, geography, and transportation.[120] China had constructed five air bases, one large-scale railway network, and more than 58,000 kilometres of roads in Tibet.[121] Moreover, it could produce the most advanced weapons, whereas India depended on the United States and Russia for arms supplies. India was also constrained by the US-Pakistan alliance and cooperation between Russia and Pakistan.[122] With respect to India, therefore, China sought to maintain the status quo by concluding border agreements to avoid armed conflict. Meanwhile, China accommodated Pakistan's improvement of its capabilities vis-à-vis India, provided

Pakistan with military and economic aid, and shared the major costs of infrastructure construction in Pakistan. Thus, in South Asia, China's selective strategies offset Indian advantages over Pakistan, while maintaining its own advantages over India.

China's maintenance of the status quo with India had two aspects. First, China acknowledged Sikkim, occupied by India since 1975, as a part of the Republic of India. In 1994, it began to consider "taking flexible measures" on the status of Sikkim.[123] In April 2005, according to the Sino-Indian joint communiqué, China removed Sikkim as a source of Sino-Indian dispute, while India reiterated Chinese sovereign rights over Tibet.[124] Second, China and India concluded agreements on the maintenance of peace and tranquility along the line of actual control in Sino-Indian border areas. Willing to resolve border issues through peaceful negotiations before concluding a final border agreement, China would abide by the line of actual control and reduce the level of its armed forces.[125] In April 2000, China and India began negotiations to demarcate the line of actual control.[126] In July 2004, China reiterated its willingness to develop a stable, friendly, and reciprocal relationship with India in the long run.[127]

India's construction of infrastructure in the disputed area since 2017 had reduced China's power advantage. From 2017 onward, both countries engaged in a "construction race" on their respective sides of the line of actual control and blamed each other for undermining the status quo. Chinese road construction in 2017 led to Indian security concerns, and Indian troops crossed the border in Donglang (Doka La). In the aftermath of the standoff, China proposed three concrete objectives with respect to India: 1) non-digression of bilateral relations; 2) non-confrontation between the two states; and 3) management of their contradictions.[128] During a talk with Indian prime minister Narendra Modi in October 2019, President Xi Jinping emphasized the importance of "smoothly managing longstanding differences."[129] In December, both sides agreed to enhance defence communication along the border, increase the number of border points of contact, and further expand border trade.[130] In the summer of 2020, however, the Sino-Indian relationship soured again. Indian road construction became a source of Chinese grievances and led to another standoff. More importantly, the Indian military fired on the PLA in the western sector of the disputed area and thus, as the Chinese Foreign Ministry put it, "broke the tranquility in the border area since 1975."[131] During the standoff, China reiterated its stance of status quo maintenance through peaceful negotiations with India. According to the Sino-Indian joint press release in Moscow that September, both sides agreed to "follow the important consensus reached by the leaders of the two countries on the development of China-India relations, including not allowing the differences between the two countries to become disputes." "The foreign ministers of the two countries believe that the current situation in the border area is not in the interests of both sides. The border defence forces of the two countries should continue dialogue, disengage contact as soon as possible, maintain the necessary distance, and ease the situation on the ground."[132]

In contrast, China made considerable concessions to Pakistan. First, it offered extensive military aid. From the 1990s onward, it offered a few Type 85-2M tanks and helped Pakistan to design Al-Khalid tanks. In 2003, China and Pakistan jointly designed the FC-1 Fierce Dragon (JF-17 Thunder) fighter,[133] and in November 2006, they agreed to develop early-warning aircraft with long-range airborne early warning radars.[134] In November 2009, China agreed to provide at least thirty-six J-10 fighters and four destroyers,[135] and in March 2011, Pakistan purchased SD-10 missiles and radars and expressed its willingness to purchase 250 JF-17 fighters within five to ten years. China provided the capital base due to Pakistan's limited financial capacity to repay Chinese loans.[136] By February 2015, China had provided Pakistan with four ZDK-03 early-warning aircraft.[137] Between 2020 and 2021, it sold four modern frigates to Pakistan.[138] In addition, China frequently conducted joint military exercises with Pakistan. By September 2017, the two countries had conducted special joint air exercises at least twelve times. In the exercises, Chinese pilots used Pakistan's Mirage fighters, while Pakistani pilots used China's J-11 fighters. Each side considered the other side as the principal antagonist during air battles.[139] These joint exercises reflected a high level of strategic trust between the two countries.

Second, China provided economic aid to Pakistan. In the aftermath of the attack on the Indian Parliament in 2001, India claimed that the gunmen had acted under the guidance of Pakistan's intelligence agency. During this standoff, China not only supported Pakistan's application for membership in the SCO but also offered RMB100 million in assistance.[140] It provided Pakistan with a civilian nuclear power plant in November 2003,[141] and the Sino-Pakistani free trade agreement became operative in July 2007. Both sides agreed to remove all tariffs for 5,104 items within three years and to collect customs duty at 0–5 percent for another 3,942 items within five years.[142] Pakistan ran a deficit in trade with China, which it needed to address by using its limited foreign currency reserves. From November

2018 onward, however, the Sino-Pakistani trade agreement allowed Pakistan to use renminbi for bilateral trade, thereby preserving Pakistan's foreign currency reserves for other purposes.[143]

Finally, China incorporated its infrastructure capabilities into its Pakistan policy. Both sides agreed to accelerate construction of Gwadar Port in August 2001.[144] By 2009, China had paid over 70 percent of the port's construction costs,[145] and by February 2013, it had invested $220 million in Gwadar Port and China Overseas Holdings Limited obtained the franchise for its administration.[146] In June 2014, China offered financial support for construction of a 1,800-kilometre railway between Gwadar Port in Pakistan and the city of Kashi (Kashgar) in China's Xinjiang that would pass through Islamabad, Pakistan's capital.[147] Based on the railway project, in February 2016, China announced a $46 billion investment in the construction of the China-Pakistan Economic Corridor,[148] which by May 2020 was providing one-third of the total electrical power capacity in Pakistan.[149] The corridor passes through the disputed region of Kashmir, however, causing India to boycott the Belt and Road Summit held in Beijing in 2017.[150] China's determination to proceed with the China-Pakistan Economic Corridor despite India's objection reflected its strong resolve to adopt selective strategies toward India and Pakistan. During talks with Pakistani premier Imran Khan, Vice President Wang Qishan called Pakistan "the only all-weather strategic partner of China." Accordingly, China would "continuously promote the all-weather strategic partnership of mutual trust toward a closer community of a shared future in the new era."[151]

In recent years, China has not only strengthened its position in Pakistan but also offered friendship to Nepal. Like Pakistan, Nepal has also had territorial disputes with India. The amount of Chinese aid to Nepal exceeded that of India in 2016.[152] China and Nepal conducted their first military exercises in 2017.[153] Following the conclusion of Sino-Nepalese transportation agreements, Nepal's use of four Chinese naval ports and three Chinese land ports enabled it to reduce its trade dependency on India.[154] In December 2020, State Councillor and Defence Minister Wei Fenghe visited Nepal and expressed China's commitment to strengthening defence cooperation with Nepal in support of the latter's territorial integrity.[155] Thus, amid its competition with the United States and Russia, China developed distinctive policies toward three non-allies in South Asia, maintaining the status quo vis-à-vis India while making considerable concessions to Pakistan and Nepal by providing extensive military and economic aid. China's selective strategies thus maintained its advantages over India and improved China's strategic environment.

Because China enjoyed tremendous advantages over its weaker neighbours in Asia, records of Chinese regional diplomacy provide opportunities for scholars to develop a theory of asymmetric statecraft. The regional competition theory not only explains Chinese historical behaviour but also provides guidance in understanding Chinese regional practice in recent years. Upholding the principle of non-alignment, Chinese Communist Party (CCP) Politburo member Yang Jiechi stated in November 2017 that "it is impractical [for a state] to seek absolute security based on the Cold War mentality and military alliances." Therefore, China should "take a new approach to developing international relations with communication, not confrontation, and with partnership, not alliance."[156] In this situation, how to engage with multiple weaker non-allied neighbours has been and will continue to be the key question in Chinese regional diplomacy. The regional competition theory offers three policy insights.

First, China will engage with different competitors in different regions. The rise of China does not resolve persistent Chinese security problems, but it does expand the power gap between China and most of its neighbours, and it also closes the gap between Chinese and American capabilities. Meanwhile, because the United States continues to possess considerable technological advantages over China, the American power projection in the Chinese neighbourhood will make Sino-American competition more intense. Sino-Russian relations will also be more complex. Tensions between the United States and Russia will result in enhanced Sino-Russian cooperation, but such cooperation is far from an alignment, as the two countries' interests are at odds in Central Asia. In light of India's potential to become a great power, Russia will seek further cooperation with India. In February 2018, Sergey Karaganov, economic and foreign policy adviser to President Putin, explained Russia's differing attitudes toward China and India: "There are some members of the Russian elite who are fearful of China ... but there is none of that with India."[157] Thus, the United States is China's only regional competitor in the South China Sea, whereas both the United States and Russia are its regional competitors in South Asia.

Second, given the above situation, China will adopt uniform strategies, in various forms, toward Vietnam, the Philippines, and Malaysia. Although China has territorial disputes with these weaker neighbours, they depend on the Chinese market to a great extent. As long as they avoid being used as US forward bases, Chinese policy will be one of uniform accommodation or status quo maintenance. Chinese accommodation of multiple weaker neighbours will consolidate and enhance cooperation, while uniform status quo maintenance will send a consistent message to the United States. The United States will have great difficulty projecting power in the Chinese neighbourhood, but uniform pressure on China's weaker neighbours cannot be ruled out if a new US "pivot" to Asia should occur in the future.

Third, China will adopt selective strategies toward India and Pakistan when the United States and Russia are Chinese competitors. China is rising relative to the United States, and India has the potential to become a great power. As China closes the gap between it and the United States, the United States will seek closer cooperation with India to counterbalance China. Meanwhile, as the gap between Chinese and Russian capabilities grows, Russia will have greater incentives to tilt toward India. At the time of writing, India does not possess independent offensive capabilities, but it obtains advanced offensive weapons from both the United States and Russia. Such military assistance will encourage India to seek a new balance of power vis-à-vis China, but Chinese selective strategies will maintain the existing Sino-Indian balance of power and thus contribute to peace and stability in South Asia.

Conclusion

Under what circumstances does China either treat weaker neighbours the same way (through uniform strategies) or differentiate among them through selective concessions or targeted coercion (selective strategies)? My argument, in a nutshell, is that the numbers of regional competitors and alignment relationships shape a great power's regional diplomacy with respect to its use of uniform strategies or selective strategies. In this book, I have proposed a regional competition theory, based on Chinese Cold War diplomacy, which I apply to explaining Chinese practices in the post–Cold War era. According to Gary King, Robert Keohane, and Sidney Verba, when a scholar, having argued that an important topic has been overlooked in the literature, then proceeds to contribute a systematic study to the area, this indeed constitutes a contribution.[1] I hope to have achieved this objective through this book. In this concluding chapter, I summarize major theoretical findings, identify the theoretical implications of historical research and area studies, and discuss future directions for research on asymmetric statecraft.

Major Theoretical Findings

International relations and foreign policy theories differ from each other, but major international relations theories – realism, liberalism, and constructivism – provide great insights into the development of foreign policy theories. In order to explain asymmetric statecraft, I draw on two major

Table C.1 Relationships between international relations and foreign policy theories

International relations theories	*Foreign policy theories*
Structural realism Offensive realism Defensive realism Institutional realism Liberal institutionalism	External threat theory
Neoclassical realism Two-level game theory Constructivism	Domestic-ideological theory

foreign policy theories – the external threat theory and the domestic-ideological theory – from the current literature. Table C.1 demonstrates the relationships between international relations and foreign policy theories. Asymmetric statecraft is a great power's particular form of foreign policy, and Chinese regional diplomacy is an important empirical foundation for a theory of asymmetric statecraft. The question, then, is how well the external threat theory and the domestic-ideological theory explain China's asymmetric statecraft. Under what circumstances has China dealt, and continues to deal, with multiple weaker neighbours through either uniform or selective strategies?

The core concept of the regional competition theory is that of a "regional competitor," which is a relational and regional concept. First, a regional competitor is a relational concept, which involves at least two actors. From a great power's perspective, its regional competitor is a state that does not share common objectives and has independent capabilities in the region. Realists and constructivists treat relational concepts as explaining variables.[2] Therefore, the regional competition theory suggests a possible synthesis of realism and constructivism toward a foreign policy theory when a relational concept becomes an explaining variable. Second, a regional competitor is a regional concept, which explains a great power's foreign policy toward multiple weaker states in its immediate neighbourhood. A great power is defined in terms of a region, and its competitor must be in the same region. The regional concept not only enables the regional competition theory to become more dynamic but also brings about a theory development based on solid empirical evidence from a regional context. To explain the use of uniform and selective strategies, this book examines China's engagement with its competitors in different regions in Asia during the Cold War and bases theory innovation on Chinese regional diplomacy. Adopting this theoretical approach paves the way for further discussion of the theoretical implications of historical research and area studies.

Theoretical Implications of Historical Research

One feature of the research presented in this book is that of theory development based on archival sources from different countries.[3] Marshalling historical evidence is crucial for testing, revisiting, and developing international relations theory. First, defining what is to be explained is the starting point of theory innovation. This book has sought to explain Chinese asymmetric statecraft toward multiple weaker neighbours. It therefore presented a historical overview of how China has engaged with weaker neighbours in East Asia, South Asia, and Indochina. Second, revisiting existing theories is a crucial step of theory development. Defining concepts begins with the revisiting process. Without solid historical knowledge, a scholar will have difficulty correctly drawing an abstract concept from complex realities. This book defines two key concepts based on historical research in archival sources: the regional competitors and alignment relationships. When and where did China form a competitive relationship with a particular country? When and where did China and another country share an expectation of mutual support in the event of war (i.e., an allied state)? Finally, examining specific causal relationships, based on historical research, offers empirical support for theory development. The external threat theory views a state's foreign policy as a response to external threat, defined mainly by the military strength of a state's main enemies. However, historical records show that, as a great power, China's regional diplomacy in maritime East Asia between 1958 and 1965 was shaped by a country without military capabilities (the Soviet Union). China's South Asia policy between 1959 and 1963 was shaped by both the United States and the Soviet Union, but neither of these two competitors possessed military strength in the region. The Sino-Soviet competition in Indochina between 1965 and 1968 was not based on their military balance in the region. The domestic-ideological theory examines domestic and ideological sources of foreign policy. However, historical records show that domestic-ideological conditions provided neither sufficient nor necessary conditions to explain China's regional diplomacy. For example, constant domestic-ideological priorities cannot fully explain China's selective strategies at a particular historical moment. Adding to international relations theories that focus on external threats, domestic politics, and ideology, this book has proposed the regional competition theory to explain China's regional diplomacy with respect to uniform strategies or selective strategies. The research on the evolution of Chinese regional diplomacy in different regions provides the empirical basis for evaluation of competing theories.

The next question, then, is: When will historical research be of greater significance to theory development? Research presented here suggests that historical research is important to understand a research puzzle, which exhibits three features. First, the number of cases, as the empirical basis of a research question, should be limited. In this scenario, a scholar can conduct empirical research for all important cases on an individual basis and examine causal relationships by taking an inductive approach. For example, available archival sources have revealed both continuities and changes in Chinese regional diplomacy between 1955 and 1975. According to the five caveats discussed in Chapter 1, I have examined all Chinese practices of asymmetric statecraft during this period. Through an examination of Chinese practices in three regions, an inductive approach to all major cases has provided an empirical basis for discussions of the features of Chinese asymmetric statecraft.

Second, subjective variables, such as (mis)perception, should play crucial roles in examining a research question. For example, defining a great power is based on military strength, but defining regional competition involves estimates of different states' objectives in a specific region. Archival research would play a more significant role in theory development when a theory examines the impact of a regional competitor (rather than a great power). Moreover, this book does not define an alignment relationship in accordance with formal alliance treaties. Rather, it defines an alignment as mutual expectation of support in the event of armed conflict. In other words, both key variables – the number of regional competitors and alignment relationships – involve how policy makers assess situations in subjective ways. These variables therefore make analyzing archival sources particularly useful and suitable for development of the regional competition theory.[4]

Third, empirical records should involve a policy process over an extended time period. Archival research would help scholars to address the following questions. Was there any real change at different historical moments? Are potential explanatory factors relatively independent or heavily intertwined? Addressing these questions would help scholars to assess existing theories and propose new hypotheses. For example, this book examines three cases of China's Cold War diplomacy. In each case, the time frame of Chinese regional practice, in terms of eight to twelve years, facilitates assessment of the explanatory power of competing theories. An investigation of policy practices in the time frame, by using the process tracing techniques, also enhances the validity of the regional competition theory.

Marshalling historical evidence for theory development requires understandings of competing theoretical approaches and archival sources from different countries. As Joseph S. Nye Jr. aptly observed, political scientists strive to generalize and develop theory, while historians probe the layers of complexity. Poor political science runs the risk of false simplicity, and poor history describes causality through irrelevant detail and confused complexity.[5] Analyzing Chinese asymmetric statecraft through the regional competition theory suggests the importance of testing, revisiting, and developing theories based on archival research. In particular, international relations scholars should identify the virtues of theoretical and historical research, choose inquiries that are of advantage to both theory and historical approaches, and deepen theoretical understandings by examining empirical sources. This would make theoretical arguments empirically more convincing. I hope the research presented in this book will contribute to an interdisciplinary inquiry into international relations theories through historical research.

Theoretical Implications of Area Studies

Another feature of the research presented in this book is theory development based on China studies. According to Alastair Iain Johnston, international relations theories are mainly developed based on the transatlantic region.[6] Do these theories offer explanations for empirical records elsewhere? Scholars have provided different answers to this crucial question. Some have given a positive answer. For example, as John Mearsheimer argues, China behaves in the same ways as other great powers in the West.[7] However, other scholars reflect limitations on the application of existing theories, based on the transatlantic region, to Asia. For instance, Barry Buzan and David C. Kang emphasize that regional orders in Asia are significantly different from those in the West.[8] Another important example is offered by Victoria Tin-bor Hui – the logics of domination in Chinese ancient history were different from the balance of power in European modern history.[9] In recent years, Amitav Acharya and his colleagues emphasize a transformation of international relations theory development from an American to a global discipline by integrating non-Western experiences into theory innovation.[10]

Despite their differences, all these scholars make contributions to international relations theory development. There are three major ways for scholars to develop theories based on area studies. In taking the first approach, scholars base empirical evidence on one region, evaluate the explanatory powers of competing theories, and reconstruct existing theories toward a better theory. For example, based on interwar European cases, Barry Posen seeks to understand the evolution of military doctrines by examining the virtues and limitations of balance of power theory and organization theory.[11] In taking the second approach, scholars base empirical evidence on one region, propose a new theory, and apply the theory to another region. For example, based on French, German, and American naval experiences, Robert Ross seeks to explain the success and failure of naval strategies and applies his theoretical frameworks to discuss trends of Chinese naval development.[12] In taking the third approach, scholars develop a new theory based on empirical evidence from more than one region. For example, based on American and Chinese archival sources, Thomas Christensen examines how domestic mobilization shapes foreign policy.[13] Interviews in China and Europe enable Avery Goldstein to analyze the central roles of nuclear deterrence in second-rank nuclear powers – China, Britain, and France.[14]

This book takes the first approach – evaluating existing theories and reconstructing a new theory; to put it in another way, this book seeks to "enrich" international relations theory by examining Chinese cases.[15] As discussed in the Introduction, traditional Chinese approaches of asymmetric statecraft shaped the People's Republic of China's leaders' mindset and practices of regional diplomacy in the Chinese neighbourhood. Contemporary scholarly communities in China have also discussed asymmetric statecraft through the "uniform-versus-selective" perspective. Relevant debates are ongoing, which suggests that Chinese policy makers engage with weaker neighbours through this perspective. Understanding the Chinese approach has motivated me to write this book. Meanwhile, debates on the uniform-versus-selective distinction have received little attention in the American, British, and German scholarly communities. Such different scholarly orientations would demonstrate that the research question concerning the uniform-versus-selective distinction exhibits strong Chinese features. This also suggests that Chinese regional diplomacy becomes a crucial empirical case for theory development of asymmetric statecraft. This book first applies the external threat and domestic-ideological theories to explain Chinese asymmetric statecraft, but, as Chapter 1 suggests, both theories have certain limitations in accounting for Chinese foreign policy. Therefore, the book proposes the regional competition theory to better explain Chinese asymmetric statecraft in its neighbourhood. In short, the book evaluates existing theories, reconstructs these theories, and proposes a new theory.

Would a theory based on Chinese cases be applicable elsewhere? Johnston provides extensive discussions on this important question. During his conversations with Chinese scholars, he identified his positions, seeking generalizable theories where possible. Acknowledging Chinese perspectives, he would extend theory applications as far as possible.[16] As he wrote to the Chinese scholarly community in a leading journal, "as a great power, China will become an essential case to develop theories of a great power's behavior, if China acts in the same way as other great powers. Otherwise, Chinese behavior can be used to revise traditional theories."[17] I agree with Johnston's positions. If other great powers behave in similar ways to China, then the regional competition theory improves the existing international relations theories and extends them toward a better and wider application. Otherwise, by Acharya's standard, the regional competition theory contributes to global international relations theory development. To what extent it can be applied elsewhere would be analyzed by scholars taking the second approach mentioned in the preceding paragraph (basing empirical evidence on one region, proposing a new theory, and applying the theory to another region), and comparing and contrasting Chinese cases with detailed empirical records elsewhere would be a fruitful area for future research.

Future Research on Asymmetric Statecraft

This book aims to open up the field of asymmetric statecraft for continued progress. There are methodological, empirical, and theoretical aspects for future research.

First, conducting comparative historical case studies presents two important challenges to causal analysis: 1) how to control variables based on a limited number of cases, and 2) how to examine the relatively independent impact of one variable on another variable. To deal with these challenges, this book has taken two measures. On the one hand, the regional competition theory refers to two independent variables – the number of regional competitors and alignment relationships – to explain asymmetric statecraft. The theory integrates the two independent variables in causal mechanisms in a succinct way. Thus, the limited number of independent variables increases the probability of successful variable control in identifying causal mechanisms. On the other hand, the two explaining variables are independent to a large extent. Chapters 2 and 3 show how China engaged with multiple weaker non-allies, while Chapter 4 focuses on Chinese approaches toward weaker allies. In each case, the alignment relationship was maintained, but the number of regional competitors varied. In other words, the changing number of regional competitors did not affect the alignment relationships. This also suggests a comparative advantage of basing the regional competition theory on Chinese cases. Of course, scholars should choose the most suitable approach to address a research question on their interests and make every effort to solve potential problems of the research methods of their choice. Therefore, it would be helpful to scholars to consider such potential virtues and limitations if they opt for other research methods to examine Chinese cases for theory development.

Second, from an empirical perspective, it would be valuable for scholars to explore further the regional competition theory's applications. On the one hand, as discussed above, the research question of the uniform-versus-selective distinction entails unique Chinese characteristics. As discussed in the Introduction, by constructing a theory of asymmetric statecraft, this book has sought to better explain China's regional diplomacy and shed light on contemporary debates over such diplomacy in the new era, thus basing its empirical foundations on Chinese experience. On the other hand, the theory of asymmetric statecraft would have more external validity if its empirical cases could be extended elsewhere. For this reason, as discussed in Chapter 1, this book has also generated hypotheses by using illustrative examples neither from Asia nor during the Cold War. Indeed, developing more generalizable theories would require a synthesis of international relations theories and area studies. Future comparative research requires close collaboration of experts in different fields, including China experts. Therefore, it would be fruitful for theoretical innovation if scholars with expertise in different areas work together to examine theoretical questions of their shared interests.

Finally, from a theoretical perspective, it would be fruitful to further explore factors that shape other forms of asymmetric statecraft. The uniform-versus-selective distinction presents only one form of asymmetric statecraft. Would external threat theory and domestic-ideological theory explain other forms of asymmetric statecraft? For example, how well do these theories explain whether a great power forms an alignment with a small/middle power? To what extent can these theories explain a great power's success or failure to create security ties among its weaker allied states? How does a great power drive a wedge between other powers in a competitive asymmetric alignment? Independent of this book, I am seeking to evaluate external threat theory and domestic-ideological theory in order to develop new theories to account for other types of asymmetric statecraft.[18] It is my hope that these projects will contribute to greater scholarly understanding of asymmetric statecraft and Chinese foreign policy.

Notes

Introduction: Understanding China's Regional Diplomacy

1 John King Fairbank, *China: The People's Middle Kingdom and the USA* (Cambridge, MA: Belknap Press of Harvard University Press, 1967).

2 John King Fairbank, "The People's Middle Kingdom," *Foreign Affairs* 44, 4 (1966): 574–76.

3 Zhonglianbu, ed., *Zhonglianbu sishinian, 1951–1991* [The CCP Central Liaison Department over forty years, 1951–1991], 1991, 154, available at China Documentation Center, Estelle and Melvin Gelman Library, George Washington University, Washington, DC.

4 Speech, Liu Huaqing at the Conference for Science and Technology of National Defense in 2000, February 1, 1989, in *Liu Huaqing junshi wenxuan* [Liu Huaqing's selected works on military affairs], vol. 2 (Beijing: Jiefangjun chubanshe, 2008), 22.

5 "Xi Jinping zai zhoubian waijiao gongzuo zuotanhui shang fabiao zhongyao jianghua" [Xi Jinping delivers an important speech at the conference on the diplomatic work with neighbouring countries], October 25, 2013, http://www.xinhuanet.com//politics/2013-10/25/c_117878897.htm.

6 Sun Ya'nan, "Douxian chuji bei Xiongnu zhanlue yanjiu" [A study of Douxian's strategy of invading the Northern Xiongnu], *Sunzi yanjiu* [*Sunzi Studies*] 4 (2018): 58–65.

7 Cui Mingde, "Lun Zhangsun Sheng 'li qiang he ruo' lilun tixi de goucheng jiqi zuoyong" [Theory and practice of Zhangsun Sheng's strategy of 'li qiang he ruo'], *Liaoning shifan daxue xuebao* [*Journal of Liaoning Normal University*] 5 (1994): 73–76.

8 Li Fang, "Dong Tujue de guifu yu Sui qianqi de bianzheng" [The eastern Turks' surrender and the border security of the early Sui Dynasty], *Xiyu yanjiu* [*Western Regions Studies*] 1 (2004): 4–10.

9 Zheng Ning, "'Bu zheng zhi guo' yu Ming chu guoji zhixu de goujian" ["Non-invasion countries" and the construction of the international order in the early Ming Dynasty], *Yanbian daxue xuebao* [*Journal of Yanbian University*] 5 (2016): 62–69.

10 Liu Shaoqi, *Lun guoji zhuyi yu minzu zhuyi* [Internationalism and nationalism] (Beijing: Renmin chubanshe, 1951).

11 Chen Si, "Mao Zedong yu 'Zizhi Tongjian'" [Mao Zedong and "Zizhi Tongjian"], April 24, 2019, http://dangshi.people.com.cn/n1/2019/0424/c85037-31046400.html; Liu Guijun, "Deng Xiaoping de zhixue zhidao" [Deng Xiaoping's way of studying], September 12, 2018, http://dangshi.people.com.cn/n1/2018/0912/c85037-30287886.html.

12 *Renmin ribao* Editorial Office, ed., *Xi Jinping yong dian* [Xi Jinping's reference to Chinese histories] (Beijing: Renmin ribao chubanshe, 2018), 164–65.

13 For more discussions, see Niu Jun, *Lengzhan shidai de Zhongguo zhanlue juece* [China's strategic decision-making during the Cold War] (Beijing: Shijie zhishi chubanshe, 2019), 24–31.

14 Shashi Bhushan Prasad, *The China Factor in Indo-Nepalese Relations, 1955–72: A Study of Linkage Phenomena* (New Delhi: Commonwealth, 1989), 76.

15 Taiwan is not an internationally acknowledged sovereign state. During the Cold War, Taipei withheld the "One China" principle and insisted on Chinese representation through the "Republic of China." The People's Republic of China has never acknowledged the so-called sovereignty of the "Republic of China."

16 Gu Dexin, "Cong zhanlue jiaodu kan Zhongguo yu Dongmeng de guanxi" [Sino-ASEAN relations from a strategic perspective], *Shijie jingji yu zhengzhi* [*World Economics and Politics*] 1 (1997): 21; Ye Zicheng, "Zhongguo shixing daguo waijiao zhanlue shizai bixing" [China should adopt a "major-power" diplomacy], *Shijie jingji yu zhengzhi* [*World Economics and Politics*] 1 (2000): 9–10; Zhuang Liwei, "Zhongguo guoji zhanlue zhong de Dongmeng keti" [ASEAN in China's international strategy], *Dangdai Yatai* [*Journal of Contemporary Asia-Pacific Studies*] 6 (2003): 22.

17 Long Xingchun, "Shilun Zhongguo yu Nanmeng duobian hezuo de jizhi yu jincheng" [The mechanisms and processes of China-SAARC relations], *Nanya yanjiu* [*South Asian Studies*] 4 (2009): 9.

18 Yan Xuetong, "Zhongguo dandang daguo zeren buyi chaoyue shili" [China should not assume a major power's responsibilities beyond its capabilities], *Cankao xiaoxi* [hereafter *RN*] [*Reference News*], March 20, 2018, 11.

19 Yuan Peng, "Guanyu goujian ZhongMei xinxing daguo guanxi de zhanlue sikao" [Strategic thoughts on constructing a new type of major-power relationship between China and the United States], *Xiandai guoji guanxi* [*Contemporary International Relations*] 5 (2012): 8; Shi Yinhong, "Guanyu Zhongguo de Yazhou Xitaipingyang zhanlue he Nanhai wenti" [China's West Pacific of Asia strategy and the South China Sea issue], *Dongnanya yanjiu* [*Southeast Asian Studies*] 5 (2016): 37.

20 Lu Jianren, "Yatai daguo zai Dongnanya diqu de liyi" [Interests of Asia-Pacific major powers in Southeast Asia], *Shijie jingji yu zhengzhi* [*World Economics and Politics*] 2 (2000): 45; Fu Ying, "Quanqiuhua jintui zhong de Zhongguo xuanze" [China's choices in the globalization era], March 1, 2018, https://finance.qq.com/a/20180301/036367.htm.

21 Yuan Zheng, "Meiguo chongfan Yatai yu Donghai, Nanhai wenti" [The US return to the Asia-Pacific region and the East China Sea and South China Sea issues], *Heping yu fazhan* [*Peace and Development*] 5 (2012): 8; Tang Yongsheng, Li Li, and Fang Ke, "Yatai zhanlue xingshi yanbian jiqi dui Zhongguo guojia an'quan de yingxiang" [The evolution of the Asia-Pacific strategic environment and its implications for Chinese national security], *Xiandai guoji guanxi* [*Contemporary International Relations*] 8 (2013): 6–7.

22 Li Chenyang, "Dui lengzhan hou Zhongguo yu Dongmeng guanxi de fansi" [Reflections on China-ASEAN relations in the post–Cold War era], *Waijiao pinglun* [*Foreign Affairs Review*] 4 (2012): 19.

23 Fu Xiaoqiang, "Yindu dui Zhongnanya diqu zhanlue pingxi" [India's strategies toward Central-South Asia], *Waijiao pinglun* [*Foreign Affairs Review*] 5 (2011): 38.

24 Tang Shiping and Zhang Yunling, "Zhongguo de diqu zhanlue" [China's regional strategy], *Shijie jingji yu zhengzhi* [*World Economics and Politics*] 6 (2004): 10.

25 Sun Xuefeng and Chen Hanxi, "Zhongguo diqu zhuyi zhengce de zhanlue xiaoying" [China's regional policy and its strategic consequences], *Shijie jingji yu zhengzhi* [*World Economics and Politics*] 5 (2006): 30.

26 Xue Li, "Renhou xiongzhang: Zhongguo zai Yazhou zhenghe zhong de juese" [A kind elder brother: China's role in Asian integration], *Shijie jingji yu zhengzhi* [*World Economics and Politics*] 10 (2008): 38.

27 Zhang Yunling, "Zhongguo de zhoubian quyuguan huigui yu xinzhixu goujian" [Recurrence of China's regional conception and new regional order], *Shijie jingji yu zhengzhi* [*World Economics and Politics*] 1 (2015): 15.

28 Zhang Yunling, "Zhongguo-Donmeng duihua 30 nian: xieshou gongchuang hezuo wenming" [Thirty years of China-ASEAN dialogue relations: working together to foster a cooperative culture], *Guoji wenti yanjiu* [*International Studies*] 3 (2021): 116.

29 Fang Changping and Zheng Ling, "Dongmeng gongtongti chengli beijing xia de Zhongguo Dongmeng guanxi" [The evolution of ASEAN community and China-ASEAN relations], *Guoji luntan* [*International Forum*] 6 (2017): 18.

30 Luo Shengrong and Zhao Qi, "Meiguo 'Yintai zhanlue' dui Zhongguo-Dongmeng gongjian '21 shiji haishang sichou zhilu' de tiaozhan yu yingdui" [Challenges facing China-ASEAN joint building of the "maritime silk road" and China's response in the context of America's Indo-Pacific strategy], *Heping yu fazhan* [*Peace and Development*] 3 (2021): 131.

31 Wu Zhicheng, "Zhongguo zhoubian waijiao xu gengjia zhongshi zhanlue mouhua" [China regional diplomacy should focus more on strategic plans], *Xiandai guoji guanxi* [*Contemporary International Relations*] 1 (2015): 26–27; Liu Feng, "Zhongguo Dongya anquan zhanlue zhuanbian jiqi jieshi" [China's security strategy toward East Asia], *Guoji zhengzhi kexue* [*Quarterly Journal of International Politics*] 3 (2016): 29–30.

32 Gao Cheng, "Zhoubian huanjing biandong dui Zhongguo jueqi de tiaozhan" [Challenges of the changing neighbourhood to China's rise], *Guoji wenti yanjiu* [*International Studies*] 5 (2013): 43–44.

33 Gao Cheng and Wang Zhen, "Zhongguo chayihua fenceng jinglue Dongnanya guojia tanxi" [An analysis of China's differentiated, multilayered strategic planning and management of Southeast Asian countries], *Shijie jingji yu zhengzhi* [*World Economics and Politics*] 12 (2019): 98–100.

34 Zhou Fangyin, "Meiguo de Yatai tongmeng tixi yu Zhongguo de yingdui" [The US Asia-Pacific alliance system and China's responses], *Shijie jingji yu zhengzhi* [*World Economics and Politics*] 11 (2013): 22.

35 Zhou Fangyin, "Zhoubian huanjing zouxiang yu Zhongguo de zhoubian zhanlue xuanze" [Regional development and China's regional strategic choices], *Waijiao pinglun* [*Foreign Affairs Review*] 1 (2014): 37–38.

36 Wei Ling, "Huoban guanxi zai shengji: Dongmeng guanqie, Zhongguo zeren yu diqu zhixu" [Upgrading partnerships again: ASEAN's concerns, Chinese responsibilities, and regional orders], *Guoji wenti yanjiu* [*International Studies*] 6 (2021): 52.

37 Qi Huaigao, "Zhongguo duobian hezuo tixi yu Meiguo shuangbian tongmeng tixi zai Dongya de maodun yu jianrong" [China's multilateral cooperative mechanism versus US

bilateral military alliances: contradictions and compatibility], *Guoji wenti yanjiu* [*International Studies*] 2 (2009): 13.

38 Qi Huaigao and Shi Yuanhua, "Zhongguo de zhoubian anquan tiaozhan yu dazhoubian waijiao zhanlue" [China's periphery security challenges and its pan-peripheral diplomatic strategy], *Shijie jingji yu zhengzhi* [*World Economics and Politics*] 6 (2013): 37–38.

39 Ling Shengli, "Quanqiu zhanlue shousuoqi yu Zhongguo 'qiangguo waijiao' xinzhengcheng" [The global strategic retrenchment period and a new journey for China's great power diplomacy], *Yatai anquan yu haiyang yanjiu* [*Asia-Pacific Security and Maritime Affairs*] 3 (2021): 14–15.

Chapter 1: A Regional Competition Theory of Asymmetric Statecraft

1 David A. Baldwin, "Power and Social Exchange," *American Political Science Review* 72, 4 (1978): 1234–38.

2 Raymond Aron, *Peace and War: A Theory of International Relations* (Garden City, NY: Doubleday, 1966), 83; Hedley Bull, *The Anarchical Society: A Study of Order in World Politics* (New York: Palgrave Macmillan, 2002), 194–96; Jack S. Levy, *War in the Modern Great Power System, 1495–1975* (Lexington: University Press of Kentucky, 1983), 16; John J. Mearsheimer, *The Tragedy of Great Power Politics* (New York: Norton, 2001), 30.

3 Arnold Wolfers, *The Small Powers and the Enforcement of Peace* (New Haven, CT: Yale Institute of International Studies, 1943), 3; Robert Rothstein, *Alliances and Small Powers* (New York: Columbia University Press, 1968), 24; Marshall R. Singer, *Weak States in a World of Powers: The Dynamics of International Relationships* (New York: Free Press, 1972), 273–75.

4 "Guns and Ghee: India's Armed Forces," *Economist* 420, 9008, September 24, 2016: n/a.

5 "Beipi buneng zhichi 10 tian 'jilie zhandou'" [(The Indian Forces are) unable to conduct sustained fighting more than 10 days], *Cankao xiaoxi* [*Reference News*] [hereafter *RN*], February 7, 2020, 6.

6 Brantly Womack, *Asymmetry and International Relationships* (Cambridge: Cambridge University Press, 2016), 10.

7 Huang Yuxing, "'Xiaoguo jituan' de zhengce xietiao" [Policy coordination of small power coalitions], *Shijie jingji yu zhengzhi* [*World Economics and Politics*] 3 (2018): 115–35.

8 Levy, *War in the Modern Great Power System,* 42–43.

9 Martin Wight, *Power Politics* (London: Royal Institute of International Affairs, 1978), 63; William C. Wohlforth, "U.S. Strategy in a Unipolar World," in *America Unrivaled: The Future of the Balance of Power,* ed. G. John Ikenberry (Ithaca, NY: Cornell University Press, 2002), 102.

10 Muthiah Alagappa, "Regionalism and Conflict Management: A Framework for Analysis," *Review of International Studies* 21, 4 (1995): 363.

11 Barry Buzan, *People, States, and Fear: The National Security Problem in International Relations* (Chapel Hill: University of North Carolina Press, 1983), 106; Barry Buzan, "Third World Regional Security in Structural and Historical Perspective," in *The Insecurity Dilemma: National Security of Third World States,* ed. Brian L. Job (Boulder, CO: Lynne Rienner, 1992), 168–69.

12 Wohlforth, "U.S. Strategy in a Unipolar World," 102.

13 Stephen G. Brooks and William C. Wohlforth, "American Primacy in Perspective," *Foreign Affairs* 81, 4 (2002): 24.
14 Samuel P. Huntington, "Lonely Superpower," *Foreign Affairs* 78, 2 (1999): 46.
15 Womack, *Asymmetry and International Relationships*, 126.
16 Brantly Womack, *China among Unequals: Asymmetric Foreign Relationships in Asia* (Singapore: World Scientific Press, 2010), 82.
17 For example, see Victor D. Cha, "Powerplay: Origins of the U.S. Alliance System in Asia," *International Security* 34, 3 (2009–10): 158–96.
18 Paul Kennedy, *Strategy and Diplomacy, 1870–1945: Eight Studies* (London and Boston: Allen and Unwin, 1983), 16; Stephen R. Rock, *Appeasement in International Politics* (Lexington: University Press of Kentucky, 2000), 12; Mearsheimer, *Tragedy of Great Power Politics*, 163–64; Alastair Iain Johnston and Robert S. Ross, eds., *Engaging China: The Management of an Emerging Power* (London/New York: Routledge, 1999), xii, xiv; Timothy Crawford, "Preventing Enemy Coalitions: How Wedge Strategies Shape Power Politics," *International Security* 35, 4 (2011): 160.
19 T.V. Paul, "The Accommodation of Rising Powers in World Politics," in *Accommodating Rising Powers: Past, Present, and Future*, ed. T.V. Paul (Cambridge: Cambridge University Press, 2016), 4–5.
20 Arnold Wolfers, *Discord and Collaboration: Essays on International Politics* (Baltimore: Johns Hopkins University Press, 1962), 140.
21 J. David Singer, "The Appeasement Option: Past and Future," in *Appeasing Fascism: Articles from the Wayne State University Conference on Munich after Fifty Years*, ed. Melvin Small and Otto Feinstein (Lanham, MD: University Press of America, 1991), 2.
22 Lawrence Freedman, ed., *Strategic Coercion: Concepts and Cases* (New York: Oxford University Press, 1998), 15.
23 Thomas C. Schelling, *Arms and Influence* (New Haven, CT: Yale University Press, 1966), 71–72; Alexander L. George and William E. Simons, eds., *The Limits of Coercive Diplomacy* (Boulder, CO: Westview Press, 1994), 8–9; Robert J. Art and Patrick M. Cronin, eds., *The United States and Coercive Diplomacy* (Washington, DC: United States Institute of Peace Press, 2003), 5–10, 361–73.
24 Alexander L. George and Richard Smoke, *Deterrence in American Foreign Policy: Theory and Practice* (New York: Columbia University Press, 1974), 537; John J. Mearsheimer, *Conventional Deterrence* (Ithaca, NY: Cornell University Press, 1983), 29–43.
25 Crawford defines selective accommodation as strategies that "mix carrots and sticks," in "Preventing Enemy Coalitions," 160.
26 My earlier research also examined China's policies toward Cambodia and Thailand between 1978 and 1982. However, I exclude this case for further discussion here given the limited access to available archival materials for examining Chinese policy decisions. See Yuxing Huang, "A Structural Theory of Multilateral Asymmetric Strategies: China's Strategies towards Neighbors before 1982," *Chinese Journal of International Politics* 8, 1 (2015): 89–113.
27 J.D. Armstrong, *Revolutionary Diplomacy: Chinese Foreign Policy and the United Front Doctrine* (Berkeley: University of California Press, 1977), 52.
28 During the Laotian civil war between 1959 and 1975, the PRC acknowledged the legitimacy of both the Laotian government and the Pathet Lao. In the history of the PRC's foreign relations, this was a unique case. This book does not discuss or explain this case.

29 Glenn H. Snyder, "Alliance Theory: A Neorealist First Cut," *Journal of International Affairs* 44, 1 (1990): 104–5.
30 Glenn H. Snyder, *Alliance Politics* (Ithaca, NY: Cornell University Press, 1997), 6.
31 Stephen M. Walt, *The Origins of Alliances* (Ithaca, NY: Cornell University Press, 1987), 1.
32 Surjit Mansingh, "China-Bhutan Relations," *China Report* 30, 2 (1994): 176–78.
33 Kenneth N. Waltz, *Theory of International Politics* (New York: McGraw-Hill, 1979), 105; Kenneth N. Waltz, "Evaluating Theories," *American Political Science Review* 91, 4 (1997): 915.
34 Mearsheimer, *Tragedy of Great Power Politics,* 2, 34.
35 Snyder, "Alliance Theory," 108; Walt, *Origins of Alliances,* 22; Charles L. Glaser, *Rational Theory of International Politics: The Logic of Competition and Cooperation* (Princeton, NJ: Princeton University Press, 2010), 3–12.
36 Stephen D. Krasner, "Regimes and the Limits of Realism: Regimes as Autonomous Variables," *International Organization* 36, 2 (1982): 497–510; Kai He, "Institutional Balancing and International Relations Theory: Economic Interdependence and Balance of Power Strategies in Southeast Asia," *European Journal of International Relations* 14, 3 (2008): 489–518.
37 Robert Axelrod and Robert O. Keohane, "Achieving Cooperation under Anarchy," *World Politics* 38, 1 (1985): 250; Lisa L. Martin, "Institutions and Cooperation: Sanctions during the Falkland Islands Conflict," *International Security* 16, 4 (1992): 143–78.
38 G. John Ikenberry, *After Victory: Institutions, Strategic Restraint, and the Rebuilding of Order after Major War* (Princeton, NJ: Princeton University Press, 2001), 5; G. John Ikenberry, "Reflections on *After Victory,*" *British Journal of Politics and International Relations* 21, 1 (2019): 9.
39 Thomas Pedersen, "Cooperative Hegemony: Power, Ideas and Institutions in Regional Integration," *Review of International Studies* 28, 4 (2002): 690–91.
40 Werner Levi, "Ideology, Interests, and Foreign Policy," *International Studies Quarterly* 14, 1 (1970): 4.
41 Jack Snyder, *Myths of Empire: Domestic Politics and International Ambition* (Ithaca, NY: Cornell University Press, 1991); Gideon Rose, "Neoclassical Realism and Theories of Foreign Policy," *World Politics* 51, 1 (1998): 151–52; Randall L. Schweller, "Unanswered Threats: A Neoclassical Realist Theory of Underbalancing," *International Security* 29, 2 (2004): 159–201; Steven E. Lobell, Norrin M. Ripsman, and Jeffrey W. Taliaferro, eds., *Neoclassical Realism, the State, and Foreign Policy* (Cambridge: Cambridge University Press, 2009).
42 Mark L. Haas, *The Ideological Origins of Great Power Politics, 1789–1989* (Ithaca, NY: Cornell University Press, 2005), 1–3; Thomas J. Christensen, *Worse Than a Monolith: Alliance Politics and Problems of Coercive Diplomacy in Asia* (Princeton, NJ: Princeton University Press, 2011).
43 Robert D. Putnam, "Diplomacy and Domestic Politics: The Logic of Two-Level Games," *International Organization* 42, 3 (1988): 434; Helen V. Milner, "Rationalizing Politics: The Emerging Synthesis of International, American and Comparative Politics," *International Organization* 52, 4 (1998): 785–86; Peter Trubowitz, *Politics and Strategy: Partisan Ambition and American Statecraft* (Princeton, NJ: Princeton University Press, 2011), 5, 16–43.
44 Judith Goldstein and Robert O. Keohane, eds., *Ideas and Foreign Policy* (Ithaca, NY: Cornell University Press, 1993); Richard Ned Lebow, "Constructive Realism," *International Studies Review* 6, 2 (2004): 346.
45 John M. Owen IV, "Transnational Liberalism and U.S. Primacy," *International Security* 26, 3 (2001–02): 122; Alastair Iain Johnston, *Cultural Realism: Strategic Culture and Grand Strategy in Chinese History* (Princeton, NJ: Princeton University Press, 1995).

46 David M. Lampton, *The Three Faces of Chinese Power: Might, Money, and Minds* (Berkeley: University of California Press, 2008), 169.

47 Robert S. Ross, "Introduction," in *Re-Examining the Cold War: U.S.-China Diplomacy, 1954–1973*, ed. Robert S. Ross and Jiang Changbin (Cambridge, MA: Harvard University Press, 2001), 8–9; Mayumi Itoh, *Pioneers of Sino-Japanese Relations: Liao and Takasaki* (New York: Palgrave Macmillan, 2012), 81–82, 87–88; Shu Guang Zhang, *Beijing's Economic Statecraft during the Cold War, 1949–1991* (Baltimore: Johns Hopkins University Press, 2014), 167.

48 A. Doak Barnett, *China and the Major Powers in East Asia* (Washington, DC: Brookings Institution, 1977), 97, 104, 122–23, 188–89; Akira Iriye, "Chinese-Japanese Relations, 1945–90," *China Quarterly* 124 (1990): 626–27.

49 Shu Guang Zhang, *Deterrence and Strategic Culture: Chinese-American Confrontations, 1949–1958* (Ithaca, NY: Cornell University Press, 1992), 228–29; M. Taylor Fravel, *Strong Borders, Secure Nation: Cooperation and Conflicts in China's Territorial Disputes* (Princeton, NJ: Princeton University Press, 2008), 243–44.

50 National Intelligence Estimate, January 5, 1956 (NIE 13-56), *Foreign Relations of the United States* [hereafter *FRUS*], *1955–1957*, vol. 3, *China*, https://history.state.gov/historicaldocuments/frus1955-57v03/d126.

51 Allen S. Whiting, *The Chinese Calculus of Deterrence: India and Indochina* (Ann Arbor: University of Michigan Press, 1975), 74.

52 John W. Garver, *Protracted Contest: Sino-Indian Rivalry in the Twentieth Century* (Seattle: University of Washington Press, 2001), 57.

53 M. Taylor Fravel, "Power Shifts and Escalation: Explaining China's Use of Force in Territorial Disputes," *International Security* 32, 3 (2007–08): 46–47.

54 Fravel, *Strong Borders, Secure Nation*, 175–76, 180, 183.

55 Memorandum for the Record, November 19, 1962, *FRUS, 1961–1963*, vol. 19, *South Asia*, https://history.state.gov/historicaldocuments/frus1961-63v19/d202.

56 Melvyn C. Goldstein, *A History of Modern Tibet*, vol. 2 (Berkeley: University of California Press, 2007), 418.

57 Letter, Chen to Zhou, December 9, 1955, in *Chen Yun wenji* [Chen Yun's collected works] [hereafter *CYWJ*], vol. 2 (Beijing: Zhongyang wenxian chubanshe, 2005), 693.

58 Fan Ming, *Xizang neibu zhizheng* [Internal rivalries in Tibet] (Hong Kong: Mingjing chubanshe, 2009), 196–97. Fan Ming used the Chinese measurement. 30 million jin = 15 million kilograms = 15,000 tons.

59 Robert S. Ross, *The Indochina Tangle: China's Vietnam Policy, 1975–1979* (New York: Columbia University Press, 1988), 4–5, 130–31; Robert S. Ross, "China and Cambodian Peace Process: The Value of Coercive Diplomacy," *Asian Survey* 31, 12 (1991): 1185.

60 Zhang, *Beijing's Economic Statecraft*, 227.

61 Anne Gilks, *The Breakdown of the Sino-Vietnamese Alliance, 1970–1979* (Berkeley: Institute of East Asian Studies, 1992), 37; Nicholas Khoo, *Collateral Damage: Sino-Soviet Rivalry and the Termination of the Sino-Vietnamese Alliance* (New York: Columbia University Press, 2011), 11–12.

62 Lien-Hang T. Nguyen, "The Sino-Vietnamese Split and the Indochina War, 1968–1975," in *The Third Indochina War: Conflict between China, Vietnam and Cambodia, 1972–79*, ed. Odd Arne Westad and Sophie Quinn-Judge (London/New York: Routledge, 2006), 25.

63 Qiang Zhai, "China and the Cambodian Conflict, 1970–1975," in *Behind the Bamboo Curtain: China, Vietnam, and the World beyond Asia*, ed. Priscilla Roberts (Washington, DC/Stanford, CA: Woodrow Wilson Center Press/Stanford University Press, 2006), 394.

64 Robert A. Scalapino, "Chinese Foreign Policy in 1979," in *China Briefing, 1980*, ed. Robert B. Oxnam and Richard C. Bush (Boulder, CO: Westview Press, 1980), 76–77; Brantly Womack, *China and Vietnam: The Politics of Asymmetry* (Cambridge: Cambridge University Press, 2006), 194; Xiaoming Zhang, *Deng Xiaoping's Long War: The Military Conflict between China and Vietnam, 1979–1991* (Chapel Hill: University of North Carolina Press, 2015).

65 Wang Taiping, ed., *Zhonghua renmin gongheguo waijiaoshi* [A diplomatic history of the People's Republic of China] [hereafter *WJS*], vol. 2 (Beijing: Shijie zhishi chubanshe, 1998), 36–37.

66 I.V. Gaĭduk, *The Soviet Union and the Vietnam War* (Chicago: I.R. Dee, 1996), 59, 61.

67 Memo, Kissinger to Nixon: Captured Communist Documents, July 16, 1970, Richard M. Nixon Presidential Library (RMNL), NSC Files, Cambodian Operations, box 588.

68 Ang Cheng Guan, *The Vietnam War from the Other Side: The Vietnamese Communists' Perspective* (London/New York: Routledge Curzon, 2002), 94–95.

69 Chen Jian, *China's Road to the Korean War: The Making of the Sino-American Confrontation* (New York: Columbia University Press, 1994), 213–14.

70 Lorenz M. Lüthi, *The Sino-Soviet Split, 1956–1966: Cold War in the Communist World* (Princeton, NJ: Princeton University Press, 2008), 81, 99.

71 Ibid., 347.

72 Ibid., 224.

73 Chen Jian, *Mao's China and the Cold War* (Chapel Hill: University of North Carolina Press, 2001), 235–37; Lüthi, *The Sino-Soviet Split*, 339; Lien-Hang T. Nguyen, *Hanoi's War: An International History of the War for Peace in Vietnam* (Chapel Hill: University of North Carolina Press, 2012), 119.

74 Alastair Iain Johnston, "China's Militarized Interstate Dispute Behavior 1949–1992: A First Cut at the Data," *China Quarterly* 153 (1998): 24.

75 Manjari Chatterjee Miller, *Wronged by Empire: Post-Imperial Ideology and Foreign Policy in India and China* (Stanford, CA: Stanford University Press, 2013), 81.

76 Chen Jian, *Mao's China and the Cold War*, 14, 173.

77 Chihiro Hosoya, "From the Yoshida Letter to the Nixon Shock," in *The United States and Japan in the Postwar World*, ed. Akira Iriye and Warren I. Cohen (Lexington: University Press of Kentucky, 1989), 30.

78 Thomas J. Christensen, "Windows and War: Trend Analysis and Beijing's Use of Force," in *New Directions in the Study of China's Foreign Policy*, ed. Alastair Iain Johnston and Robert S. Ross (Stanford, CA: Stanford University Press, 2006), 59–60.

79 Thomas J. Christensen, *Useful Adversaries: Grand Strategy, Domestic Mobilization, and Sino-American Conflict, 1947–1958* (Princeton, NJ: Princeton University Press, 1996), 6, 194–241.

80 Garver, *Protracted Contest*, 43–54; John W. Garver, "China's Decision for War with India in 1962," in Johnston and Ross, *New Directions in the Study of China's Foreign Policy*, 86–132.

81 Fravel, *Strong Borders, Secure Nation*, 70.

82 Morton A. Kaplan, "Problems of Theory Building and Theory Confirmation in International Politics," *World Politics* 14, 1 (1961): 16.

83 Hans J. Morgenthau, "A Political Theory of Foreign Aid," *American Political Science Review* 56, 2 (1962): 301–9.

84 Walt, *Origins of Alliances*, 225, 241–42.

85 David A. Baldwin, "Foreign Aid, Intervention, and Influence," *World Politics* 21, 3 (1969): 437.

86 Doris A. Graber, "Are Foreign Aid Objectives Attainable?" *Western Political Quarterly* 19, 1 (1966): 80.

87 Paul M. McGarr, *The Cold War in South Asia: Britain, the United States and the Indian Subcontinent, 1945–1965* (Cambridge: Cambridge University Press, 2013), 116–17.

88 Snyder, *Alliance Politics*, 9–10. For example, Chinese leaders felt pressures to fight for allies' interests during the Cold War. See Yuxing Huang, "China's Security and the Use of Force: Lessons from the Cold War," in *The Legacy of the Cold War: Perspectives on Security, Cooperation, and Conflict*, ed. Vojtech Mastny and Zhu Liqun (Lanham, MD: Rowman and Littlefield, Lexington Books, 2014), 277–322.

89 James D. Morrow, "The Strategic Setting of Choices: Signaling, Commitment, and Negotiation in International Relations," in *Strategic Choice and International Relations*, ed. David A. Lake and Robert Powell (Princeton, NJ: Princeton University Press, 1999), 106; Huang Yuxing, "Nengli fenyi yu junshi xiezuo" [Capability differentials and military coordination], *Shijie jingji yu zhengzhi* [*World Economics and Politics*] 5 (2021): 108–30.

90 Glenn H. Snyder, "The Security Dilemma in Alliance Politics," *World Politics* 36, 4 (1984): 466–67.

91 Patrick Morgan, *Deterrence Now* (Cambridge: Cambridge University Press, 2003), 80–81.

92 Speech, Brezhnev at the Central Committee of the Communist Party of the Soviet Union, December 12, 1966, in *E'luosi jiemi dang'an: ZhongSu guanxi* [Sino-Soviet relations: declassified documents from Russian archives], vol. 11, ed. Shen Zhihua (Shanghai: Dongfang chuban zhongxin, 2015), 248.

93 Robert Jervis argues that "a pattern of behavior" is one type of "indices." Robert Jervis, *The Logic of Images in International Relations* (Princeton, NJ: Princeton University Press, 1970), 18–19.

94 Randall Everest Newnham, *Economic Linkage in German-Polish Relations, 1918–1939* (Pittsburgh: Center for Russian and East European Studies, 2006), 22.

95 Józef Lipski, *Diplomat in Berlin, 1933–1939* (New York: Columbia University Press, 1968), 377, 395.

96 Kenneth N. Waltz, "The Origins of War in Neorealist Theory," in *The Origins and Prevention of Major Wars*, ed. Robert I. Rotberg and Theodore K. Rabb (Cambridge: Cambridge University Press, 1989), 45.

97 James D. Morrow, "Alliances and Asymmetry: An Alternative to the Capability Aggregation Model of Alliances," *American Journal of Political Science* 35, 4 (1991): 914–16.

98 Mancur Olson and Richard Zeckhauser, "An Economic Theory of Alliances," *Review of Economics and Statistics* 48, 3 (1966): 266–79.

99 Piotr Stefan Wandycz, *The Twilight of French Eastern Alliances, 1926–1936: French-Czechoslovak-Polish Relations from Locarno to the Remilitarization of the Rhineland* (Princeton, NJ: Princeton University Press, 1988), 147.

100 Waltz, *Theory of International Politics;* Kenneth N. Waltz, "International Politics Is Not Foreign Policy," *Security Studies* 6, 1 (1996) 54–57.

101 Glenn H. Snyder, "Process Variables in Neorealist Theory," *Security Studies* 5, 3 (1996): 173.

102 As will be discussed in Chapter 3, after 1962, China and Pakistan formed an alignment directed against India. The regional competition theory requires policy targets to be either

allied states or non-allied states. Therefore, the theory seeks to explain only China's South Asia policy between 1955 and 1962.

103 *Nie Rongzhen nianpu* [A chronicle of Nie Rongzhen's life] [hereafter *NRZNP*], vol. 1 (Beijing: Renmin chubanshe, 1999), 527; *Peng Dehuai nianpu* [A chronicle of Peng Dehuai's life] [hereafter *PDHNP*] (Beijing: Renmin chubanshe, 1998), 557, 631, 673–74.

104 The Secretary of State to the Embassy in Japan, October 14, 1953, *FRUS, 1952–1954,* vol. 14, *China and Japan,* https://history.state.gov/historicaldocuments/frus1952-54v14p2/d701; Memorandum of a Conversation, Department of State, Washington, December 9, 1957, *FRUS, 1955–1957,* vol. 3, *China,* https://history.state.gov/historicaldocuments/frus1955-57v03/d303; Memorandum of Conversation, July 11, 1961, *FRUS, 1961–1963,* vol. 19, *South Asia,* https://history.state.gov/historicaldocuments/frus1961-63v19/d30; Ang Cheng Guan, *The Vietnam War from the Other Side,* 94–95; Memo, Helms to Kissinger: Delivery of Arms and Ammunitions to the Cambodian Government, April 15, 1970, RMNL, NSC Files, Alexander M. Haig Chronological Files, box 965.

105 Wang Li et al., Dangdai Zhongguo de bingqi gongye [*The military industry of contemporary China*] (Beijing: Dangdai zhongguo chubanshe, 1993), 61–62; Telegram from the Embassy in India to the Department of State, October 25, 1962, *FRUS, 1961–1963,* vol. 19, *South Asia,* https://history.state.gov/historicaldocuments/frus1961-63v19/d180.

106 *NRZNP,* vol. 2, 1035.

107 *Zhongguo hangkong gongye dashiji, 1951–2011* [A chronicle of major events of the Chinese aviation industry, 1951–2011] [hereafter *HKDSJ*] (Beijing: Hangkong gongye chubanshe, 2011), 29.

108 Zhu Ying et al., *Su Yu zhuan* [Biography of Su Yu] (Beijing: Dangdai zhongguo chubanshe, 2000), 877; Han Huaizhi and Tan Jingqiao, eds., *Dangdai Zhongguo jundui de junshi gongzuo* [Military work of contemporary China's armed forces], vol. 2 (Beijing: Zhongguo shehui kexue chubanshe, 1989), 161.

109 According to Stephen Van Evera's list, the first nine criteria are as follows: 1) data richness; 2) extreme values on the independent variable, dependent variable, or condition variable; 3) large within-case variance in values on the independent, dependent, or condition variables; 4) divergence of predictions made of the case by competing theories; 5) the resemblance of case background conditions to the conditions of current policy problems; 6) prototypicality of case background conditions; 7) appropriateness for controlled comparison with other cases (mainly using Mill's method of difference); 8) outlier character; 9) intrinsic importance. Stephen Van Evera, *Guide to Methods for Students of Political Science* (Ithaca, NY: Cornell University Press, 1997), 77–78.

110 John W. Garver, "Sino-Indian Rapproachement and the Sino-Pakistan Entente," *Political Science Quarterly* 111, 2 (1996): 327–33.

111 Van Evera, *Guide to Methods for Students of Political Science,* 54.

112 John Gerring, *Case Study Research: Principles and Practices* (Cambridge: Cambridge University Press, 2007), 184.

113 James Mahoney, "Process Tracing and Historical Explanation," *Security Studies* 24, 2 (2015): 200–18.

114 Alexander L. George and Andrew Bennett, *Case Studies and Theory Development in the Social Sciences* (Cambridge, MA: MIT Press, 2005), 99–100; Marc Trachtenberg, *The Craft of International History: A Guide to Method* (Princeton, NJ: Princeton University Press, 2006).

115 Mahoney, "Process Tracing and Historical Explanation," 202.

116 Jack S. Levy, "Explaining Events and Developing Theories: History, Political Science, and the Analysis of International Relations," in *Bridges and Boundaries: Historians, Political Scientists, and the Study of International Relations,* ed. Colin Elman and Miriam Fendius Elman (Cambridge, MA: MIT Press, 2001), 59, 61.

Chapter 2: East Asia, 1955–65

1 Report by the CCP Investigation Department, May 12, 1950, in *E'luosi jiemi dang'an: ZhongSu guanxi* [Sino-Soviet relations: declassified documents from Russian archives] [hereafter *ZSGX*], vol. 2, ed. Shen Zhihua (Shanghai: Dongfang chuban zhongxin, 2015), 409.

2 Memo by the US Central Intelligence Agency, November 13, 1951, in *Meiguo dui Hua qingbao jiemi dang'an (1948–76)* [Declassified archives on US China policy (1948–76)], vol. 5, ed. Shen Zhihua (Beijing: Dongfang chubanshe, 2009), 241.

3 Shi Zhe, *Zai lishi juren shenbian: Shi Zhe huiyilu* [Side in the history of the giants: Shi Zhe's memoirs] (Beijing: Zhongyang wenxian chubanshe, 1991), 412.

4 Lin Li, *Wangshi suoyi* [Reminiscence of past events] (Beijing: Zhongyang wenxian chubanshe, 2006), 134.

5 "Treaty of Friendship, Alliance and Mutual Assistance between the Union of Soviet Socialist Republics and the People's Republic of China," February 14, 1950, http://www.ioc.u-tokyo.ac.jp/~worldjpn/documents/texts/docs/19500214.T1E.html.

6 *Zhongguo hangkong gongye dashiji, 1951–2011* [A chronicle of major events of the Chinese aviation industry, 1951–2011] [hereafter *HKDSJ*] (Beijing: Hangkong gongye chubanshe, 2011), 55, 73, 89. The Soviet designs of the MiG-21 were incomplete.

7 Wang Yazhi, *Peng Dehuai junshi canmou huiyi: 1950 niandai ZhongSu junshi guanxi jianzheng* [Memoirs of Peng Dehuai's secretary on Sino-Soviet military cooperation in the 1950s], ed. Shen Zhihua and Li Danhui (Shanghai: Fudan daxue chubanshe, 2009), 60–61, 95.

8 Liang Dongyuan, *596 mishi* [Stories behind China's first atomic bomb] (Wuhan: Hubei renmin chubanshe, 2007), 331–32.

9 Memo, Langer to Smith, June 25, 1951, *Foreign Relations of the United States* [hereafter *FRUS*], *1951,* vol. 3, *Korea and China, Part 2,* 1997. William L. Langer was the assistant director of the Central Intelligence Agency (CIA). Walter Bedell Smith was the director of the CIA.

10 Speech, Lei at the International Economic Conference, April 7, 1952, in *Zhonghua renmin gongheguo yu Yazhou guojia guanxi* [The People's Republic of China's relations with Asian countries], ed. Intelligence Department of the PRC Foreign Ministry (Beijing: 1954), available at China Foreign Affairs University Library, Beijing.

11 Shen Zhihua, *Lengzhan de zhuanxing: ZhongSu tongmeng de jianli yu yuandong geju bianhua* [The transformation of the Cold War: the formation of the Sino-Soviet alliance and the change of strategic environment in the Far East] (Beijing: Jiuzhou chubanshe, 2013), 196.

12 Jay Taylor, *The Generalissimo: Chiang Kai-shek and the Struggle for Modern China* (Cambridge, MA: Harvard University Press, 2009), 484.

13 Draft Statement of Policy Prepared by the National Security Council Planning Board, December 28, 1954, *FRUS, 1952–1954,* vol. 14, *China and Japan, Part I,* https://history.state.gov/historicaldocuments/frus1952-54v14p1/d459.

14 Shen Weiping, *8/23 Jinmen dapaozhan* [The shelling over Jinmen on August 23] (Jinan: Huanghe chubanshe, 2008), 76.

15 Minutes, Antonov's Talk with Zhang, September 21, 1958, in *ZSGX,* vol. 8, 241. Sergei Antonov was Soviet chargé d'affaires in China. Zhang Wentian was the PRC's deputy foreign minister.

16 Shen Weiping, *8/23 Jinmen dapaozhan,* 245.

17 Speech, Zhou at the Fourth Meeting of the First Chinese People's Consultative Conference, February 4, 1953, in *Zhonghua renmin gongheguo yu Yazhou guojia guanxi.*

18 *Riben wenti wenjian huibian* [hereafter *RBWT*] [Collected documents on Japan], vol. 1 (Beijing: Shijie zhishi chubanshe, 1955), 99.

19 Speech, Zhou on the United Front, July 6, 1952, Guangdong Provincial Archive, 204-4-33-001, 8.

20 Feng Ruiyun et al., *ZhongRi guanxishi* [A history of Sino-Japanese relations], vol. 3 (Beijing: Shehui kexue wenxian chubanshe, 2006), 87, 89.

21 Intelligence Department of the PRC Foreign Ministry, ed., *Meiguo qinzhan Taiwan wenti* [The question of American aggressions in Taiwan], vol. 2 (Beijing: 1954), available at China Foreign Affairs University Library, Beijing.

22 *Peng Dehuai nianpu* [A chronicle of Peng Dehuai's life] [hereafter *PDHNP*] (Beijing: Renmin chubanshe, 1998), 574–75.

23 Ibid., 582–83.

24 Nie Fengzhi, "Peihe luhaijun jiefang Yijiangshan dao" [In collaboration with the army and the navy to liberate the Yijiangshan Islands], in *Kongjun huiyi shiliao* [Recollections and historical materials of the Air Force] (Beijing: Jiefangjun chubanshe, 1992), 450.

25 *PDHNP,* 587–88.

26 Report by Liao Chengzhi, December 10, 1954, Tianjin Municipal Archive, X0053-C-000781, 1.

27 Draft Report by the PRC Foreign Trade Ministry, 1955, Zhejiang Provincial Archive, J127-002-066, 16.

28 Li De'an et al., *Zhou Enlai yu Riben pengyou men* [Zhou Enlai and his Japanese friends] (Beijing: Zhongyang wenxian chubanshe, 1992), 19.

29 Zhang Xiangshan, *ZhongRi guanxi guankui yu jianzheng* [Personal accounts on Sino-Japanese relations through a bamboo tube] (Beijing: Dangdai shijie chubanshe, 1998), 226–27.

30 Report, Zhou to Mao, February 2, 1955, Foreign Ministry Archive of the People's Republic of China (CFMA), 113-00224-01, 1–3.

31 Minutes, Zhou's Talk with Paranjpe, February 6, 1955, CFMA, 105-00057-01, 3. V.V. Paranjpe was the Indian ambassador to China.

32 *Zhonghua renmin gongheguo waijiao dang'an xuanbian* [Selected Foreign Ministry Archive of the People's Republic of China], vol. 2 (Beijing: Shijie zhishi chubanshe, 2007), 42.

33 Speech, Zhou at the Second Meeting of the First National People's Congress, July 30, 1955, in *Zhonghua renmin gongheguo duiwai guanxi wenjian ji* [hereafter *ZGDWGXWJ*] [Documents on foreign relations of the People's Republic of China] (Beijing: Shijie zhishi chubanshe, 1954–55), 330.

34 Minutes, Zhou's Talk with U Nu (Excerpt), April 15, 1955, in *Zhou Enlai nianpu, 1949–1976* [hereafter *ZELNP*] [A chronicle of Zhou Enlai's life, 1949–1976], vol. 1 (Beijing: Zhongyang wenxian chubanshe, 1997), 463–64.

35 Telegram, US Embassy in Djakarta to the Department of State, April 25, 1955, US National Archive II, College Park, MD, RG 59, Central Decimal File 1955–59, file 793, box 3917.

36 *PDHNP,* 606–7.

37 Minutes, Lomakin's Talk with Zhou, May 21, 1955, in *ZSGX,* vol. 5, 349.
38 Feng Ruiyun et al., *ZhongRi guanxishi,* vol. 3, 129.
39 Speech, Li at the Foreign Trade Ministerial Meeting, August 11, 1955, Henan Provincial Archive, J142-1-6, 4. Li Zheren was the PRC's deputy foreign trade minister.
40 Interview, Zhou's Talk with Japanese Correspondents, August 17, 1955, in *Riben wenti wenjian huibian* [hereafter *RBWT*] [Collected documents on Japan], vol. 2 (Beijing: Shijie zhishi chubanshe, 1958), 14.
41 *ZELNP,* vol. 1, 531.
42 Minutes, Yudin's Talk with Liu, January 10, 1956, in *ZSGX,* vol. 6, 143. Pavel F. Yudin was Soviet ambassador to China. Liu Shaoqi was the CCP vice chairman.
43 Speech, Mao at the Conference on Intellectuals, January 20, 1956, in "Mao Zedong sixiang wansui" [hereafter *MZDSX*] [Long live Mao Zedong thought] (1969), 33, available at Smith College Library, Northampton, MA.
44 Minutes, Zhou's Talk with Cheng (Excerpt), May 13, 1956, in *Mao Zedong sixiang xingcheng yu fazhan dashiji* [Chronicle of major events in the formation and evolution of Mao Zedong's thought] (Beijing: Zhongyang wenxian chubanshe, 2011), 637; Cheng Siyuan, *Wode huiyi* [My memoirs] (Beijing: Huayi chubanshe, 1994), 249. Cheng Siyuan was the intermediary between Beijing and former president of the "Republic of China" Li Zongren.
45 Minutes, Mao's Talk with Cao (Except), October 3, 1956, in *Mao Zedong nianpu, 1949–1976* [A chronicle of Mao Zedong's life, 1949–1976] [hereafter *MZDNP*], vol. 3 (Beijing: Zhongyang wenxian chubanshe, 2013), 4–5. Cao Juren was the intermediary between Beijing and Taipei.
46 Minutes, Lomakin's Talk with Zhou, May 21, 1955, *ZSGX,* vol. 5, 347–48.
47 Ji Ming, "Mao Zedong, Zhou Enlai wei zuguo tongyi yu Taiwan dangju de jiaowang" [Mao Zedong and Zhou Enlai approaching the Taiwan Authority for National Unification], in *Taihai fengyunlu* [The story over the Taiwan Strait], ed. Xu Shiquan (Beijing: Huayi chubanshe, 1998), 150.
48 Wu Xuexian et al., *Hongse Huarun* [The red "China resources"] (Beijing: Zhonghua shuju, 2010), 281–82.
49 Minutes, Mao's Talk with Sukarno (Excerpt), October 4, 1956, *MZDNP,* vol. 3, 5–6. Sukarno was president of Indonesia.
50 Report, Zhou's Talk with Katsumata, October 9, 1956, in *Zhanhou ZhongRi guanxi wenxian ji, 1945–1970* [Collected documents of Sino-Japanese relations in the postwar era, 1945–1970], ed. Tian Huan (Beijing: Zhongguo shehui kexue chubanshe, 1996), 294. Katsumata Seiichi was the head of JSP Diet Strategy Committee.
51 Minutes, Zhou's Talk with the Japanese Education Delegation (Excerpt), February 16, 1957, in *Zhou Enlai junshi huodong jishi, 1918–1975* [hereafter *ZELJSHDJS*] [A chronicle of Zhou Enlai's military activities], vol. 2 (Beijing: Zhongyang wenxian chubanshe, 2000), 417.
52 Minutes, Mao and Zhou's Talk with the JSP Delegation, April 21, 1957, Guizhou Provincial Archive, 1-1-1526, 6; Wu Xuewen, *Fengyu yinqing: wo suo jingli de ZhongRi guanxi* [Rain and sunshine: my personal experience in Sino-Japanese relations] (Beijing: Shijie zhishi chubanshe, 2002), 284.
53 Minutes, Zhou's Talk with Yudin (Excerpt), May 22, 1957, *ZELJSHDJS,* vol. 2, 423.
54 Minutes, Mao's Talk Voroshilov (Excerpt), May 25, 1957, *MZDNP,* vol. 3, 162. Kliment Voroshilov was the chairman of the Presidium of the Supreme Soviet of the Soviet Union.
55 Minutes, Zhou's Talk with Singh, October 14, 1957, CFMA, 113-00264-01, 126. Singh was Indian chargé d'affaires in China.

56 Zhongguo ZhongRi guanxishi xuehui, ed., *Youyi zhu chunqiu: Wei Xinzhongguo zuochu gongxian de Riben ren* [Friendship forever: Japanese contribution to the new China], vol. 1 (Beijing: Xinhua chubanshe, 2002), 374.
57 Minutes, Peng's Talk with the Japanese Veterans Delegation, July 1, 1957, Guizhou Provincial Archive, 1-1-1526, 7.
58 Speech, Chen to Directors of Foreign Trade Departments of Various Provinces (Excerpt), December 6, 1957, in Wu Xuexian et al., *Hongse Huarun,* 284.
59 Instruction, Zhu to Lei (Excerpt), December 16, 1957, in *Zhu De nianpu, xinbianben* [A chronicle of Zhu De's life, new edition], vol. 3 (Beijing: Zhongyang wenxian chubanshe, 2006), 1641–42. Lei Renmin was the PRC's deputy foreign trade minister.
60 Minutes, Mao's Talk with Yudin, February 28, 1958, in Lorenz M. Lüthi, *The Sino-Soviet Split, 1956–1966: Cold War in the Communist World* (Princeton, NJ: Princeton University Press, 2008), 96.
61 Instruction, Mao to Peng, March 8, 1958, in *Jianguo yilai Mao Zedong wengao* [hereafter *JGYLMZDWG*] [Manuscripts of Mao Zedong since the founding of the nation], vol. 7 (Beijing: Zhongyang wenxian chubanshe, 1992), 107.
62 Tian Huan, *Zhanhou ZhongRi guanxi wenxian ji, 1945–1970,* 103.
63 Feng Ruiyun et al., *ZhongRi guanxishi,* 154.
64 Minutes, Zhou's Talk with Nehru, March 1, 1956, CFMA, 105-00327-02, 6. Ratan Kumar Nehru was the Indian ambassador to China.
65 Letter, Wang to Johnson, January 14, 1958, in *ZGDWGXWJ* (1958), 89–90. Wang Bingnan was the PRC's ambassador to Poland.
66 Letter, Martin to Wang, March 12, 1958, in *ZGDWGXWJ* (1958), 92–93. Edwin Webb Martin was the first secretary of the US Embassy in the United Kingdom.
67 Mao's Speech Guideline at Chengdu Conference, March 9, 1958, in *JGYLMZDWG,* vol. 7, 110.
68 Speech, Zhou at Chengdu Conference (Excerpt), March 19, 1958, in *ZELNP,* vol. 2, 133.
69 Tian Huan, ed., *Zhanhou ZhongRi guanxishi nianbiao, 1945–1993* [A chronicle of major events of Sino-Japanese relations in the postwar era, 1945–1993] (Beijing: Zhongguo shehui kexue chubanshe, 1994), 105.
70 *ZGDWGXWJ* (1958), 271.
71 Minutes, Yudin's Talk with Zhou, April 15, 1958, in *ZSGX,* vol. 8, 32.
72 Speech, Zhou to the CCP Cadres of Guangzhou, July 10, 1958, Guizhou Provincial Archive, 1-1-1735, 6–8.
73 Speech, Wu to the CCP Cadres of Shaanxi Province, June 13, 1958, Guizhou Provincial Archive, 1-1-1735, 5–6. Wu Xiuquan was the PRC's deputy foreign minister.
74 *ZGDWGXWJ* (1958), 140.
75 Chen Xiaolu, "Chen Yi and China's Diplomacy," in *Toward a History of Chinese Communist Foreign Relations, 1920s–1960s,* ed. Michael H. Hunt and Niu Jun (Washington, DC: Woodrow Wilson Center Asia Program, 1992), 92.
76 *PDHNP,* 691–92.
77 Yang Chengwu, "Paoji Jinmen" [Shelling of Jinmen Islands], in *Zong canmoubu huiyi shiliao* [Recollections and historical materials of the headquarters of the General Staff] (Beijing: Jiefangjun chubanshe, 1995), 495.
78 Memo, Background Information and Recommendations Relating to the Situation in the Taiwan Straits, August 30, 1958, US National Archive II, College Park, MD, RG 59, Central Decimal File 1955–59, file 794, box 3976.

79 Yao Jun, ed., *Zhongguo hangkongshi* [A history of China's aviation] (Zhengzhou: Daxiang chubanshe, 1998), 301.
80 Yang Chengwu, "Paoji Jinmen," 498–99.
81 Shen Weiping, *8/23 Jinmen dapaozhan,* 167.
82 Sun Weitao, ed., *Liu Yalou jiangjun chuanqi* [The story of General Liu Yalou], vol. 1 (Beijing: Zhongguo wenhua chubanshe, 2010), 390.
83 Reference Materials on the 19th International Red Cross Committee's General Assembly, October 12, 1956, CFMA, 113-00264-01, 87.
84 Kong Hanbing, *Hanbing fang Luoming* [Kong Hanbing's interviews with Romulus Ioan Budura] (Shanghai: Shanghai renmin chubanshe, 2013), 60.
85 Memorandum from the Director of Intelligence and Research (Cumming) to the Under Secretary of State (Herter), November 29, 1957, *FRUS, 1955–1957,* vol. 3, *China,* https://history.state.gov/historicaldocuments/frus1955-57v03/d299. Hugh S. Cumming Jr. was director of intelligence and research. Christian A. Herter was the under secretary of state.
86 *Susiluofu yanlun xuan* [Selected speeches of Suslov], vol. 2 (Shanghai: Shanghai renmin chubanshe, 1976), 497.
87 Minutes, Zhou's Talk with Yudin (Excerpt), January 27, 1958, in *ZELNP,* vol. 2, 121–22.
88 Minutes, Krutikov's Talk with Zhou, February 1, 1958, in *ZSGX,* vol. 7, 393–94. Konstantin Krutikov was Soviet chargé d'affaires in China.
89 Telegram, US Embassy in Tokyo to the Department of State, June 20, 1958, US National Archive II, College Park, MD, RG 59, Central Decimal File 1955–59, file 692, box 2718.
90 Reference Materials by the Far East Division of the Soviet Foreign Ministry, December 9, 1960, in *ZSGX,* vol. 9, 251–52.
91 Zi Ding, *Li Qiang zhuan* [Biography of Li Qiang] (Beijing: Renmin chubanshe, 2004), 181.
92 Minutes of Conversation, Mao Zedong and Ambassador Yudin, July 22, 1958, Wilson Center Digital Archive, http://digitalarchive.wilsoncenter.org/document/116982.
93 Shen Zhihua, "Paoji jinmen: Sulian de yingdui yu ZhongSu fenqi" [Shelling over Jinmen: The Soviet Response and Sino-Soviet Differences], in *Jinmen: Neizhan yu lengzhan* [Jinmen: the civil war and the Cold War], ed. Shen Zhihua and Tang Qihua (Beijing: Jiuzhou chubanshe, 2010), 152.
94 Minutes, Zhou's Talk with Sudarikov (Excerpt), September 5, 1958, in *ZELNP,* vol. 2, 166. Nikolai G. Sudarikov was the Soviet counsellor in China.
95 Draft Report, "On the Trip of the Soviet Party-Governmental Delegation to the PRC," December 18, 1959, Wilson Center Digital Archive, http://digitalarchive.wilsoncenter.org/document/112989.
96 Speech, Mao Zedong at the Fifteenth Meeting of the Supreme State Council (Excerpt), September 5, 1958, Wilson Center Digital Archive, http://digitalarchive.wilsoncenter.org/document/117013.
97 Shen Weiping, *8/23 Jinmen dapaozhan,* 252.
98 Yang Chengwu, "Paoji Jinmen," 508.
99 Han Nianlong, ed., *Diplomacy of Contemporary China* (Hong Kong: New Horizon Press, 1990), 133–34.
100 *HKDSJ,* 66.
101 Minutes of Conversation, Mao Zedong and Ambassador Yudin, July 22, 1958, Wilson Center Digital Archive, http://digitalarchive.wilsoncenter.org/document/116982.
102 Telegram, Zhou to Mao (Excerpt), September 23, 1958; Telegram, Mao to Zhou (Excerpt), September 24, 1958, in *ZELJSHDJS,* vol. 2, 467–68.

103 *ZELNP,* vol. 2, 171–72.
104 Telegram from the Embassy in Poland to the Department of State, September 22, 1958, *FRUS, 1958–1969,* vol. 19, *China,* https://history.state.gov/historicaldocuments/frus1958-60v19/d120.
105 Shen Zhihua, "Paoji jinmen," 153–54.
106 Minutes, Antonov's Talk with Zhou, September 27, 1958, in *ZSGX,* vol. 8, 251; Shen Zhihua, "Paoji jinmen," 153–54.
107 Minutes, Antonov's Talk with Zhou, September 27, 1958, in *ZSGX,* vol. 8, 250.
108 *ZELNP,* vol. 2, 177–78.
109 *ZGDWGXWJ* (1958), 284; *RBWT,* vol. 3, 397.
110 Liu Shilong, *Xinzhongguo duiRi zhengce, 1949–1972* [The PRC's policy toward Japan, 1949–1972] (Beijing: Shijie zhishi chubanshe, 2020), 279–82.
111 *Heluxiaofu yanlun* [Collected speeches of Khrushchev], vol. 10 (Beijing: Shijie zhishi chubanshe, 1965), 571.
112 Record of Conversation between Soviet and Chinese Party Delegations, January 25, 1959, in *Xinzhongguo yu Sulian de gaoceng wanglai* [Interactions between the new China and the Soviet Union on the summit level], vol. 2, ed. Xu Xiaotian et al. (Changchun: Jilin renmin chubanshe, 2001), 545.
113 *HKDSJ,* 71; Liang Dongyuan, *596 mishi,* 332.
114 Liang Dongyuan, *596 mishi,* 141–42. The withdrawal occurred on August 23, 1959. The author mistakenly put the date as "August 23, 1960." For another source regarding the date, see Shen Zhihua, *Wunai de xuanze: lengzhan yu ZhongSu tongmeng de mingyun, 1945–1959* [Reluctant choices: the Cold War and the fate of the Sino-Soviet alliance, 1945–1959] (Beijing: Shehui kexue wenxian chubanshe, 2013), 719.
115 Liang Dongyuan, *596 mishi,* 332; Shen Zhihua, *Wunai de xuanze,* 718–19.
116 Discussion between N.S. Khrushchev and Mao Zedong, October 2, 1959, Wilson Center Digital Archive, http://digitalarchive.wilsoncenter.org/document/112088.
117 Minutes, Zhou's Talk with Matsumura (Excerpt), October 25, 1959, in *ZELJSHDJS,* vol. 2, 505–6. Matsumura Kenzo was the LDP's adviser.
118 Liu Shilong, *Xinzhongguo duiRi zhengce, 1949–1972,* 283–84.
119 *RBWT,* vol. 3, 98.
120 Statement by Asanuma Inejiro, July 24, 1954, in Intelligence Department of the PRC Foreign Ministry, *Meiguo qinzhan Taiwan wenti,* vol. 2.
121 Liu Deyou, *Shiguang zhilü: wo jingli de ZhongRi guanxi* [The time travel: my personal experience in Sino-Japanese relations] (Beijing: Shangwu yinshuguan, 1999), 334–36; Wang Junyan, *Liao Chengzhi zhuan* [Biography of Liao Chengzhi] (Beijing: Renmin chubanshe, 2006), 357.
122 Speech, Zhou to Cadres in Charge of Economic Policies, May 11, 1959, in *Zhou Enlai jingji wenxuan* [Zhou Enlai's selected works on economic affairs] (Beijing: Zhongyang wenxian chubanshe, 1993), 400.
123 Walter LaFeber, *The Clash: A History of U.S.-Japan Relations* (New York: W.W. Norton, 1997), 319.
124 Statement by the PRC Foreign Ministry, January 14, 1960, in *ZGDWGXWJ* (1960), 7.
125 Junshi kexueyuan junshi lishiyanjiusuo, ed., *Renmin Jiefangjun gaige fazhan 30 nian* [The reform and development of the People's Liberation Army over 30 years] (Beijing: Junshi kexue chubanshe, 2008), 17–18.

126 Minutes, Zhou's Talk with Chervonenko (Excerpt), January 19, 1960, in *ZELJSHDJS,* vol. 2, 517–18. Stepan Chervonenko was the Soviet ambassador to China.
127 Oral Message, Mao to Khrushchev, January 13, 1960, in *JGYLMZDWG,* vol. 9, 8.
128 Speech, Kang at the Meeting of the Warsaw Pact Political Consultative Committee, February 4, 1960, http://www.php.isn.ethz.ch/lory1.ethz.ch/collections/colltopice7f9-2.html?lng=en&id=16320&navinfo=16034. Kang Sheng was an alternative member of the CCP Politburo.
129 Speech, Lu at the Conference on Foreign Exports to Capitalist Countries, February 13, 1960, Fujian Provincial Archive, 0293-009-0003-0001, 2; *Deng Xiaoping nianpu, 1904–1974* [hereafter *DXPNP*] [A chronicle of Deng Xiaoping's life, 1904–1974], vol. 3 (Beijing: Zhongyang wenxian chubanshe, 2009), 1546–47. Lu Xuzhang was the PRC's deputy foreign trade minister.
130 Shen Weiping, *8/23 Jinmen dapaozhan,* 256.
131 *Dulesi yanlun xuanji* [Selected speeches of John F. Dulles] (Beijing: Shijie zhishi chubanshe, 1960), 451.
132 Pang Xianzhi and Jin Chongji, eds., *Mao Zedong zhuan, 1949–1976* [hereafter *MZDZ*] [Biography of Mao Zedong, 1949–1976] (Beijing: Zhongyang wenxian chubanshe, 2003), 880–81.
133 Speech, Zhou at the CCP Central Propaganda Department, November 10, 1958, Shanghai Municipal Archive, A23-1-544, 9–10.
134 Conlon Associates, *United States Foreign Policy: Asia* (Washington, DC: US Government Printing Office, 1959), 147, 153–55.
135 Chen Zhiqi, *Meiguo duihua zhengce sanshinian* [The US policy toward China over thirty years] (Taipei: Zhonghua ribaoshe, 1981), 189–91.
136 Report by the PRC Foreign Ministry, January 8, 1960, CFMA, 113-00377-01, 6.
137 Interview, Mao with Snow, in *Mao Zedong waijiao wenxuan* [hereafter *MZDWJ*] [Mao Zedong's selected works on diplomacy] (Beijing: Zhongyang wenxian chubanshe/Shijie zhishi chubanshe, 1994), 449. Edgar Snow was an American journalist.
138 "Aktenvermerk über den Abshiedsbesuch beim Stellv. Ministerpräsidenten und Minister für Auswärtige Angelegenheiten der VR China, Genossen Tschen I, am Montag, den 30. Januar 1961, 10.00 bis 11.00 Uhr," in *Die DDR und China 1949 bis 1990: Politik, Wirtschaft, Kultur: eine Quellensammlung,* ed. Werner Meißner (Berlin: Akademie, 1995), 194.
139 *DXPNP,* vol. 3, 1563–64.
140 Gao Feng et al., *Lin Haiyun zhuan* [A biography of Lin Haiyun] (Beijing: Duiwai jingji maoyi daxue chubanshe, 2000), 361–62.
141 Speech, Zhou at the CCP Work Conference in Beidaihe, July 31, 1960, in *1958–1965 Zhonghua renmin gongheguo jingji dang'an ziliao xuanbian* [hereafter *JJDA*] [Selected archival materials on the PRC's economic affairs, 1958–1965] (Beijing: Zhongguo caizheng jingji chubanshe, 2011), the volume "Investment in Fixed Assets and Construction," 355; *MZDNP,* vol. 4, 436.
142 Gao Feng et al., *Lin Haiyun zhuan,* 362.
143 Li Enmin, *ZhongRi minjian jingji waijiao 1945–1972* [The Sino-Japanese non-governmental economic diplomacy, 1945–1972] (Beijing: Renmin chubanshe, 1997), 260.
144 Instruction by the PRC Foreign Trade Ministry, February 2, 1961, Jiangsu Provincial Archive, 4066-003-0186, 13–14.
145 Memorandum of Conversation, June 21, 1961, *FRUS, 1961–63,* vol. 22, *Northeast Asia,* https://history.state.gov/historicaldocuments/frus1961-63v22/d337.

146 Speech, Ye at the Naval Training Conference, May 19, 1961, in *Ye Jianying junshi wenxuan* [Ye Jianying's selected works on military affairs] (Beijing: Jiefangjun chubanshe, 1997), 509.

147 Minutes, Zhang's Talk with Kuznetsov, August 2, 1961, CFMA, 113-00442-02, 2. Zhang Dequn was the PRC's chargé d'affaires in the Soviet Union. Vasily Kuznetsov was the first Soviet deputy foreign minister.

148 *RBWT,* vol. 4, 130–31.

149 *ZGDWGXWJ* (1961), 401.

150 *Zhongguo waiwenju wushinian dashiji* [hereafter *WWJDSJ*] [A chronicle of major events of the China International Publishing Group over fifty years], vol. 1 (Beijing: Xinxing chubanshe, 1999), 140 and 142–43.

151 Memorandum of Conversation, June 21, 1961, *FRUS, 1961–1963,* vol. 22, *Northeast Asia,* https://history.state.gov/historicaldocuments/frus1961-63v22/d337.

152 Wang Yongqin, ed., *Tongyi zhilu: liang'an guanxi wushinian dashiji* [The road toward unification: a chronicle of major events across the strait over fifty years] (Guangzhou: Guangdong renmin chubanshe, 1999), 71.

153 Yang Chengwu, "Paoji Jinmen," 515.

154 Minutes, Liu and Zhou's Talk with Mahendra, September 30, 1961, CFMA, 204-01473-04, 4. Mahendra was the king of Nepal.

155 Li Fusheng and Fang Yingkai, eds., *Xinjiang bingtuan tunken shubian shi* [A history of the Xinjiang Corps' stationing and reclaiming of land], vol. 1 (Wulumuqi: Xinjiang keji weisheng chubanshe, 1997), 711.

156 Ibid., 712; Li Fengyou and Zhang Ye, "Pingxi Yita shijian zhong de wuzhuang jingcha budui" [The armed security forces in the Yita incident], in *Gong'an budui huiyi shiliao* [Recollections and historical materials of public security forces] (Beijing: Jiefangjun chubanshe, 1997), 381.

157 Li Sheng, ed., *Zhongguo Xinjiang lishi yu xianzhuang* [China's Xinjiang in historical and contemporary perspectives] (Wulumuqi: Xinjiang renmin chubanshe, 2006), 284.

158 Central Intelligence Bulletin, Daily Brief, April 15, 1961, John F. Kennedy Library (JFKL), National Security Files (NSF), Chester V. Clifton, box 349.

159 Intelligence Memo, Soviet Military Strategy and the Chinese Problem, April 26, 1963, JFKL, NSF Departments and Agencies, box 272.

160 Chen Donglin, *Sanxian jianshe: beizhan shiqi de xibu kaifa* [The third front construction: the western development in the war preparation era] (Beijing: Zhonggong zhongyang dangxiao chubanshe, 2003), 80.

161 Intelligence Memo, October 29, 1963, JFKL, NSF Countries, box 138A.

162 Speech, Peng to College Students in Beijing, August 7, 1965, Tianjin Municipal Archive, X0003-C-016618, 9–10.

163 Speech, Zhou at the Military-Industry Meeting in Northeast China, June 8, 1962, in *Zhou Enlai junshi wenxuan* [Zhou Enlai's selected works on military affairs], vol. 4 (Beijing: Renmin chubanshe, 1997), 434.

164 Telegram, US Embassy in Moscow to the Department of State, June 30, 1962, JFKL, NSF Countries, box 25.

165 Telegram from the Embassy in Poland to the Department of State, June 23, 1962, *FRUS, 1961–63,* vol. 22, *Northeast Asia,* https://history.state.gov/historicaldocuments/frus1961-63v22/d131.

166 Mei Zi, ed., *MeiTai guanxi zhongyao ziliao xuanbian, 1948.11–1996.4* [hereafter *MTGX*] [Selected important materials on US-Taiwan relations, 1948.11–1996.4] (Beijing: Shishi chubanshe, 1997), 342.

167 Ibid., 344.
168 Zhu Wenquan, "Taiwan dangju junshi zhengce bange shiji de tiaozheng shanbian" [The adjustment and evolution in military policies of the Taiwan authorities in the latter half of the twentieth century], *Zhongguo junshi kexue* [*China Military Science*] 3 (2002): 41.
169 Frank Langdon, *Japan's Foreign Policy* (Vancouver: UBC Press, 1973), 47.
170 Douglas Mendel, *The Japanese People and Foreign Policy* (Berkeley: University of California Press, 1961), 98.
171 Department of State Guidelines Paper, n.d., *FRUS, 1961–1963*, vol. 22, *Northeast Asia*, https://history.state.gov/historicaldocuments/frus1961-63v22/d354.
172 Airgram, US Embassy in Tokyo to the Department of State, August 22, 1962, JFKL, Countries box 25A, JFKL.
173 Speech, Marshal Ye Jianying at the PLA's Military Training Conference, November 23, 1962, in *Gongzuo tongxun* [Working bulletin], vol. 69, ed. People's Liberation Army, General Political Department, 3, available at China Documentation Center, Estelle and Melvin Gelman Library, George Washington University, Washington, DC.
174 Intelligence Memo, Possible Chinese Plans to Shell the Offshore Islands, September 20, 1963, JFKL, NSF Departments and Agencies, box 272.
175 Intelligence Memo, Discussions between President Diem and Vice President Chen Cheng, March 19, 1963, JFKL, NSF Countries, box 197.
176 *Yang Chengwu nianpu* [A chronicle of Yang Chengwu's life] (Beijing: Jiefangjun chubanshe, 2014), 374.
177 Intelligence Memo, Possible Chinese Plans to Shell the Offshore Islands, September 20, 1963, JFKL, NSF Departments and Agencies, box 272.
178 Geng Zhonglin, ed., *Wu Ruilin shiliao* [Historical evidence on Wu Ruilin], vol. 2, 1343–44, available at Tsinghua University Libraries, Beijing.
179 Wang Shangrong jiangjun bianxiezu, ed., *Wang Shangrong jiangjun* [General Wang Shangrong] (Beijing: Dangdai zhongguo chubanshe, 2000), 494–95.
180 "Xinzhongguo zuida haizhan" [The largest naval battle in the history of the People's Republic of China], https://www.sohu.com/a/283445152_166075.
181 *ZELNP,* vol. 2, 764.
182 Huang Qinghua, *ZhongFa jianjiao shimo: 20 shiji 40–60 naindai ZhongFa guanxi* [The establishment of the Sino-French relationship: the relationship from the 1940s to the 1960s] (Hefei: Huangshan shushe, 2014), 319–21.
183 Minutes, Mao's Talk with Heads of Japanese Youth Delegations, November 25, 1965, Shanghai Municipal Archive, C21-1-1099, 9–10.
184 Zhai Xin, *Songcunqiansan jituan he Zhongguo* [Matsumura Kenzo Group, Japan's diplomatic pipe to China] (Beijing: Shehui kexue wenxuan chubanshe, 2007), 138, 146; Liu Shilong, *Xinzhongguo duiRi zhengce, 1949–1972,* 53.
185 Speech, Sun Pinghua on Matsumura's Visit to China, November 23, 1962, Tianjin Municipal Archive, X0003-C-016567.17-18. Sun Pinghua was a Chinese official who joined the Sino-Japanese negotiations. Also see Gao Feng et al., *Lin Haiyun zhuan,* 391–92.
186 Minutes, Zhou's Talk with Japanese former Prime Minister Ishibashi Tanzan, October 9, 1963, in *Zhou Enlai waijiao wenxuan* [hereafter *ZELWJ*] [Zhou Enlai's selected works on diplomacy] (Beijing: Zhongyang wenxian chubanshe, 1990), 343–45.
187 Wang Junyan, *Liao Chengzhi zhuan,* 371.
188 Memorandum, Soviet Government to Japanese Government, January 27, 1960, in *RBWT,* vol. 3, 405.

189 *RBWT,* vol. 3, 260–61.
190 Li De'an, ed., *Zhou Enlai yu Riben pengyou men* [Zhou Enlai and his Japanese friends] (Beijing: Zhongyang wenxian chubanshe, 1992), 60–62.
191 *ZELNP,* vol. 2, 725–26.
192 Wang Taiping, *Wang Taiping wencun: ZhongRi jianjiao qianhou zai Dongjing* [Wang Taiping's selected works: observing the Sino-Japanese normalization in Tokyo] (Beijing: Shehui kexue wenxian chubanshe, 2012), 64.

Chapter 3: South Asia, 1955–63

1 Letter Exchanged with the Treaty, July 31, 1950, in S.D. Muni, *Foreign Policy of Nepal* (New Delhi: National Publishing House, 1973), 286.
2 Shaheen Irshad Khan, *Rejection Alliance? A Case-Study of U.S.-Pakistan Relations, 1947–1967* (Lahore: Ferozsons, 1972), 68; Foreign Trade Institute of the PRC Foreign Trade Ministry, ed., *Sulian duiwai maoyi jiben tongji, 1954–1975* [The foundation of the foreign trade statistics of the Soviet Union, 1954–1975] [hereafter *SLWM*] (Beijing: Renmin chubanshe, 1977), 155–57.
3 Telegram, the Acting Secretary of State to the Embassy in Pakistan, October 22, 1954, *Foreign Relations of the United States* [hereafter *FRUS*], *1952–1954,* vol. 11, *Africa and South Asia, Part II,* https://history.state.gov/historicaldocuments/frus1952-54v11p2/d1165. Herbert Hoover Jr. was the acting secretary of state.
4 Memorandum from the Assistant Secretary of State for Near Eastern and South Asian Affairs (Jones) and the Under Secretary of State's Special Assistant for Communist Economic Affairs (Terrill) to the Acting Secretary of State, September 12, 1959, *FRUS, 1958–1960,* vol. 15, *South and Southeast Asia,* https://history.state.gov/historicaldocuments/frus1958-60v15/d135. G. Lewis Jones was the assistant secretary of state for Near Eastern and South Asian affairs.
5 Airgram from the Embassy in Afghanistan to the Department of State, February 21, 1961, *FRUS, 1961–1963,* vol. 19, *South Asia,* https://history.state.gov/historicaldocuments/frus1961-63v19/d7.
6 Memo, Rusk to Matthews, United States Military Assistance Program in Southeast Asia, January 31, 1951, *FRUS, 1951,* vol. 6, *Asia and the Pacific, Part I,* 19. Dean Rusk was the assistant secretary of state for Far Eastern affairs. H. Freeman Matthews was the deputy under secretary of state.
7 Memorandum from the Assistant Secretary of State for Far Eastern Affairs (Robertson) to the Secretary of State, February 9, 1956, *FRUS, 1955–1957,* vol. 22, *Southeast Asia,* https://history.state.gov/historicaldocuments/frus1955-57v22/d24.
8 Telegram from the Department of State to the Embassy in Burma, June 28, 1956, *FRUS, 1955–1957,* vol. 22, *Southeast Asia,* https://history.state.gov/historicaldocuments/frus1955-57v22/d48.
9 John W. Garver, *Protracted Contest: Sino-Indian Rivalry in the Twentieth Century* (Seattle: University of Washington Press, 2001), 142.
10 Memorandum by the Executive Secretary (Lay) to the National Security Council, March 2, 1954, *FRUS, 1952–1954,* vol. 11, *Africa and South Asia, Part II,* https://history.state.gov/historicaldocuments/frus1952-54v11p2/d625.
11 Aftab Alam, *U.S. Military Aid to Pakistan and India's Security* (New Delhi: Raj Publications, 2001), 54–55.

12 Memorandum from the Under Secretary of State (Herter) to the President, November 8, 1958, *FRUS, 1958–1960,* vol. 15, *South and Southeast Asia,* https://history.state.gov/historicaldocuments/frus1958-60v15/d118.

13 Zhao Weiwen, *YinZhong guanxi fengyunlu, 1949–1999* [A history of the Sino-Indian relationship, 1949–1999] (Beijing: Shishi chubanshe, 2000), 35; Editorial Note, *FRUS, 1951,* vol. 6, *Asia and the Pacific, Part II,* 2113.

14 Draft Instruction by Yunnan Military Region, July 7, 1952, in *Yunnan jiaofei douzheng* [Anti-rebellion struggles in Yunnan] (Kunming: Yunnan daxue chubanshe, 2011), 351.

15 Prime Minister Nu to President Eisenhower, March 15, 1954, *FRUS, 1952–1954,* vol. 12, *East Asia and the Pacific, Part II,* https://history.state.gov/historicaldocuments/frus1952-54v12p2/d154.

16 Xie Yixian, ed., *Zhonghua renmin gongheguo waijiaoshi, 1949–1995* [A diplomatic history of the PRC, 1949–1995] (Beijing: Zhongguo qingnian chubanshe, 1997), 93.

17 Speech, Chen Yi at the First Party Congress of the East China Military Region, April 19, 1954, in *Chen Yi junshi wenxuan* [Chen Yi's selected works on military affairs] (Beijing: Jiefangjun chubanshe, 1996), 578.

18 Speech, Khrushchev in Kashmir, December 10, 1955, in *Bu'erjianing, Heluxiaofu fangwen Yindu, Miandian, he Afuhan qijian de jianghua* [Collected speeches of Bulganin and Khrushchev during their visits to India, Burma, and Afghanistan] (Beijing: Renmin chubanshe, 1956), 113.

19 Minutes, Zhou's Talk with Ahmed, January 4, 1956, Foreign Ministry Archive of the People's Republic of China (CFMA), 105-00351-01, 1. Sultanuddin Ahmed was Pakistan's ambassador to China.

20 Sun Shihai and Jiang Yili, eds., *Erzhanhou Nanya guojia duiwai guanxi yanjiu* [Foreign relations in South Asia since the end of the Second World War] (Beijing: Fangzhi chubanshe, 2007), 352.

21 Telegram, Geng to Zhou, April 6, 1956, CFMA, 105-00473-02, 1–2.

22 Zhang Minqiu, ed., *ZhongYin guanxi yanjiu, 1947–2003* [Sino-Indian relations, 1947–2003] (Beijing: Beijing daxue chubanshe, 2004), 23.

23 Jin Chongji, ed., *Zhou Enlai zhuan* [hereafter *ZELZ*] [Biography of Zhou Enlai] (Beijing: Zhongyang wenxian chubanshe, 1998), 1492.

24 Minutes, Mao's Talk with Nehru, October 21, 1954, CFMA, 204-00007-08, 2.

25 Minutes, Zhou's Talk with Nehru, June 25, 1954, CFMA, 203-00006-01, 14–15.

26 *ZELZ,* 1149–50.

27 Memorandum of Conversation, February 18, 1973, *FRUS, 1969–1976,* vol. 18, *China,* 165.

28 Minutes, Zhou's Talk with the Pakistan Women's Delegation, October 7, 1954, CFMA, 204-00004-03, 7, 11, 12, 22–23.

29 Minutes, Zhou's Talk with U Nu, June 28, 1954, CFMA, 203-00007-03, 10, 14, and 19.

30 Minutes, Mao's Talk with U Nu, December 1, 1954, in *Mao Zedong waijiao wenxuan* [hereafter *MZDWJ*] [Mao Zedong's selected works on diplomacy] (Beijing: Zhongyang wenxian chubanshe/Shijie zhishi chubanshe, 1994), 184–85, 187–89.

31 Speech, Zhou to the PRC Delegation for the World Peace Conference in Helsinki (Excerpt), June 7, 1955, in *Zhou Enlai waijiao wenxuan* [hereafter *ZELWJ*] [Zhou Enlai's selected works on diplomacy] (Beijing: Zhongyang wenxian chubanshe, 1990), 150–51.

32 Report by Lei, August 20, 1953, CFMA, 105-00109-01, 1. Lei Renmin was the PRC's deputy foreign trade minister.

33 Telegram, the Secretary of State to the Department of State, February 27, 1955, *FRUS, 1955–1957,* vol. 22, *Southeast Asia,* https://history.state.gov/historicaldocuments/frus1955-57v22/d3.
34 Memorandum of a Conversation, June 29, 1955, *FRUS, 1955–1957,* vol. 22, *Southeast Asia,* https://history.state.gov/historicaldocuments/frus1955-57v22/d12.
35 Speech, Chen Yun at the PRC State Council, September 23, 1955, in *Chen Yun wenji* [Chen Yun's collected works] [hereafter *CYWJ*], vol. 2 (Beijing: Zhongyang wenxian chubanshe, 2005), 659.
36 Speech, Ye to Directors of Foreign Trade Departments and Trade Representatives from Various Provinces, January 20, 1956, Zhejiang Provincial Archive, J127-003-136, 15–16.
37 Speech, Li at the Foreign Trade Ministerial Meeting, August 11, 1955, Henan Provincial Archive, J142-1-6, 4.
38 Minutes, Zhou's Talk with Nehru (Excerpt), June 18, 1956, in *Zhou Enlai yu waiguo shounao ji zhengyao huitanlu* [Zhou Enlai's talks with foreign leaders and politicians] (Beijing: Taihai chubanshe, 2012), 105–6. Ratan Kumar Nehru was India's ambassador to China.
39 Lin Liangguang, Ye Zhengjia, and Han Hua, *Dang dai Zhongguo yu Nanya guojia guan xi* [Contemporary China–South Asia relations] (Beijing: Shehui kexue wenxian chubanshe, 2001), 129.
40 Telegram, PRC Foreign Ministry to the Embassy in Burma: Zhou's Talk with U Hla Maung, August 7, 1956, CFMA, 105-00757-02, 3.
41 Report, On Unsettled Questions in Sino-Burmese Relations, March 17, 1956, CFMA, 105-00447-03, 9–10.
42 Minutes, Zhou's Talk with U Hla Maung, June 22, 1956, CFMA, 105-00307-02, 4.
43 Telegram from the Department of State to the Embassy in Burma, June 28, 1956, *FRUS, 1955–1957,* vol. 22, *Southeast Asia,* https://history.state.gov/historicaldocuments/frus1955-57v22/d48.
44 Minutes, Zhou's Talk with U Hla Maung (Excerpt), August 15, 1956, in Li Lianqing, *Da waijiaojia Zhou Enlai* [hereafter *DWJJ*] [Zhou Enlai: a great diplomat], vol. 4 (Hong Kong: Tiandi tushu youxian gongsi, 1999), 236–37.
45 Zhuo Renzheng, ed., *Yinyin baobo qing: 1956 nian ZhongMian bianmin dalianhuan* [The friendship of relatives: the Sino-Burmese border festival in 1956] (Beijing: Zhongyang wenxian chubanshe, 2003), 119.
46 Minutes, Zhou's Talk with U Hla Maung, August 25, 1956, CFMA, 105-00307-03, 8.
47 Ibid.
48 Telegram from the Department of State to the Embassy in Burma, September 20, 1956, *FRUS, 1955–1957,* vol. 22, *Southeast Asia,* https://history.state.gov/historicaldocuments/frus1955-57v22/d55.
49 Report by the PRC Embassy in Burma, December 25, 1958, CFMA, 105-00846-05, 10–12.
50 Speech, Zhou at the National Political Consultative Conference (Excerpt), March 16, 1957, in *DWJJ,* vol. 4, 243.
51 *DWJJ,* vol. 4, 247.
52 Ibid., 247–48.
53 Maung Aung Myoe, *In the Name of Pauk-Phaw: Myanmar's China Policy since 1948* (Singapore: Institute of Southeast Asian Studies, 2011), 45.
54 Minutes, Mao's Talk with U Ba Swe, December 14, 1957, CFMA, 105-00339-01, 3.
55 Report by the PRC Embassy in India, February 1, 1956, CFMA, 105-00788-01, 1.

56 Speech, Chen Yi on Reception of International Guests, September 10, 1956, Fujian Provincial Archive, 0136-008-0461-0017, 7.
57 Report by the PRC Foreign Ministry, August 28, 1956, CFMA, 204-00033-01, 3.
58 Sanjay Upadhya, *Nepal and the Geo-Strategic Rivalry between China and India* (London/New York: Routledge, 2012), 76; *Zhou Enlai yu Xizang* [Zhou Enlai and Tibet] (Beijing: Zhongguo zangxue chubanshe, 1998), 468–69.
59 Minutes, Zhou's Talk with Acharya, September 27, 1956, in *Zhou Enlai yu waiguo shounao ji zhengyao huitanlu,* 115; Minutes, Zhou's Talk with R.K. Nehru, September 27, 1956, CFMA, 105-00327-10, 2. Tanka Prasad Acharya was Nepal's prime minister.
60 Record of Conversation between Chinese and Soviet Government Delegations (Excerpt), January 9, 1957, in *Zhou Enlai junshi huodong jishi* [hereafter *ZELJSHDJS*] [A chronicle of Zhou Enlai's military activities], vol. 2 (Beijing: Zhongyang wenxian chubanshe, 2000), 413.
61 Report by the PRC Foreign Ministry, September 10, 1956, CFMA, 105-00594-01, 5–6.
62 Letter, Zhou to Nehru, January 22, 1959 (Excerpt), in *Zhou Enlai nianpu, 1949–1976* [hereafter *ZELNP*] [A chronicle of Zhou Enlai's life, 1949–1976], vol. 2 (Beijing: Zhongyang wenxian chubanshe, 1997), 201–2.
63 Yang Yizhen, *Pingxi 1959 nian Xizang wuzhuang panluan jishi: Yang Yizhen huiyilu* [Anti-rebellions in Tibet in 1959: Yang Yizhen's memoirs] (Beijing: Zhongguo zangxue chubanshe, 2010), 150–51.
64 Wu Lengxi, *Shinian lunzhan, 1956–1966: ZhongSu guanxi huiyilu* [Ten years polemical war, 1956–1966: a memoir of Sino-Soviet relations] (Beijing: Zhongyang wenxian chubanshe, 1999), 194–95.
65 Sun Shihai and Jiang Yili, *Erzhanhou Nanya guojia duiwai guanxi yanjiu,* 354.
66 Minutes, Mao's Talk with the Tenth Panchen Lama, May 7, 1959, in *Mao Zedong Xizang gongzuo wenxuan* [Mao Zedong's selected works on Tibetan affairs] (Beijing: Zhongyang wenxian chubanshe/Zhongguo zangxue chubanshe, 2008), 201.
67 Instruction by Mao, May 13, 1959, in *Jianguo yilai Mao Zedong wengao* [hereafter *JGYLMZDWG*] [Manuscripts of Mao Zedong since the founding of the nation], vol. 8 (Beijing: Zhongyang wenxian chubanshe, 1993), 268–70.
68 Instruction to Luo, August 5, 1959, CFMA, 113-00272-01, 53–54. Luo Guibo was the PRC's deputy foreign minister.
69 Sun Shihai and Jiang Yili, *Erzhanhou Nanya guojia duiwai guanxi yanjiu,* 354.
70 Minutes, Mao's Talk with Naim Khan, September 8, 1959, CFMA, 105-00399-08, 6–7, 9.
71 Memorandum from the Under Secretary of State for Economic Affairs (Ball) to President Kennedy, April 19, 1961, *FRUS, 1961–1963,* vol. 19, *South Asia,* https://history.state.gov/historicaldocuments/frus1961-63v19/d14.
72 Telegram from the White House to the Embassy in the United Kingdom, June 9, 1962, *FRUS, 1961–1963,* vol. 19, *South Asia,* https://history.state.gov/historicaldocuments/frus1961-63v19/d134.
73 Memorandum of Conversation, June 14, 1962, *FRUS, 1961–1963,* vol. 19, *South Asia,* https://history.state.gov/historicaldocuments/frus1961-63v19/d136.
74 Vojtech Mastny, "The Soviet Union's Partnership with India," *Journal of Cold War Studies* 12, 3 (2010): 50–90.
75 Annual Report for the Year 1960, Embassy of India to the Soviet Union, January 5, 1961, https://www.php.isn.ethz.ch/kms2.isn.ethz.ch/serviceengine/Files/PHP/94130/ipublicationdocument_singledocument/b031a29d-128c-4a80-88b2-f7bb474d08d3/en/AnnualReport_Embassy_1961_01.pdf.

76 Press Reports on Visit of Soviet First Deputy Premier (Alexsei Kosygin) to India, February 28, 1961, https://www.php.isn.ethz.ch/kms2.isn.ethz.ch/serviceengine/Files/PHP/94104/ipublicationdocument_singledocument/ed448628-6e7d-46e5-9948-32f25d6e0c08/en/PressConference_Kosygin_1961_02.pdf.

77 Annual Report for the Year 1960, Embassy of India to the Soviet Union, January 5, 1961, https://www.php.isn.ethz.ch/kms2.isn.ethz.ch/serviceengine/Files/PHP/94130/ipublicationdocument_singledocument/b031a29d-128c-4a80-88b2-f7bb474d08d3/en/AnnualReport_Embassy_1961_01.pdf.

78 Memorandum from the Joint Chiefs of Staff to the Secretary of Defense (Gates), November 15, 1960, *FRUS, 1958–1960,* vol. 15, *South and Southeast Asia,* https://history.state.gov/historicaldocuments/frus1958-60v15/d271.

79 Shen Zhihua, ed., *ZhongSu guanxi shigang, 1917–1991, zengdingban* [A history of Sino-Soviet relations, 1917–1991, revised edition] (Beijing: Shehui kexue wenxian chubanshe, 2011), 316.

80 Telegram from the Embassy in India to the Department of State, May 18, 1962, *FRUS, 1961–1963,* vol. 19, *South Asia,* https://history.state.gov/historicaldocuments/frus1961-63v19/d122.

81 *SLWM,* 156.

82 Memorandum of Conversation, March 7, 1961, *FRUS, 1961–1963,* vol. 19, *South Asia,* https://history.state.gov/historicaldocuments/frus1961-63v19/d8.

83 *SLWM,* 155–57.

84 Minutes, Zhou's Talk with Diplomatic Representatives from Socialist Countries (Excerpt), May 2, 1959, in *ZELNP,* vol. 2, 224–25; Minutes, Zhou's Talk with Diplomatic Representatives from Socialist Countries, May 6, 1959, in *ZELWJ,* 270.

85 Khrushchev's Interview with Karanjia, May 7, 1959, in *Youguan Xizang wenti de wenjian he cailiao xuanbian (guoji bufen)* [Selected documents and materials on the question of Tibet (international aspects)], ed. Xinhua News Agency (Beijing: 1959), 164, available at China Foreign Affairs University Library, Beijing.

86 Li Lianqing, *Lengnuan suiyue: Yyibosanzhe de ZhongSu guanxi* [Ups and downs of Sino-Soviet relations] (Beijing: Shijie zhishi chubanshe, 1999), 292.

87 Minutes, Yudin's Talk with Chen Yi, May 8, 1959, in *E'luosi jiemi dang'an: ZhongSu guanxi* [Sino-Soviet relations: declassified documents from Russian archives] [hereafter *ZSGX*], vol. 8, ed. Shen Zhihua (Shanghai: Dongfang chuban zhongxin, 2015), 353–54.

88 Li Lianqing, *Lengnuan suiyue,* 294.

89 Telegram, Embassy in Moscow to the Department of State, September 10, 1959, US National Archive II, College Park, MD, RG 59, Central Decimal File 1955–59, file 690, box 2716.

90 Telegram, Embassy in Moscow to the Department of State, September 12, 1959, US National Archive II, College Park, MD, RG 59, Central Decimal File 1955–59, file 690, box 2716.

91 Discussion between N.S. Khrushchev and Mao Zedong, October 2, 1959, Wilson Center Digital Archive, http://digitalarchive.wilsoncenter.org/document/112088.

92 Paul Robinson and Jay Dixon, *Aiding Afghanistan: A History of Soviet Assistance to a Developing Country* (New York: Columbia University Press, 2013), 48.

93 Telegram, the PRC Embassy in Burma to the Foreign Ministry, November 28, 1959, CFMA, 105-00912-05, 7.

94 Minutes, Zhou's Talk with the Indian Communist Party Delegation (Excerpt), October 3, 1959, in *ZELZ,* 1499.

95 Pang Xianzhi and Jin Chongji, eds., *Mao Zedong zhuan, 1949–1976* [hereafter *MZDZ*] [Biography of Mao Zedong, 1949–1976] (Beijing: Zhongyang wenxian chubanshe, 2003), 1023–24.

96 Zhao Weiwen, *YinZhong guanxi fengyunlu, 1949–1999,* 156–57.
97 Minutes, Mao's Talk with Wang Jiaxiang et al. (Excerpt), November 12, 1959, in *Mao Zedong nianpu, 1949–1976* [A chronicle of Mao Zedong's life, 1949–1976] [hereafter *MZDNP*], vol. 4 (Beijing: Zhongyang wenxian chubanshe, 2013), 236–39.
98 Wu Lengxi, *Shinian lunzhan, 1956–1966,* 229–30.
99 Speech, Chen Yi to the CCP Cadres of Guizhou Province, November 24, 1959, Guizhou Provincial Archive, 1-1-1844, 16–17.
100 Minutes, Zhou's Talk with Rau (Excerpt), January 18, 1960, in *ZELNP,* vol. 2, 279. Heinrich Rau was the deputy premier of the German Democratic Republic.
101 Minutes, Zhou's Talk with Chervonenko (Excerpt), January 26, 1960, *ZELNP,* vol. 2, 283–84.
102 Minutes, Chen's Talk with Chervonenko, January 29, 1960, CFMA, 204-00113-02, 2–4.
103 Speech, Kang at the Meeting of the Warsaw Pact Political Consultative Committee, February 4, 1960, http://www.php.isn.ethz.ch/lory1.ethz.ch/collections/colltopice7f9-2.html?lng=en&id=16320&navinfo=16034.
104 *Heluxiaofu yanlun* [Collected speeches of Khrushchev], vol. 14 (Beijing: Shijie zhishi chubanshe, 1966), 166.
105 Wu Lengxi, *Shinian lunzhan, 1956–1966,* 252–53.
106 Trends and Implications of Soviet Policy, approved on April 7, 1960, NATO Archives, C-M (60) 38, 8.
107 Minutes, Zhou's Talk with Ledovskii, April 17, 1960, CFMA, 203-00036-05, 2.
108 Minutes, Zhou's Talk with U Nu, April 17, 1960, CFMA, 203-00036-07, 8. The report, for the talk held on April 17, was made on April 20.
109 *DWJJ,* vol. 4, 286–95; K. Natwar Singh, *My China Diary 1956–1988* (New Delhi: Rupa and Company, 2009), 100–1.
110 Minutes, Zhou's Talk with Nehru (Excerpt), April 24, 1960, in *ZELNP* vol. 2, 312.
111 Telegram, Zhou to Mao (Excerpt), May 4, 1960, in *ZELNP* vol. 2, 315–16.
112 Minutes, Ding's Talk with Ayub, February 10, 1960, CFMA, 105-00402-02, 2–3. Ding Guoyu was the PRC's ambassador to Pakistan.
113 Minutes, Geng's Talk with Malik, April 5, 1960, CFMA, 105-00991-11, 4–5. After his tenure in Pakistan, Geng became the PRC's deputy foreign minister. A.M. Malik was Pakistan's ambassador to China.
114 Minutes, Chen Yi's Talk with Pakistan's Ambassador in Afghanistan, August 22, 1960, CFMA, 203-00033-09, 1.
115 Minutes, Zhou's Talk with the Nepalese Delegation of the Sino-Nepalese Joint Border Committee, February 9, 1961, CFMA, 105-01063-04, 1–2.
116 Minutes, Zhou's Talk with R.K. Nehru, July 16, 1961, CFMA, 105-01774-03, 23–24.
117 Minutes, Zhou's Talk with King Mahendra, September 30, 1961, CFMA, 204-01473-08, 7.
118 Minutes, Chen Yi's Talk with the Afghan Ambassador to China, July 28, 1960, CFMA, 203-00032-08, 3.
119 Minutes, Chen Yi's Talk with the Soviet Ambassador to Afghanistan, August 22, 1960, CFMA, 203-00032-08, 2.
120 Minutes, Chen Yi's Talk with Daoud, August 26, 1960, CFMA, 203-00033-06, 2.
121 Speech, Chen Yi at the United Front Department, September 16, 1960, Fujian Provincial Archive, 0101-006-0208, 10–11.
122 Report by the CCP Committee of the PRC's Foreign Trade Ministry, December 20, 1959, in *1958–1965 Zhonghua renmin gongheguo jingji dang'an ziliao xuanbian* [hereafter *JJDA*]

[Selected archival materials on the PRC's economic affairs, 1958–1965] (Beijing: Zhongguo caizheng jingji chubanshe, 2011), the volume on "Foreign Trade," 109.

123 Letter, Zhou to Koirala, December 22, 1959, CFMA, 105-00409-03, 7–8.

124 Letter, Zhou to Ne Win, December 22, 1959, CFMA, 105-00385-02, 2–3.

125 Speech, Chen Yi at the National Culture and Education Conference, February 18, 1960, Shanghai Municipal Archive, A22-2-851, 13–14.

126 Minutes, Zhou's Talk with Koirala, March 13 and 15, 1960, CFMA, 204-00101-03, 15–16, 18, 21.

127 Minutes, Zhou's Talk with Giri, October 9, 1959, CFMA, 204-00079-09, 3. Tulsi Giri was Nepal's foreign minister.

128 Minutes, Mao's Talk with Koirala, March 18, 1960, CFMA, 204-00101-02, 12.

129 Minutes, Zhou's Talk with Koirala, March 15, 1960, CFMA, 204-00101-03, 24.

130 *ZELNP,* vol. 2, 328–29.

131 Telegram, the PRC Embassy in Nepal to the Foreign Ministry, February 16, 1961, CFMA, 105-01458-08, 10.

132 Minutes, Zhou's Talk with Bahadur, August 19, 1961, CFMA, 105-01063-09, 5. Bahadur was Nepal's ambassador to China.

133 Upadhya, *Nepal and the Geo-Strategic Rivalry between China and India,* 87.

134 Minutes, Zhou's Talk with Ne Win (Excerpt), January 25, 1960, in *DWJJ,* vol. 4, 255–56.

135 Minutes, Li's Talk with Barrington, July 11, 1960, CFMA, 105-01422-02, 1–4. Li Yimang was the PRC's ambassador to Burma. James Barrington was Burma's secretary-general.

136 Minutes, Mao's Talk with U Nu, September 29, 1960, in *MZDWJ,* 445. Kachin people, as well as the BCP, launched an armed struggle against Burma's government.

137 Report by the PRC Foreign Ministry, December 31, 1960, CFMA, 105-01026-01, 1.

138 Myoe, *In the Name of Pauk-Phaw,* 50.

139 Report by the PRC Foreign Ministry, January 1961, CFMA, 105-01026-01, 5.

140 Report by the PRC Embassy in Burma, August 26, 1961, CFMA, 105-01079-01, 20.

141 Airgram from the Embassy in Pakistan to the Department of State, December 3, 1960, *FRUS, 1958–1960,* vol. 15, *South and Southeast Asia,* https://history.state.gov/historicaldocuments/frus1958-60v15/d394.

142 Telegram from the Embassy in Pakistan to the Department of State, March 22, 1961, fn 4, *FRUS, 1961–1963,* vol. 19, *South Asia,* https://history.state.gov/historicaldocuments/frus1961-63v19/d11.

143 Minutes, Geng's Talk with Rashdi, January 13, 1962, CFMA, 105-01512-02, 7. Pir Ali Muhammad Rashdi was Pakistan's ambassador to China.

144 Minutes, Ding's Talk with Pakistan's Secretary-General, January 13, 1962, CFMA, 105-01800-02, 1–2.

145 Minutes, Zhou's Talk with Rashdi, March 8, 1962, CFMA, 105-01799-02, 7.

146 "Aktenvermerk über eine Besprechung im Außenministerium der VR China zwischen dem stellvertretenden Außenminister Dsöng und Botschafter Hegen am 3. Januar 1962 in der Zeit von 16.00 Uhr bis 18.15 Uhr," in *Die DDR und China 1949 bis 1990: Politik, Wirtschaft, Kultur: eine Quellensammlung,* ed. Werner Meißner (Berlin: Akademie, 1995), 128.

147 Telegram from the Embassy in Pakistan to the Department of State, March 3, 1962, *FRUS, 1961–1963,* vol. 19, *South Asia,* https://history.state.gov/historicaldocuments/frus1961-63v19/d107.

148 Minutes, Zhou's Talk with Penm Nouth (Excerpt), June 4, 1962, in *ZELNP,* vol. 2, 481. Penm Nouth was Cambodia's prince.

149 Speech, Zhou at the Military-Industry Meeting in Northeast China, June 8, 1962, in *Zhou Enlai junshi wenxuan* [Zhou Enlai's selected works on military affairs], vol. 4 (Beijing: Renmin chubanshe, 1997), 434–35.

150 Speech, Wang at the Enlarged Meeting of Xinjiang's People's Committee, June 21, 1962, *Wang Enmao wenji* [Wang Enmao's collected works], vol. 1 (Beijing: Zhongyang wenxian chubanshe, 1997), 387–89.

151 Minutes, Cherkasov's Talk with Pan, July 14, 1962, in Shen Zhihua, *Lengzhan de zaizhuanxing: ZhongSu tongmeng de neizai fenqi jiqi jieju* [The retransformation of the Cold War: the inherent differences within the Sino-Soviet alliance and the fate of the alliance] (Beijing: Jiuzhou chubanshe, 2013), 391. Mikhail Cherkasov was Soviet chargé d'affaires in India.

152 Minutes, Zhou's Talk with Kim (Excerpt), October 11, 1962, in *Zhou Enlai waijiao huodong dashiji, 1949–1975* [A chronicle of major events of Zhou Enlai's foreign affairs activities, 1949–1975] [hereafter *ZELWJHDDSJ*] (Beijing: Shijie zhishi chubanshe, 1993), 337–38.

153 *MZDZ,* 1223.

154 Ibid.

155 *ZELJSHDJS,* vol. 2, 564.

156 Zhonggong Xizang zizhiqu weiyuanhui dangshiyanjiushi, ed., *Tan Guansan yu lao Xizang jingshen* [Tan Guansan and the spirit of "senior Tibetans"] (Beijing: Zhonggong dangshi chubanshe, 2011), 271.

157 Speech, Zhou at the Tenth Plenary Session of the Eighth Central Committee (Excerpt), September 26, 1962, *ZELNP,* vol. 2, 498.

158 Instruction by Zhou, September 29, 1962, in Gu Yongzhong, *He Long yu gongheguo yuanshuai* [He Long and marshals of the republic] (Beijing: Renmin chubanshe, 2007), 279.

159 Lin Liangguang, Ye Zhengjia, and Han Hua, *Dang dai Zhongguo yu Nanya guojia guan xi,* 133.

160 Memo, The Sino-Indian Border Dispute and Its Ramifications, May 7, 1962, John F. Kennedy Library (JFKL), National Security Files (NSF) Countries, box 106A.

161 Minutes, Zhang's Talk with Giri, February 7, 1962, CFMA, 105-01521-01, 22. Zhang Shijie was the PRC's ambassador to Nepal.

162 *Zhonghua renmin gongheguo duiwai guanxi wenjian ji* [hereafter *ZGDWGXWJ*] [Documents on foreign relations of the People's Republic of China] (Beijing: Shijie zhishi chubanshe, 1962), 96.

163 Lin Liangguang, Ye Zhengjia, and Han Hua, *Dang dai Zhongguo yu Nanya guojia guan xi,* 133.

164 Instruction, October 20, 1962, in *Gongzuo tongxun* [Working bulletin], vol. 65, ed. People's Liberation Army, General Political Department, 19, available at China Documentation Center, Estelle and Melvin Gelman Library, George Washington University, Washington, DC.

165 Letter, Nehru to Khrushchev, October 27, 1962, CFMA, 109-03804-03, 25.

166 Minutes, Zhou's Talk with Burma's Ambassador in China, October 29, 1962, CFMA, 105-01781-02, 2–3.

167 ZhongYin bianjing ziwei fanji zuozhan shi bianxiezu, ed., *ZhongYin bianjing ziwei fanji zuozhan shi* [A history of the self-defence and counterattack operations on the Sino-Indian border] (Beijing: Junshi kexue chubanshe, 1994), 480.

168 *MZDZ,* 1263.
169 *ZELNP,* vol. 2, 504.
170 Minutes, Geng's Talk with Raza, December 13, 1962, CFMA, 105-01116-04, 3–4. Nawabzada Agha Mohammad Raza was Pakistan's ambassador to China.
171 Instruction by the PRC Foreign Ministry (Excerpt), December 25, 1962, in *Zhongguo waiwenju wushinian dashiji* [hereafter *WWJDSJ*] [A chronicle of major events of the China International Publishing Group over fifty years], vol. 1 (Beijing: Xinxing chubanshe, 1999), 151–52.
172 Minutes, Zhou's Talk with Zedenbal, December 26, 1962, *Cold War International History Project Bulletin* 8–9 (1996–97): 267. J. Zedenbal was a Mongolian leader.
173 Ibid.
174 Gao Feng et al., *Lin Haiyun zhuan* [A biography of Lin Haiyun] (Beijing: Duiwai jingji maoyi daxue chubanshe, 2000), 420.
175 M. Taylor Fravel, *Strong Borders, Secure Nation: Cooperation and Conflicts in China's Territorial Disputes* (Princeton, NJ: Princeton University Press, 2008), 46.
176 Minutes, Mao's Talk with Bhutto, March 3, 1963, CFMA, 204-01502-01, 8.
177 Memo, CIA: Possible Defense Agreement between Communist China and Pakistan, 5 June 1965, Lyndon B. Johnson Library (LBJL), NSF Files of Robert W. Komer, box 47.
178 Sun Shihai and Jiang Yili, *Erzhanhou Nanya guojia duiwai guanxi yanjiu,* 429.
179 William J. Barnds, *India, Pakistan, and the Great Powers* (New York: Praeger, 1972), 206–7.
180 Li Zongyu, ed., *Ou'Mei gongyun fengyunlu (1945–1991)* [A chronicle of major events of international communist movements in Europe and America (1945–1991)] (Beijing: Renmin chubanshe, 1994), 70.
181 Minutes, Geng's Talk with Afghan Ambassador to China, July 19, 1960, CFMA, 203-00032-07, 5–6.
182 Instruction, Chen Yi to First Asian Department of the PRC Foreign Ministry, June 4, 1963, CFMA, 105-01175-01, 1–2; Fravel, *Strong Borders, Secure Nation*, 46.
183 Fravel, *Strong Borders, Secure Nation*, 46.

Chapter 4: Indochina, 1962–75

1 Li Ke and Hao Shengzhang, *Wenhua dageming zhong de renmin jiefangjun* [The People's Liberation Army during the great cultural revolution] (Beijing: Zhonggong dangshi ziliao chubanshe, 1989), 409.
2 Memo, the Joint Chiefs of Staff to Military Aide to the President: Comparative Forces in Laos, May 1, 1961, John F. Kennedy Presidential Library (JFKL), National Security Files (NSF) Departments and Agencies, box 276; Arthur J. Dommen, *Conflict in Laos: The Politics of Neutralization* (New York: Praeger, 1965), 104.
3 Xie Yixian, ed., *Zhongguo waijiaoshi: Zhonghua renmin gongheguo shiqi, 1949–1979* [A diplomatic history of the PRC, 1949–1979] (Kaifeng: Henan renmin chubanshe, 1988), 232–33.
4 Telegram, the PRC Embassy in Cambodia to the Foreign Ministry, April 10, 1962, Foreign Ministry Archive of the People's Republic of China (CFMA), 117-00986-01, 33–34.
5 *Zhonghua renmin gongheguo duiwai guanxi wenjian ji* [hereafter *ZGDWGXWJ*] [Documents on foreign relations of the People's Republic of China] (Beijing: Shijie zhishi chubanshe, 1963), 222.

6 Gina Chon and Thet Sambath, *Behind the Killing Fields: A Khmer Rouge Leader and One of His Victims* (Philadelphia: University of Pennsylvania Press, 2010), 64.
7 Stephen Heder, "Kampuchea's Armed Struggle: The Origins of an Independent Revolution," *Bulletin of Concerned Asian Scholars* 11, 1 (1979): 3–4.
8 Intelligence Brief, October 16, 1964, Lyndon B. Johnson Presidential Library (LBJL), Declassified and Sanitized Documents from Unprocessed Files (DSDUF), box 5.
9 Intelligence Memorandum, Cambodia's Foreign Policy, December 11, 1965, LBJL, NSF Country File, box 237.
10 Minutes, Yudin's Talk with Zhou, April 30, 1956, in *E'luosi jiemi dang'an: ZhongSu guanxi* [Sino-Soviet relations: declassified documents from Russian archives] [hereafter *ZSGX*], vol. 6, ed. Shen Zhihua (Shanghai: Dongfang chuban zhongxin, 2015), 257.
11 Discussion between N.S. Khrushchev and Mao Zedong, October 2, 1959, Wilson Center Digital Archive, http://digitalarchive.wilsoncenter.org/document/112088.
12 Minutes, Chervonenko's Talk with Zhou, June 5, 1961, in *ZSGX*, vol. 9, 306.
13 Telegram, Harriman's Talk with Pushkin, October 12, 1961, LBJL, NSF Intelligence File, box 3. W. Averell Harriman was the US representative to the Geneva Conference. Georgy Pushkin, Soviet deputy foreign minister, was the Soviet delegate to the Geneva Conference.
14 "Diskussionsbereitrag des Genossen Towmasjan auf der Konferenz der vier Parteien über Laos, 7., 8. und 9. März, 1962," Bundesarchiv-Militärarchiv, Freiburg, DVW/1/6426a.
15 Minutes, Han's Talk with Binh, August 20, 1964, CFMA, 117-01700-01, 20. Han Nianlong was the PRC's deputy foreign minister. Tran Tu Binh was the DRV's ambassador to China.
16 Telegram, US Embassy in Paris to the Department of State, December 27, 1968, Richard M. Nixon Presidential Library (RMNL), NSC Files, Vietnam Subject Files, box 66.
17 Wang Taiping, ed., *Zhonghua renmin gongheguo waijiaoshi* [A diplomatic history of the People's Republic of China] [hereafter *WJS*], vol. 2 (Beijing: Shijie zhishi chubanshe, 1998), 34.
18 Minutes, Mao's Talk with the DRV's Economic Delegation (Excerpt), June 4, 1963, in *Mao Zedong jingji nianpu* [A chronicle of Mao Zedong's life on economic affairs], ed. Gu Longsheng (Beijing: Zhonggong zhongyang dangxiao chubanshe, 1993), 581.
19 Telegram, the PRC Embassy in Hanoi to the Foreign Ministry, October 5, 1963, CFMA, 117-01365-06, 2.
20 Minutes, Deng's Talk with the Lao Dong Party Delegation (Excerpt), February 25, 1964, in *Deng Xiaoping nianpu, 1904–1974* [hereafter *DXPNP*] [A chronicle of Deng Xiaoping's life, 1904–1974], vol. 3 (Beijing: Zhongyang wenxian chubanshe, 2009), 1800–1.
21 Li Ke and Hao Shengzhang, *Wenhua dageming zhong de renmin jiefangjun*, 409.
22 Memorandum for the President, March 16, 1964, in *The Pentagon Papers: The Defense Department History of United States Decision-Making on Vietnam, Vol. 3, The Senator Gravel Edition* (Boston: Beacon Press, 1971), 501.
23 Minutes, Zhou's Talk with Ne Win (Excerpt), July 10, 1964, in *Zhou Enlai nianpu, 1949–1976* [hereafter *ZELNP*] [A chronicle of Zhou Enlai's life, 1949–1976], vol. 2 (Beijing: Zhongyang wenxian chubanshe, 1997), 655.
24 Minutes, Mao's Talk with Three Vietnamese Delegations (Excerpt), July 27, 1964, in *Mao Zedong nianpu, 1949–1976* [A chronicle of Mao Zedong's life, 1949–1976] [hereafter *MZDNP*], vol. 5 (Beijing: Zhongyang wenxian chubanshe, 2013), 378.
25 Minutes, Zhou's Talk with Truong Cang (Excerpt), August 5, 1964, in *ZELNP*, vol. 2, 662–63. Truong Cang was the Cambodian ambassador to China.
26 *ZELNP*, vol. 2, 663.

27 Memo, The Situation in South Vietnam, August 13, 1964, LJBL, NSF Country File Vietnam, box 7.
28 Letter, Zhou to Sihanouk, August 27, 1962, in *ZGDWGXWJ* (1962), 289–90.
29 Telegram, US Embassy in Phnom Penh to the Department of State, November 6, 1962, JFKL, NSF Countries, box 17.
30 Telegram, US Embassy in Phnom Penh to the Department of State, November 8, 1962, JFKL, NSF Countries, box 17.
31 Speech, Liu to Sihanouk, February 12, 1963, in *ZGDWGXWJ* (1963), 156; Roger M. Smith, *Cambodia's Foreign Policy* (Ithaca, NY: Cornell University Press, 1965), 226–38.
32 Minutes, Deng's Talk with Lon Nol (Excerpt), March 14, 1964, in *DXPNP,* vol. 3, 1804.
33 Instruction, Mao to the National Planning Leadership Group, May 11, 1964, in "Mao Zedong sixiang wansui" [hereafter *MZDSX*] [Long live Mao Zedong thought] (1969), 496, available at Smith College Library, Northampton, MA.
34 Telegram, the PRC Embassy in Hanoi to the Foreign Ministry, August 5, 1964, CFMA, 113-00439-02, 37.
35 Telegram, the PRC's Chargé d'Affaires in Laos to the Foreign Ministry, August 11, 1964, CFMA, 113-00439-02, 39–40.
36 Telegram from the Embassy in Cambodia to the Department of State, March 26, 1964, *Foreign Relations of the United States* [hereafter *FRUS*], *1964–1968,* vol. 27, *Mainland Southeast Asia, Regional Affairs,* https://history.state.gov/historicaldocuments/frus1964-68v27/d123.
37 Memorandum of Conversation, August 12, 1964, *FRUS, 1964–1968,* vol. 27, *Mainland Southeast Asia, Regional Affairs,* https://history.state.gov/historicaldocuments/frus1964-68v27/d144.
38 Minutes, Mao's Talk with Sihanouk, September 28, 1964, in "77 Conversations between Chinese and Foreign Leaders on the Wars in Indochina, 1964–1977" [hereafter "77 Conversations"], *Cold War International History Project Working Paper* 22 (1998), 71.
39 Minutes, Zhou's Talk with Sihanouk, October 1, 1964, CFMA, 204-01548-01, cited in Zhai Qiang, "Zhou Enlai yu ZhongJian hezuo guanxi de jianli, 1954–1965" [Zhou Enlai and the establishment of cooperative relations between China and Cambodia, 1954–1965], *Nankai xuebao* [*Nankai Journal*] 1 (2014): 30.
40 Minutes, Zhou's Talk with Sihanouk (Excerpt), October 4, 1964, in Li Lianqing, *Da waijiaojia Zhou Enlai* [hereafter *DWJJ*] [Zhou Enlai: a great diplomat], vol. 5 (Hong Kong: Tiandi tushu youxian gongsi, 2001), 269.
41 *Dierci bujiemeng guojia de guojia huo zhengfu shounao huiyi wenjian huibian* [Collected documents of the second summit of non-aligned countries] (Beijing: 1964), 181–82, available at China Foreign Affairs University Library, Beijing.
42 Melvin Gurtov, *China and Southeast Asia: The Politics of Survival: A Study of Foreign Policy Interaction* (Baltimore: Johns Hopkins University Press, 1975), 67–68.
43 Memo, The Situation in South Vietnam, October 28, 1964, LBJL, NSF Country File Vietnam, box 9.
44 The Department of State: Daily Summary, November 10, 1964, LBJL, NSF Agency File, box 48.
45 Memo, The Situation in South Vietnam, n.d. [November 12–18, 1964], LBJL, NSF Country File Vietnam, box 10.
46 Memo, The Situation in South Vietnam, December 16, 1964, LBJL, NSF Country File Vietnam, box 11.

47 Memo, The Situation in South Vietnam, December 23, 1964, LBJL, NSF Country File Vietnam, box 11.
48 Memo, Sino-Vietnamese Frictions, June 21, 1967, LBJL, NSF Country File Vietnam, box 201.
49 Memo, The Situation in South Vietnam, August 13, 1964, LBJL, NSF Country File Vietnam, box 7.
50 Telegram, the PRC Embassy in Hanoi to the Foreign Ministry, September 30, 1964, CFMA, 113-00404-08, 10.
51 *Bolieriniefu yanlun* [Collected speeches of Brezhnev], vol. 1 (Shanghai: Shanghai renmin chubanshe, 1974), 60.
52 Li Ke and Hao Shengzhang, *Wenhua dageming zhong de renmin jiefangjun,* 409.
53 "Minutes of Conversations, A.N. Kosygin and Mao Zedong, 11 February, 1965," in Sergey Radchenko, *Two Suns in the Heavens: The Sino-Soviet Struggle for Supremacy, 1962–1967* (Stanford, CA: Stanford University Press, 2009), 228.
54 Memo, Communist Differences over Political Settlement in Indochina, March 5, 1965, LBJL, NSF Country File Vietnam, box 14.
55 Speech, Li Xiannian at the Political Work Conference in Tianjin, February 22, 1965, Tianjin Municipal Archive, X0003-Y-011876, 2–3.
56 Intelligence Brief, October 2, 1964, LBJL, DSDUF, box 5; Intelligence Brief, October 16, 1964, LBJL, DSDUF, box 5; Intelligence Memorandum, Cambodia's Role in the Movement of Arms and Ammunition to the Vietnamese Communists, July 1968, LBJL, NSF Country File, box 237; International Department of Xinhua News Agency, ed., *Yinduzhina wenti ziliao: Jianpuzhai wenti dashiji (1954 nian zhi 1972 naindi)* [hereafter *YZWT*] [Materials on the question of Indochina: a chronicle of major events on the question of Cambodia, 1954–1972] (1973), 26, available at Tsinghua University Libraries, Beijing; Tan Shi et al., *Jianpuzhai* [Cambodia] (Nanning: Guangxi renmin chubanshe, 1985), 140.
57 NIE (National Intelligence Estimate): Soviet Military Posture and Policies in the Third World, vol. 2, August 2, 1973, RMNL, Mandatory Review Opening, May 20, 2015, box 1.
58 Economic Intelligence Statistical Handbook: 1968, July 1968, LBJL, NSF Agency File, box 10.
59 Memo, The Situation in Vietnam, February 24, 1965, LBJL, NSF Country File Vietnam, box 49.
60 Memo, The Situation in Vietnam, February 23, 1965, LBJL, NSF Country File Vietnam, box 49.
61 Memo, Vietnam Checklist for the Director of Central Intelligence, March 17, 1965, LBJL, RAC (Remote Archives Capture) Project File, box 3.
62 Speech, Xu at the Teleconference of Nanjing Military Region, April 19, 1965, in *Xu Shiyou junshi wenxuan* [Xu Shiyou's selected works on military affairs] (Beijing: Junshi kexue chubanshe, 2012), 666.
63 Memo, The Situation in the Far East, April 29, 1965, NATO Archives, C-M (65) 34.
64 She Chunshu, *Jianpuzhai: baojing cangsang* [Cambodia: many vicissitudes in history] (Hong Kong: City University of Hong Kong Press, 2004), 56.
65 Intelligence Memorandum, Cambodia and the Vietnamese Communists: A New Phase? June 13, 1966, LBJL, NSF Country File, box 237.
66 Memo, The Situation in South Vietnam, March 10, 1965, LBJL, NSF Country File Vietnam, box 15 [2 of 2].
67 Memo, Negotiating Initiatives on Vietnam, August 2, 1965, LBJL, NSF Country File Vietnam, box 197.

68 Memo, Communist Positions on a New Geneva Conference on Cambodia, April 26, 1965, LBJL, NSF Country File, box 236.
69 Memo, The Situation in South Vietnam, April 28, 1965, LBJL, NSF Country File Vietnam, box 16 [2 of 2].
70 Memo, Vietnam Checklist for the Director of Central Intelligence, April 25, 1965, LBJL, RAC Project File, box 3.
71 Zhang Aiping, ed., *Zhongguo renmin jiefangjun* [The Chinese People's Liberation Army], vol. 1 (Beijing: Dangdai zhongguo chubanshe, 1994), 274.
72 *WJS,* vol. 2, 36–37.
73 Intelligence Information Cable, April 29, 1965, LBJL, NSF Country File, box 238.
74 Memo, The Situation in South Vietnam, April 28, 1965, LBJL, NSF Country File Vietnam, box 16 [2 of 2].
75 *YZWT,* 21.
76 *Zhou Enlai waijiao huodong dashiji, 1949–1975* [A chronicle of major events of Zhou Enlai's foreign affairs activities, 1949–1975] [hereafter *ZELWJHDDSJ*] (Beijing: Shijie zhishi chubanshe, 1993), 450.
77 Telegram, Zhou to Sihanouk (Excerpt), May 20, 1965, in *ZELNP,* vol. 2, 731.
78 Kang Daisha, "Zai Jianpuzhai de rizi" [The days in Cambodia], in *Nü waijiaoguan* [The female diplomats], ed. Cheng Xiangjun (Beijing: Renmin tiyu chubanshe, 1995), 478.
79 Minutes, Zhou's Talk with Dong, September 9, 1965, in "77 Conversations," 88.
80 Speech, Zhou at the National Planning Meeting, November 11, 1965, Hunan Provincial Archive, 192-1-400, 12–13.
81 Memo, Vietnam Checklist for the Director of Central Intelligence, November 21, 1965, LBJL, RAC Project File, box 7.
82 Memo, Vietnam Checklist for the Director of Central Intelligence, December 12, 1965, LBJL, RAC Project File, box 7.
83 Memo, The Situation in South Vietnam, March 30, 1966, LBJL, NSF Country File Vietnam, box 29.
84 Foreign Broadcast Information Service (FBIS), Cambodian Ministers' Resignation, September 11, 1967, LBJL, NSF Country File, box 242.
85 *DWJJ,* vol. 6, 101.
86 Ibid., 101–2.
87 Intelligence Memorandum, Cambodia and the Vietnamese Communists, November 16, 1967, LBJL, NSF Country File Vietnam, box 92.
88 DRV-Cambodia Joint Communiqué, January 12, 1968, LBJL, NSF Country File Vietnam, box 92.
89 Minutes, Zhou's Talk with Cambodian Communist Leaders (Excerpt), November 30, 1968, in *ZELNP,* vol. 3, 267.
90 Information Intelligence Cable, March 18, 1970, Gerald R. Ford Presidential Library, NSC Vietnam Information Group Intelligence and Other Reports, 1967–1975, box 10.
91 Minutes, Zhou's Talk with Le Duan et al., April 13, 1966, in "77 Conversations," 94.
92 Memo, Hanoi Lays Down "Basis" for Vietnam Talks, April 15, 1965, LBJL, NSF Country File Vietnam, box 16 [1 of 2].
93 Memo, The Situation in South Vietnam, August 18, 1965, LBJL, NSF Country File Vietnam, box 22.
94 Intelligence Information Cable, December 29, 1966, LBJL, NSF Country File Vietnam, box 38.

95 Text of Central Intelligence Agency (CIA) Report on Soviet Officials' Views on the Vietnam War and the USSR's Aims in Europe, April 3, 1967, LBJL, NSF Country File Vietnam, box 92.
96 Intelligence Information Cable, July 20, 1967, LBJL, NSF Country File Vietnam, box 84.
97 Memorandum of Conversation, February 12, 1968, LBJL, NSF Country File Vietnam, box 140.
98 Memo, Chronology of US-DRV Exchanges on Meeting Site, May 6, 1968, LBJL, NSF Country File Vietnam, box 131.
99 Ibid.
100 Zhang Aiping, *Zhongguo renmin jiefangjun,* 274; Xie Lifu, "Mao Zedong miandui Meiguo" [Mao Zedong facing the United States], in *Waijiao zhanluejia Mao Zedong* [Mao Zedong: a diplomatic strategist], ed. Deng Liqun (Beijing: Zhongyang minzu daxue chubanshe, 2003), 523–24.
101 Li Ke and Hao Shengzhang, *Wenhua dageming zhong de renmin jiefangjun,* 423.
102 Memo, The Situation in South Vietnam, September 22, 1965, LBJL, NSF Country File Vietnam, box 22.
103 Minutes, Mao's Talk with Le Duan (Excerpt), November 8, 1966, in *MZDNP,* vol. 6, 14–15.
104 Minutes, Zhou's Talk with Pham Van Dong, April 13, 1968, in "77 Conversations," 121–23.
105 Minutes, Zhou's Talk with Pham Van Dong et al., April 29, 1968, in "77 Conversations," 127.
106 Telegram, US Consulate in Hong Kong to the Department of State: Beijing and the Vietnam Peace Talks, May 16, 1968, RMNL, NSC Files, Paris Talks Meetings, box 165; Intelligence Memorandum, Sino-Vietnamese Frictions, June 27, 1968, LBJL, NSF Intelligence File, box 14.
107 "1965–1973 nian Zhongguo dui Yuenan de yuanzhu" [Chinese Aid to Vietnam, 1965–1973], https://www.sohu.com/a/280367117_120049412.
108 Robert S. Ross, *Negotiating Cooperation: The United States and China, 1969–1989* (Stanford, CA: Stanford University Press, 1995), 24.
109 Minutes, Zhou's Talk with Xuan Thuy (Excerpt), July 1, 1969, cited in Liao Xinwen, "Ershi shiji liuqishiniandai Mao Zedong, Deng Xiaoping deng dapo Sulian baowei de zhanlue sixiang yu juece licheng" [Strategic thoughts and decision making of Mao Zedong and Deng Xiaoping on breaking Soviet encirclement in the 1960s–70s], *Dangde wenxian* [*The Party's Documents*] 6 (2010): 36. Xuan Thuy was the DRV's foreign minister.
110 Letter, Zhou to the CCP Vice Chairman Lin Biao (Excerpt), June 27, 1969, in Gao Wenqian, *Wannian Zhou Enlai* [Zhou Enlai's later years] (Hong Kong: Mirror Books, 2003), 410.
111 Memo, Lynn to Kissinger, May 28, 1970, RMNL, NSC Files, Cambodian Operations, box 585. Lawrence E. Lynn was a staff member of the National Security Council.
112 *WJS,* vol. 3, 73.
113 *MZDNP,* vol. 6, 296–97; Benshu bianjizu, ed., *Mao Zedong guoji jiaowanglu* [Records of Mao Zedong's international activities] (Beijing: Zhonggong dangshi chubanshe, 1995), 77.
114 Miyazaki Seon, *Gongqishimin huiyilu* [Miyazaki Seon's memoirs], trans. Yang Guiyan (Beijing: Zhongguo shehui kexue chubanshe, 2012), 121–22.
115 Memo, The Department of State to Kissinger, May 20, 1970, RMNL, NSC Files, Cambodian Operations, box 579.
116 FBIS, Soviet Statements on Nixon's Speech, May 4, 1970, RMNL, NSC Files, Cambodian Operations, box 584.

117 *YZWT,* 66.
118 Memo, The Department of State to Kissinger, May 28, 1970, RMNL, NSC Files, Cambodian Operations, box 580.
119 Memo, The Department of State to Kissinger: Daily Report on Cambodia, No. 60, June 24, 1970, RMNL, NSC Files, Cambodian Operations, box 580.
120 Memo, Holdridge to Kissinger: Soviet Shipping to North Vietnam, July 8, 1970, RMNL, NSC Files, Vietnam Country Files, box 148. John H. Holdridge was a staff member of the National Security Council.
121 Xie Lifu, "Mao Zedong miandui Meiguo," 534.
122 Statements by Prince Norodom Sihanouk, 1965–1973, GRFL, NSC East Asian and Pacific Affairs Staff Files, box 17.
123 Yuichi Kubota, *Armed Groups in Cambodian Civil War: Territorial Control, Rivalry, and Recruitment* (New York: Palgrave Macmillan, 2013), 53.
124 Memo, Direct and Specific Messages between the US and PRC, n.d., RMNL, NSC Files for the President's Files, China/Vietnam Negotiations, box 1031.
125 Gao Wenqian, *Wannian Zhou Enlai,* 414.
126 Memo, Kissinger to Nixon: China at Warsaw Talks Suggest US Send High-Level Representative to Beijing, February 20, 1970, RMNL, NSC Files for the President's Files, China/Vietnam Negotiations, box 1031.
127 *MZDNP,* vol. 6, 286.
128 Memo, Direct and Specific Messages between the US and PRC, n.d., RMNL, NSC Files for the President's Files, China/Vietnam Negotiations, box 1031.
129 Ibid.
130 Minutes, Zhou's Talk with Pakistan's President Yahya Khan, November 13, 1970, in *Zhou Enlai waijiao wenxuan* [hereafter *ZELWJ*] [Zhou Enlai's selected works on diplomacy] (Beijing: Zhongyang wenxian chubanshe, 1990), 466–67.
131 Memo, Direct and Specific Messages between the US and PRC, n.d., RMNL, NSC Files for the President's Files, China/Vietnam Negotiations, box 1031.
132 Lu Guang, "Xiaoqiu zhuandong diqiu: 'pingpang waijiao' qinliji" [The small ball shapes the earth: my experience in the "ping-pong diplomacy"], in *Jianzheng Aolinpike* [Witnessing the Olympics], ed. Tang Mingxin, Feng Guijia, and Zhang Bing (Beijing: Xinhua chubanshe, 2007), 264.
133 Message, Nixon to Zhou, May 10, 1971, RMNL, NSC Files for the President's Files, China/Vietnam Negotiations, box 1031.
134 Recent Messages between US and PRC, n.d., RMNL, NSC Files for the President's Files, China/Vietnam Negotiations, box 1031.
135 Ibid.
136 Telegram, Ousarma in Vientiane to the Defense Department: Conversation with Polish Military Adviser to the ICC, June 1, 1971, RMNL, NSC Files, Vietnam Country Files, box 155.
137 Memorandum, Kissinger to Nixon, April 17, 1971, *FRUS, 1969–1976,* vol. 7, *Vietnam, July 1970–January 1972,* 554.
138 Kang Maozhao, *Waijiaoguan huiyilu* [A diplomat's memoirs] (Beijing: Zhongyang wenxian chubanshe, 2000), 207.
139 Fan Shuo, *Ye Jianying zai feichang shiqi, 1966–1976* [Ye Jianying at critical moments, 1966–1976] (Beijing: Huawen chubanshe, 2006), 280.
140 Memorandum of Conversation, July 10, 1971, *FRUS, 1969–1976,* vol. 17, *China,* 420.

141 Ibid., 416–18. China continued to maintain its diplomatic relationship with the government of Laos. Therefore, the term "the people of Laos" referred to communists in Laos.

142 FBIS, July 19, 1971, RMNL, NSC Files, President's Trip Files, box 499.

143 Memo, Negroponte to Haig: Hanoi Concerned about Diminished Worldwide Interest in Vietnam, October 20, 1971, RMNL, NSC Files, Alexander M. Haig Chronological Files, box 989.

144 Kang Maozhao, *Waijiaoguan huiyilu,* 205.

145 Zhou Enlai, "Chou En-lai's Report on the International Situation, December 1971," *Issues and Studies* 14, 1 (1977): 114.

146 Li Yongming, *Wode jizhe shengya* [My career as a journalist] (Singapore: Renmin chubanshe siren youxian gongsi, 2007), 143.

147 *YZWT,* 113.

148 FBIS, Sihanouk Says PRC, DRV Have Assured Him of Continued Aid, October 4, 1972, RMNL, Systemic Review Opening (August 21, 2013), box 48.

149 Intelligence Memo, CIA: Developments in Indochina, July 4, 1972, RMNL, Systemic Review Opening (August 21, 2013), box 46.

150 Memo, Holdridge to Kissinger: Appraisal of the May 8 Measure, One Month Later, June 7, 1972, RMNL, NSC Files, Vietnam Country Files, box 160.

151 *FRUS, 1969–1976,* vol. 17, *China,* 1110.

152 Telegram, The Situation Room to Kissinger, May 18, 1973, RMNL, NSC Files, Kissinger Office Files, HAK Trip Files, box 34.

153 Speech, Li at the National Physical Education Work Conference, January 22, 1973, Shanghai Municipal Archive, B246-2-840-47, 5–6.

154 Liu Wanzhen and Li Qinggui, eds., *Mao Zedong guoji jiaowanglu, zengdingben* [Records of Mao Zedong's international activities, expanded version] (Beijing: Zhonggong dangshi chubanshe, 2003), 377–78.

155 Minutes, Mao's Talk with Le Duan et al. (Excerpt), February 1, 1973, in *MZDNP,* vol. 6, 466–68.

156 Minutes, Vernon Walters's Talk with Vo Van Sung, November 3, 1971, RMNL, NSC Files for the President's Files, Vietnam Negotiations, box 854.

157 "ZhongYue Beibuwan huajie shuangfang haiyu mianji xiangdang, wei sheji daoyu zhuquan" [China and Vietnam equally share the Beibu Gulf, no reference to sovereignty disputes over islands], August 3, 2004, http://news.sina.com.cn/c/2004-08-03/04203274593s.shtml.

158 Huang Guo'an et al., *ZhongYue guanxishi jianbian* [A concise history of the Sino-Vietnamese relationship] (Nanning: Guangxi renmin chubanshe, 1986), 242.

159 Fan Shuo, ed., *Ye Jianying zhuan* [Biography of Ye Jianying] (Beijing: Dangdai Zhongguo chubanshe, 1995), 615; "Guanyu Huangsha qundao he Changsha qundao de baipishu" [The South Vietnamese White Book on the South China Sea], in Zhongguo guojifa xuehui, ed., *Guojifa ziliao* [International law materials], vol. 5 (Beijing: Falü chubanshe, 1990), 86.

160 Xiao Xiqing, *ZhongFei waijiao guanxishi* [Chinese-Philippine diplomatic relations] (Taipei: Zhengzhong shuju, 1995), 881–82.

161 "Information, über Gespräch mit führenden Genossen des ZK der KPdSU während der internen Chinaberatung von 16.-18. Mai 1973 in Moskau," May 24, 1973, Stiftung Archiv der Parteien und Massenorganisationen der DDR im Bundesarchiv [Archive of the Foundation of the Parties and Mass Organizations of the GDR in the Federal Archives] (SAPMO), DY 30/IV B 2/20/582, Berlin-Lichterfelde.

162 Telegram, US Embassy in Moscow to the Department of State, August 21, 1973, GRFL, NSC Vietnam Information Group Intelligence and Other Reports, 1967–1975, box 12.
163 Sydney H. Schanberg, "Moscow, Backing Sihanouk, Will Leave Only 'Caretakers' in Phnom Penh," *New York Times,* October 22, 1973; Sydney H. Schanberg, "All but 3 Soviet Aides Leave Cambodia," *New York Times,* October 26, 1973.
164 Telegram, US Embassy in Moscow to the Department of State, November 9, 1973, GRFL, NSC Vietnam Information Group Intelligence and Other Reports, 1967–1975, box 12.
165 Memorandum of Conversation, November 13 and 14, 1973, *FRUS, 1969–1976,* vol. 18, *China,* 424.
166 Intelligence Information Cable, December 14, 1973, GRFL, NSC Vietnam Information Group Intelligence and Other Reports, 1967–1975, box 10.
167 Radio TV Report: Sihanouk to CBS News, September 3, 1973, RMNL, NSC Files, Kissinger Office Files, Country Files Far East, box 99.
168 Minutes, Mao's Talk with Sihanouk et al. (Excerpt), April 2, 1974, in *MZDNP,* vol. 6, 526.
169 Telegram, US Consulate in Hong Kong to the Department of State, May 28, 1974, GRFL, NSC Vietnam Information Group Intelligence and Other Reports, 1967–1975, box 1.
170 Minutes, Qiao's Talk with Kissinger, October 2, 1974, *FRUS, 1969–1976,* vol. 18, *China,* 540–41.
171 Minutes, Deng's Talk with Mansfield, December 12, 1974, GRFL, Presidential Country Files for East Asia and the Pacific, box 14.
172 *WJS,* vol. 3, 77.
173 Robert S. Ross, *The Indochina Tangle: China's Vietnam Policy, 1975–1979* (New York: Columbia University Press, 1988); Xiaoming Zhang, *Deng Xiaoping's Long War: The Military Conflict between China and Vietnam, 1979–1991* (Chapel Hill: University of North Carolina Press, 2015).

Chapter 5: Regional Diplomacy in the New Era

1 Dennis Hickey and Lilly Kelan Lu, "Japan's Military Modernization: The Chinese Perspective," in *China and Japan at Odds: Deciphering the Perpetual Conflict,* ed. James C. Hsiung (New York: Palgrave Macmillan, 2007), 105–6.
2 Richard C. Bush, *The Perils of Proximity: China-Japan Security Relations* (Washington, DC: Brookings Institution Press, 2010), 41; Eric Heginbotham and Richard J. Samuels, "Active Denial: Redesigning Japan's Response to China's Military Challenge," *International Security* 42, 4 (2018): 166.
3 Michael Beckley, "The Emerging Military Balance in East Asia," *International Security* 42, 2 (2017): 95–98.
4 Kai He, "China and Southeast Asia: Strategic Interdependence in the Making," *Asia Policy* 13, 4 (2018): 17.
5 Manjeet Pardesi, "Explaining the Asymmetry in the Sino-Indian Strategic Rivalry," *Australian Journal of International Affairs* 75, 3 (2021): 347–48.
6 John W. Garver, "Sino-Indian Rapproachement and the Sino-Pakistan Entente," *Political Science Quarterly* 111, 2 (1996): 327–33.
7 "Zhongguo changzhu lianheguo daibiaotuan fayanren jiu anlihui shenyi Keshimi'er wenti da jizhe wen" [The spokesman of the PRC's Permanent Mission to the United Nations at the press conference: on the question of Kashmir at the UN Security Council],

August 6, 2020, https://baijiahao.baiducom/s?id=1674221423062328152&wfr=spider&for=pc.

8 Tan Xinmu, "Meikongjun ni zai Guandao bushu zhanji" [The US Air Force will be deployed in Guam], *Jiefangjun bao* [hereafter *JFJB*] [*People's Liberation Army Daily*], January 15, 2004, 5; "Mei zai Guandao bushu dingji zhanji 'Youling'" [The United States will deploy B-2 in Guam], *Cankao xiaoxi* [hereafter *RN*] [*Reference News*], October 14, 2007, 1; "Mei F-22 'Mengqin' zhanji bushu Guandao" [The F-22 Raptors will be deployed in Guam], *RN*, August 9, 2008, 2.

9 Pete Brush, "U.S., Philippines Joint Exercises," April 23, 2002, https://www.cbsnews.com/news/us-philippines-joint-exercises-23-04-2002/.

10 "US Troops Arrive in Philippines for Military Exercises," February 16, 2004, https://www.globalsecurity.org/military/library/news/2004/02/mil-040216-pla-daily03.htm.

11 "Mei jiang dafu zengjia dui Feilübin de junyuan" [The United States will significantly enhance military support to the Philippines], October 25, 2004, https://news.sina.com.cn/o/2004-10-25/10504028674s.shtml.

12 Jeffrey Hill, "Ex-Im Bank Issues $118 Million Loan to Vietnam for Lockheed Satellite," October 2, 2012, https://www.satellitetoday.com/government-military/2012/10/02/ex-im-bank-issues-118-million-loan-to-vietnam-for-lockheed-satellite/.

13 Matthew Lee, "US Pledges $32.5m in Naval Aid to Southeast Asia Nations," *Boston Globe*, December 17, 2013, https://www.bostonglobe.com/news/world/2013/12/17/increases-naval-aid-southeast-asia/I5b60Of3OJiaBTPTLyp61I/story.html.

14 "Malaixiya zhuangbei F/A-18 zhanji yiyou 22 nian" [It has been 22 years since Malaysia received F/A-18 fighters], May 11, 2019, https://baijiahao.baidu.com/s?id=1633189462577619555&wfr=spider&for=pc.

15 "Vietnam, Japan Ink Defense Cooperation Deal," October 25, 2011, http://www.thanhniennews.com/politics/vietnam-japan-ink-defense-cooperation-deal-9866.html.

16 Scott Cheney-Peters, "Japan to Provide Vietnam Patrol Boats Next Year," June 2, 2014, https://news.usni.org/2014/06/02/japan-provide-vietnam-patrol-boats-next-year.

17 "Anbei fangwen Yuenan" [Abe's visit to Vietnam], January 17, 2013, http://world.people.com.cn/n/2013/0117/c157278-20239419.html.

18 "Japan Pledges Patrol Vessels, Loans to Vietnam," September 16, 2015, http://www.thanhniennews.com/politics/japan-pledges-patrol-vessels-loans-to-vietnam-51406.html.

19 "Japan Pledges $820 Million Loan to Support Ho Chi Minh City Metro Project," May 31, 2016, https://e.vnexpress.net/news/business/japan-pledges-820-million-loan-to-support-ho-chi-minh-city-metro-project-3411692.html.

20 "E'bao cheng E'Zhong junshi hezuo shengwen" [Russian media say Sino-Russian military cooperation will be advanced], *RN*, March 2, 2007, 5; "Zhong'E lianhe junyan dierlun cuoshang jieshu" [The conclusion of the second round negotiations of the Sino-Russian joint exercises], *RN*, June 7, 2009, 5; "E waizhang: Zhong'E junyan wuguan Nanhai zhengduan" [The Russian foreign minister: the Sino-Russian exercises are irrelevant to the South China Sea disputes], *RN*, August 7, 2015, 16; Sam LaGrone, "China, Russia Kick Off Joint South China Sea Naval Exercise; Includes 'Island Seizing' Drill," September 12, 2016, https://news.usni.org/2016/09/12/china-russia-start-joint-south-china-sea-naval-exercise-includes-island-seizing-drill; "Zhong'E jiangzai Xi Jinping daofang shi qiandadan" [China and Russia will conclude a big contract during Xi Jinping's visit], *RN*, July 3, 2017, 16; Franz-Stefan Gady, "China, Russia Kick Off Anti-Ballistic Missile Defense Exercise,"

December 12, 2017, https://thediplomat.com/2017/12/china-russia-kick-off-anti-ballistic-missile-defense-exercise/; "Zhongguo jundui di E canjia Shanghe junyan" [The PLA arrived in Russia for SCO military exercises], *RN,* August 18, 2018, 8; "Zhong E haijun xiazhou qingdao lianhe junyan" [China and Russia will conduct joint naval exercises in Qingdao next week], *RN,* April 26, 2019, 16; "Daji guoji kongbu zhuyi juyou chuncui fangyu xingzhi Zhong E deng duoguo kaiqi daguimo junyan" [China, Russia, and other countries will conduct large-scale military exercises for self-defence and anti-terrorism purposes], *RN,* September 16, 2019, 1; "Shenhua junshi hezuo weihu diqu wending Zhong'E junyan zhanxian liangguo guanxi xingaodu" [Strengthening military cooperation for regional stability, the Sino-Russian cooperation has been upgraded by joint military exercises], *RN,* August 12, 2021, 16; "Zhong'E haijun chuanyue Jinqing haixia" [Chinese and Russian navies pass through the Strait of Tsugaru], *RN,* October 20, 2021, 16; "Gangmei shuping Zhong'E'Yi Amanwan junyan ju zhanlueyiyi" [The Hong Kong media: the Sino-Russian-Iranian military exercise has strategic implications in the Sea of Oman], *RN,* January 23, 2022, 8.

21 Alexander Korolev, "Systemic Balancing and Regional Hedging: China-Russia Relations," *Chinese Journal of International Politics* 9, 4 (2016): 391–93; Alexander Korolev, "Russia in the South China Sea: Balancing and Hedging," *Foreign Policy Analysis* 15, 2 (2019): 263–82.

22 "E 2005 nian jiang xiang Yuenan tigong S-300PMU1 fangkong daodan" [Russia will provide S-300PMU1 air defence missiles to Vietnam in 2005], August 25, 2003, http://news.sina.com.cn/w/2003-08-25/0842628484s.shtml; "E nishou Yue liebao huweijian" [Russia will provide frigates to Vietnam], *RN,* November 20, 2006, 2; "E xiang Yuenan chushou duosou qianting" [Russia will sell several submarines to Vietnam], *RN,* December 17, 2009, 2; "Jiakan ping Yue haijun goumai liusou 'Jiluo' 636" [The Canadian media: Vietnam's navy purchases six Project 636 Kilo-class submarines], *RN,* April 27, 2010, 5.

23 "Malaixiya dasuan zenggou Su-30 zhanji" [Malaysia will purchase more Su-30s], *RN,* December 14, 2007, 5; "Russia's Su-30MKM to Remain Malaysian Air Force's Major Fighter – Source," March 26, 2019, https://tass.com/defense/1050532.

24 "E'luosi jiangyu Yuenan lianhe kaifa Nanhai liangge daxing tianranqitian" [Russia will conduct joint exploitations with Vietnam for two large gas fields in the South China Sea], April 10, 2012, http://mil.news.sina.com.cn/2012-04-10/0838687158.html; "Russia State Oil Firm Starts Drilling at New Well Offshore Vietnam," May 15, 2018, https://www.rigzone.com/news/wire/russia_state_oil_firm_starts_drilling_at_new_well_offshore_vietnam-15-may-2018-154614-article.

25 "E fandui waibu shili jieru Nanhai zhengduan" [Russia opposes any extra-regional power's intervention in the South China Sea disputes], *RN,* May 22, 2012, 16.

26 "E waizhang: Zhong'E junyan wuguan Nanhai zhengduan," 16.

27 "Wang Yi Talks about South China Sea Issue: Facts Will Tell and Justice Will Prevail," May 24, 2016, http://www.chinese-embassy.org.uk/eng/HotTopics/errorpath/t1367176.htm.

28 "China, Russia Plan Joint Military Drills in South China Sea," July 28, 2016, https://www.militarytimes.com/2016/07/28/china-russia-plan-joint-military-drills-in-south-china-sea/.

29 "Pujing: Zhichi Zhongguo buchengren Nanhai zhongcai" [Putin: supporting Chinese positions against the South China Sea Arbitration], September 6, 2016, http://world.

huanqiu.com/exclusive/2016-09/9404788.html; "South China Sea: China Praises Putin, Slams Obama," September 8, 2016, https://www.thebricspost.com/south-china-sea-china-praises-putin-slams-obama/.

30 Joshua P. Rowan, "US-Japan Security Alliance, ASEAN, and the South China Sea Dispute," *Asian Survey* 45, 3 (2005): 419–20.

31 Speech, Zhu Rongji at the 57th Meeting of the Standing Committee of the PRC's State Council, April 30, 2002, in *Zhu Rongji jianghua shilu* [Zhu Rongji's collected speeches], vol. 4 (Beijing: Renmin chubanshe, 2011), 357.

32 "Zhongguo yu Dongmeng qianshu 'Nanhai gefang xingwei xuanyan' huxin jiaqiang" [The Chinese-ASEAN "Declaration of the Conduct of Parties in the South China Sea" promotes mutual trust], November 4, 2002, http://news.sohu.com/63/43/news204124363.shtml.

33 "Yuenan he Malaixiya lianshou kance Nansha" [Vietnam and Malaysia jointly explore the Nansha Islands], March 17, 2006, http://news.sohu.com/20060317/n242338169.shtml; Prashanth Parameswaran, "Vietnam-Malaysia Navy Ties in Focus with Bilateral Visit," July 5, 2018, https://thediplomat.com/2018/07/vietnam-malaysia-navy-ties-in-focus-with-bilateral-visit/.

34 Congress of the Philippines, Fourteenth Congress, Second Regular Session, "An Act to Amend Certain Provisions of Republic Act No. 3046, as Amended by Republic Act No. 5446, to Define the Archipelagic Baseline of the Philippines and for Other Purposes," March 10, 2009, https://www.lawphil.net/statutes/repacts/ra2009/ra_9522_2009.html.

35 "Zhongguo 'yuzheng jujian' Nanhai xuanshi zhuquan" [Large patrol ships of the fishery administration demonstrate China's sovereignty in the South China Sea], *RN*, March 16, 2009, 1.

36 Christopher Bodeen, "China Criticizes Clinton Comments on Island Chains," July 30, 2010, http://archive.boston.com/news/world/asia/articles/2010/07/30/china_criticizes_clinton_comments_on_island_chains/.

37 "US, Vietnam to Launch Unprecedented Naval Exercises," August 10, 2010, https://www.globalsecurity.org/military/library/news/2010/08/mil-100810-voa09.htm.

38 Deng Yingwen, "Shilun Yuenan jiang Nanhai wenti guojihua zhi jucuo" [Vietnam's attempts to internationalize the South China Sea issue], *Dongnanya yanjiu* [*Southeast Asian Studies*] 6 (2010): 30–31.

39 "Feilübin kuochong junbei kongzhi Nansha daoyu la meijun wei ziji 'chengyao'" [The Philippines is building its armed forces and calling for American support], April 14, 2011, http://www.china.com.cn/military/txt/2011-04/14/content_22358086.htm; Renato Cruz De Castro and Walter Lohman, "U.S.-Philippines Partnership in the Cause of Maritime Defense," *Heritage Foundation Backgrounder*, August 8, 2011, https://www.heritage.org/asia/report/us-philippines-partnership-the-cause-maritime-defense.

40 "Wen Jiabao fangwen Malaixiya Yinni qianxi tan Nanhai zhengduan" [Wen Jiabao's talks on the South China Sea dispute prior to his visit to Malaysia and Indonesia], April 26, 2011, https://www.chinanews.com.cn/gn/2011/04-26/3000123_2.shtml.

41 "Dongmeng xiugai youguan Nanzhongguohai shengming" [ASEAN revises its statement on the South China Sea], *RN*, May 19, 2011, 16.

42 "China to Neighbors: Keep out of Spratlys," *Philippine Daily Inquirer*, June 10, 2011, https://newsinfo.inquirer.net/13613/china-to-neighbors-keep-out-of-spratlys; "Spratly Islands: A New Geo-Strategic Game?" June 22, 2011, https://www.c3sindia.org/geopolitics-strategy/spratly-islands-a-new-geo-strategic-game/.

43 "Statement of the Presidential Spokesperson on the Peaceful Settlement of Disputes in the West Philippine Sea," June 13, 2011, https://www.officialgazette.gov.ph/2011/06/13/statement-of-the-presidential-spokesperson-on-the-peaceful-settlement-of-disputes-in-the-west-philippine-sea-june-13-2011/.

44 "Mei yu Dongmeng liuguo juxing lianhe junyan" [The United States will conduct joint exercises with six ASEAN members], *RN,* June 15, 2011, 1.

45 Hillary Rodham Clinton, "Remarks with Philippines Foreign Secretary Albert del Rosario after Their Meeting," June 23, 2011, https://www.globalsecurity.org/military/library/news/2011/06/mil-110623-state01.htm.

46 Rodel Rodis, "The Dragon and the Mosquito," *Philippine Daily Inquirer,* July 13, 2011, https://globalnation.inquirer.net/5816/the-dragon-and-the-mosquito.

47 "Chen Bingde: Mei canyu Nanhai junyan butuo" [Chen Bingde: it is inappropriate that the United States joins the military exercise in the South China Sea], July 12, 2011, http://news.sohu.com/20110712/n313101154.shtml.

48 "Vietnam, Philippines Sign MoU on Naval Cooperation," October 27, 2011, http://www.thanhniennews.com/politics/vietnam-philippines-sign-mou-on-naval-cooperation-9865.html.

49 "PHL, Vietnam Agree to Enhance Cooperation at Hanoi Talks," October 8, 2011, https://www.officialgazette.gov.ph/2011/10/08/phl-vietnam-agree-to-enhance-cooperation-at-hanoi-talks/; "Yuenan yuanshou fang Fei: zhichi Fei Nanhai fang'an jiang jiaqiang haijun hezuo" [Vietnam's president visits the Philippines, supports the proposal in the South China Sea and enhances naval cooperation], October 27, 2011, http://news.sohu.com/20111027/n323581164.shtml.

50 "Ao'bama Xilali tongshi fangwen Yatai" [Obama and Hillary pay visits to the Asia-Pacific region], November 17, 2011, http://news.sohu.com/20111117/n325911171.shtml; Melissa Hellmann, "The U.S. Will Increase Its Military Presence in Australia," *Time,* August 12, 2014, https://time.com/3102616/us-military-presence-australia/.

51 In a speech at the fortieth-anniversary celebration of the Shanghai Communiqué. Cui Tiankai, "Jianding buyi tuijin ZhongMei hezuo huoban guanxi" [Resolutely pushing forward the Sino-American cooperative partnership], *Guoji wenti yanjiu* [*International Studies*] 2 (2012): 4.

52 "US, Vietnam Hold Joint Naval Drills amid China Tensions," April 23, 2012, http://www.nationmultimedia.com/breakingnews/US-Vietnam-hold-joint-naval-drills-amid-China-tens-30180505.html.

53 "The China-Philippine Banana War," June 6, 2012, https://www.asiasentinel.com/society/the-china-philippine-banana-war/.

54 "Sanshashi sheli lishun Nanhai ziyuan bantu" [The establishment of Sansha City sorts out a resource map in the South China Sea], June 22, 2012, https://business.sohu.com/20120622/n346287010.shtml.

55 Le Yucheng, "Dui guoji bianju yu Zhongguo waijiao de ruogan sikao" [Some reflections on the changing international environment and Chinese foreign policy], *Xiandai guoji guanxi* [*Contemporary International Relations*] 8 (2012): 6.

56 "Ribao baodao Zhongguo yong 'xingwei zhunze' xiang Dongmeng shiya" [The Japanese media: China is applying pressures upon the ASEAN by the 'Code of Conduct'], *RN,* March 29, 2013, 6.

57 Michael Green et al., "Counter-Coercion Series: Second Thomas Shoal Incident," June 9, 2017, https://amti.csis.org/counter-co-2nd-thomas-shoal/.

58 "Malaixiya lianshou FeiYue" [Malaysia cooperates with the Philippines and Vietnam], February 28, 2014, http://world.cankaoxiaoxi.com/2014/0228/353450.shtml; Prashanth Parameswaran, *Playing It Safe: Malaysia's Approach to the South China Sea and Implications for the United States* (Washington, DC: Center for a New American Security, February 2015), https://www.files.ethz.ch/isn/189746/CNAS%20Maritime%206_Parameswaran_Final.pdf.

59 Michael Green et al., "Counter-Coercion Series: China-Vietnam Oil Rig Standoff," June 12, 2017, https://amti.csis.org/counter-co-oil-rig-standoff/.

60 "Fei chao chiguajiao kuojian huati jiaoju Nanhai" [The Philippines is carrying out provocations in the South China Sea by making propaganda on the construction of the Chigua Island], *RN*, May 15, 2014, 16; Felix K. Chang, "China's (Is)land Reclamation in the South China Sea," May 16, 2014, https://www.fpri.org/2014/05/chinas-island-reclamation-in-the-south-china-sea/.

61 "Guofang daxue jiaoshou: Nanhai daojiao jianshe hui henkuai jieshu" [A professor of the National Defence University: construction on South China Sea islands will end soon], May 31, 2015, http://news.ifeng.com/a/20150531/43876134_0.shtml.

62 "Chiguajiao jichang jungong" [The completion of the airfield on Chigua Island], *RN*, March 16, 2016, 14.

63 "Tichu jiejue Nanhai wenti 'shuanggui silu' shi wushi weitiao" [The 'dual track' proposal is a practical adjustment to solve the South China Sea dispute], August 11, 2014, http://opinion.china.com.cn/opinion_14_106414.html.

64 "ZhongFei haijing jiang juxing gongtong xunlian" [China and the Philippines will conduct joint exercises for coast guards], *RN*, March 3, 2017, 16.

65 "China Commits $3.4bn for Philippine Projects," March 8, 2017, http://www.arabnews.com/node/1064751/business-economy.

66 "Vietnam, China to Strengthen Defense Cooperation," August 31, 2016, https://en.qdnd.vn/military/intl-relations-and-cooperation/vietnam-china-to-strengthen-defense-cooperation-473099.

67 "Zhongguo haijun qianting shoufang Malaixiya" [The Chinese navy pays the first visit to Malaysia], *RN*, January 8, 2017, 8; "Chinese Submarine Confirmed a Stopover in Malaysia," January 10, 2017, http://www.china.org.cn/china/2017-01/10/content_40067691.htm.

68 "Zhongguo tiyi she Nanhai yan'anguo hezuo jizhi" [China proposes to establish cooperative mechanisms with neighbours in the South China Sea], *RN*, March 28, 2017, 16.

69 "Zhongguo Dongmeng tongguo Nanhai xingwei zhunze kuangjia" [China and the ASEAN conclude a framework agreement over the COC], *RN*, May 19, 2017, 16.

70 "Nanhai youle 'zhunze' kuangjia yuwai ganshe ke xiu yi" [When the "framework" agreement of the COC is available, extra-regional interventions should be over], August 7, 2017, https://www.sohu.com/a/163025731_162758.

71 "Xi Jinping jiu Dongmeng chengli 50 zhounian xiang Dongmeng lunzhi zhuxiguo Feilübin zongtong Dutu'erte zhi hedian" [Xi Jinping's congratulatory remarks to President Duterte on ASEAN's 50th anniversary year], August 8, 2017, http://news.xinhuanet.com/politics/2017-08/08/c_1121449525.htm.

72 "Di qici Zhongguo-Dongmeng fangzhang feizhengshi huiwu juxing" [The seventh informal meeting of Chinese and ASEAN defence ministers], October 24, 2017, https://baijiahao.baidu.com/s?id=1582092330864549582&wfr=spider&for=pc.

73 "Xi Jinping zaici huijian Yuegong zhonngyang zongshuji Ruan Zhonngfu" [Xi's second talk with Nguyen Phu Trong, general secretary of the Communist Party of Vietnam Central

Committee], November 13, 2017, http://www.gov.cn/xinwen/2017-11/13/content_5239332.htm.

74 "ZhongYue lianhe shengming" [The Sino-Vietnamese joint statement], November 13, 2017, http://www.rmzxb.com.cn/c/2017-11-13/1868510_1.shtml.

75 "Fu Ying Mu'anhui shang bochi 'Zhongguo weixie lun' Madisi wei Mei dui Hua zhengce bianhu," [The Munich Security Conference: Fu Ying criticizes the "China threat theory" and Mattis justifies US China policy], *RN,* February 20, 2018, 16.

76 "Ri lalong Yue Fei Yinni jiankong Zhong Chao dianbo" [Japan monitors China and North Korea by inviting Vietnam, the Philippines, and Indonesia], *RN,* February 17, 2018, 8.

77 Fu Ying, "Quanqiuhua jintui zhong de Zhongguo xuanze" [China's choices in the globalization era], March 1, 2018, https://finance.qq.com/a/20180301/036367.htm.

78 "Meimei baodao Mei B-52 hongzhaji dijin Nansha feixing" [US news reports says that B-52 bombers are approaching the Nansha Islands], *RN,* June 6, 2018, 16.

79 "Mei jiang xiang Dongnanya chushou 'Saomiaoying' ke yongyu jianshi Nanhai" [The United States will sell 'Scan Eagle' to Southeast Asia for monitor use in the South China Sea], *RN,* June 5, 2019, 16.

80 "Wang Yi: Chengdan gongtong zeren, weihu Nanhai wending" [Wang Yi: assuming the common responsibilities for peace and stability in the South China Sea], October 29, 2018, https://www.fmprc.gov.cn/ce/cekp/chn/zgxw/t1610576.htm.

81 "Jiefangjun yu waijun pinmi haishang junyan" [The PLA frequently conducts joint naval exercises with foreign armed forces], *RN,* April 28, 2019, 8.

82 "Zhongfang zhenggao yuwai guojia wu jiaoju Nanhai" [China issues a warning against extra-regional powers' interventions in the South China Sea], *RN,* August 1, 2019, 16.

83 "Wang Yi chuxi jinian Zhongguo-Dongmeng duihua guanxi 30 zhounian tebie waizhang huiyi he MeiLan hezuo waizhang huihou jieshou meiti caifang" [Wang Yi at the press conference of the ASEAN-China foreign ministers' meeting in celebration of the 30th anniversary of dialogue relations and Lancang-Mekong cooperation foreign ministers' meeting], June 10, 2021, http://www.xinhuanet.com/world/2021-06/10/c_1127550934.htm.

84 Li Keqiang, "Zai di 22 ci Zhongguo Dongmeng lingdaoren huiyi shang de jianghua" [Speech at the 22nd China-ASEAN summit meeting], November 3, 2019, http://www.xinhuanet.com/politics/leaders/2019-11/04/c_1125187703.htm.

85 "Waimei shuping Zhongfang tui 'Nanhai xingwei zhunze' zaori dacheng" [Foreign media reports: China will contribute to the conclusion of the COD in the South China Sea as early as possible], *RN,* November 14, 2020, 8.

86 "U.S. Military in Pakistan," October 8, 2001, https://www.cbsnews.com/news/us-military-in-pakistan/; Vernon Loeb, "Footprints in Steppes of Central Asia: New Bases Indicate U.S. Presence Will Be Felt after Afghan War," February 9, 2002, https://www.globalsecurity.org/org/news/2002/020209-attack01.htm.

87 "US Sells Six C-130 Hercules Planes to Pakistan," August 19, 2003, http://www.spacewar.com/2003/030819171205.dgsyovc4.html.

88 "Baowei'er huiwu Bazongtong" [Powell meets Pakistan's president], March 19, 2004, http://news.sina.com.cn/w/2004-03-19/00202083394s.shtml; "How Much Did the U.S. Give Pakistan?" May 11, 2011, https://www.foxbusiness.com/markets/how-much-did-the-u-s-give-pakistan.

89 "Mei ni shou Ba 'Yucha' daodan" [The United States will provide harpoon missile to Pakistan], *RN,* June 2, 2006, 5.

90 Andrew Healey, "Pakistan Takes Bell 412EP," March 22, 2007, https://www.ainonline.com/aviation-news/aviation-international-news/2007-03-22/pakistan-takes-bell-412ep; "Meijun yuan Bajisitan yi duikang 'jidi'" [The United States supports Pakistan to counter Al-Qaeda], *RN,* August 1, 2007, 2.

91 "Yinbao cheng Ba keneng liyong meijunyuan yu Yin zuozhan" [Indian media report that Pakistan could use US aid to fight against India], *RN,* June 8, 2009, 5.

92 "Yindu jiang xiang Meiguo goumai batao 'Yuancheng wuqi suoding leida' xitong" [India will purchase eight long-range radar systems from the United States], May 14, 2002, http://news.sohu.com/40/98/news200849840.shtml; Pete Brush, "U.S., India in Military Exercise," May 16, 2002, https://www.cbsnews.com/news/us-india-in-military-exercise/.

93 "Mei qudai E cheng Yin zuida wuqi gongying guo" [The United States replaces Russia as the largest military supplier to India], *RN,* August 14, 2014, 6.

94 Jafar Syed, "Israeli Phalcons for Brother in Arms India," January 2, 2002, https://www.mediamonitors.net/israeli-phalcons-for-brother-in-arms-india/; "Yixiang lichengbei yiyi de hexin jishu bei Meiguo kabozi" [The United States is cutting off supply of a technology with significant implications], June 20, 2019, https://baijiahao.baidu.com/s?id=1636850510426632341&wfr=spider&for=pc.

95 "Yindu 'rujisike' goumai wuqi" [India purchases weapons at its disposal], *RN,* January 8, 2007, 5; "India and Israel's Barak-8 SAM Development Project(s)," February 15, 2019, https://www.defenseindustrydaily.com/india-israel-introducing-mr-sam-03461.

96 "Riben dui Yindu daikuan zengzhi linian zuigao" [Japanese loans to India break the historical record], *RN,* April 2, 2006, 1; "Japan-India Relations (Basic Data)," November 12, 2018, https://www.mofa.go.jp/region/asia-paci/india/data.html.

97 Sushant Singh, "India, US Sign Key Defence Pact to Use Each Other's Bases for Repair, Supplies," August 31, 2016, https://indianexpress.com/article/india/india-news-india/manohar-parrikar-signs-key-logistics-defence-pact-with-us-3004581/.

98 "Xinwen fenxi: Mei chushou dingjian hangmu shebei yitu lalong Yindu" [The news analysis: the United States will provide the most advanced aircraft carrier equipment to India], October 23, 2017, https://baijiahao.baidu.com/s?id=1582050632393526398&wfr=spider&for=pc.

99 "7200 wan meiyuan! Yindu jiang caigou baiyumei Yizhi diduikong daodan" [$72 million: India will purchase about 100 Israeli-made land-to-air missiles], January 4, 2018, https://baijiahao.baidu.com/s?id=1588615102294119665&wfr=spider&for=pc.

100 "Xinwen fenxi: Yindu jungou zai Mei E jian 'zuoyoufengyuan'" [The news analysis: India seeks to play the United States and Russia off one another for arms], July 31, 2018, https://baijiahao.baidu.com/s?id=1607495588596090495&wfr=spider&for=pc.

101 "E guanzhu ZhongTu tianranqi hezuo" [Russia pays attention to the Sino-Turkmenistan gas cooperation], *RN,* August 24, 2006, 8; "E'bao baodao ZhongTu tianranqi jiaoyi dui E 'jiwei buli'" [Russian media say that the Sino-Turkmenistan gas deals are significantly to Russian disadvantage], *RN,* August 1, 2007, 8; "ZhongWu qianshu tianranqi xieyi" [China and Uzbekistan sign a gas agreement], *RN,* June 12, 2010, 8; "Zhong'E shiyou yunfei fenqi jianruihua" [China and Russia have a more serious difficulty on oil transportation price], *RN,* June 1, 2011, 16; "Waimei: Hasakesitan jiang dui Hua chukou tianranqi shenhua shuangbian youhao guanxi" [Foreign media say Kazakhstan began to export gas to China on a large scale to promote friendship], October 5, 2017, https://baijiahao.baidu.com/

s?id=1580392445973874483&wfr=spider&for=pc; "Hasakesitan meinian xiang Zhongguo chukou tianranqi guimo jiang zengzhi 100 yi lifangmi" [Kazakhstan increases the scale of its annual gas export to China to 10 billion cubic metres], January 16, 2018, https://baijiahao.baidu.com/s?id=1589709556748928306&wfr=spider&for=pc.

102 Morena Skalamera, "Russia's Lasting Influence in Central Asia," *Survival* 59, 6 (2017–18): 131–35; Farkhod Aminjonov, "Central Asian Gas Exports Dependency," *RUSI Journal* 163, 2 (2018): 66–77.

103 "Wang Yi tong E'luosi waizhang Lafuluofu tongdianhua" [Wang Yi's telephone conversation with Russian foreign minister Lavrov], January 11, 2022, http://www.news.cn/world/2022-01/11/c_1128250390.htm.

104 "E Yin qianshu shinian fangwu hezuo xieyi" [Russia and India conclude a ten-year defence cooperation agreement], *RN,* December 8, 2009, 1; Dipanjan Roy Chaudhury, "India, Russia Sign Civil Nuclear Action Plan for Second Plant; Third Country Project," October 5, 2018, https://economictimes.indiatimes.com/industry/energy/power/india-russia-sign-civil-nuclear-action-plan-for-second-plant-third-country-project/articleshow/66085647.cms.

105 "Jiekou 'Zhongguo weixie' kuojunbei" [Significant military expansions under the excuse of "Chinese threats"], March 15, 2001, http://mil.news.sina.com.cn/2001-03-15/15479.html; "Yindu kongjun jiang cong E'luosi jieshou 6 jia Yi'er 78 kongzhong jiayouji" [Indian air forces will receive six IL-78 tanker aircraft from Russia], October 12, 2002, http://news.sohu.com/07/98/news203639807.shtml.

106 "Yin'E qianshu ju'e wuqi zujie xieyi" [India and Russia conclude a large-scale weapon lease agreement], January 20, 2003, http://news.sina.com.cn/w/2003-01-20/1350881106.shtml; "India Nuclear Update – 2003," September 1, 2003, https://www.wisconsinproject.org/india-nuclear-update-2003/.

107 "E'Yin hezuo shengchan chaoyinsu fanjian daodan" [Russia and India jointly produce supersonic speed anti-ship missiles], *RN,* July 24, 2006, 5.

108 "Yindu dinggou 300 liang T-90 tanke" [India will purchase 300 T-90 tanks], *RN,* December 27, 2006, 5.

109 "E wei Yin jianzao huweijian jinzhan shunli" [Russian construction of Indian frigates works well], *RN,* June 20, 2010, 5; "Russia to Float India's First Krivak III Frigate," November 18, 2009, https://www.naval-technology.com/news/news70242-html/.

110 "India to Buy 42 More Russian Made Su-30MKI Aircraft," March 3, 2010, http://www.brahmand.com/news/India-to-buy-42-more-Russian-made-Su30MKI-aircraft/3285/1/11.html; "Mi-17V-5 Military Transport Helicopter," April 3, 2020, https://www.airforce-technology.com/projects/mi-17v-5-military-transport-helicopter/.

111 "E Yin qianshu S-400 junshou xieyi" [Russia and India conclude an agreement over arms sales of S-400s], *RN,* October 6, 2018, 2.

112 "Yin zaici daliang dinggou E T-90 tanke" [India requests a new deal for a large number of Russian-produced T-90 tanks], *RN,* April 12, 2019, 6.

113 "Maigei Yindu wuqi geng xianjin" [Weapons sold to India are more advanced], December 19, 2002, http://news.sohu.com/10/68/news205076810.shtml.

114 "Yindu zenggou Su-30 zhanji duifu Zhongguo" [India purchases more Su-30 aircraft to deal with China], *RN,* October 4, 2009, 1.

115 "Yin ni zai Zangnan bushu xindaodan budui yingdui Zhongguo de weishe wuqi" [India will deploy new missile troops in southern Tibet to deal with Chinese deterrent weapons], August 4, 2016, http://news.sina.com.cn/c/2016-08-04/doc-ifxutfyw0568014.shtml.

116 E. Denisov and I.A. Safranchuk, "Four Problems of the SCO in Connection with Its Enlargement," *Russian Politics and Law* 54, 5–6 (2016): 502–4.

117 Lei Jianfeng, "Pingheng ZhongMei yu yi Yin duichong: E dui Hua zhanlue xindongxiang" [Striking a US-China balance and hedging by Russian-Indian relations: recent development of Russia's China policy], *E'luoṣi yanjiu* [*Russian Studies*] 1 (2021): 56.

118 Li Ziguo, "Shanghai hezuo zuzhi de kuoyuan yu mingyun gongtongti jianshe" [The SCO membership extension and construction of the community of a shared future], *E'luosi dong'ou zhongya yanjiu* [*Russian, Eastern European and Central Asian Studies*] 4 (2021): 13.

119 "Lafuluofu fangYin qianghua E'Yin guanxi qiangdiao E'Zhong guanxi 'yida zuigao shuiping'" [During the visit to India, Lavrov strengthened Russian-Indian cooperation and emphasized the Sino-Russian cooperation had reached the highest level], *RN,* April 8, 2021, 2.

120 "Yindu zongli Xin'ge benyue zhong fanghua" [Indian prime minister Singh will visit China this month], January 7, 2008, http://news.sohu.com/20080107/n254502162.shtml; "ZhongYin bianjing junli" [The Sino-Indian military balance in the border areas], August 16, 2009, http://www.china.com.cn/military/txt/2009-08/16/content_18342936.htm; "Yinbao baodao Yin fangzhang danyou Zhongguo jiaqiang bianjing junli" [The Indian media say that India's defence minister shows great concerns about Chinese enhanced capabilities along the border], *RN,* March 9, 2011, 16.

121 "Yin junfang cheng yingdui Jiefangjun you zhunbei" [India military indicates preparations to deal with the PLA], *RN,* April 14, 2012, 8.

122 Vinay Kaura, "India's Changing Relationship with Russia," *RUSI Journal* 163, 1 (2018): 52–54.

123 Cheng Ruisheng, *Mulin waijiao sishinian* [The good neighbours diplomacy in forty years] (Chengdu: Sichuan renmin chubanshe, 2006), 271.

124 "The Sino-Indian Joint Communiqué," *JFJB,* April 13, 2005, 5.

125 Wang Taiping, ed., *Xinzhongguo waijiao 50 nian* [New China's foreign relations in 50 years], vol. 1 (Beijing: Beijing chubanshe, 1999), 338–39.

126 "Waijiaobu fayanren cheng ZhongYin bianjie wenti you xinjinzhan" [The foreign ministry spokesman says that China and India have achieved a new agreement on border issues], April 27, 2000, http://news.sina.com.cn/china/2000-04-27/85647.html.

127 Jiang Yaping, "Dai Bingguo shuo ZhongYin hezuo qianjing guangkuo" [Dai Bingguo says that the prospect of Sino-Indian cooperation is great], *JFJB,* July 29, 2004, 5.

128 "Wang Yi pan Nibo'er chongdang ZhongYin jian qiaoliang" [Wang Yi hopes Nepal will become a bridge between China and India], *RN,* September 8, 2017, 16.

129 "Xi Jinping tong Yindu zongli Modi zai Jinnai jixu juxing huiwu" [Xi meets with Indian prime minister Modi in Chennai for more talks], October 12, 2019, http://www.xinhuanet.com/politics/leaders/2019-10/12/c_1125097242.htm.

130 "ZhongYin juxing bianjie wenti tebie daibiao huiwu" [China and India hold meetings for special representatives on border issues], *Renmin ribao* [*People's Daily*], December 22, 2019, 3.

131 "Yinfang zai ZhongYin bianjing shouxian mingqiang weixie, Waijiaobu: duncu Yinfang yansu chachu tiaoxin renyuan" [India fired guns along the Sino-Indian border: the Chinese foreign ministry called for Indian serious investigations], September 8, 2020, http://www.xinhuanet.com/world/2020-09/08/c_1126469113.htm.

132 "ZhongYin waizhang fabiao lianhe xinwengao, shuangfang dacheng wudian gongshi" [The Chinese and Indian foreign ministers issued a joint press release, and the two sides reached a five-point consensus], September 11, 2020, http://www.xinhuanet.com/world/2020-09/11/c_1126479682.htm. For an English version of the press release, see https://www.tellerreport.com/news/2020-09-11-the-chinese-and-indian-foreign-ministers-issued-a-joint-press-release--and-the-two-sides-reached-a-five-point-consensus.B1LR12SQED.html.

133 "Mushalafu fanghua daidong ZhongBa fangwu xinsiwei" [Musharraf's visit brings about new thinking in Sino-Pakistan defence cooperation], November 7, 2003, http://news.sina.com.cn/w/2003-11-07/15362090636.shtml.

134 "ZhongBa qianshu ziyou maoyi xieding" [China and Pakistan sign a free trade agreement], *RN,* November 25, 2006, 1.

135 "Zhongguo shou Ba jian-10 zhanji rang Yindu jinzhang" [China's export of JF-10 to Pakistan makes India nervous], *RN,* November 12, 2009, 1–2.

136 "Miqie junbei hezuo shenhua ZhongBa guanxi" [Closer military cooperation improves Sino-Pakistani relations], *RN,* March 28, 2011, 14.

137 "Kalakunlun ying" [The eagle of the Karakoram], October 30, 2021, https://www.163.com/dy/article/GNIFG2JM05529MC6.html.

138 "Meimei baodao Zhongguo wei Ba jianzao 'zuixianjin' junjian xiashui" [The US media: China constructed the most advanced battleships for Pakistan's navy], *RN,* August 25, 2020, 16.

139 "ZhongBa kongjun feixingyuan tongcheng duifang zhanji duikang xunlian zhanxian shendu huxin" [The Sino-Pakistan exchange of aircraft for joint military exercises reflected the high level of strategic trust], September 22, 2017, http://news.xinhuanet.com/politics/2017-09/22/c_1121710008.htm.

140 "Zhang Qiyue jiu Mushalafu fanghua zhu A shiguan gongzuo da jizhewen" [Zhang Qiyue answers questions on Pakistan president's visit to China, etc.], December 25, 2001, https://news.sina.com.cn/c/2001-12-25/428822.html.

141 "Mushalafu fanghua daidong ZhongBa fangwu xinsiwei" [Musharraf's visit brings about new thinking in the Sino-Pakistan defence cooperation], November 7, 2003, http://news.sina.com.cn/w/2003-11-07/15362090636.shtml.

142 "ZhongBa zimao xieding shenhua shuangbian guanxi" [The Sino-Pakistan free trade agreement promotes bilateral relations], *RN,* July 8, 2007, 4.

143 "ZhongBa tongyi yi Renminbi jiesuan shuangbian maoyi" [China and Pakistan agree to use renminbi for their trade], *RN,* November 7, 2018, 14.

144 "Zhu Rongji huijian Bajisitan caizheng buzhang he jiaotong buzhang" [Zhu Rongji meets with Pakistan's finance and transportation ministers], August 9, 2001, https://news.sina.com.cn/c/2001-08-09/325164.html.

145 "Ribao wangcheng Zhongguo zai Yinduyang gouzhu dui Yin 'baoweiquan'" [Japanese media say that China is encircling India at the Indian Ocean], *RN,* May 26, 2009, 8.

146 "Guade'ergang cheng Zhongguo xunzhao nengyuan yaodi" [Gwadar Port becomes a key place for China to look for resources], *RN,* February 13, 2013, 14.

147 "Zhongguo diaoyan ZhongBa tielu xiangmu" [China investigates the Sino-Pakistani railway project], *RN,* June 30, 2014, 16.

148 "Zhuanjia renwei ZhongBa jingji zoulang mianlin sanda tiaozhan" [Experts believe that the China-Pakistan Economic Corridor faces three challenges], *RN,* February 17, 2016, 14.

149 "Guowu weiyuan jian waijiao buzhang Wang Yi huida zhongwai jizhe tiwen" [State Councillor and Foreign Minister Wan Yi's interview with Chinese and foreign journalists], May 24, 2020, http://www.xinhuanet.com/politics/2020lh/2020-05/24/c_139083738.htm.

150 "ZhongYin gaojibie huitan weipo jiangju" [The Sino-Indian high-level talks have not broken the stalemate], *RN,* February 24, 2017, 16.

151 "Wang Qishan huijian Bajisitan zongli Yimulan Han" [Wang Qishan's meeting with Pakistan's premier, Imran Khan], November 4, 2018, https://baijiahao.baidu.com/s?id=1616176660526937137&wfr=spider&for=pc.

152 "Zhongguo dui Nibo'er yuanzhu yuanchao Yindu" [China's aid to Nepal far exceeds that from India], *RN,* May 10, 2016, 14.

153 "ZhongNi shouci lianhe junyan zhouri qidong" [The first Sino-Nepalese joint military exercises will begin on Sunday], *RN,* April 15, 2017, 8.

154 "Rimei baodao Nibo'er jiang shiyong Zhongguo gangkou" [Japanese news sources: Nepal will use Chinese ports], *RN,* September 9, 2018, 8.

155 "Wei Fenghe fang Nanya hangshi fangwu hezuo" [Wei Fanghe strengthened practical defence cooperation during his visit to South Asia], *RN,* December 2, 2020, 16.

156 Yang Jiechi, "Tuidong goujian renlei mingyun gongtongti" [Promoting the construction of a community of shared future], November 19, 2017, http://cpc.people.com.cn/n1/2017/1119/c64094-29654801.html.

157 "China and Russia Are Quasi Allies ... On Strategic Affairs Russia and India Have Serious Conversations Only at Top Level," February 28, 2018, https://blogs.timesofindia.indiatimes.com/Globespotting/china-and-russia-are-quasi-allies-on-strategic-affairs-russia-and-india-have-serious-conversations-only-at-top-level.

Conclusion

1 Gary King, Robert O. Keohane, and Sidney Verba, *Designing Social Inquiry: Scientific Inference in Qualitative Research* (Princeton, NJ: Princeton University Press, 1994), 16–17.

2 Glenn H. Snyder, "Process Variables in Neorealist Theory," *Security Studies* 5, 3 (1996): 173; Yaqing Qin, *A Relational Theory of World Politics* (Cambridge: Cambridge University Press, 2018).

3 For more discussions, see Huang Yuxing, "Guoji guanxishi yanjiu de lilun yiyi" [Theoretical significance of studies on international relations history], *Lengzhan guojishi yanjiu* [*Cold War International History Studies*] 2 (2019): 171–75.

4 Independent of this book, I am seeking to explain how ideological matching among different states shapes a power transition between a rising power and a hegemon. It is a recent example that a research question enables me to better use archival sources for theory development. For some preliminary results, see Huang Yuxing, "Jueqiguo ruhe yanpan baquanguo jiemeng de kenengxing" [How does a rising power estimate the possibility of a hegemon's alliance formation?], *Shijie jingji yu zhengzhi* [*World Economics and Politics*] 5 (2022): 77–100.

5 Joseph S. Nye Jr., "Old Wars and Future Wars: Causation and Prevention," in *The Origins and Prevention of Major Wars,* ed. Robert I. Rotberg and Theodore K. Rabb (Cambridge: Cambridge University Press, 1989), 4.

6 Alastair Iain Johnston, "What (if Anything) Does East Asia Tell Us about International Relations Theory?" *Annual Review of Political Science* 15 (2012): 53–78.

7 John J. Mearsheimer, "The Gathering Storm: China's Challenge to US Power in Asia," *Chinese Journal of International Politics* 3, 4 (2010): 389–91.

8 Barry Buzan, "Security Architecture in Asia: The Interplay of Regional and Global Levels," *Pacific Review* 16, 2 (2003): 143–73; David C. Kang, "Hierarchy in Asian International Relations: 1300 to 1900," *Asian Security* 1, 1 (2005): 53–79.

9 Victoria Tin-bor Hui, *War and State Formation in Ancient China and Early Modern Europe* (Cambridge: Cambridge University Press, 2005).

10 Amitav Acharya, "Global International Relations (IR) and Regional Worlds: A New Agenda for International Studies," *International Studies Quarterly* 58, 4 (2014): 647–59; Amitav Acharya, "Theorising the International Relations of Asia: Necessity or Indulgence? Some Reflections," *Pacific Review* 30, 6 (2017): 816–28.

11 Barry Posen, *The Sources of Military Doctrine: France, Britain, and Germany between the World Wars* (Ithaca, NY: Cornell University Press, 1984).

12 Robert S. Ross, "Nationalism, Geopolitics and Naval Expansionism: From the Nineteenth Century to the Rise of China," *Naval War College Review* 71, 4 (2018): 11–44.

13 Thomas J. Christensen, *Useful Adversaries: Grand Strategy, Domestic Mobilization, and Sino-American Conflict, 1947–1958* (Princeton, NJ: Princeton University Press, 1996).

14 Avery Goldstein, *Deterrence and Security in the 21st Century: China, Britain, France, and the Enduring Legacy of the Nuclear Revolution* (Stanford, CA: Stanford University Press, 2000).

15 Xuetong Yan, *Ancient Chinese Thought, Modern Chinese Power* (Princeton, NJ: Princeton University Press, 2011), 259.

16 Wang Jun and Dan Xingwu, *Zhongguo guoji guanxi yanjiu sishinian* [International relations studies in China in the past forty years] (Beijing: Zhongyang bianyi chubanshe, 2008), 345.

17 Alastair Iain Johnston, "Zhongguo waijiao zhengce yanjiu: lilun qushi ji fangfa bianxi" [Trends in theory and method in the study of Chinese foreign policy], *Shijie jingji yu zhengzhi* [*World Economics and Politics*] 8 (2006): 70.

18 Huang Yuxing, "Tanpan nengli yu lianmeng zhuanxing" [Negotiating power and alliance transformation], *Shijie jingji yu zhengzhi* [*World Economics and Politics*] 6 (2017): 77–101; Huang Yuxing, "Gongneng fenyi yu lianmeng xingcheng" [Functional division and alliance formation], *Shijie jingji yu zhengzhi* [*World Economics and Politics*] 2 (2019): 101–22; Yuxing Huang, "An Interdependence Theory of Wedge Strategies," *Chinese Journal of International Politics* 13, 2 (2020): 253–86.

Bibliography

Bibliographic Note

This book seeks to reach theoretical conclusions based on a wide range of sources from Chinese, Russian, German, American, and NATO archives. Chinese sources provide direct evidence for an investigation of Chinese regional diplomacy. Between 2009 and 2013, the Foreign Ministry Archive of the People's Republic of China (CFMA) released thousands of original documents produced during the period 1949–66. In this book, I analyze these documents, which were created by various departments of the Ministry of Foreign Affairs, including the General Office, the Department of Asian Affairs, the Department of International Organizations and Conferences, the Protocol Department, and People's Republic of China (PRC) embassies in various Asian countries. I also examine documents created by other ministries and forwarded to the Ministry of Foreign Affairs, including documents produced by the People's Liberation Army (PLA) General Political Department, the PLA General Staff Headquarters, and the Chinese Ministry of Foreign Trade. The key documents discussed in the book are those pertaining to records of conversations between Chinese and foreign leaders and documents that involve implementation of Chinese foreign policy.

Moreover, each provincial and municipal archive in China includes a complete set of documents from the Chinese Communist Party (CCP) Central Committee and the State Council. Local archives may include records of Chinese leaders' speeches at internal party meetings, of CCP Central Committee directives related to foreign affairs, and of documents created by the CCP Propaganda Department, the CCP Liaison Department, and the Ministry of Foreign Affairs of the People's Republic of China, all of which enable me to examine Chinese leaders' perceptions at the national level. Different archives provide different degrees of archival access to different scholars at different moments. Each archive provides a list of documents available for research. However, different archives approve specific documents, on an individual basis, in accordance with archival sources and submitted research topics. Between 2012 and 2014, I visited twenty provincial/municipal archives in China, and in this book I analyze documents from nine local archives, those of Fujian, Guangdong, Guizhou, Henan, Hunan, Jiangsu, Shanghai, Tianjin, and Zhejiang.

I also exploit pertinent sources under three categories: 1) unpublished documentary collections; 2) CCP leaders' works and chronicles of major events; and 3) documentary collections or chronicles of major events on selected topics.

1 Unpublished documentary collections are archival sources edited by the Chinese government but not published for various reasons. The Chinese government made significant efforts to collect reports by foreign news agencies on various key issues of Chinese regional diplomacy. For example, some documentary collections on Asian affairs, edited by the Intelligence Department of the PRC Foreign Ministry between 1954 and 1959, were available at China Foreign Affairs University Libraries in 2013. Approaches to the editing of the documentary collections revealed principal concerns of the Chinese government in the 1950s. Another example is a chronicle of major events on the question of Cambodia, edited by the International Department of Xinhua News Agency in 1973, available at Tsinghua University Libraries in 2016. The chronology provided an excellent survey of continuity and change in various parties' policies toward armed conflict in Cambodia. "Gongzuo tongxun" [Working bulletin], edited by the PLA's General Political Department, available at the Estelle and Melvin Gelman Library of George Washington University, is also worth noting. The 160 volumes provided a few hundred PLA instructions down to the regiment level.
2 CCP leaders' works and chronicles of major events are official documentary collections, released by the Chinese government. Since 1979, the Chinese government has compiled and published selected works and chronicles of major events of almost all top CCP leaders. Although released selectively, the documents are important for scholars who wish to understand Chinese foreign policy. Selected works may include (in)complete internal talks by Chinese leaders or (in)complete records of conversations between Chinese and foreign leaders. A chronicle of major events may summarize how Chinese leaders made foreign policy decisions or put those decisions into practice. With respect to Chinese regional diplomacy, some official documentary collections are helpful sources, such as *Jianguo yilai Mao Zedong wengao* [Manuscripts of Mao Zedong since the founding of the nation] (Beijing: Zhongyang wenxian chubanshe, various years); *Mao Zedong waijiao wenxuan* [Mao Zedong's selected works on diplomacy] (Beijing: Zhongyang wenxian chubanshe/Shijie zhishi chubanshe, 1994); *Mao Zedong nianpu, 1949–1976* [A chronicle of Mao Zedong's life, 1949–1976] (Beijing: Zhongyang wenxian chubanshe, 2013); *Zhou Enlai waijiao wenxuan* [Zhou Enlai's selected works on diplomacy] (Beijing: Zhongyang wenxian chubanshe, 1990); and *Zhou Enlai nianpu, 1949–1976* [A chronicle of Zhou Enlai's life, 1949–1976] (Beijing: Zhongyang wenxian chubanshe, 1997). Sources with respect to high-ranking PLA officials are also worth noting.
3 Documentary collections or chronicles of major events on selected topics provide a new perspective for scholars in examining the PRC's history and its regional diplomacy in particular. During the Cold War, the Chinese government released important foreign policy statements on a regular basis in *Zhonghua renmin gongheguo duiwai guanxi wenjian ji* [Documents on foreign relations of the People's Republic of China] (Beijing: Shijie zhishi chubanshe, various years). In particular, *Riben wenti wenjian huibian* [Collected documents on Japan] (Beijing: Shijie zhishi chubanshe, various years) are helpful sources for scholars in tracing China's Japan policy. In the post–Cold War era, the Chinese

government also compiled and published documentary collections on foreign affairs, such as *Zhanhou ZhongRi guanxi wenxian ji, 1945–1970* [Collected documents of Sino-Japanese relations in the postwar era, 1945–1970] (Beijing: Zhongguo shehui kexue chubanshe, 1996) and *Zhonghua renmin gongheguo waijiao dang'an xuanbian* [Selected Foreign Ministry Archive of the People's Republic of China], vol. 2 (Beijing: Shijie zhishi chubanshe, 2007). These sources provide evidence for scholars in assessing implementation of the PRC's foreign policy. Moreover, the Chinese government released documents on economic affairs, such as *1958–1965 Zhonghua renmin gongheguo jingji dang'an ziliao xuanbian* [Selected archival materials on the PRC's economic affairs, 1958–1965] (Beijing: Zhongguo caizheng jingji chubanshe, 2011). This documentary collection provides important evidence concerning the PRC's foreign trade data and foreign aid decisions. I also use some rare chronicles of major events, such as *Zhongguo hangkong gongye dashiji, 1951–2011* [A chronicle of major events of the Chinese aviation industry, 1951–2011] (Beijing: Hangkong gongye chubanshe, 2011) and *Zhongguo waiwenju wushinian dashiji* [A chronicle of major events of the China International Publishing Group over fifty years] (Beijing: Xinxing chubanshe, 1999). These sources offer evidence for scholars regarding the PRC's military strength and foreign propaganda initiatives.

In addition to Chinese sources, Russian and German archival sources provide indirect support for understanding Chinese regional diplomacy. During the Cold War, the Soviet Union and East Germany were allies of the PRC and the Democratic Republic of Vietnam (DRV). After the collapse of the Soviet Union, the Russian Federation declassified some Soviet archives, and the Federal Republic of Germany released extensive East German archives. Sino-Soviet, Soviet–East German, Sino–East German, and East German–DRV records of conversations offer new opportunities for scholars to advance understandings of Chinese regional diplomacy. Russian archives reveal the rise and fall of Sino-Soviet relations and the nature and limitations of Soviet-Vietnamese cooperation. The Soviet Union and East Germany maintained various intelligence exchange channels on a regular basis. Therefore, East German archives reveal the dynamics of the Sino-Soviet relations and features of Moscow's China policy after 1959. I analyze Soviet declassified documents, translated into English or Chinese. The most important Russian archives, translated into English, include those released by the Cold War International History Project and Wilson Center Digital Archive. The most important Russian archives, translated into Chinese, include Shen Zhihua, ed., *E'luosi jiemi dang'an: ZhongSu guanxi* [Sino-Soviet relations: declassified documents from Russian archives] (Shanghai: Dongfang chuban zhongxin, 2015). The most important East German archival sources include documents that I obtained, between 2018 and 2020, from Stiftung Archiv der Parteien und Massenorganisationen der DDR im Bundesarchiv (SAPMO) (Archive of the Foundation of the Parties and Mass Organizations of the GDR in the Federal Archives), Berlin-Lichterfelde; Bundesarchiv-Militärarchiv, Freiburg; and Werner Meißner, Hrsg., *Die DDR und China 1949 bis 1990: Politik, Wirtschaft, Kultur: eine Quellensammlung* [The GDR and China from 1949 to 1990: politics, economics, and culture: a source collection] (Berlin: Akademie, 1995).

Finally, US and NATO archives provide evidence for important observations and critical assessments of Chinese regional diplomacy. In this book, I extensively exploit US archival sources with respect to China, the Soviet Union, and regional competition in Asia, and I compare and contrast them with evidence from Chinese, Russian, and German archives. Between 2014 and 2018, I collected US archival sources at the US National Archives and

Records Administration and the Kennedy, Johnson, Nixon, and Ford Presidential Libraries. The most significant evidence comes from national security files of US presidencies and Department of State documents of US administrations. I also analyze essential evidence in published documentary collections, such as documents available at *Foreign Relations of the United States*. The United States and its allies collected evidence and conducted analysis, based on a wide range of sources, with respect to China, the Soviet Union, and many other countries in Asia. These sources involve records of conversations between Chinese and Soviet leaders and other foreign leaders and offer key information about military deployment and foreign aid.

Unpublished Primary Sources

Chinese Archives

Foreign Ministry Archive of the People's Republic of China
Fujian Provincial Archive
Guangdong Provincial Archive
Guizhou Provincial Archive
Henan Provincial Archive
Hunan Provincial Archive
Jiangsu Provincial Archive
Shanghai Municipal Archive
Tianjin Municipal Archive
Zhejiang Provincial Archive

US Archives

Gerald R. Ford Presidential Library, Michigan
John F. Kennedy Presidential Library, Massachusetts
Lyndon B. Johnson Presidential Library, Texas
Richard M. Nixon Presidential Library, California
US National Archive II, College Park, Maryland

European Archives

Berlin-Lichterfelde
  Stiftung Archiv der Parteien und Massenorganisationen der DDR im Bundesarchiv (SAPMO)
Bundesarchiv-Militärarchiv, Freiburg
NATO Archives, Brussels

China Foreign Affairs University Library

Dierci bujiemeng guojia de guojia huo zhengfu shounao huiyi wenjian huibian 第二次不结盟国家的国家或政府首脑会议文件汇编 [Collected documents of the second summit of non-aligned countries]. Beijing: 1964.

Intelligence Department of the PRC Foreign Ministry 外交部情报司, ed. *Meiguo qinzhan Taiwan wenti* 美国侵占台湾问题 [The question of American aggressions in Taiwan], vol. 2. Beijing: 1954.

–, ed. *Zhonghua renmin gongheguo yu Yazhou guojia guanxi* 中华人民共和国与亚洲国家关系 [The People's Republic of China's relations with Asian countries]. Beijing: 1954.

Xinhua News Agency 新华通讯社, ed. *Youguan Xizang wenti de wenjian he cailiao xuanbian (guoji bufen)* 有关西藏问题的文件和材料选编 (国际部分) [Selected documents and materials on the question of Tibet (international aspects)]. Beijing: 1959.

Library of Chinese Academy of International Trade and Economic Cooperation, Ministry of Commerce

Institute of Southeast Asia of Yunnan Province and Institute of Southwest Asia of Yunnan University 云南省东南亚研究所, 云南大学西南亚研究所, eds. "Liangci shiyou weiji dui shijie jingji de yingxiang" 两次石油危机对世界经济的影响 [Impact of two oil crises upon world economy]. 1983.

Tsinghua University Libraries

Geng Zhonglin 耿仲琳, ed. *Wu Ruilin shiliao* 吴瑞林史料 [Historical evidence on Wu Ruilin].

International Department of Xinhua News Agency 新华社国际部, ed. *Yinduzhina wenti ziliao: Jianpuzhai wenti dashiji (1954 nian zhi 1972 naindi)* 印度支那问题资料: 柬埔寨问题大事记 (1954年至1972年底) [Materials on the question of Indochina: a chronicle of major events on the question of Cambodia, 1954–1972], 1973.

Estelle and Melvin Gelman Library, George Washington University

People's Liberation Army, General Political Department 中国人民解放军总政治部, ed. *Gongzuo tongxun* 工作通讯 [Working bulletin].

Zhonglianbu 中联部, ed. *Zhonglianbu sishinian, 1951–1991* 中联部四十年 1951–1991 [The CCP Central Liaison Department over forty years, 1951–1991], 1991.

Smith College Library

"Mao Zedong sixiang wansui" 毛泽东思想万岁 [Long live Mao Zedong thought]. 1969.

Published Primary Sources

Chinese Documentary Collections

1958–1965 Zhonghua renmin gongheguo jingji dang'an ziliao xuanbian 1958–1965 中华人民共和国经济档案资料选编 [Selected archival materials on the PRC's economic affairs, 1958–1965]. Beijing: Zhongguo caizheng jingji chubanshe, 2011.

Chen Yi junshi wenxuan 陈毅军事文选 [Chen Yi's selected works on military affairs]. Beijing: Jiefangjun chubanshe, 1996.

Chen Yun wenji 陈云文集 [Chen Yun's collected works]. Beijing: Zhongyang wenxian chubanshe, 2005.

Deng Xiaoping nianpu, 1904–1974 邓小平年谱 1904–1974 [A chronicle of Deng Xiaoping's life, 1904–1974]. Beijing: Zhongyang wenxian chubanshe, 2009.

Gu Longsheng 顾龙生, ed. *Mao Zedong jingji nianpu* 毛泽东经济年谱 [A chronicle of Mao Zedong's life on economic affairs]. Beijing: Zhonggong zhongyang dangxiao chubanshe, 1993.

Jianguo yilai Mao Zedong wengao 建国以来毛泽东文稿 [Manuscripts of Mao Zedong since the founding of the nation]. Beijing: Zhongyang wenxian chubanshe, various years.

Liu Huaqing junshi wenxuan 刘华清军事文选 [Liu Huaqing's selected works on military affairs]. Beijing: Jiefangjun chubanshe, 2008.

Liu Shaoqi 刘少奇. *Lun guoji zhuyi yu minzu zhuyi* 论国际主义与民族主义 [Internationalism and nationalism]. Beijing: Renmin chubanshe, 1951.

Mao Zedong nianpu, 1949–1976 毛泽东年谱 1949–1976 [A chronicle of Mao Zedong's life, 1949–1976]. Beijing: Zhongyang wenxian chubanshe, 2013.

Mao Zedong sixiang xingcheng yu fazhan dashiji 毛泽东思想形成与发展大事记 [Chronicle of major events in the formation and evolution of Mao Zedong's thought]. Beijing: Zhongyang wenxian chubanshe, 2011.

Mao Zedong waijiao wenxuan 毛泽东外交文选 [Mao Zedong's selected works on diplomacy]. Beijing: Zhongyang wenxian chubanshe/Shijie zhishi chubanshe, 1994.

Mao Zedong Xizang gongzuo wenxuan 毛泽东西藏工作文选 [Mao Zedong's selected works on Tibetan affairs]. Beijing: Zhongyang wenxian chubanshe/Zhongguo zangxue chubanshe, 2008.

Nie Rongzhen nianpu 聂荣臻年谱 [A chronicle of Nie Rongzhen's life]. Beijing: Renmin chubanshe, 1999.

Peng Dehuai nianpu 彭德怀年谱 [A chronicle of Peng Dehuai's life]. Beijing: Renmin chubanshe, 1998.

Riben wenti wenjian huibian 日本问题文件汇编 [Collected documents on Japan]. Beijing: Shijie zhishi chubanshe, various years.

Tian Huan 田桓, ed. *Zhanhou ZhongRi guanxi wenxian ji, 1945–1970* 战后中日关系文献集 1945–1970 [Collected documents of Sino-Japanese relations in the postwar era, 1945–1970]. Beijing: Zhongguo shehui kexue chubanshe, 1996.

–, ed. *Zhanhou ZhongRi guanxishi nianbiao, 1945–1993* 战后中日关系史年表 1945–1993 [A chronicle of major events of Sino-Japanese relations in the postwar era, 1945–1993]. Beijing: Zhongguo shehui kexue chubanshe, 1994.

Wang Enmao wenji 王恩茂文集 [Wang Enmao's collected works]. Beijing: Zhongyang wenxian chubanshe, 1997.

Xu Shiyou junshi wenxuan 许世友军事文选 [Xu Shiyou's selected works on military affairs]. Beijing: Junshi kexue chubanshe, 2012.

Yang Chengwu nianpu 杨成武年谱 [A chronicle of Yang Chengwu's life]. Beijing: Jiefangjun chubanshe, 2014.

Ye Jianying junshi wenxuan 叶剑英军事文选 [Ye Jianying's selected works on military affairs]. Beijing: Jiefangjun chubanshe, 1997.

Yunnan jiaofei douzheng 云南剿匪斗争 [Anti-rebellion struggles in Yunnan]. Kunming: Yunnan daxue chubanshe, 2011.

Zhongguo hangkong gongye dashiji, 1951–2011 中国航空工业大事记 1951–2011 [A chronicle of major events of the Chinese aviation industry, 1951–2011]. Beijing: Hangkong gongye chubanshe, 2011.

Zhongguo waiwenju wushinian dashiji 中国外文局五十年大事记 [A chronicle of major events of the China International Publishing Group over fifty years]. Beijing: Xinxing chubanshe, 1999.

Zhonghua renmin gongheguo duiwai guanxi wenjian ji 中华人民共和国对外关系文件集 [Documents on foreign relations of the People's Republic of China]. Beijing: Shijie zhishi chubanshe, various years.

Zhonghua renmin gongheguo waijiao dang'an xuanbian 中华人民共和国外交档案选编 [Selected Foreign Ministry Archive of the People's Republic of China], vol. 2. Beijing: Shijie zhishi chubanshe, 2007.

Zhou Enlai jingji wenxuan 周恩来经济文选 [Zhou Enlai's selected works on economic affairs]. Beijing: Zhongyang wenxian chubanshe, 1993.

Zhou Enlai junshi huodong jishi, 1918–1975 周恩来军事活动纪事 1918–1975 [A chronicle of Zhou Enlai's military activities, 1918–1975]. Beijing: Zhongyang wenxian chubanshe, 2000.

Zhou Enlai junshi wenxuan 周恩来军事文选 [Zhou Enlai's selected works on military affairs]. Beijing: Renmin chubanshe, 1997.

Zhou Enlai nianpu, 1949–1976 周恩来年谱 1949–1976 [A chronicle of Zhou Enlai's life, 1949–1976]. Beijing: Zhongyang wenxian chubanshe, 1997.

Zhou Enlai waijiao huodong dashiji, 1949–1975 周恩来外交活动大事记 1949–1975 [A chronicle of major events of Zhou Enlai's foreign affairs activities, 1949–1975]. Beijing: Shijie zhishi chubanshe, 1993.

Zhou Enlai waijiao wenxuan 周恩来外交文选 [Zhou Enlai's selected works on diplomacy]. Beijing: Zhongyang wenxian chubanshe, 1990.

Zhou Enlai yu waiguo shounao ji zhengyao huitanlu 周恩来与外国首脑及政要会谈录 [Zhou Enlai's talks with foreign leaders and politicians]. Beijing: Taihai chubanshe, 2012.

Zhou Enlai yu Xizang 周恩来与西藏 [Zhou Enlai and Tibet]. Beijing: Zhongguo zangxue chubanshe, 1998.

Zhu De nianpu, xinbianben 朱德年谱 (新编本) [A chronicle of Zhu De's life, new edition]. Beijing: Zhongyang wenxian chubanshe, 2006.

Zhu Rongji jianghua shilu 朱镕基讲话实录 [Zhu Rongji's collected speeches]. Beijing: Renmin chubanshe, 2011.

US Documentary Collections

Conlon Associates. *United States Foreign Policy: Asia.* Washington, DC: US Government Printing Office, 1959.

Foreign Relations of the United States. Washington, DC: US Government Printing Office, various years.

The Pentagon Papers: The Defense Department History of United States Decision-Making on Vietnam, vol. 3. *The Senator Gravel Edition.* Boston: Beacon Press, 1971.

German Documentary Collections

Werner Meißner, ed. *Die DDR und China 1949 bis 1990: Politik, Wirtschaft, Kultur: eine Quellensammlung.* Berlin: Akademie, 1995.

US, Russian, and Vietnamese Documentary Collections Translated into Chinese

Bolieriniefu yanlun 勃列日涅夫言论 [Collected speeches of Brezhnev]. Shanghai: Shanghai renmin chubanshe, various years.

Bu'erjianing, Heluxiaofu fangwen Yindu, Miandian, he Afuhan qijian de jianghua 布尔加宁, 赫鲁晓夫访问印度, 缅甸和阿富汗期间的讲话 [Collected speeches of Bulganin and Khrushchev during their visits to India, Burma, and Afghanistan]. Beijing: Renmin chubanshe, 1956.

Dulesi yanlun xuanji 杜勒斯言论选集 [Selected speeches of John F. Dulles]. Beijing: Shijie zhishi chubanshe, 1960.

Heluxiaofu yanlun 赫鲁晓夫言论 [Collected speeches of Khrushchev]. Beijing: Shijie zhishi chubanshe, various years.

Mei Zi 梅孜, ed. *MeiTai guanxi zhongyao ziliao xuanbian, 1948.11–1996.4* 美台关系重要资料选编: 1948.11–1996.4 [Selected important materials on US-Taiwan relations, 1948.11–1996.4]. Beijing: Shishi chubanshe, 1997.

Shen Zhihua 沈志华, ed. *Meiguo duiHua qingbao jiemi dang'an (1948–76)* 美国对华情报解密档案 1948–76 [Declassified archives on US China policy (1948–76)]. Beijing: Dongfang chubanshe, 2009.

–, ed. *E'luosi jiemi dang'an: ZhongSu guanxi* 俄罗斯解密档案选编: 中苏关系 [Sino-Soviet relations: declassified documents from Russian archives]. Shanghai: Dongfang chuban zhongxin, 2015.

Susiluofu yanlun xuan 苏斯洛夫言论选集 [Selected speeches of Suslov]. Shanghai: Shanghai renmin chubanshe, various years.

Xigong weizhengquan waijiaobu 西贡伪政权外交部, ed. "Guanyu Huangsha qundao he Changsha qundao de baipishu" [The South Vietnamese White Book on the South China Sea]. In *Guojifa ziliao* 国际法资料 [International law materials], vol. 5, edited by the Zhongguo guojifa xuehui 中国国际法学会. Beijing: Falü chubanshe, 1990.

Statistical Sources

Foreign Trade Institute of the PRC Foreign Trade Ministry 对外贸易部国际贸易研究所, ed. *Sulian duiwai maoyi jiben tongji, 1954–1975* 苏联对外贸易基本统计 1954–1975 [The foundation of the foreign trade statistics of the Soviet Union, 1954–1975]. Beijing: Renmin chubanshe, 1977.

The Military Balance. London: Institute for Strategic Studies, various years.

SIPRI Yearbook of World Armaments and Disarmament. Stockholm: Almquist and Wiksell, various years.

Websites

Airforce Technology. https://www.airforce-technology.com/
Arab News. http://www.arabnews.com/
Asia Maritime Transparency Initiative. https://amti.csis.org/
Asia Sentinel. https://www.asiasentinel.com/
Aviation International News. https://www.ainonline.com/
Baijiahao 百家号. https://baijiahao.baidu.com/
Brahmand. http://www.brahmand.com/
Cankao xiaoxi 参考消息. http://www.cankaoxiaoxi.com/
CBS News. https://www.cbsnews.com/
Chennai Centre for China Studies. https://www.c3sindia.org/
Dangshi xuexi jiaoyu guanwang 党史学习教育官网. http://dangshi.people.com.cn/
Dawn. https://www.dawn.com/
Defense Industry Daily. https://www.defenseindustrydaily.com/
Fenghuang wang 凤凰网. http://news.ifeng.com/
Fox Business. https://www.foxbusiness.com/
Freedom of Information Act. http://www.foia.cia.gov/
Globalsecurity. https://www.globalsecurity.org/
Guandian Zhongguo 观点中国. http://opinion.china.com.cn/
Huanqiu wang 环球网. http://world.huanqiu.com/
Institute for Advanced Study on Asia (Japan). http://www.ioc.u-tokyo.ac.jp/

Inquirer.Net. https://www.inquirer.net/
Media Monitors Network. https://www.mediamonitors.net/
Military Times. https://www.militarytimes.com/
Ministry of Foreign Affairs of Japan. https://www.mofa.go.jp/
Naval Technology. https://www.naval-technology.com/
Official Gazette. https://www.officialgazette.gov.ph/
People's Army Newspaper (Vietnam). https://en.qdnd.vn/
Renmin wang guoji 人民网 (国际). http://world.people.com.cn/
Renminzhengxie wang 人民政协网. http://www.rmzxb.com.cn/
Rigzone. https://www.rigzone.com/
Russia Business Today. https://russiabusinesstoday.com/
Souhu caijing 搜狐财经. https://business.sohu.com/
Souhu wang 搜狐网. http://www.sohu.com/
TASS Russian News Agency. https://tass.com/
Teller Report. https://www.tellerreport.com/
Tengxun wang 腾讯网. https://news.qq.com/
Thanh Nien News. http://www.thanhniennews.com/
The Boston Globe. https://www.bostonglobe.com/
The Boston Globe's Newspaper Article Archive. http://archive.boston.com/
The BRICS Post. https://www.thebricspost.com/
The Diplomat. https://thediplomat.com/
The Economic Times. https://economictimes.indiatimes.com/
The Foreign Policy Research Institute. https://www.fpri.org/
The Heritage Foundation. https://www.heritage.org/
The Indian Express. https://indianexpress.com/
The LAWPHIL Project. https://www.lawphil.net/
The Nation (Thailand). http://www.nationmultimedia.com/
The Parallel History Project on Cooperative Security. https://www.php.isn.ethz.ch/lory1.ethz.ch/index-2.html/
The Space Daily. http://www.spacewar.com/
The Times of India. https://blogs.timesofindia.indiatimes.com/
The Wilson Center Digital Archive. http://digitalarchive.wilsoncenter.org/
The Wisconsin Project on Nuclear Arms Control. https://www.wisconsinproject.org/
Time. https://time.com/
US Naval Institute. https://news.usni.org/
Via Satellite. https://www.satellitetoday.com/
VnExpress. https://e.vnexpress.net/
Wangyi 网易. https://www.163.com/
Xinhua wang 新华网. http://xinhuanet.com/
Xinlang junshi 新浪军事. http://mil.news.sina.com.cn/
Xinlang xinwen 新浪新闻. http://news.sina.com.cn/
Zhongguo gongchandang xinwenwang 中国共产党新闻网. http://cpc.people.com.cn/
Zhongguo wang 中国网. http://www.china.com.cn/, http://www.china.org.cn/
Zhongguo xinwen wang 中国新闻网. https://www.chinanews.com.cn/
Zhonghua renmin gongheguo waijiaobu 中华人民共和国外交部. http://www.fmprc.gov.cn/
Zhonghua renmin gongheguo zhongyang renmin zhengfu 中华人民共和国中央人民政府. http://www.gov.cn/

Zhonghua renmin gongheguo zhu Dabuliedian ji Bei'ai'er'lan lianhe wangguo dashiguan 中华人民共和国驻大不列颠及北爱尔兰联合王国大使馆. http://www.chinese-embassy.org.uk/

Periodicals

Cankao xiaoxi [Reference News]
The Economist
Jiefangjun bao [People's Liberation Army Daily]
New York Times
Renmin ribao [People's Daily]

Published Secondary Sources

Acharya, Amitav. "Global International Relations (IR) and Regional Worlds: A New Agenda for International Studies." *International Studies Quarterly* 58, 4 (2014): 647–59.

–. "Theorising the International Relations of Asia: Necessity or Indulgence? Some Reflections." *Pacific Review* 30, 6 (2017): 816–28.

Alagappa, Muthiah. "Regionalism and Conflict Management: A Framework for Analysis." *Review of International Studies* 21, 4 (1995): 359–87.

Alam, Aftab. *U.S. Military Aid to Pakistan and India's Security.* New Delhi: Raj Publications, 2001.

Aminjonov, Farkhod. "Central Asian Gas Exports Dependency." *RUSI Journal* 163, 2 (2018): 66–77.

Ang Cheng Guan. *The Vietnam War from the Other Side: The Vietnamese Communists' Perspective.* London/New York: Routledge Curzon, 2002.

Armstrong, J.D. *Revolutionary Diplomacy: Chinese Foreign Policy and the United Front Doctrine.* Berkeley: University of California Press, 1977.

Aron, Raymond. *Peace and War: A Theory of International Relations.* Garden City, NY: Doubleday, 1966.

Art, Robert J., and Patrick M. Cronin, eds. *The United States and Coercive Diplomacy.* Washington, DC: United States Institute of Peace Press, 2003.

Axelrod, Robert, and Robert O. Keohane. "Achieving Cooperation under Anarchy." *World Politics* 38, 1 (1985): 226–54.

Baldwin, David A. "Foreign Aid, Intervention, and Influence." *World Politics* 21, 3 (1969): 425–47.

–. "Power and Social Exchange." *American Political Science Review* 72, 4 (1978): 1229–42.

Barnds, William J. *India, Pakistan, and the Great Powers.* New York: Praeger, 1972.

Barnett, A. Doak. *China and the Major Powers in East Asia.* Washington, DC: Brookings Institution, 1977.

Beckley, Michael. "The Emerging Military Balance in East Asia." *International Security* 42, 2 (2017): 78–119.

Benshu bianjizu 本书编辑组, ed. *Mao Zedong guoji jiaowanglu* 毛泽东国际交往录 [Records of Mao Zedong's international activities]. Beijing: Zhonggong dangshi chubanshe, 1995.

Brooks, Stephen G., and William C. Wohlforth. "American Primacy in Perspective." *Foreign Affairs* 81, 4 (2002): 20–33.

Bull, Hedley. *The Anarchical Society: A Study of Order in World Politics.* New York: Palgrave Macmillan, 2002.

Bush, Richard C. *The Perils of Proximity: China-Japan Security Relations.* Washington, DC: Brookings Institution Press, 2010.

Buzan, Barry. *People, States, and Fear: The National Security Problem in International Relations.* Chapel Hill: University of North Carolina Press, 1983.

–. "Security Architecture in Asia: The Interplay of Regional and Global Levels." *Pacific Review* 16, 2 (2003): 143–73.

–. "Third World Regional Security in Structural and Historical Perspective." In *The Insecurity Dilemma: National Security of Third World States,* edited by Brian L. Job, 167–89. Boulder, CO: Lynne Rienner, 1992.

Cha, Victor D. "Powerplay: Origins of the U.S. Alliance System in Asia." *International Security* 34, 3 (2009–10): 158–96.

Chaudhri, Mohammed Ahsen. *Pakistan and the Great Powers.* Karachi: Council for Pakistan Studies, 1970.

Chen, Jian. *China's Road to the Korean War: The Making of the Sino-American Confrontation.* New York: Columbia University Press, 1994.

–. *Mao's China and the Cold War.* Chapel Hill: University of North Carolina Press, 2001.

Chen Donglin 陈东林. *Sanxian jianshe: beizhan shiqi de xibu kaifa* 三线建设: 备战时期的西部开发 [The third front construction: The western development in the war preparation era]. Beijing: Zhonggong zhongyang dangxiao chubanshe, 2003.

Chen, Xiaolu. "Chen Yi and China's Diplomacy." In *Toward a History of Chinese Communist Foreign Relations, 1920s–1960s,* edited by Michael H. Hunt and Niu Jun, 89–112. Washington, DC: Woodrow Wilson Center Asia Program, 1992.

Chen Zhiqi 陈志奇. *Meiguo duihua zhengce sanshinian* 美国对华政策三十年 [The US policy toward China over thirty years]. Taipei: Zhonghua ribaoshe, 1981.

Cheng Ruisheng 程瑞生. *Mulin waijiao sishinian* 睦邻外交四十年 [The good neighbours diplomacy in forty years]. Chengdu: Sichuan renmin chubanshe, 2006.

Cheng Siyuan 程思远. *Wode huiyi* 我的回忆 [My memoirs]. Beijing: Huayi chubanshe, 1994.

Chon, Gina, and Thet Sambath. *Behind the Killing Fields: A Khmer Rouge Leader and One of His Victims.* Philadelphia: University of Pennsylvania Press, 2010.

Christensen, Thomas J. *Useful Adversaries: Grand Strategy, Domestic Mobilization, and Sino-American Conflict, 1947–1958.* Princeton, NJ: Princeton University Press, 1996.

–. "Windows and War: Trend Analysis and Beijing's Use of Force." In *New Directions in the Study of China's Foreign Policy,* edited by Alastair Iain Johnston and Robert S. Ross, 50–85. Stanford, CA: Stanford University Press, 2006.

–. *Worse Than a Monolith: Alliance Politics and Problems of Coercive Diplomacy in Asia.* Princeton, NJ: Princeton University Press, 2011.

Crawford, Timothy. "Preventing Enemy Coalitions: How Wedge Strategies Shape Power Politics." *International Security* 35, 4 (2011): 155–89.

Cui Mingde 崔明德. "Lun Zhangsun Sheng 'li qiang he ruo' lilun tixi de goucheng jiqi zuoyong" 论长孙晟"离强合弱"理论体系的构成及其作用 [Theory and practice of Zhangsun Sheng's strategy of "li qiang he ruo"]. *Liaoning shifan daxue xuebao* 辽宁师范大学学报 *[Journal of Liaoning Normal University]* 5 (1994): 73–76.

Cui Tiankai 崔天凯. "Jianding buyi tuijin ZhongMei hezuo huoban guanxi" 坚定不移推进中美合作伙伴关系 [Resolutely pushing forward the Sino-American cooperative partnership]. *Guoji wenti yanjiu* 国际问题研究 *[International Studies]* 2 (2012): 1–5.

Deng Yingwen 邓应文. "Shilun Yuenan jiang Nanhai wenti guojihua zhi jucuo" 试论越南将南海问题国际化之举措 [Vietnam's attempts to internationalize the South China Sea issue]. *Dongnanya yanjiu* 东南亚研究 *[Southeast Asian Studies]* 6 (2010): 29–36.

Denisov, E., and I.A. Safranchuk. "Four Problems of the SCO in Connection with Its Enlargement." *Russian Politics and Law* 54, 5–6 (2016): 494–515.

Dommen, Arthur J. *Conflict in Laos: The Politics of Neutralization.* New York: Praeger, 1965.

Du Jidong 杜继东. *Meiguo dui Taiwan diqu yuanzhu yanjiu 1950–1965* 美国对台湾地区援助研究 1950–1965 [US assistance to Taiwan, 1950–1965]. Nanjing: Fenghuang chubanshe, 2011.

Fairbank, John King. *China: The People's Middle Kingdom and the USA.* Cambridge, MA: Belknap Press of Harvard University Press, 1967.

–. "The People's Middle Kingdom." *Foreign Affairs* 44, 4 (1966): 574–86.

Fan Ming 范明. *Xizang neibu zhizheng* 西藏内部之争 [Internal rivalries in Tibet]. Hong Kong: Mingjing chubanshe, 2009.

Fan Shuo 范硕. *Ye Jianying zai feichang shiqi, 1966–1976* 叶剑英在非常时期 1966–1976 [Ye Jianying at critical moments, 1966–1976]. Beijing: Huawen chubanshe, 2006.

–, ed. *Ye Jianying zhuan* 叶剑英传 [Biography of Ye Jianying]. Beijing: Dangdai Zhongguo chubanshe, 1995.

Fang Changping, and Zheng Ling 方长平, 郑凌. "Dongmeng gongtongti chengli beijing xia de Zhongguo Dongmeng guanxi" 东盟共同体成立背景下的中国东盟关系 [The evolution of ASEAN community and China-ASEAN Relations]. *Guoji luntan* 国际论坛 *[International Forum]* 6 (2017): 13–18.

Feng Ruiyun et al. 冯瑞云. *ZhongRi guanxishi* 中日关系史 [A history of Sino-Japanese relations]. Beijing: Shehui kexue wenxian chubanshe, 2006.

Forsberg, Aaron. *America and the Japanese Miracle: The Cold War Context of Japan's Postwar Economic Revival, 1950–1960.* Chapel Hill: University of North Carolina Press, 2000.

Fravel, M. Taylor. "Power Shifts and Escalation: Explaining China's Use of Force in Territorial Disputes." *International Security* 32, 3 (2007–08): 44–83.

–. *Strong Borders, Secure Nation: Cooperation and Conflicts in China's Territorial Disputes.* Princeton, NJ: Princeton University Press, 2008.

Freedman, Lawrence, ed. *Strategic Coercion: Concepts and Cases.* New York: Oxford University Press, 1998.

Fu Xiaoqiang 傅小强. "Yindu dui Zhongnanya diqu zhanlue pingxi" 印度对中南亚地区战略评析 [India's strategies toward Central-South Asia]. *Waijiao pinglun* 外交评论 *[Foreign Affairs Review]* 5 (2011): 28–38.

Fu Ying 傅莹. "Quanqiuhua jintui zhong de Zhongguo xuanze" 全球化进退中的中国选择 [China's choices in the globalization era]. March 1, 2018, https://finance.qq.com/a/20180301/036367.htm.

Gaĭduk, I.V. *The Soviet Union and the Vietnam War.* Chicago: I.R. Dee, 1996.

Gao Cheng 高程. "Zhoubian huanjing biandong dui Zhongguo jueqi de tiaozhan" 周边环境变动对中国崛起的挑战 [Challenges of the changing neighbourhood to China's rise]. *Guoji wenti yanjiu* 国际问题研究 *[International Studies]* 5 (2013): 33–45.

Gao Cheng, and Wang Zhen 高程, 王震. "Zhongguo chayihua fenceng jinglue Dongnanya guojia tanxi" 中国差异化分层经略东南亚国家探析 [An analysis of China's differentiated, multilayered strategic planning and management of Southeast Asian countries]. *Shijie jingji yu zhengzhi* 世界经济与政治 *[World Economics and Politics]* 12 (2019): 69–100.

Gao Feng et al. 高峰. *Lin Haiyun zhuan* 林海云传 [A biography of Lin Haiyun]. Beijing: Duiwai jingji maoyi daxue chubanshe, 2000.

Gao Wenqian 高文谦. *Wannian Zhou Enlai* 晚年周恩来 [Zhou Enlai's later years]. Hong Kong: Mirror Books, 2003.

Garver, John W. "China's Decision for War with India in 1962." In *New Directions in the Study of China's Foreign Policy,* edited by Alastair Iain Johnston and Robert S. Ross, 86–130. Stanford, CA: Stanford University Press, 2006.

–. *Protracted Contest: Sino-Indian Rivalry in the Twentieth Century.* Seattle: University of Washington Press, 2001.

–. "Sino-Indian Rapprochement and the Sino-Pakistan Entente." *Political Science Quarterly* 111, 2 (1996): 323–47.

George, Alexander L., and Andrew Bennett. *Case Studies and Theory Development in the Social Sciences.* Cambridge, MA: MIT Press, 2005.

George, Alexander L., and William E. Simons, eds. *The Limits of Coercive Diplomacy.* Boulder, CO: Westview Press, 1994.

George, Alexander L., and Richard Smoke. *Deterrence in American Foreign Policy: Theory and Practice.* New York: Columbia University Press, 1974.

Gerring, John. *Case Study Research: Principles and Practices.* Cambridge: Cambridge University Press, 2007.

Gilks, Anne. *The Breakdown of the Sino-Vietnamese Alliance, 1970–1979.* Berkeley: Institute of East Asian Studies, 1992.

Glaser, Charles L. *Rational Theory of International Politics: The Logic of Competition and Cooperation.* Princeton, NJ: Princeton University Press, 2010.

Goldstein, Avery. *Deterrence and Security in the 21st Century: China, Britain, France, and the Enduring Legacy of the Nuclear Revolution.* Stanford, CA: Stanford University Press, 2000.

Goldstein, Judith, and Robert O. Keohane, eds. *Ideas and Foreign Policy.* Ithaca, NY: Cornell University Press, 1993.

Goldstein, Melvyn C. *A History of Modern Tibet.* Vol. 2. Berkeley: University of California Press, 2007.

Graber, Doris A. "Are Foreign Aid Objectives Attainable?" *Western Political Quarterly* 19, 1 (1966): 68–84.

Gu Dexin 顾德欣. "Cong zhanlue jiaodu kan Zhongguo yu Dongmeng de guanxi" 从战略角度看中国与东盟的关系 [Sino-ASEAN relations from a strategic perspective]. *Shijie jingji yu zhengzhi* 世界经济与政治 *[World Economics and Politics]* 1 (1997): 21–22.

Gu Yongzhong 顾永忠. *He Long yu gongheguo yuanshuai* 贺龙与共和国元帅 [He Long and marshals of the republic]. Beijing: Renmin chubanshe, 2007.

Gurtov, Melvin. *China and Southeast Asia: The Politics of Survival: A Study of Foreign Policy Interaction.* Baltimore: Johns Hopkins University Press, 1975.

Haas, Mark L. *The Ideological Origins of Great Power Politics, 1789–1989.* Ithaca, NY: Cornell University Press, 2005.

Han Huaizhi and Tan Jingqiao 韩怀智, 谭旌樵, eds. *Dangdai Zhongguo jundui de junshi gongzuo* 当代中国军队的军事工作 [Military work of contemporary China's armed forces]. Beijing: Zhongguo shehui kexue chubanshe, 1989.

Han Nianlong, ed. *Diplomacy of Contemporary China.* Hong Kong: New Horizon Press, 1990.

He, Kai. "China and Southeast Asia: Strategic Interdependence in the Making." *Asia Policy* 13, 4 (2018): 17–23.

–. "Institutional Balancing and International Relations Theory: Economic Interdependence and Balance of Power Strategies in Southeast Asia." *European Journal of International Relations* 14, 3 (2008): 489–518.

Heder, Stephen. "Kampuchea's Armed Struggle: The Origins of an Independent Revolution." *Bulletin of Concerned Asian Scholars* 11, 1 (1979): 2–23.

Heginbotham, Eric, and Richard J. Samuels. "Active Denial: Redesigning Japan's Response to China's Military Challenge." *International Security* 42, 4 (2018): 128–69.

Hickey, Dennis, and Lilly Kelan Lu. "Japan's Military Modernization: The Chinese Perspective." In *China and Japan at Odds: Deciphering the Perpetual Conflict,* edited by James C. Hsiung, 95–112. New York: Palgrave Macmillan, 2007.

Hosoya, Chihiro. "From the Yoshida Letter to the Nixon Shock." In *The United States and Japan in the Postwar World,* edited by Akira Iriye and Warren I. Cohen, 21–35. Lexington: University Press of Kentucky, 1989.

Huang Guo'an et al. 黄国安. *ZhongYue guanxishi jianbian* 中越关系史简编 [A concise history of Sino-Vietnamese relationship]. Nanning: Guangxi renmin chubanshe, 1986.

Huang Qinghua 黄庆华. *ZhongFa jianjiao shimo: 20 shiji 40–60 naindai ZhongFa guanxi* 中法建交始末: 20 世纪 40–60 年代中法关系 [The establishment of the Sino-French relationship: the relationship from the 1940s to the 1960s]. Hefei: Huangshan shushe, 2014.

Huang, Yuxing. "China's Security and the Use of Force: Lessons from the Cold War." In *The Legacy of the Cold War: Perspectives on Security, Cooperation, and Conflict,* edited by Vojtech Mastny and Liqun Zhu, 277–322. Lanham, MD: Rowman and Littlefield, Lexington Books, 2014.

–. "An Interdependence Theory of Wedge Strategies." *Chinese Journal of International Politics* 13, 2 (2020): 253–86.

–. "A Structural Theory of Multilateral Asymmetric Strategies: China's Strategies towards Neighbors before 1982." *Chinese Journal of International Politics* 8, 1 (2015): 89–113.

Huang Yuxing 黄宇兴. "Gongneng fenyi yu lianmeng xingcheng" 功能分异与联盟形成 [Functional division and alliance formation]. *Shijie jingji yu zhengzhi* 世界经济与政治 *[World Economics and Politics]* 2 (2019): 101–22.

–. "Guoji guanxishi yanjiu de lilun yiyi" 国际关系史研究的理论意义 [Theoretical significance of studies on international relations history]. *Lengzhan guojishi yanjiu* 冷战国际史研究 *[Cold War International History Studies]* 2 (2019): 171–75.

–. "Jueqiguo ruhe yanpan baquanguo jiemeng de kenengxing" 崛起国如何研判霸权国结盟的可能性 [How does a rising power estimate the possibility of a hegemon's alliance formation?]. *Shijie jingji yu zhengzhi* 世界经济与政治 *[World Economics and Politics]* 5 (2022): 77–100.

–. "Nengli fenyi yu junshi xiezuo" 能力分异与军事协作 [Capability differentials and military coordination]. *Shijie jingji yu zhengzhi* 世界经济与政治 *[World Economics and Politics]* 5 (2021): 108–30.

–. "Tanpan nengli yu lianmeng zhuanxing" 谈判能力与联盟转型 [Negotiating power and alliance transformation]. *Shijie jingji yu zhengzhi* 世界经济与政治 *[World Economics and Politics]* 6 (2017): 77–101.

–. "'Xiaoguo jituan' de zhengce xietiao" "小国集团" 的政策协调 [Policy coordination of small power coalitions]. *Shijie jingji yu zhengzhi* 世界经济与政治 *[World Economics and Politics]* 3 (2018): 115–35.

Hui, Victoria Tin-bor. *War and State Formation in Ancient China and Early Modern Europe.* Cambridge: Cambridge University Press, 2005.

Huntington, Samuel P. "Lonely Superpower." *Foreign Affairs* 78, 2 (1999): 35–49.

Ikenberry, G. John. *After Victory: Institutions, Strategic Restraint, and the Rebuilding of Order after Major War.* Princeton, NJ: Princeton University Press, 2001.

–. "Reflections on *After Victory.*" *British Journal of Politics and International Relations* 21, 1 (2019): 5–19.

Iriye, Akira. "Chinese-Japanese Relations, 1945–90." *China Quarterly* 124 (1990): 624–38.

Itoh, Mayumi. *Pioneers of Sino-Japanese Relations: Liao and Takasaki.* New York: Palgrave Macmillan, 2012.

Jervis, Robert. *The Logic of Images in International Relations.* Princeton, NJ: Princeton University Press, 1970.

Ji Ming 纪明. "Mao Zedong, Zhou Enlai wei zuguo tongyi yu Taiwan dangju de jiaowang" 毛泽东，周恩来为祖国统一与台湾当局的交往 [Mao Zedong and Zhou Enlai approaching the Taiwan Authority for National Unification]. In *Taihai fengyunlu* 台海风云录 [The story over the Taiwan Strait], edited by Xu Shiquan 许世铨, 146–60. Beijing: Huayi chubanshe, 1998.

Jin Chongji 金冲及, ed. *Zhou Enlai zhuan* 周恩来传 [Biography of Zhou Enlai]. Beijing: Zhongyang wenxian chubanshe, 1998.

Johnston, Alastair Iain. "China's Militarized Interstate Dispute Behavior 1949–1992: A First Cut at the Data." *China Quarterly* 153 (1998): 1–30.

–. *Cultural Realism: Strategic Culture and Grand Strategy in Chinese History.* Princeton, NJ: Princeton University Press, 1995.

–. "What (if Anything) Does East Asia Tell Us about International Relations Theory?" *Annual Review of Political Science* 15 (2012): 53–78.

–. "Zhongguo waijiao zhengce yanjiu: lilun qushi ji fangfa bianxi" 中国外交政策研究：理论趋势及方法辨析 [Trends in theory and method in the study of Chinese foreign policy]. *Shijie jingji yu zhengzhi [World Economics and Politics]* 8 (2006): 64–73.

Johnston, Alastair Iain, and Robert S. Ross, eds. *Engaging China: The Management of an Emerging Power.* London/New York: Routledge, 1999.

Junshi kexueyuan junshi lishiyanjiusuo 军事科学院军事历史研究所, ed. *Renmin Jiefangjun gaige fazhan 30 nian* 人民解放军改革发展 30 年 [The reform and development of the People's Liberation Army over 30 years]. Beijing: Junshi kexue chubanshe, 2008.

Kang, David C. "Hierarchy in Asian International Relations: 1300 to 1900." *Asian Security* 1, 1 (2005): 53–79.

Kang Daisha 康岱沙. "Zai Jianpuzhai de rizi" 在柬埔寨的日子 [The days in Cambodia]. In *Nüwaijiaoguan* 女外交官 [The female diplomats], edited by Cheng Xiangjun 程湘君, 474–89. Beijing: Renmin tiyu chubanshe, 1995.

Kang Maozhao 康矛召. *Waijiaoguan huiyilu* 外交官回忆录 [A diplomat's memoirs]. Beijing: Zhongyang wenxian chubanshe, 2000.

Kaplan, Morton A. "Problems of Theory Building and Theory Confirmation in International Politics." *World Politics* 14, 1 (1961): 6–24.

Kaura, Vinay. "India's Changing Relationship with Russia." *RUSI Journal* 163, 1 (2018): 48–60.

Kennedy, Paul. *Strategy and Diplomacy, 1870–1945: Eight Studies.* London and Boston: Allen and Unwin, 1983.

Khan, Shaheen Irshad. *Rejection Alliance? A Case-Study of U.S.-Pakistan Relations, 1947–1967.* Lahore: Ferozsons, 1972.

Khoo, Nicholas. *Collateral Damage: Sino-Soviet Rivalry and the Termination of the Sino-Vietnamese Alliance.* New York: Columbia University Press, 2011.

King, Gary, Robert O. Keohane, and Sidney Verba. *Designing Social Inquiry: Scientific Inference in Qualitative Research.* Princeton, NJ: Princeton University Press, 1994.

Kong Hanbing 孔寒冰. *Hanbing fang Luoming* 寒冰访罗明 [Kong Hanbing's interviews with Romulus Ioan Budura]. Shanghai: Shanghai renmin chubanshe, 2013.

Korolev, Alexander. "Russia in the South China Sea: Balancing and Hedging." *Foreign Policy Analysis* 15, 2 (2019): 263–82.

–. "Systemic Balancing and Regional Hedging: China-Russia Relations." *Chinese Journal of International Politics* 9, 4 (2016): 375–97.

Krasner, Stephen D. "Regimes and the Limits of Realism: Regimes as Autonomous Variables." *International Organization* 36, 2 (1982): 497–510.

Kubota, Yuichi. *Armed Groups in Cambodian Civil War: Territorial Control, Rivalry, and Recruitment.* New York: Palgrave Macmillan, 2013.

LaFeber, Walter. *The Clash: A History of U.S.-Japan Relations.* New York: W.W. Norton, 1997.

Lampton, David M. *The Three Faces of Chinese Power: Might, Money, and Minds.* Berkeley: University of California Press, 2008.

Langdon, Frank. *Japan's Foreign Policy.* Vancouver: UBC Press, 1973.

Le Yucheng 乐玉成. "Dui guoji bianju yu Zhongguo waijiao de ruogan sikao" 对国际变局与中国外交的若干思考 [Some reflections on the changing international environment and Chinese foreign policy]. *Xiandai guoji guanxi* 现代国际关系 *[Contemporary International Relations]* 8 (2012): 1–6.

Lebow, Richard Ned. "Constructive Realism." *International Studies Review* 6, 2 (2004): 346–48.

Lei Jianfeng 雷建锋. "Pingheng ZhongMei yu yi Yin duichong: E dui Hua zhanlue xindongxiang" 平衡中美与以印对冲：俄对华战略新动向 [Striking a US-China balance and hedging by Russian-Indian relations: recent development of Russia's China policy]. *E'luosi yanjiu* 俄罗斯研究 *[Russian Studies]* 1 (2021): 43–73.

Levi, Werner. "Ideology, Interests, and Foreign Policy." *International Studies Quarterly* 14, 1 (1970): 1–31.

Levy, Jack S. "Explaining Events and Developing Theories: History, Political Science, and the Analysis of International Relations." In *Bridges and Boundaries: Historians, Political Scientists, and the Study of International Relations,* edited by Colin Elman and Miriam Fendius Elman, 39–83. Cambridge, MA: MIT Press, 2001.

–. *War in the Modern Great Power System, 1495–1975.* Lexington: University Press of Kentucky, 1983.

Li Chenyang 李晨阳. "Dui lengzhan hou Zhongguo yu Dongmeng guanxi de fansi" 对冷战后中国与东盟关系的反思 [Reflections on China-ASEAN relations in the post–Cold War era]. *Waijiao pinglun* 外交评论 *[Foreign Affairs Review]* 4 (2012): 10–20.

Li De'an et al. 李德安. *Zhou Enlai yu Riben pengyou men* 周恩来与日本朋友们 [Zhou Enlai and his Japanese friends]. Beijing: Zhongyang wenxian chubanshe, 1992.

Li Enmin 李恩民. *ZhongRi minjian jingji waijiao 1945–1972* 中日民间经济外交 1945–1972 [The Sino-Japanese non-governmental economic diplomacy 1945–1972]. Beijing: Renmin chubanshe, 1997.

Li Fang 李方. "Dong Tujue de guifu yu Sui qianqi de bianzheng" 东突厥的归附与隋前期的边政 [The eastern Turks' surrender and the border security of the early Sui Dynasty]. *Xiyu yanjiu* 西域研究 *[Western Regions Studies]* 1 (2004): 4–10.

Li Fengyou and Zhang Ye 李凤友, 张野. "Pingxi Yita shijian zhong de wuzhuang jingcha budui" 平息伊塔事件中的武装警察部队 [The armed security forces in the Yita incident].

In *Gong'an budui huiyi shiliao* 公安部队回忆史料 [Recollections and historical materials of public security forces], 380–84. Beijing: Jiefangjun chubanshe, 1997.

Li Fusheng and Fang Yingkai 李福生, 方英楷, eds. *Xinjiang bingtuan tunken shubian shi* 新疆兵团屯垦戍边史 [A history of the Xinjiang Corps' stationing and reclaiming of land]. Wulumuqi: Xinjiang keji weisheng chubanshe, 1997.

Li Ke and Hao Shengzhang 李可, 郝生章. *Wenhua dageming zhong de renmin jiefangjun* "文化大革命" 中的人民解放军 [The People's Liberation Army during the Great Cultural Revolution]. Beijing: Zhonggong dangshi ziliao chubanshe, 1989.

Li Lianqing 李连庆. *Da waijiaojia Zhou Enlai* 大外交家周恩来 [Zhou Enlai: a great diplomat]. Hong Kong: Tiandi tushu youxian gongsi, various years.

–. *Lengnuan suiyue: Yibosanzhe de ZhongSu guanxi* 冷暖岁月——一波三折的中苏关系 [Ups and downs of Sino-Soviet relations]. Beijing: Shijie zhishi chubanshe, 1999.

Li Sheng 厉声, ed. *Zhongguo Xinjiang lishi yu xianzhuang* 中国新疆历史与现状 [China's Xinjiang in historical and contemporary perspectives]. Wulumuqi: Xinjiang renmin chubanshe, 2006.

Li Yongming 李永明. *Wode jizhe shengya* 我的记者生涯 [My career as a journalist]. Singapore: Renmin chubanshe siren youxian gongsi, 2007.

Li Ziguo 李自国. "Shanghai hezuo zuzhi de kuoyuan yu mingyun gongtongti jianshe" 上海合作组织的扩员与命运共同体建设 [The SCO membership extension and construction of the community of a shared future]. *E'luosi dong'ou zhongya yanjiu* 俄罗斯, 东欧中亚研究 *[Russian, Eastern European and Central Asian Studies]* 4 (2021): 7–28.

Li Zongyu 李宗禹, ed. *Ou'Mei gongyun fengyunlu (1945–1991)* 欧美共运风云录 1945–1991 [A chronicle of major events of international communist movements in Europe and America (1945–1991)]. Beijing: Renmin chubanshe, 1994.

Liang Dongyuan 梁东元. *596 mishi* 596 秘史 [Stories behind China's first atomic bomb]. Wuhan: Hubei renmin chubanshe, 2007.

Liao Xinwen 廖心文. "Ershi shiji liuqishiniandai Mao Zedong, Deng Xiaoping deng dapo Sulian baowei de zhanlue sixiang yu juece licheng" 二十世纪六七十年代毛泽东, 邓小平等打破苏联包围的战略思想与决策历程 [Strategic thoughts and decision making of Mao Zedong and Deng Xiaoping on breaking Soviet encirclement in the 1960s–1970s]. *Dangde wenxian* 党的文献 *[The Party's Documents]* 6 (2010): 35–42.

Lin Li 林利. *Wangshi suoyi* 往事琐忆 [Reminiscence of past events]. Beijing: Zhongyang wenxian chubanshe, 2006.

Lin Liangguang, Ye Zhengjia, and Han Hua 林良光, 叶正佳, 韩华. *Dang dai Zhongguo yu Nanya guojia guan xi* 当代中国与南亚国家关系 [Contemporary China–South Asia relations]. Beijing: Shehui kexue wenxian chubanshe, 2001.

Ling Shengli 凌胜利. "Quanqiu zhanlue shousuoqi yu Zhongguo 'qiangguo waijiao' xinzhengcheng" 全球战略收缩期与中国 "强国外交" 新征程 [The global strategic retrenchment period and a new journey for China's great power diplomacy]. *Yatai anquan yu haiyang yanjiu* 亚太安全与海洋研究 *[Asia-Pacific Security and Maritime Affairs]* 3 (2021): 1–17.

Lipski, Józef. *Diplomat in Berlin, 1933–1939*. New York: Columbia University Press, 1968.

Liu Deyou 刘德有. *Shiguang zhilü: wo jingli de ZhongRi guanxi* 时光之旅——我经历的中日关系 [The time travel: my personal experience in Sino-Japanese relations]. Beijing: Shangwu yinshuguan, 1999.

Liu Feng 刘丰. "Zhongguo Dongya anquan zhanlue zhuanbian jiqi jieshi" 中国东亚安全战略转变及其解释 [China's security strategy toward East Asia]. *Guoji zhengzhi kexue* 国际政治科学 *[Quarterly Journal of International Politics]* 3 (2016): 29–52.

Liu Shilong 刘世龙. *Xinzhongguo duiRi zhengce, 1949–1972* 新中国对日政策1949–1972 [The PRC's policy toward Japan, 1949–1972]. Beijing: Shijie zhishi chubanshe, 2020.

Liu Wanzhen and Li Qinggui 刘万镇, 李庆贵, eds. *Mao Zedong guoji jiaowanglu, zengdingben* 毛泽东国际交往录（增订本）[Records of Mao Zedong's international activities, expanded version]. Beijing: Zhonggong dangshi chubanshe, 2003.

Lobell, Steven E., Norrin M. Ripsman, and Jeffrey W. Taliaferro, eds. *Neoclassical Realism, the State, and Foreign Policy.* Cambridge: Cambridge University Press, 2009.

Long Xingchun 龙兴春. "Shilun Zhongguo yu Nanmeng duobian hezo de jizhi yu jincheng" 试论中国与南盟多边合作的机制与进程 [The mechanisms and processes of China-SAARC relations]. *Nanya yanjiu* 南亚研究 *[South Asian Studies]* 4 (2009): 1–9.

Lu Guang 鲁光. "Xiaoqiu zhuandong diqiu: 'pingpang waijiao' qinliji" 小球转动地球: "乒乓外交" 亲历记 [The small ball shapes the earth: my experience in the "ping-pong diplomacy"]. In *Jianzheng Aolinpike* 见证奥林匹克 [Witnessing the Olympics], edited by Tang Mingxin, Feng Guijia, and Zhang Bing 汤铭新, 冯贵家, 张兵, 262–74. Beijing: Xinhua chubanshe, 2007.

Lu Jianren 陆建人. "Yatai daguo zai Dongnanya diqu de liyi" 亚太大国在东南亚地区的利益 [Interests of Asia-Pacific major powers in Southeast Asia]. *Shijie jingji yu zhengzhi* 世界经济与政治 *[World Economics and Politics]* 2 (2000): 41–45.

Luo Shengrong and Zhao Qi 罗圣荣, 赵祺. "Meiguo 'Yintai zhanlue' dui Zhongguo-Dongmeng gongjian '21 shiji haishang sichou zhilu' de tiaozhan yu yingdui" 美国 "印太战略" 对中国 - 东盟共建 "21世纪海上丝绸之路" 的挑战与应对 [Challenges facing China-ASEAN joint building of the "maritime silk road" and China's response in the context of America's Indo-Pacific strategy]. *Heping yu fazhan* 和平与发展 *[Peace and Development]* 3 (2021): 115–34.

Lüthi, Lorenz M. *The Sino-Soviet Split, 1956–1966: Cold War in the Communist World.* Princeton, NJ: Princeton University Press, 2008.

Ma Jianguang 马建光. *E'luosi duiwai junshi jishu hezuo: xianzhuang yu qianzhan* 俄罗斯对外军事技术合作: 现状与前瞻 [Russia's foreign technological cooperation: current situations and future trends]. Beijing: Guofang gongye chubanshe, 2013.

Mahoney, James. "Process Tracing and Historical Explanation." *Security Studies* 24, 2 (2015): 200–18.

Mansingh, Surjit. "China-Bhutan Relations." *China Report* 30, 2 (1994): 175–84.

Martin, Lisa L. "Institutions and Cooperation: Sanctions during the Falkland Islands Conflict." *International Security* 16, 4 (1992): 143–78.

Mastny, Vojtech. "The Soviet Union's Partnership with India." *Journal of Cold War Studies* 12, 3 (2010): 50–90.

McGarr, Paul M. *The Cold War in South Asia: Britain, the United States and the Indian Subcontinent, 1945–1965.* Cambridge: Cambridge University Press, 2013.

Mearsheimer, John J. *Conventional Deterrence.* Ithaca, NY: Cornell University Press, 1983.

–. "The Gathering Storm: China's Challenge to US Power in Asia." *Chinese Journal of International Politics* 3, 4 (2010): 381–96.

–. *The Tragedy of Great Power Politics.* New York: Norton, 2001.

Mendel, Douglas. *The Japanese People and Foreign Policy.* Berkeley: University of California Press, 1961.

Meng Xianzhang 孟宪章, ed. *ZhongSu maoyi shi ziliao* 中苏贸易史资料 [Sources on the Sino-Soviet trade history]. Beijing: Zhongguo duiwai jingji maoyi chubanshe, 1991.

Miller, Manjari Chatterjee. *Wronged by Empire: Post-Imperial Ideology and Foreign Policy in India and China.* Stanford, CA: Stanford University Press, 2013.

Milner, Helen V. "Rationalizing Politics: The Emerging Synthesis of International, American and Comparative Politics." *International Organization* 52, 4 (1998): 759–86.

Miyazaki Seon 宫崎世民. *Gongqishimin huiyilu* 宫崎世民回忆录 [Miyazaki Seon's memoirs], translated by Yang Guiyan 杨贵言. Beijing: Zhongguo shehui kexue chubanshe, 2012.

Morgan, Patrick. *Deterrence Now.* Cambridge: Cambridge University Press, 2003.

Morgenthau, Hans J. "A Political Theory of Foreign Aid." *American Political Science Review* 56, 2 (1962): 301–9.

Morrow, James D. "Alliances and Asymmetry: An Alternative to the Capability Aggregation Model of Alliances." *American Journal of Political Science* 35, 4 (1991): 903–33.

–. "The Strategic Setting of Choices: Signaling, Commitment, and Negotiation in International Relations." In *Strategic Choice and International Relations,* edited by David A. Lake and Robert Powell, 77–114. Princeton, NJ: Princeton University Press, 1999.

Muni, S.D. *Foreign Policy of Nepal.* New Delhi: National Publishing House, 1973.

Myoe, Maung Aung. *In the Name of Pauk-Phaw: Myanmar's China Policy since 1948.* Singapore: Institute of Southeast Asian Studies, 2011.

Newnham, Randall Everest. *Economic Linkage in German-Polish Relations, 1918–1939.* Pittsburgh: Center for Russian and East European Studies, 2006.

Nguyen, Lien-Hang T. *Hanoi's War: An International History of the War for Peace in Vietnam.* Chapel Hill: University of North Carolina Press, 2012.

–. "The Sino-Vietnamese Split and the Indochina War, 1968–1975." In *The Third Indochina War: Conflict between China, Vietnam and Cambodia, 1972–79,* edited by Odd Arne Westad and Sophie Quinn-Judge, 12–32. London/New York: Routledge, 2006.

Nie Fengzhi 聂凤智. "Peihe luhaijun jiefang Yijiangshan dao" 配合陆海军解放一江山岛 [In collaboration with the army and the navy to liberate the Yijiangshan Islands]. In *Kongjun huiyi shiliao* 空军: 回忆史料 [Recollections and historical materials of the Air Force], 444–53. Beijing: Jiefangjun chubanshe, 1992.

Niu Jun 牛军. *Lengzhan shidai de Zhongguo zhanlue juece* 冷战时代的中国战略决策 [China's strategic decision-making during the Cold War]. Beijing: Shijie zhishi chubanshe, 2019.

Nye, Joseph S. Jr. "Old Wars and Future Wars: Causation and Prevention." In *The Origins and Prevention of Major Wars,* edited by Robert I. Rotberg and Theodore K. Rabb, 3–12. Cambridge: Cambridge University Press, 1989.

Olson, Mancur, and Richard Zeckhauser. "An Economic Theory of Alliances." *Review of Economics and Statistics* 48, 3 (1966): 266–79.

Owen, John M. IV. "Transnational Liberalism and U.S. Primacy." *International Security* 26, 3 (2001–02): 117–52.

Pang Xianzhi and Jin Chongji 逄先知, 金冲及, eds. *Mao Zedong zhuan, 1949–1976* 毛泽东传 1949–1976 [Biography of Mao Zedong, 1949–1976]. Beijing: Zhongyang wenxian chubanshe, 2003.

Parameswaran, Prashanth. *Playing It Safe: Malaysia's Approach to the South China Sea and Implications for the United States.* Washington, DC: Center for a New American Security, February 2015.

Pardesi, Manjeet. "Explaining the Asymmetry in the Sino-Indian Strategic Rivalry." *Australian Journal of International Affairs* 75, 3 (2021): 341–65.

Paul, T.V. "The Accommodation of Rising Powers in World Politics." In *Accommodating Rising Powers: Past, Present, and Future,* edited by T.V. Paul, 3–32. Cambridge: Cambridge University Press, 2016.

Pedersen, Thomas. "Cooperative Hegemony: Power, Ideas and Institutions in Regional Integration." *Review of International Studies* 28, 4 (2002): 677–96.

Posen, Barry. *The Sources of Military Doctrine: France, Britain, and Germany between the World Wars.* Ithaca, NY: Cornell University Press, 1984.

Prasad, Shashi Bhushan. *The China Factor in Indo-Nepalese Relations, 1955–72: A Study of Linkage Phenomena.* New Delhi: Commonwealth, 1989.

Putnam, Robert D. "Diplomacy and Domestic Politics: The Logic of Two-Level Games." *International Organization* 42, 3 (1988): 427–60.

Qi Huaigao 祁怀高. "Zhongguo duobian hezuo tixi yu Meiguo shuangbian tongmeng tixi zai Dongya de maodun yu jianrong" 中国多边合作体系与美国双边同盟体系在东亚的矛盾与兼容 [China's multilateral cooperative mechanism versus US bilateral military alliances: contradictions and compatibility]. *Guoji wenti yanjiu* 国际问题研究 *[International Studies]* 2 (2009): 9–16.

Qi Huaigao, and Shi Yuanhua 祁怀高, 石源华. "Zhongguo de zhoubian an'quan tiaozhan yu dazhoubian waijiao zhanlue" 中国的周边安全挑战与大周边外交战略 [China's periphery security challenges and its pan-peripheral diplomatic strategy]. *Shijie jingji yu zhengzhi* 世界经济与政治 *[World Economics and Politics]* 6 (2013): 25–46.

Qin, Yaqing. *A Relational Theory of World Politics.* Cambridge: Cambridge University Press, 2018.

Radchenko, Sergey. *Two Suns in the Heavens: The Sino-Soviet Struggle for Supremacy, 1962–1967.* Stanford, CA: Stanford University Press, 2009.

Renmin ribao Editorial Office 《人民日报》评论部, ed. *Xi Jinping yong dian* 习近平用典 [Xi Jinping's reference to Chinese histories]. Beijing: Renmin ribao chubanshe, 2018.

Robinson, Paul, and Jay Dixon. *Aiding Afghanistan: A History of Soviet Assistance to a Developing Country.* New York: Columbia University Press, 2013.

Rock, Stephen R. *Appeasement in International Politics.* Lexington: University Press of Kentucky, 2000.

Rose, Gideon. "Neoclassical Realism and Theories of Foreign Policy." *World Politics* 51, 1 (1998): 144–72.

Ross, Robert S. "China and Cambodian Peace Process: The Value of Coercive Diplomacy." *Asian Survey* 31, 12 (1991): 1170–85.

–. *The Indochina Tangle: China's Vietnam Policy, 1975–1979.* New York: Columbia University Press, 1988.

–. "Introduction." In *Re-Examining the Cold War: U.S.-China Diplomacy, 1954–1973,* edited by Robert S. Ross and Jiang Changbin, 1–24. Cambridge, MA: Harvard University Press, 2001.

–. "Nationalism, Geopolitics and Naval Expansionism: From the Nineteenth Century to the Rise of China." *Naval War College Review* 71, 4 (2018): 11–44.

–. *Negotiating Cooperation: The United States and China, 1969–1989.* Stanford, CA: Stanford University Press, 1995.

Rothstein, Robert. *Alliances and Small Powers.* New York: Columbia University Press, 1968.

Rowan, Joshua P. "US-Japan Security Alliance, ASEAN, and the South China Sea Dispute." *Asian Survey* 45, 3 (2005): 414–36.

Scalapino, Robert A. "Chinese Foreign Policy in 1979." In *China Briefing, 1980,* edited by Robert B. Oxnam and Richard C. Bush, 75–85. Boulder, CO: Westview Press, 1980.

Schanberg, Sydney H. "All but 3 Soviet Aides Leave Cambodia." *New York Times,* October 26, 1973.

–. "Moscow, Backing Sihanouk, Will Leave Only 'Caretakers' in Phnom Penh." *New York Times,* October 22, 1973.

Schelling, Thomas C. *Arms and Influence.* New Haven, CT: Yale University Press, 1966.

Schweller, Randall L. "Unanswered Threats: A Neoclassical Realist Theory of Underbalancing." *International Security* 29, 2 (2004): 159–201.

She Chunshu 佘春树. *Jianpuzhai: baojing cangsang* 柬埔寨：饱经沧桑 [Cambodia: many vicissitudes in history]. Hong Kong: City University of Hong Kong Press, 2004.

Shen Jueren 沈觉人, ed. *Dangdai Zhongguo duiwai maoyi* 当代中国对外贸易 [Foreign trade of contemporary China]. Beijing: Dangdai zhongguo chubanshe, 1992.

Shen Weiping 沈卫平. *8/23 Jinmen dapaozhan* 8/23 金门大炮战 [The big shelling over Jinmen on August 23]. Jinan: Huanghe chubanshe, 2008.

Shen Zhihua 沈志华. *Lengzhan de zaizhuanxing: ZhongSu tongmeng de neizai fenqi jiqi jieju* 冷战的再转型：中苏同盟的内在分歧及其结局 [The retransformation of the Cold War: the inherent differences within the Sino-Soviet alliance and the fate of the alliance]. Beijing: Jiuzhou chubanshe, 2013.

–. *Lengzhan de zhuanxing: ZhongSu tongmeng jianli yu yuandong geju bianhua* 冷战的转型：中苏同盟建立与远东格局变化 [The transformation of the Cold War: the formation of the Sino-Soviet alliance and the change of strategic environment in the Far East]. Beijing: Jiuzhou chubanshe, 2013.

–. "Paoji jinmen: Sulian de yingdui yu ZhongSu fenqi" 炮击金门：苏联的应对与中苏分歧 [Shelling over Jinmen: The Soviet response and Sino-Soviet differences]. In *Jinmen: neizhan yu lengzhan* 金门：内战与冷战 [Jinmen: the civil war and the Cold War], edited by Shen Zhihua and Tang Qihua 沈志华, 唐启华, 131–57. Beijing: Jiuzhou chubanshe, 2010.

–. *Wunai de xuanze: lengzhan yu ZhongSu tongmeng de mingyun, 1945–1959* 无奈的选择：冷战与中苏同盟的命运 1945–1959 [Reluctant choices: the Cold War and the fate of the Sino-Soviet alliance, 1945–1959]. Beijing: Shehui kexue wenxian chubanshe, 2013.

–, ed. *ZhongSu guanxi shigang, 1917–1991, zengdingban* 中苏关系史纲 1917–1991 增订版 [A history of Sino-Soviet relations, 1917–1991, revised edition]. Beijing: Shehui kexue wenxian chubanshe, 2011.

Shi Yinhong 时殷弘. "Guanyu Zhongguo de Yazhou Xitaipingyang zhanlue he Nanhai wenti" 关于中国的亚洲西太平洋战略和南海问题 [China's West Pacific of Asia strategy and the South China Sea issue]. *Dongnanya yanjiu* 东南亚研究 *[Southeast Asian Studies]* 5 (2016): 33–38.

Shi Zhe 师哲. *Zai lishi juren shenbian: Shi Zhe huiyilu* 在历史巨人身边：师哲回忆录 [Side in the history of the giants: Shi Zhe's memoirs]. Beijing: Zhongyang wenxian chubanshe, 1991.

Singer, J. David. "The Appeasement Option: Past and Future." In *Appeasing Fascism: Articles from the Wayne State University Conference on Munich after Fifty Years,* edited by Melvin Small and Otto Feinstein, 1–8. Lanham, MD: University Press of America, 1991.

Singer, Marshall R. *Weak States in a World of Powers: The Dynamics of International Relationships.* New York: Free Press, 1972.

Singh, K. Natwar. *My China Diary 1956–1988*. New Delhi: Rupa and Company, 2009.

Skalamera, Morena. "Russia's Lasting Influence in Central Asia." *Survival* 59, 6 (2017–18): 123–42.

Smith, Roger M. *Cambodia's Foreign Policy*. Ithaca, NY: Cornell University Press, 1965.

Snyder, Glenn H. *Alliance Politics*. Ithaca, NY: Cornell University Press, 1997.

–. "Alliance Theory: A Neorealist First Cut." *Journal of International Affairs* 44, 1 (1990): 103–23.

–. "Process Variables in Neorealist Theory." *Security Studies* 5, 3 (1996): 167–92.

–. "The Security Dilemma in Alliance Politics." *World Politics* 36, 4 (1984): 461–95.

Snyder, Jack. *Myths of Empire: Domestic Politics and International Ambition*. Ithaca, NY: Cornell University Press, 1991.

Sun Shihai, and Jiang Yili 孙士海, 江亦丽, eds. *Erzhanhou Nanya guojia duiwai guanxi yanjiu* 二战后南亚国家对外关系研究 [Foreign relations in South Asia since the end of the Second World War]. Beijing: Fangzhi chubanshe, 2007.

Sun Weitao 孙维韬, ed. *Liu Yalou jiangjun chuanqi* 刘亚楼将军传奇 [The story of General Liu Yalou]. Beijing: Zhongguo wenhua chubanshe, 2010.

Sun Xuefeng and Chen Hanxi 孙学峰, 陈寒溪. "Zhongguo diqu zhuyi zhengce de zhanlue xiaoying" 中国地区主义政策的战略效应 [China's regional policy and its strategic consequences]. *Shijie jingji yu zhengzhi* 世界经济与政治 *[World Economics and Politics]* 5 (2006): 26–30.

Sun Ya'nan 孙亚男. "Douxian chuji bei Xiongnu zhanlue yanjiu" 窦宪出击北匈奴战略研究 [A study of Douxian's strategy of invading the Northern Xiongnu]. *Sunzi yanjiu* 孙子研究 *[Sunzi Studies]* 4 (2018): 58–65.

Tan Shi et al. 谭实. *Jianpuzhai* 柬埔寨 [Cambodia]. Nanning: Guangxi renmin chubanshe, 1985.

Tang Shiping and Zhang Yunling 唐世平, 张蕴岭. "Zhongguo de diqu zhanlue" 中国的地区战略 [China's regional strategy]. *Shijie jingji yu zhengzhi* 世界经济与政治 *[World Economics and Politics]* 6 (2004): 8–13.

Tang Yongsheng, Li Li, and Fang Ke 唐永胜, 李莉, 方珂. "Yatai zhanlue xingshi yanbian jiqi dui Zhongguo guojia an'quan de yingxiang" 亚太战略形势演变及其对中国国家安全的影响 [The evolution of the Asia-Pacific strategic environment and its implications for Chinese national security]. *Xiandai guoji guanxi* 现代国际关系 *[Contemporary International Relations]* 8 (2013): 1–9.

Taylor, Jay. *The Generalissimo: Chiang Kai-shek and the Struggle for Modern China*. Cambridge, MA: Harvard University Press, 2009.

Trachtenberg, Marc. *The Craft of International History: A Guide to Method*. Princeton, NJ: Princeton University Press, 2006.

Trubowitz, Peter. *Politics and Strategy: Partisan Ambition and American Statecraft*. Princeton, NJ: Princeton University Press, 2011.

Upadhya, Sanjay. *Nepal and the Geo-Strategic Rivalry between China and India*. London/New York: Routledge, 2012.

Van Evera, Stephen. *Guide to Methods for Students of Political Science*. Ithaca, NY: Cornell University Press, 1997.

Walt, Stephen M. *The Origins of Alliances*. Ithaca, NY: Cornell University Press, 1987.

Waltz, Kenneth N. "Evaluating Theories." *American Political Science Review* 91, 4 (1997): 913–17.

–. "International Politics Is Not Foreign Policy." *Security Studies* 6, 1 (1996): 54–57.

–. "The Origins of War in Neorealist Theory." In *The Origins and Prevention of Major Wars*, edited by Robert I. Rotberg and Theodore K. Rabb, 39–52. Cambridge: Cambridge University Press, 1989.

–. *Theory of International Politics*. New York: McGraw-Hill, 1979.

Wandycz, Piotr Stefan. *The Twilight of French Eastern Alliances, 1926–1936: French-Czechoslovak-Polish Relations from Locarno to the Remilitarization of the Rhineland*. Princeton, NJ: Princeton University Press, 1988.

Wang Jun, and Dan Xingwu 王军, 但兴悟. *Zhongguo guoji guanxi yanjiu sishinian* 中国国际关系研究四十年 [International relations studies in China in the past forty years]. Beijing: Zhongyang bianyi chubanshe, 2008.

Wang Junyan 王俊彦. *Liao Chengzhi zhuan* 廖承志传 [Biography of Liao Chengzhi]. Beijing: Renmin chubanshe, 2006.

Wang Li et al. 王立. *Dangdai Zhongguo de bingqi gongye* 当代中国的兵器工业 [The military industry of contemporary China]. Beijing: Dangdai zhongguo chubanshe, 1993.

Wang Shangrong jiangjun bianxiezu 《王尚荣将军》编写组, ed. *Wang Shangrong jiangjun* 王尚荣将军 [General Wang Shangrong]. Beijing: Dangdai Zhongguo chubanshe, 2000.

Wang Taiping 王泰平. *Wang Taiping wencun: ZhongRi jianjiao qianhou zai Dongjing* 王泰平文存: 中日建交前后在东京 [Wang Taiping's selected works: observing the Sino-Japanese normalization in Tokyo]. Beijing: Shehui kexue wenxian chubanshe, 2012.

–, ed. *Xinzhongguo waijiao 50 nian* 新中国外交50年 [New China's foreign relations in 50 years]. Vols. 1–3. Beijing: Beijing chubanshe, 1999.

–, ed. *Zhonghua renmin gongheguo waijiaoshi* 中华人民共和国外交史 [A diplomatic history of the People's Republic of China]. Beijing: Shijie zhishi chubanshe, 1998.

Wang Yazhi 王亚志. *Peng Dehuai junshi canmou huiyi: 1950 niandai ZhongSu junshi guanxi jianzheng* 彭德怀军事参谋的回忆: 1950 年代中苏军事关系见证 [Memoirs of Peng Dehuai's secretary on Sino-Soviet military cooperation in the 1950s], edited by Shen Zhihua and Li Danhui 沈志华, 李丹慧. Shanghai: Fudan daxue chubanshe, 2009.

Wang Yongqin 王永钦, ed. *Tongyi zhilu: liang'an guanxi wushinian dashiji* 统一之路: 两岸关系五十年大事记 [The road toward unification: a chronicle of major events across the strait over fifty years]. Guangzhou: Guangdong renmin chubanshe, 1999.

Wei Ling 魏玲. "Huoban guanxi zai shengji: Dongmeng guanqie, Zhongguo zeren yu diqu zhixu" 伙伴关系再升级: 东盟关切, 中国责任与地区秩序 [Upgrading partnerships again: ASEAN's concerns, Chinese responsibilities, and regional orders]. *Guoji wenti yanjiu* 国际问题研究 *[International Studies]* 6 (2021): 32–52.

Whiting, Allen S. *The Chinese Calculus of Deterrence: India and Indochina*. Ann Arbor: University of Michigan Press, 1975.

Wight, Martin. *Power Politics*. London: Royal Institute of International Affairs, 1978.

Wohlforth, William C. "U.S. Strategy in a Unipolar World." In *America Unrivaled: The Future of the Balance of Power*, edited by G. John Ikenberry, 98–118. Ithaca, NY: Cornell University Press, 2002.

Wolfers, Arnold. *Discord and Collaboration: Essays on International Politics*. Baltimore: Johns Hopkins University Press, 1962.

–. *The Small Powers and the Enforcement of Peace*. New Haven, CT: Yale Institute of International Studies, 1943.

Womack, Brantly. *Asymmetry and International Relationships*. Cambridge: Cambridge University Press, 2016.

–. *China among Unequals: Asymmetric Foreign Relationship in Asia*. Singapore: World Scientific Press, 2010.

–. *China and Vietnam: The Politics of Asymmetry*. Cambridge: Cambridge University Press, 2006.

Wu Lengxi 吴冷西. *Shinian lunzhan, 1956–1966: Zhang Su guanxi huiyilu* 十年论战 1956–1966: 中苏关系回忆录 [Ten years polemical war, 1956–1966: a memoir of Sino-Soviet relations]. Beijing: Zhongyang wenxian chubanshe, 1999.

Wu Xuewen 吴学文. *Fengyu yinqing: wo suo jingli de ZhongRi guanxi* 风雨阴晴: 我所经历的中日关系 [Rain and sunshine: my personal experience in Sino-Japanese relations]. Beijing: Shijie zhishi chubanshe, 2002.

Wu Xuexian et al. 吴学先. *Hongse Huarun* 红色华润 [The red "China resources"]. Beijing: Zhonghua shuju, 2010.

Wu Zhicheng 吴志成. "Zhongguo zhoubian waijiao xu gengjia zhongshi zhanlue mouhua" 中国周边外交需更加重视战略谋划 [China regional diplomacy should focus more on strategic plans]. *Xiandai guoji guanxi* 现代国际关系 *[Contemporary International Relations]* 1 (2015): 25–27.

Xiao Xiqing 萧曦清. *ZhongFei waijiao guanxishi* 中菲外交关系史 [Chinese-Philippine diplomatic relations]. Taipei: Zhengzhong shuju, 1995.

Xie Lifu 解力夫. "Mao Zedong miandui Meiguo" 毛泽东面对美国 [Mao Zedong facing the United States]. In *Waijiao zhanluejia Mao Zedong* 外交战略家毛泽东 [Mao Zedong: a diplomatic strategist], edited by Deng Liqun 邓力群, 491–572. Beijing: Zhongyang minzu daxue chubanshe, 2003.

Xie Yixian 谢益显, ed. *Zhongguo waijiaoshi: Zhonghua renmin gongheguo shiqi, 1949–1979* 中国外交史: 中华人民共和国时期 1949–1979 [A diplomatic history of the PRC, 1949–1979]. Kaifeng: Henan renmin chubanshe, 1988.

–. *Zhonghua renmin gongheguo waijiaoshi, 1949–1995* 中华人民共和国外交史 1949–1995 [A diplomatic history of the PRC, 1949–1995]. Beijing: Zhongguo qingnian chubanshe, 1997.

Xu Guangyi 胥光义, ed. *Dangdai Zhongguo jundui de houqin gongzuo* 当代中国军队的后勤工作 [Logistical work of armed forces in contemporary China]. Beijing: Zhongguo shehui kexue chubanshe, 1990.

Xu Xiaotian et al. 徐晓天, eds. *Xinzhongguo yu Sulian de gaoceng wanglai* 新中国与苏联的高层往来 [Interactions between the new China and the Soviet Union on the summit level]. Changchun: Jilin renmin chubanshe, 2001.

Xue Li 薛力. "Renhou xiongzhang: Zhongguo zai Yazhou zhenghe zhong de juese" 仁厚兄长: 中国在亚洲整合中的角色 [A kind elder brother: China's role in Asian integration]. *Shijie jingji yu zhengzhi* 世界经济与政治 *[World Economics and Politics]* 10 (2008): 36–39.

Yan, Xuetong. *Ancient Chinese Thought, Modern Chinese Power*. Princeton, NJ: Princeton University Press, 2011.

Yan Xuetong 阎学通. "Zhongguo dandang daguo zeren buyi chaoyue shili" 中国担当大国责任不宜超越实力 [China should not assume a major power's responsibilities beyond its capabilities]. *Cankao xiaoxi* 参考消息 *[Reference News]*, March 20, 2018, 11.

Yang Chengwu 杨成武. "Paoji Jinmen" 炮击金门 [Shelling of Jinmen Islands]. In *Zong canmoubu huiyi shiliao* 总参谋部回忆史料 [Recollections and historical materials of the headquarters of the General Staff], 492–517. Beijing: Jiefangjun chubanshe, 1995.

Yang Yizhen 杨一真. *Pingxi 1959 nian Xizang wuzhuang panluan jishi: Yang Yizhen huiyilu* 平息 1959 年西藏武装叛乱纪实——杨一真回忆录 [Anti-rebellions in Tibet in 1959: Yang Yizhen's memoirs]. Beijing: Zhongguo zangxue chubanshe, 2010.

Yao Jun 姚峻, ed. *Zhongguo hangkongshi* 中国航空史 [A history of China's aviation]. Zhengzhou: Daxiang chubanshe, 1998.

Ye Zicheng 叶自成. "Zhongguo shixing daguo waijiao zhanlue shizai bixing" 中国实行大国外交战略势在必行 [China should adopt a "major-power" diplomacy]. *Shijie jingji yu zhengzhi* 世界经济与政治 *[World Economics and Politics]* 1 (2000): 5–10.

Yuan Peng 袁鹏. "Guanyu goujian ZhongMei xinxing daguo guanxi de zhanlue sikao" 关于构建中美新型大国关系的战略思考 [Strategic thoughts on constructing a new type of major-power relationship between China and the United States]. *Xiandai guoji guanxi* 现代国际关系 *[Contemporary International Relations]* 5 (2012): 1–8.

Yuan Zheng 袁征. "Meiguo chongfan Yatai yu Donghai, Nanhai wenti" 美国重返亚太与东海, 南海问题 [The US return to the Asia-Pacific region and the East China Sea and South China Sea issues]. *Heping yu fazhan* 和平与发展 *[Peace and Development]* 5 (2012): 7–9.

Zaman, Arshad. "Economic Relations between Pakistan and the United States: Aid, Trade, and North-South Relations." In *United States–Pakistan Forum: Relations with Major Powers,* edited by Leo E. Rose and Noor A. Hussain, 56–69. Lahore: Vanguard Books, 1987.

Zhai, Qiang. "China and the Cambodian Conflict, 1970–1975." In *Behind the Bamboo Curtain: China, Vietnam, and the World beyond Asia,* edited by Priscilla Roberts, 369–403. Washington, DC/Stanford, CA: Woodrow Wilson Center Press/Stanford University Press, 2006.

Zhai Qiang 翟强. "Zhou Enlai yu ZhongJian hezuo guanxi de jianli, 1954–1965" 周恩来与中柬合作关系的建立 1954–1965 [Zhou Enlai and the establishment of cooperative relations between China and Cambodia, 1954–1965]. *Nankai xuebao* 南开学报 *[Nankai Journal]* 1 (2014): 24–32.

Zhai Xin 翟新. *Songcunqiansan jituan he Zhongguo* 松村谦三集团和中国 [Matsumura Kenzo Group, Japan's diplomatic pipe to China]. Beijing: Shehui kexue wenxuan chubanshe, 2007.

Zhang, Shu Guang. *Beijing's Economic Statecraft during the Cold War, 1949–1991.* Baltimore: Johns Hopkins University Press, 2014.

–. *Deterrence and Strategic Culture: Chinese-American Confrontations, 1949–1958.* Ithaca, NY: Cornell University Press, 1992.

Zhang, Xiaoming. *Deng Xiaoping's Long War: The Military Conflict between China and Vietnam, 1979–1991.* Chapel Hill: University of North Carolina Press, 2015.

Zhang Aiping 张爱萍, ed. *Zhongguo renmin jiefangjun* 中国人民解放军 [The Chinese People's Liberation Army]. Beijing: Dangdai zhongguo chubanshe, 1994.

Zhang Minqiu 张敏秋, ed. *ZhongYin guanxi yanjiu, 1947–2003* 中印关系研究 1947–2003 [Sino-Indian relations, 1947–2003]. Beijing: Beijing daxue chubanshe, 2004.

Zhang Xiangshan 张香山. *ZhongRi guanxi guankui yu jianzheng* 中日关系管窥与见证 [Personal accounts on Sino-Japanese relations through a bamboo tube]. Beijing: Dangdai shijie chubanshe, 1998.

Zhang Yunling 张蕴岭. "Zhongguo de zhoubian quyuguan huigui yu xinzhixu goujian" 中国的周边区域观回归与新秩序构建 [Recurrence of China's regional conception and new regional order]. *Shijie jingji yu zhengzhi* 世界经济与政治 *[World Economics and Politics]* 1 (2015): 5–25.

–. "Zhongguo-Donmeng duihua 30 nian: xieshou gongchuang hezuo wenming" 中国–东盟对话30年：携手共创合作文明 [Thirty years of China-ASEAN dialogue relations: working together to foster a cooperative culture]. *Guoji wenti yanjiu [International Studies]* 3 (2021): 107–17.

Zhanhou diguo zhuyi jingji bianxiezu《战后帝国主义经济》编写组, ed. *Zhanhou diguo zhuyi jingji* 战后帝国主义经济 [Economics of imperialist countries in the postwar era]. Shanghai: Shanghai renmin chubanshe, 1972.

Zhao Weiwen 赵蔚文. *YinZhong guanxi fengyunlu, 1949–1999* 印中关系风云录 1949–1999 [A history of the Sino-Indian relationship, 1949–1999]. Beijing: Shishi chubanshe, 2000.

Zheng Ning 郑宁. "'Bu zheng zhi guo' yu Ming chu guoji zhixu de goujian" "不征之国"与明初国际秩序的构建 ["Non-invasion countries" and the construction of the international order in the early Ming Dynasty]. *Yanbian daxue xuebao* 延边大学学报 *[Journal of Yanbian University]* 5 (2016): 62–69.

Zhonggong Xizang zizhiqu weiyuanhui dangshiyanjiushi 中共西藏自治区委员会党史研究室, ed. *Tan Guansan yu lao Xizang jingshen* 谭冠三与老西藏精神 [Tan Guansan and the spirit of "senior Tibetans"]. Beijing: Zhonggong dangshi chubanshe, 2011.

Zhongguo ZhongRi guanxishi xuehui 中国中日关系史学会, ed. *Youyi zhu chunqiu: Wei Xinzhongguo zuochu gongxian de Riben ren* 友谊铸春秋: 为新中国作出贡献的日本人 [Friendship forever: Japanese contribution to the new China]. Beijing: Xinhua chubanshe, 2002.

ZhongYin bianjing ziwei fanji zuozhan shi bianxiezu《中印边境自卫反击作战史》编写组, ed. *ZhongYin bianjing ziwei fanji zuozhan shi* 中印边境自卫反击作战史 [A history of the self-defence and counterattack operations on the Sino-Indian border]. Beijing: Junshi kexue chubanshe, 1994.

Zhou Enlai. "Chou En-lai's Report on the International Situation, December 1971." *Issues and Studies* 14, 1 (1977): 113–27.

Zhou Fangyin 周方银. "Meiguo de Yatai tongmeng tixi yu Zhongguo de yingdui" 美国的亚太同盟体系与中国的应对 [The US Asia-Pacific alliance system and China's responses]. *Shijie jingji yu zhengzhi* 世界经济与政治 *[World Economics and Politics]* 11 (2013): 4–24.

–. "Zhoubian huanjing zouxiang yu Zhongguo de zhoubian zhanlue xuanze" 周边环境走向与中国的周边战略选择 [Regional development and China's regional strategic choices]. *Waijiao pinglun* 外交评论 *[Foreign Affairs Review]* 1 (2014): 28–42.

Zhu Wenquan 朱文泉. "Taiwan dangju junshi zhengce ban'ge shiji de tiaozheng shanbian" 台湾当局军事政策半个世纪的调整嬗变 [The adjustment and evolution in military policies of the Taiwan authorities in the latter half of the twentieth century]. *Zhongguo junshi kexue* 中国军事科学 *[China Military Science]* 3 (2002): 40–49.

Zhu Ying et al. 朱楹. *Su Yu zhuan* 粟裕传 [Biography of Su Yu]. Beijing: Dangdai Zhongguo chubanshe, 2000.

Zhuang Liwei 庄礼伟. "Zhongguo guoji zhanlue zhong de Dongmeng keti" 中国国际战略中的东盟课题 [ASEAN in China's international strategy]. *Dangdai Yatai* 当代亚太 *[Journal of Contemporary Asia-Pacific Studies]* 6 (2003): 21–24.

Zhuo Renzheng 卓人政, ed. *Yinyin baobo qing: 1956 nian ZhongMian bianmin dalianhuan* 殷殷胞波情: 1956 年中缅边民大联欢 [The friendship of relatives: the Sino-Burmese border festival in 1956]. Beijing: Zhongyang wenxian chubanshe, 2003.

Zi Ding 紫丁. *Li Qiang zhuan* 李强传 [Biography of Li Qiang]. Beijing: Renmin chubanshe, 2004.

Index

Note: "(t)" after a page number indicates a table